TRANSNATIONAL CAPITALISM AND NATIONAL DEVELOPMENT

New Perspectives on Dependence

HUMANITIES STUDIES IN DEVELOPMENT
in association with the Institute of Development Studies,
University of Sussex

This is a new series of books on the politics, economics
and sociology of development.

TRANSNATIONAL CAPITALISM AND NATIONAL DEVELOPMENT

New Perspectives on Dependence

Edited by

JOSÉ J. VILLAMIL

*Professor at the Graduate School of Planning,
University of Puerto Rico*

*Formerly Visiting Fellow at the Institute of
Development Studies, University of Sussex*

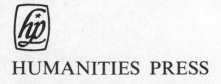

HUMANITIES PRESS

First published in the USA in 1979 by
HUMANITIES PRESS INC.
Atlantic Highlands, New Jersey 07716

© The Institute of Development Studies, 1979

Library of Congress Cataloging in Publication Data

Main entry under title:

Transnational capitalism and national development.

    (Humanities studies in development)
    Includes index.
    1. Underdeveloped areas—Addresses, essays, lectures.
    2. Economic development—Addresses, essays, lectures.
    3. International business enterprises—Addresses,
    essays, lectures.   I. Villamil, José Joaquín.
    II. Series.
    HC59.7.T7385   1979   330.9′172′4   78–26672
    ISBN 0–391–00963–X

Photosetting by Thomson Press (India) Limited, New Delhi
Printed in England by
Redwood Burn Ltd., Trowbridge and Esher

CONTENTS

PREFACE

The essays included in this volume reflect some of the work done, over the past three years, by members of the Dependence Cluster at the Institute of Development Studies. Most of the authors have been associated with the Cluster either as members of the I.D.S. staff or as Visiting Fellows. This permitted the members of the group to meet throughout the period and discuss their work. Although no claim is made to a uniform point of view, the essays do reflect common points of reference.

During the Fall of 1977, Osvaldo Sunkel and myself co-directed a Study Group on *International Relations and National Development* in which the pieces included in the volume were discussed and from which many useful suggestions were incorporated. One objective of the Study Group was to bring together a group of researchers working on topics related to those dealt with in the book. A number of the participants in the Study Group are currently carrying out case studies of country experiences as well as studies on various institutions and processes.

In many ways, most of the articles in the book represent work in progress rather than the final results of research projects. They are the result of discussions on the dependence framework and its implications, in the context of changes in the global organization and operation of capitalism over the past three decades.

Many thanks are due to the secretaries of the Dependence Cluster at I.D.S., who provided excellent support in the preparation of this book. Special thanks are due to Mrs. Trinidad Ball. My colleagues and fellow contributors to this volume, I wish to thank for their collaboration and their friendly acceptance of my frequent reminders of impending deadlines. Ann Segrave of the I.D.S. Publications Office was most helpful and efficient in handling a number of matters related to the publication of the book.

I also wish to thank *Development and Change* for permission to publish Martin Godfrey's 'The International Market in Skills and the Transmission of Inequality' which had previously appeared in that Journal; Frank Cass & Co. Ltd., for permission to publish 'Partners in Underdevelopment? The Transnationalization Thesis in a Kenyan Context' by Martin Godfrey and Steven Langdon, previously published in the *Journal of Commonwealth and*

Comparative Politics; and *Comparative Politics* for permission to publish 'Modernization and Dependence: Alternative Perspectives in the Study of Latin America', by J. Samuel Valenzuela and Arturo Valenzuela.

The I.D.S. provided me with a Visiting Fellowship for a seven month period, beginning in June 1977, during which this book was completed, and for which I am most grateful.

José J. Villamil
Editor
Brighton
January, 1978

CONTRIBUTORS

Rita Cruise O'Brien—Fellow, Institute of Development Studies
Carlos Fortin—Fellow, Institute of Development Studies
Edmundo Fuenzalida—Research Fellow, Institute of Development Studies
Martin Godfrey—Fellow, Institute of Development Studies
Steven Langdon—Assistant Professor of Economics, Carleton University Toronto
Robin Luckham—Fellow, Institute of Development Studies
Enrique Oteiza—Research Fellow, Institute of Development Studies
Dudley Seers—Fellow and former Director, Institute of Development Studies
Osvaldo Sunkel—Fellow, Institute of Development Studies
Arturo Valenzuela—Associate Professor of Political Science, Duke University and Visiting Fellow, Institute of Development Studies, 1977–1978
Samuel Valenzuela—Assistant Professor of Sociology, Yale University
José J. Villamil—Associate Professor, Graduate School of Planning, University of Puerto Rico and Visiting Fellow, Institute of Development Studies, 1975–1976, 1977–1978

INTRODUCTION

José J. Villamil

DEPENDENCE AND DEVELOPMENT

Dependence entered the vocabulary of development studies not much more than a decade ago. As an analytical category it arose from the experience of the underdeveloped world in the post World War II years, and as a reaction to the prevailing orthodoxy in the field. What has come to be called the dependence approach implied a significant rethinking of the basic theoretical explanations of underdevelopment. It was, initially, and still primarily a Latin American phenomenon, and only recently has it extended to other parts of the world. That the reaction to the neo-classical and modernization approaches to development should have occurred in Latin America and not elsewhere in the developing world, was to be expected. Countries in Asia and Africa were mostly, until very recently, colonies of various European countries. Their underdevelopment was clearly and obviously related to their colonial status.

Latin America, on the other hand, had been independent for the most part for well over a century, and still many of the symptoms of a colonial regime existed and still persist. In the early years of the present century, most Latin American countries were extremely poor, dependent on the export of raw materials, politically impotent and dominated by a land owning oligarchy which took over from the old viceroys. During the thirties and forties some of the countries industrialized by adopting import substitution policies. Sectors of Latin American society experienced rapid modernization. But, twenty years after the end of World War II, Latin America was still underdeveloped, the mass of the population poor, and the countries just as dependent as ever, now on the United States.

In the late forties, the U.N. Economic Commission for Latin America (ECLA), had put forward an explanation for Latin America's underdevelopment in terms of external 'bottlenecks'. Prices of Latin American exports had a secular downward trend, while prices of imports were increasing. These deteriorating terms of trade, plus the fact that the markets for Latin American commodity exports were growing slowly, meant that Latin America could not rely on its traditional exports for stimulating growth. This assault on

1

the comparative advantage theories of trade and development met with much resistance from the established academic circles, but it undoubtedly touched upon one of the critical factors affecting Latin American development. Furthermore, ECLA's analysis emphasized that there were conditions which made the problem a secular, structural one. Among these, the monopolistic structures of the economies of the industrialized countries was pointed out as an important one. From ECLA's early work the idea that the world is made up of a 'centre' and a 'periphery' and that the relationship between the two was not necessarily harmonious, but conflictive and asymmetrical, was born. One policy prescription which followed was that the Latin American countries should adopt a strategy of import substitution industrialization.

However important it may have been, ECLA's analysis and the 'centre-periphery' approach left out a number of important aspects. ECLA's work was for the most part related to trade aspects, leaving out of the analysis factors related to the class structure of the region's countries, the dependent nature of import substitution industrialization, the changing nature of the world capitalist economy and other aspects. The nation was conceived as the unit of analysis, as the economic actor. In part, the failure of the import substitution industrialization strategy and the concomitant integration attempts, can be explained by these gaps in ECLA's early work.

The dependence perspective arose, in part, as an extension of the structuralist thinking associated with ECLA and partly as a reaction to the failure of import substitution industrialization (Cardoso, 1977; O'Brien, 1975). Drawing from the Marxist tradition, it sought to integrate class analysis with structuralist views, and to move away from both the static nature of structuralism and the narrow economic base of most of development thinking, including that of ECLA (Cardoso, 1977). Although others in this book discuss the evolution and content of dependence thinking (Valenzuela and Valenzuela; Sunkel), it is important to consider, however briefly some of its basic themes.

It must be recognized, first, that dependence thinking does not pretend to be a precisely articulated theoretical model. Rather, as Fagen (1977) has written, '. . . dependency theory is in reality a conceptual framework, a set of concepts, hypothesized linkages, and an optic that attempts to locate and clarify a wide range of problems'. It is a 'way of framing' many of the issues that relate to underdevelopment (Fagen, 1977). Critics of dependence thinking frequently forget this point and, as Cardoso (1977) has mentioned, consider it as a theory, 'implying a corpus of formal and testable propositions', something which the Latin American social scientists working in this tradition had been unwilling to do.

The particular historical context of national societies is given much emphasis in dependence thinking; thus, the importance attached to the study of concrete experiences. In this sense, it provides a marked contrast to modernization and neo-classical approaches to questions of underdevelopment. Furthermore, it recognizes that history is not made up of the parallel evolution of different societies, but rather that the history of the 'periphery' was also a part of that of the 'centre', and that they could not be separated. The pattern of Latin American history in the recent past was related to its previous colonial experience and that, in turn, to the expansion of European capitalism.

A second aspect of dependence thinking, which relates to the above, is that obstacles to development are not only, or even primarily, national but also extra-national, and that there are crucial structural linkages between them. ECLA's analysis, together with the literature on Imperialism, provided much of the basis for this conception. Particular modes of incorporation into the world economy were emphasized in the analysis of underdevelopment. As Sunkel suggests in his article in this volume, underdevelopment in the periphery is a consequence of the development of capitalism in the centre. This view, of course, stands in direct contrast to those which attributed underdevelopment exclusively to inadequacies in the populations of underdeveloped countries (low achievement motivation, resistance to innovation and modernization) or their institutions.

Another component of the dependence view is that the process of development cannot be considered as a smooth, evolutionary transition between two stages (traditional and modern, for example), in which change is continuous, incremental and harmonious. Change involves conflict because it necessarily means transforming a society's structures, as well as severing the links with the capitalist economy (or, at least, modifying the means of incorporation), and these actions will be resisted, not by the groups which could be classified as 'traditional', but precisely by those most closely associated with the 'modern' economy. This is a point clearly suggested by Sunkel and Fuenzalida in this volume.

A country's social formations and the nature of its dependent relationships are closely interrelated. Integration into the world capitalist system has meant the formation of particular economic and social structures, but the precise nature of these is frequently determined by the nature of a society's class structure (see, for example, Vasconi, 1970; Sunkel and Fuenzalida; Langdon, in this volume). Critics of dependence thinking have frequently taken it to task for being 'nationalist' and excluding the class component from its analysis of underdevelopment. Certainly, some of the early works did create the impression that external factors (i.e. external to the nation) were exclusively to blame for underdevelopment, echoing the main thrust of ECLA's line of attack. However, it is now generally recognized that the interaction between internal structure and external factors is more complex (see, for example, Cardoso, 1977; and various of the articles in this volume).

Another implication of the dependence perspective is the need to adopt a holistic approach. The problems of underdevelopment are complex, multi-dimensional ones which cannot be segregated into economic, social, cultural and political compartments. In certain respects the dependence approach closely resembles some of the work done from a systems' theory perspective and, in fact, many of the concepts utilized in systems' theory—openness, integration and disintegration, for example—are also found in the dependence literature (see, for examples, Gutierrez, Ortiz and Villamil, 1971; Gonzalez Casanova, 1972).

Attention has been focused on a new set of variables in development thinking. In fact, what had been considered pluses in the traditional approaches, became minuses when looked at through dependence 'glasses'. Technological dependence was re-cognized as a problem, rather than as a manifestation of modernization and progress. The impact of mass communications in peripheral countries is considered in most cases to be negative. In general, the adoption of norms, criteria and models of organization from the industrialized countries is seen as harmful, and not, as previously, the objective of a process of modernization (see the articles by Cruise O'Brien; Godfrey; Fuenzalida; Luckham in this volume; also Sauvant, 1976; Schiller, 1976; Michalet, 1976).

This meant that development objectives had to be re-defined, criteria for decision-making in development policy modified (a suggestion made by Seers in his article in this volume). Attention is focused on achieving national independence and self reliant development as primary objectives of development policy. But, the modification of a country's dependent condition entails concomitant transformations in its mode of production and class structure. This carries the further implication that much of the conventional wisdom of development planning becomes irrelevant if what is pursued is major structural transformations along the lines mentioned (see, for example, the article by Villamil on planning, included in this volume).

In seeking to answer the question as to why industrialization has failed to produce the changes expected and bring with it development, attention was focused on the changing nature of the world capitalist system and, in particular, the increasing importance of multinational corporations (O'Brien, 1975; Fajnzylber, 1976; Sunkel, 1971). Most of the articles in this book are addressed, precisely, to issues related to the impact of a changing world economy, in which a relatively small number of large transnational corporations are dominant, on the countries of the periphery. In many ways, the new thinking on development is a reaction to the changes which have taken place in the world economy, particularly after World War II.

THE WORLD CAPITALIST ECONOMY SINCE 1945

The nature of the changes in the world economy since 1945 have been discussed by others in this volume (Sunkel and Fuenzalida; Valenzuela and Valenzuela; Oteiza; Seers) and elsewhere (Vaitsos, 1976; Widstrand, 1975; Sunkel, 1971; Barnet and Muller, 1974) and need not be discussed in great detail. Perhaps the salient characteristic of the post-1945 period has been the increasing transnationalization of capitalism. The magnitude and importance of the large transnational enterprises has been amply documented as have their impacts.[1] Thus, a recent study dealing with the consequences of dismemberment of U.S. oil companies, a measure suggested by some members of Congress, concluded that the implications to the U.S. economy were such in financial, economic and research and development terms, that the move best be abandoned (Johnson and Messick, 1976). If this is the impact of these eighteen companies on the world's most powerful economy it is not difficult to imagine the impact on smaller, less powerful ones.

In more general terms, the growing importance of transnational enterprises and their mode of operation have lead to the disappearance of the market as an allocator of resources and determinant of international trade. Increasingly, trade transactions between countries are in fact between divisions or affiliates of the same corporation. For example, it is estimated that approximately thirty per cent of Third World exports of manufactured goods to the United States are intra-firm transactions (Cox, 1976). In the case of Mexico, over seventy-five per cent of its manufacturing exports to the United States are intra-firm transactions, which ECLA estimates to be undervalued by as much as forty per cent (Villamil, 1978). It is obvious then that prices have ceased to perform the role assigned to them in traditional economic thinking. But the same can be said for many other concepts and terms in development economics. Thus, the meaning of foreign investment is questionable when investment by multinationals is for the most part financed by sources of the host country.[2] Technology transfers between countries have been questioned (in Michalet, 1976), and it is argued that what really takes place is a process of diffusion of technology within the corporation, between its main office where it is developed, and its affiliates and subsidiaries where it is utilized. The meaning of profits must assume a different character in a context in which the firm does not necessarily maximize profits at the national level but, through transfer pricing, contributes to profit maximization for the whole corporate system. There is not much meaning in profit figures in any one country when there is a possibility of transfer pricing and shifting of profits through other means. One implication of the growing importance of multinationals in the world economy is that the distinction between micro and macro economics has become progressively less useful. To understand the dynamics of national economies one must understand the behaviour of the large transnational firm.

But, changes in the organization of capitalism are just one aspect of the changes that have characterized the global capitalist economy over the past three decades. These have been years of cyclical fluctuations and recently of prolonged recession, the magnitude of which is summarized by Chenery (1975): 'The world economy is currently in a state of disequilibrium of a magnitude not seen since the aftermath of World War II. The symptoms of underlying stress have been manifested over the past two years in the form of raw material shortages, a food and fertilizer crisis, a dramatic rise in petroleum prices and, finally, worldwide inflation and threats of impending financial disaster'. Although the causes of the current crisis are frequently associated with OPEC's actions, the fact is that the foundations for it were laid much before the increase in petroleum prices. Witness, for example, the devaluation of the dollar in 1971.

Whatever the causes of the present crisis, undoubtedly it exists and goes beyond a cyclical downswing in the capitalist system. Furthermore, it has not been responding to the standard fiscal and monetary remedies. Partly because of this, there have been increasing calls for a re-organization of the world economic order and for modification of the rules of the game, both from the centre and the periphery. Although three items are of particular importance in the present crisis—food, petroleum and the external debt of developing countries[3]—and many of the measures proposed at the international level have tried to deal with them, there have been other reactions to the changes in the world capitalist economy which go further.

Third World Countries had for some time been acting in concert on many issues. UNCTAD I, for example, met in 1964 to consider a report by Raúl Prebisch on 'A new trade policy for development' in which access to markets and higher prices for Third World exports were given attention (Maizels, 1976). But UNCTAD and other attempts at improving the position of Third World countries in the world economy have not been particularly successful. We are nearly into the third Development Decade of the United Nations, and not much improvement has occurred. In 1973, at a meeting of the non-aligned countries held in Algiers, the heads of state of those countries approved a declaration which called for a new international economic order and alternative development strategies. Mostly as a result of this initiative, the Sixth Special Session of the U.N. General Assembly approved a *Declaration and Action Programme on the Establishment of a New International Economic Order* (Resolutions 3201 (S-VI) and 3202 (S-VI) of 1 May 1974). The contents of the Declaration and Action Programme are well known. Most of the important issues in the area of North-South relationships are included. Some were non-controversial, but other proposed measures proved to be quite sensitive and were vehemently opposed by the industrialized capitalist countries: the rights of countries to sovereignty over their natural resources, the right to regulate multinationals, indexation of export prices and others. Regardless of whether the NIEO proposals are approved and implemented, they have provided a rallying point for Third World countries. The crisis in the world economy called attention to the role of multinationals and to the need for new ways of dealing with them and the changing circumstances of world capitalism.

However, two *caveats* are in order. The first refers to the fact that despite the many meetings, the good intentions and the rhetoric, very little has been advanced in the negotiations for a new international economic order, or even for more limited changes in UNCTAD. This is partly due to the fact that the OECD countries have resisted making concessions. Whereas the developing countries have taken the position of negotiating the changes in the order of things as a whole, the developed capitalist countries have held out for piecemeal negotiations on specific points. So that, in fact, as

Oteiza makes clear in this volume, there is no new international economic order, or at least not the new international order proposed by the meeting in Algiers.

The second *caveat* refers to a different matter, for it deals with the question of who benefits from a new economic order. The proposals included in the Declaration and Action Programme are sometimes contradictory among themselves and many questions are left unanswered. What type of society will result or is envisioned in the proposals? What is the perceived future of the Third World in the new order? For whose benefit is it being created? How is the additional surplus from the proposed measures to be used?

One reading of the NIEO proposals is that reforms in the international system are being sought by national elites in the developing countries to forego the need for significant structural transformations in their countries, that these measures are little more than an attempt on their part to adjust to a changing world situation. As Farer (1975) has put it, these groups 'are talking about greater equality between states. And in their largely authoritarian systems, the state is they'. It is clear then that changes in the international context alone will not bring about the transformations required to benefit the vast majority of the world's population.

Although the discussions on the NIEO, UNCTAD and other such Third World initiatives have received most of the attention from the press and from students of development problems, they are not the only responses to changes in the world capitalist economy. After the second World War a number of institutions were created and entrusted with the task of managing the world economy, or at least playing an important part in this process. Among them was the World Bank, the International Monetary Fund and others such as the OECD. It became evident with the recent crisis that the previously existing institutions were not able to cope with the new conditions, including a more aggressive Third World.

Partly to deal with the new situation in the world economy, partly to try to improve the relationships among the developed capitalist countries, and as a reaction against the policies of the Nixon Administration in the early seventies, which smacked of a certain economic nationalism contrary to the needs of the new transnational organization of capitalism, a new organization was established in 1973, the Trilateral Commission (Ullman, 1976). This commission is made up of leading figures from the world of transnational capitalism and from politics, from the United States, Japan and Western Europe. It is interesting to note that President Carter and a large number of leading figures in his Administration are members of the Commission (including his National Security Advisor, Secretary of the Treasury, Secretary of State, Secretary of Defence, the Vice-President and a number of others in high positions).

The Commission represents 'an ideological perspective representing the transnational outlook of the multinational corporation. . .' (Falk, 1975), in effect a 'transnational ideology' (Cox, 1976). It stands for a 'much more far reaching coordination among all the trilateral governments' (Ullman, 1976), the ultimate result of which would be 'a community of the developed nations', according to Zbigniew Brzezinski, former Director of the Commission, and now President Carter's National Security Advisor. Initially, the aims were more closely related to uniting the developed countries so as to be able to negotiate with the developing world from a position of strength. Lately, the Commission has been associated with positions which go much beyond that relatively limited objective and pursue a much greater control of the world economy, aimed at assuring its stability.

The Commission's positions are most often in direct conflict with the interests of developing countries (and in some cases even the developed ones), such as when it has argued against state intervention with foreign investment or the control of multinationals. But this conflict is not always in evidence, at least not with the officially expressed positions of the Third World. Thus, it has argued that there should be a reduction of tariffs in OECD countries on industrial products from developing countries, a proposal also made in the *Declaration and Action Programme for a New International Economic Order*. In a world in which trade in manufactured goods is increasingly being taken over by multinationals, this is an eminently sensible posture to adopt. A recent Trilateral Commission report, cited in the *International Herald Tribune* of 15 December, 1977, makes wide ranging recommendations which, in substance, would imply that the countries represented in the Commission should be responsible for managing the world economy. Thus, it is stated, the core of a future international monetary system must be 'agreed and operated' by the five to ten biggest countries. The other countries could then adopt 'a wide variety of arrangements. . . around that central core'. The report, one of whose authors is Undersecretary of State for Economic Affairs of the U.S., explicitly argues that wide participation by a large number of countries would merely hinder the decision-making process. Another recommendation made in this report, and one with which the Trilateral Commission has been associated almost from its inception, has to do with transforming the IMF into an international Central Bank. In effect, what the Trilateral Commission is proposing is the creation of a world state apparatus to manage the global economy in its new phase of transnationalization.

Obviously much more could be said about the changes in the world capitalist economy in the past three decades and the responses which these changes have called forth. The point which must be made, and is in a number of articles in this volume, is that this new phase of capitalist expansion is not just an extension of previous ones but is qualitatively different, a point emphasized by Sunkel and Fuenzalida in this volume, as well as by others (Schiller, 1976; Frobel, 1977; Vaitsos, 1976). Perhaps the primary distinction with previous phases is the global extension of industrial production, both for export and for serving local markets. This has given rise to the practice of international sub-contracting, as in the case of the Mexican frontier with the U.S. (Villamil, 1978) and the proliferation of export platforms, in addition to the establishment of manufacturing subsidiaries in the larger countries to serve local markets.[4] This process of diffusion of industrial production has made it more difficult to differentiate First and Third World concerns, just as the transnational corporations have had negative impacts on the latter, their impacts on sectors of the former have also been negative.

Thus, tensions begin to develop between *national* sectors in the central countries, and those most closely identified with transnational capitalism. An example is provided by the conflict between the Nixon Administration's moves in imposing an import surcharge and the views of members of the Trilateral Commission. But even more dramatic is the response of U.S. labour unions (and those of some European countries) to the new tendencies in the transnationalization of capitalism. There have been two reactions from the labour unions: to organize at the international level by bringing together unions in different countries but associated with the same corporation or industry, and to try to promote national policies that would restrict multinationals, and thus protect immobile labour against mobile capital (Cox, 1976). So far, success has been very limited in either case. This is due to a number of reasons which may be obvious, one being that competition is in many cases from 'export platforms' where unions are forbidden or severely restricted in their scope for action. Also, what could happen if the transnational strategy is pursued, is that the workers affected—those that work for the multinationals—may realize that their interests are not necessarily in conflict with those of the corporations, thus generating a symbiotic relationship between them, creating a new international labour aristocracy, a point mentioned by Cox (1976).

As mentioned previously, many of the actions initiated by the developing countries have had as their motive the regulation and control of multinationals. An example is the *Charter of Economic Rights and Duties of States* (U.N. General Assembly Resolution 3281 (XXIX), 12 December, 1974), proposed by the then President of Mexico. In many ways, the approaches of the developing countries parallel the 'transnational' and 'national' strategies of labour as described above. The former haven't been particularly successful, except in minor ways. With respect to national strategies, one thing has become apparent and it is that many of the approaches utilized in a previous phase of capitalist expansion, are no longer effective as means of curtailing the influence of transnational capitalism. Nationalizations, for example, have been found wanting, for how does one nationalize technology?[5] There are ways of maintaining profit levels without ownership. In fact, ownership by the multinationals may be counterproductive and alternative arrangements can be made to assure a supply of a given commodity or a given level of profits. Thus, outright ownership has come to be substituted by a number of other mechanisms; management contracts, for example (see the article by Fortín in this volume). Many of the traditional instruments of nationalist economic policy such as nationalizations, localization of staffs in foreign enterprises, requirements for local participation in ownership, have all proven to be compatible with an extended role for transnational capital in developing countries. The degree of dependence remaining as it was or even increasing.

One option which has been suggested as a possible way of counteracting the impact of multinationals is that of creating producers' associations similar to OPEC in other areas. However, the possibilities for success along these lines appear limited (Radetzki, 1976). It has become increasingly clearer that transforming a society's structures and reducing its external dependence can only come about by conscious disengagement from the world capitalist economy. This will, in turn, require changes in the distribution of power in most societies, changes in development strategy and in the criteria utilized in making development decisions (see the comments on this subject by Oteiza, Seers, Godfrey, and Villamil).

ON THE ORGANIZATION OF THE VOLUME

The book is divided into four parts. Articles included in the first section deal with some theoretical issues which relate to changes in the world system and the theoretical schemes which interpret these changes. The articles by Sunkel and by Valenzuela and Valenzuela trace the development of dependence thinking and contrast it with the other prevailing interpretations. Sunkel in particular places the development of development thinking within the context of changes in the world economy and the international system generally. The article by Seers reinterprets the concept and meaning of dependence in terms of three main variables: dependence on food, technology and oil, and argues that dependence on technology is perhaps the most basic. Seers' article places particular emphasis on expanding the 'room for manouvre' of countries in their development policy, and the fact that this may entail trade-offs with income growth. Sunkel and Fuenzalida trace through the develop-ment of the transnational capitalist system and the implications for the developing countries of being incorporated into it. They describe a process in which integration into that system leads to the disintegration of national structures. Their article provides a clear rationale for substituting the nation state with the global system as the unit of analysis in development studies.

The second section of the book deals with transnational structures and processes: technological innovation, com-munications, the military and the international market for skills. One conclusion from these articles is that the mechanisms of incorporation into the global capitalist system and the impacts of this incorporation are different and more subtle than those which characterized capitalist expansion in previous phases. All four articles point to the existence of a network of contacts between different groups in the periphery—professionals, generally including the military, scientists and public administrators—with their coun-terparts in the developed centre, and how these contacts, through the universities, conferences, journals, joint activities, lead to a deformation of the various areas of activity. They all suggest the fruitlessness of attempting partial solutions such as localization of jobs in the absence of more far reaching reforms (such as those related to language in Tanzania) and reducing the international mobility of these groups (by adopting standards of professional qualification defined on the basis of national need, rather than international norms).

The third section includes two studies on the impact of capitalist development, and two which deal with the role of the state. Langdon's article on the state and multinationals in Africa points to a symbiotic relationship between them and the state's role in promoting through various means the penetration of multi-nationals. Fortín's piece deals more specifically with the natural resources sector and points to the adaptation of multinationals to nationalist policies, concluding that ways have been found of satisfying both nationalist aspirations and the surplus extraction requirements of the corporations. The articles on Kenya and Puerto Rico, although dealing with two countries quite different in most respects, show certain similarities with respect to the disintegrative impacts of dependent capitalist development.

The articles included in the final section look at alternative strategies to dependent capitalist growth. Oteiza considers the possibilities of collective self reliance as a means of overcoming the limitations of dependent growth, and the obstacles which exist for adopting such a strategy. Villamil considers the implications for planning of adopting an alternative development strategy which emphasizes national self-reliance, redistribution of income and wealth, and the concomitant transformations of the mode of production and class structure. The planning model suggested differs in important respects from that which is derived from the neo-classical and modernization perspectives.

NOTES

1 The U.N. estimates that value added by multinationals amounted in 1971 to approximately $500 billion, or twenty per cent of total GNP of the non-socialist world. This proportion, quoted in Girvan (1975), has probably been exceeded by now as it is estimated that the multinational sector has grown much faster than the rest of the economy. In any case, it underestimates the importance of these firms which is much greater if one considers their role in research and development, total investment and share of total profits.
2 A U.S. Senate Committee investigating multinationals calculated that over 85 per cent of the financial needs of multinationals from the U.S. operating abroad, were met from local sources (U.S. Senate, 1973).
3 By the end of 1976, the total external debt of the developing countries had reached $212,600 millions, having almost doubled in three years (*Bulletin of the IMF*, Vol. 6, No. 17, September, 1977). With the increasing burden of servicing the external debt and the depressed conditions in the world economy a number of countries are in risk of defaulting on their loans, with grave consequences for the international financial system. This situation has lead to a number of proposals for turning over the debt of a number of these countries.
4 The extension of capitalism, and particularly of industrial capitalism, to countries in the periphery has been accompanied by an extension of a series of superstructural activities aimed at creating a favorable environment for the development of capitalism. Thus, of the largest 25 advertising firms in the world, 23 are American. By 1971, the advertising expenditure of U.S. companies abroad had reached $5 billion, most of which was channelled through American advertising companies. As Schiller (1971) has stated, 'The internationalization of the American advertising business is an integral part of the expansion of U.S. industry abroad'.

5 The Saudi government nationalized ARAMCO, the large oil company, but is still dependent on the large multinational corporations which owned ARAMCO, for its technology. In any case, as Apgar (1977) has stated, '. . . ARAMCO is generally managed like a U.S. multinational . . . Goods and services can be marketed directly to ARAMCO more or less as they would be to major corporations in the United States'.

REFERENCES

Apgar, M., 1977, 'Succeeding in Saudi Arabia', *Harvard Business Review*, January–February.

Barnet, R. J. and Muller, R. E., 1974, *Global Reach: The Power of the Multinational Corporations*, Simon and Schuster, New York.

Cardoso, F. H., 1977, 'The Consumption of Dependency Theory in the United States', *Latin American Research Review*, Vol. XII, no. 3.

Chenery, H ., 1975, 'Restructuring the World Economy', *Foreign Affairs*, Vol. 53, no. 2.

Cox, R. W., 1976, 'Labour and the Multinationals', *Foreign Affairs*, Vol. 54, no. 2.

Fagen, R., 1977, 'Studying Latin American Politics: Some Implications of a *Dependencia* Approach', *Latin American Research Review*, Vol. XII, no. 2.

Fajnzylber, F., 1976, 'Oligopolio, Empresas Transnacionales y Estilos de Desarrollo', *El Trimestre Económico*, Vol. XLIII (3), Num. 171, Julio–Septiembre.

Falk, R., 1975, 'A New Paradigm for International Legal Studies', *The Yale Law Journal*, Vol. 84, no. 5.

Farer, T., 1975, 'The United States and the Third World: A Basis for Accommodation', *Foreign Affairs*, Vol. 54, no. 1.

Frobel, F., *et al.*, 1977, *The New International Division of Labour*, published in German as *Die Neue Internationale Arbeitsteilung*, Rowohlt, Taschenbuch Verlag GmbH, Reinbek bei Hamburg, Germany, Chs. 1 and 2, mimeo, in English.

Girvan, N., 1975, 'Economic Nationalists v. Multinational Corporations: Revolutionary or Evolutionary Change?', in Widstrand, 1975.

González Casanova, P., 1972, 'Sistemas Históricos', *Sociedad y Desarrollo*, Num. 2, Abril–Junio.

Gutierrez, E., Ortiz, H. and Villamil, J., 1971, 'Open Systems Planning', *Northeast Regional Science Review*, Vol. 1, April.

Helleiner, G. (ed.) 1976, *A World Divided: The Less Developed Countries in the International Economy*, Cambridge University Press, Cambridge.

Johnson, W. and Messick, R., 1976, *The Journal of Energy and Development*, Vol. ii, no. 1, Autumn.

Maizels, A., 1976, 'A New International Strategy for Primary Commodities', in Helleiner, 1976.

Michalet, C. A., 1976, *Le Capitalisme Mondial*, Presses Universitaires de France, Paris.

O'Brien, P., 1975, 'A Critique of Latin American Theories of Dependency', in Oxaal, I, *et al.*, *Beyond the Sociology of Development*, Routledge and Kegan Paul, London.

Radetzki, M., 1976, 'The Potential for Monopolistic Commodity Pricing by Developing Countries', in Helleiner, 1976.

Sauvant, K., 1976, 'His Master's Voice', *CERES*, Vol. 9, no. 5.

Schiller, H., 1971, 'Madison Avenue Imperialism', *Transaction*, Vol. 8, nos. 5 & 6.

———, 1976, *Communication and Cultural Domination,* International Arts and Sciences Press, New York.

Sunkel, O., 1971, 'Capitalismo Transnacional y Desintegración Nacional en América Latina', *Estudios Internacionales*, Num. 4, Enero–Marzo.

Ullman, R., 1976, 'Trilateralism: 'Partnership' For What?', *Foreign Affairs*, Vol. 55, no. 1.

U.S. Senate, Committee on Finance, 1973, *Implications of Multinational Firms for World Trade and Investment and for U.S. Trade and Labor*, Washington.

Vaitsos, C., 1976, 'Power, Knowledge and Development Policy: Relations Between Transnational Enterprises and Developing Countries', in Helleiner, 1976.

Vasconi, T., 1970, 'De la Dependencia Como una Categoría Básica para el Análisis del Desarrollo Latinoamericano', *Cuadernos de la Sociedad Venezolana de Planificación*, Nos. 82–83, Noviembre–Diciembre.

Villamil, J., 1978 (forthcoming), 'Core Periphery in the Western Hemisphere', in Seers, D., Schaffer, B., and Kiljunen, M. L., (eds.), *Underdeveloped Europe: Studies in Core-Periphery Relations*, Harvester Press, Hassocks.

Widstrand, C. (ed.), *Multinational Firms in Africa*, Scandinavian Institute of African Studies, Uppsala.

PART ONE

THEORETICAL PERSPECTIVES

1

THE DEVELOPMENT OF DEVELOPMENT THINKING

Osvaldo Sunkel

The development of capitalism was at the centre of economic thought during the century that followed the publication in 1776 of Adam Smith's *The Wealth of Nations*. It was the fundamental concern of classical political economy. From the last quarter of the nineteenth century until the 1950s, that concern, and political economy itself, were removed from the mainstream of economic thought. Neoclassical economic theory, with its focus on the behaviour of individual producers and consumers in perfect or imperfect markets, and theories that attempted to explain the cyclical instability of capitalism, took over.

The subject of development started to reappear in economic thought only in the 1950s, but now referred to the economic problems of the countries that had *not* become industrialized by that time. The economic development of underdeveloped countries, which is what we really have in mind when we now speak of development thinking, is a very recent subject in the evolution of economic thought. Hardly any book published before 1950 had the word development in its title, universities did not offer courses on the subject, special development institutes did not exist, nor did development experts. Technical assistance as we know it now became a substantial operation only with President Truman's Point IV Programme and the U.N. Technical Assistance Programme.

The recent first inter-regional meeting of the four Associations that represent hundreds of institutions devoted to development studies in Africa, Asia, Europe and Latin America attests to the importance that the subject has acquired in just over two decades.[1] But the boom that it enjoys is in stark contrast to the crisis of the development process itself. One of the consequences of this disparity is the need for a critical reappraisal. At a moment when new policies, strategies and models are being proposed it is worth looking back upon the interaction between development thinking and development practice over the last two decades, because it may have important lessons for the future.

I propose to examine the evolution of development thinking from

19

three main perspectives: the nature of the political economies that have constituted the object of development thought since the 1950s and of their international context; the nature of economic thought when development became a fundamental issue at this time; and the ways in which development thinking responded to the development process itself.

Before embarking on this difficult exercise—a sort of sociology of knowledge of development thinking—I would like to point out that it is not based on systematic research, but rather on personal experience; that this experience is essentially that of Latin America and therefore of the overwhelming hegemonic presence of the United States; and that it is the experience of an economist.

Let me start by identifying some of the basic structural characteristics of the underdeveloped economies around 1950 as well as some basic changes that were taking place internally and in the international context. Most underdeveloped countries were still colonies at that time, though a few had just become independent, and some—most of the Latin American countries—had been independent for over a century. All were economically, politically and culturally linked to one or other of the industrial countries to which they exported primary products and surplus, and from which they imported manufactures, human resources, investments, technology, institutions, ideas, values, culture.

The size of the sector that consumed these imports—the so-called modern sector—depended on three factors: the size of the total surplus generated in the export sector; the proportion of it that the local ruling groups managed to keep and consume or invest (the more they invested locally the more their productive base expanded); and the degree to which the ruling groups exploited the rest of society, which they achieved partly by preserving the pre-existing local institutions and culture and partly by destroying them in order to generate an abundant supply of cheap labour. As a consequence the national economy, society, polity and culture were highly heterogeneous. Differing socio-economic, political and cultural forms interacted, though all were to a greater or a lesser extent dominated by capitalist relations of trade and/or production.

The Great Depression, World War II, decolonization and the Cold War, changed the power balance within the ruling classes of many countries. The groups linked more closely to the traditional export interests were weakened, and new middle-class sectors (professionals, small entrepreneurs, industrialists, where some industry had developed previously, and new political leaders and groups to represent them) were strengthened. The basic objective of these new groups was the promotion of industrialization as a means to generalize the consumption patterns and life styles acquired by importing the life styles of the industrial countries (the de-monstration effect, as it was then called). To make this possible, they had to increase their control over the foreign sector in order to capture a larger proportion of the surplus needed to finance increased consumption and investment. The state became in this way the active instrument of a new policy aimed at the local reproduction of the characteristics of mature capitalist countries: industrialization, agricultural modernization, infrastructure, in-creased provision of social services and so forth.

The countries that had all these things were the developed countries, those that lacked them were underdeveloped, and de-velopment was the process of transition from one situation to the other.

This way of thinking about development was furthermore intensely promoted from abroad, particularly by the United States, the new capitalist centre, as a foreign policy instrument in the context of the Cold War. The external support of national ruling classes against challenges from the left became an all-important objective in the capitalist camp. (This was the case not only in the underdeveloped world, but even more so in Europe, where the main instruments were NATO, the Marshall Plan and European eco-nomic integration). Correspondingly, the national ruling classes in the underdeveloped countries saw the USA and Western Europe as guardians of their interests and as socio-political and economic models. The development of modern industrial capitalism in these countries therefore became their long-term aim, held in common with the ruling classes of the major Western powers. This frequently contributed to an acceleration of the disintegration of the European colonial empires and to a further strengthening of the USA as the capitalist superpower.

Let us now look quickly at the economic thought available around 1950 to help policy-makers, experts and advisers formulate the best policies for the development of underdeveloped countries. There was, of course, political economy, the *locus classicus* of the analysis of the emergence and expansion of industrial capitalism in Great Britain. But the writings of the founding fathers of economics were considered to have been overtaken by the scientific progress of the discipline, and had therefore been relegated to museum pieces. Their great analytical strength, the attempt to relate the growth of the capitalist mode of production and the operation of the economics of the market to the changing nature of social classes and the consequent redistribution of power, within the historical context of the world-wide expansion of industrial capitalism and imperialism, was precisely what had been expurgated and replaced by positive economic theory. The most important body of thought inherited from classical political economy—Marxism—had been suppressed everywhere: in the capitalist world by McCarthyism, in the socialist camp by Stalinism. In the name of scientific progress and the Cold War, the dynamics of capitalism had been exorcised from economics, and we were left with the two main paradigms of pure economics: neo-classical economic theory (including the comparative cost theory of international trade) and Keynesian macroeconomics, and microdynamics.

These schools corresponded to the needs and characteristics of mature capitalism; the efficient operation of individual firms and consumers in national and international markets, and the avoidance of cyclical instability with short-term policies of full employment and long-term strategies of growth. But for underdeveloped countries the policies derived from these theories amounted to a drastic programme of economic, political, social and cultural transformation. Few of them satisfied the assumptions underlying neoclassical and Keynesian economics, or, to be more precise, these assumptions corresponded only to a partial segment of reality: that more closely related to the export sector and the main cities. Money was not a universal means of exchange, it was used in urban and to some extent in urban-rural transactions, but less frequently within rural communities. With the exception of some export activities and the urban sector there was hardly a labour market, as most people remained attached to rural communities and institutions of one type or another. The modern capitalist type of enterprise was largely foreign, and was to be found mainly in the export sector and in trade, and only to a small extent in manufacture. Basic social capital—such as roads, energy, communications, railroads, ports—was again available only to the export sector and main cities. These were in fact in better contact with the metropolitan centres than with their own hinterlands. Education was restricted to a small urban elite. Financial institutions, apart from some branches of foreign banks, hardly existed. The State apparatus was limited in geographical and operational scope, and had a weak and highly unstable tax base, mainly in the foreign sector.

If theory did not correspond to reality, so much the worse for reality: it would have to be changed so that it would correspond to the assumptions of neoclassical and macrodynamic theory. Two main lines of thinking and policy emerged. On the one hand were the conservatives—intellectual representatives of the old order—who maintained that the traditional specialization in primary exports constituted the best engine of growth, provided that the industrial countries also achieved full employment and growth. The benefits of specialization and comparative advantage would then be spread from the export sector to the rest of society and development would eventually be achieved.

This line of thinking, however, went against the interests of the new social groups that were emerging out of the struggle against the old alliance of the local oligarchy and imperialism. Emerging national bourgeoisies were trying to gain control of the state in order to capture a larger share of the surplus generated in the export sector and to use it to promote industrialization and modernization generally. Macrodynamic theory provided the rationalization for an active state role and for a heavy emphasis on capital accumulation as the basis for economic growth, although for different reasons and in different circumstances than those envisaged by Keynes. Growth models—including models of capital accumulation used in Soviet planning—and social accounting and input-output analysis provided practical instruments for planning.

Theories that were critical of the doctrines of free trade and international specialization and that attributed underdevelopment to the lack of industrial development (such as those of Prebisch, Singer, Lewis, Mandelbaum, Rosenstein-Rodan, Nurkse—none of them, interestingly enough, of Anglo-Saxon origin), provided the rationalization for protection, for investment in infrastructure and manufacturing and for planning. The contrast between the heterogeneous reality of underdeveloped countries and the assumptions of neo-classical theory provided the rationale for policies of institutional reform and modernization in agriculture, education, taxation, public administration and finance.

A more radical version of this programme for the development of national capitalism strongly influenced by an undercurrent of Marxist thinking about internal and international exploitation, surfaced here and there, when political conditions allowed. Heavy emphasis was placed on nationalization of foreign investment in the primary export sector and public utilities, state ownership of basic industries, trade with socialist countries and much more drastic agrarian reform and state planning.

In Latin America these various lines of thinking crystallized during the 1950s around the work of Raul Prebisch and a group of young economists at the U.N. Economic Commission for Latin America. This institution became the intellectual and technical base for the support of progressive nationalist and reformist movements and governments throughout the region, and the object of bitter attack by conservative groups in Latin America, as well as by the U.S. government, academic and business interests.

It is easy now with hindsight to point to the weaknesses and limitations of the new development policies pursued since the 1950s. But at a time when the socio-political and economic interests related to the primary export sectors were still very strong, and when threats to them were automatically labelled a communist plot and harshly suppressed, it is convenient to recall that these programmes of nationalist and social democratic reform were regarded as a revolutionary challenge to the existing internal and international order.

All this changed dramatically at the end of the 1950s with the Cuban Revolution and the fall of the dictatorships of Perez Jimenez in Venezuela, Odria in Peru and Rojas Pinilla in Colombia, as well as the change from the Eisenhower to the Kennedy administration in the U.S.A. These political events reflected the crisis of the old order, which could no longer be supported because it had been substantially eroded inside Latin America and, as we shall suggest later, internationally also. The alternatives appeared clear: either a socialist revolution, or full support for the new emerging social forces behind industrialization and modernization policies.

It was thought that the latter, including the expansion of education, rural modernization, and urbanization, would promote social mobility and diversify the social structure, widening the middle and entrepreneurial classes which were thought to be the indispensable social base of modern capitalist society. The creation of modern bourgeois societies of this kind would in turn facilitate the development of political democracy, as practised in Western Europe and the U.S.A.

Economic, sociological and political theories which gave an idealized version of the contemporary nature of countries that had reached the stage of mature industrial capitalism were transfromed into a programme of capitalist development in the periphery, into an ideology of development, of which Rostow's *The Stages of Economic Growth: a non Communist Manifesto* is probably the most extreme and explicit version. The Alliance for Progress, the response of the new ruling coalitions of the U.S.A. and Latin America to the Cuban Revolution, which had established a socialist state in the Americas, was the practical expression of a full fledged capitalist modernization programme.

Thus the Cold War and the Cuban Revolution together with the changing internal power structure in Latin America were critical factors in the promotion of development and modernization programmes in Latin America. These were one aspect of historical trends of a more economic and global nature. In particular the emergence of the U.S.A. as the superpower in the capitalist camp, with its vast endowment of natural resources and its dynamic and expanding industrial system, was beginning to change the nature of the international economic order built up by Britain and Western Europe in the nineteenth century. After World War II, the massive expansion of U.S. overseas investment was concentrated in manufacturing and related marketing and financial services rather than in primary products, apart from oil. Looked at in institutional terms this is the period of the phenomenal expansion of the transnational corporation. The Alliance for Progress represented therefore a coalition of the new transnational industrial elites of the centre and the modernizing elites of the peripheral countries. For some years, in the early 1960s, national and international development efforts seemed well on the way towards accelerating industrialization, modernization, urbanization, social mobility, decolonization and political democracy in the countries that used to be called 'underdeveloped'. Marx's dictum: 'the country that is more developed only shows to the less developed the image of its own future', seemed about to be proved correct.

But the development record of the 1960s and early 1970s eventually turned out to be ambivalent. Although accelerated economic growth was supposed to increase employment opportunities, it soon became apparent that unemployment and underemployment, particularly in the urban areas, was rising dramatically and creating staggering problems of urban poverty. At the same time skills, income and wealth were concentrated in the hands of a small entrepreneurial and professional elite and income inequality was accentuated. Although industrial expansion and diversification had gone quite far in many countries, the benefits associated with this process in the developed countries did not materialize. Rather than the export structure being diversified, primary product exports continued to predominate. Instead of the local entrepreneurial class being strengthened, the subsidiaries of transnational corporations took over the more dynamic industrial activities and larger scale enterprises. With foreign control of industry, capital-intensive innovations were continuously introduced, intensifying conspicuous consumption and the waste of existing capital stock, and increasing imports and other foreign exchange requirements.

In the absence of structural reforms in the rural areas, which proved to be politically unviable, agricultural modernization increased yields and productivity per man in the larger estates, generated additional rents for the landowning class, and contributed to the disruption and stagnation of rural communities and smallholders, thereby accelerating rural emigration. The same phenomena of the 'subsidiarization' and expansion of the larger enterprises, and the consequent displacement and stagnation of the smaller national firms, can be seen to a greater or lesser extent in every branch of economic activity: trade, construction, finance, transport, mass media, sometimes even bringing in the state itself through its association with foreign subsidiaries.

Urban unemployment and social polarization led to a stronger emphasis on 'social' policies: new attempts at introducing progressive taxation, increased government expenditure on education, housing and health services, special programmes in support of the urban poor, regional policies for backward areas. Given the underlying structural situation and processes which these policies attempted to redress, their effects were at best negligible, and at worst a contribution to the negative trends enumerated above.

The situation became even more dramatic in the early 1970s. Governments had been expanding their activities and expenditures heavily, while their revenues continued to be derived essentially from a relatively stagnant and unstable foreign sector. Similarly, foreign payments on current and capital account rose rapidly with the increase in investment, consumption, foreign ownership and private and public foreign debt, while the export structure remained essentially unchanged. Urban income and population growth frequently outran the increase in marketable rural production. These and other disequilibria fuelled internal inflation and balance-of-payments crises, accentuating foreign indebtedness. The need to control inflation, to limit imports and expand exports, to control the urban poor and repress rural uprisings led several countries to introduce severe deflationary policies implemented by authoritarian regimes. Rather than easing tensions and facilitating political democracy, development has aggravated economic, class, cultural and political polarization and conflict.

Faced with this situation, development thinking took two different directions. One argued that this was the inevitable consequence of the transition to capitalist development, the price to be paid in order to achieve development. The other elaborated a radical critique, suggesting that capitalist development in the periphery would not reproduce the historical capitalist development path, that the current crisis would not be overcome with more of the same kind of development policies. The first approach is still followed by the

majority of development practitioners. But although much development thinking in academic circles, particularly in the developed
countries, continued to be based on the modernization paradigm
because of the internal dynamics—or rather, statics—of the academic establishment, development thinking among social scientists
involved in development planning in the developing countries began
to change radically in the mid-1960s, particularly in Latin America.

To begin with, it became increasingly clear that there had been a
reification of economics in development thinking almost to the
exclusion of other social sciences. It was also apparent that the
solution was not to put the other disciplines side by side with
economics, to engage in the kind of interdisciplinary approach by
aggregation which had begun to surface in some writing on
development. The problem went much deeper; it had to do with the
static functionalist paradigm of all the modern social sciences—the
study of the economic, social and political operation of a national
society, given the structural-historical conditions of modern urban-
industrial capitalism. The problem of development, on the contrary,
was increasingly seen to be the study of the changes brought about
by the expansion of the capitalist mode of production into semi
and/or pre-capitalist social formations. Furthermore, it also became
clear that modern capitalism itself was not static, that it was
undergoing significant change under the influence of the new central
role played by the transnational business sector in symbiosis with
the State, upon the processes of capital accumulation, technological
innovation and demand manipulation on a global scale.
Development thought had therefore to start addressing itself to
understanding the contemporary dynamics of capitalism, in terms
both of its core and of its peripheries, the relationship between them
and—last but not least—of their relations with socialism.

In other words, it became evident that the unit of analysis of
development can no longer be the nation-state alone. Even if one
must still begin from the particular country one is interested in, its
specific historical development process must be put into the context
of the evolution of capitalism globally and of its local, internal
manifestations. These have typically been the determining factors
that have triggered off profound processes of structural transformation. The establishment of colonies, the struggle against the
colonizers, decolonization, the development of primary product
exports, foreign investment in local manufacturing, the effects of
world wars and crises, transfers of foreign institutions and culture
generally—these all play a central role in the historical evolution of
every underdeveloped country.

Although they have occurred at different times and take different forms, such phenomena constitute the common historical legacy of dependence. But the way in which they work themselves out in specific national and local societies depends essentially on the antecedent nature of these societies and their historical reaction to external stimulae. Therefore there are both common elements and great differences among the underdeveloped countries. A eurocentric or global perspective tends to stress homogeneity; a national perspective, on the contrary, stresses heterogeneity and singularity. Both perspectives are biased, and must complement each other.

The growing body of literature in Latin America, Africa and Asia on the historical evolution of countries and regions, in the context of the development of global capitalism, is throwing new light on the real nature of the development process. Economic and social history has received a great stimulus in the last decade from the questions raised by the crisis of development, and comparative history has been a particularly useful exercise for a better understanding of how contemporary situations have come about. The reincorporation of the historical dimension into development thinking has had other positive efforts. For economics itself, it has had the healthy consequence of forcing the analytical apparatus of the discipline to adapt to actual historical reality, rather than the reverse. Traditional micro and macro theory is being reformulated in an effort to determine the *relevant* variables and relationships, and a corresponding effort is under way to develop operational categories in terms of *appropriate* statistical frameworks. The recovery of the historical dimension has also made it clear that the disciplinary specialialization of the social sciences under the functionalist paradigm has made them inherently incapable of grasping the nature of the development process, despite their usefulness for the analysis of concrete partial situations.

Even if not wholly satisfactory, the analytical frameworks of classical political economy and particularly of Marxism do at least go in the directions required to analyse development: globalism and wholism. But to be useful they require historical specificity, in terms of the analysis of the structural characteristics of particular societies at given times and places. Even if we assume that the basic laws of capitalist development are unchanged, the mode of operation of capitalist economies varies under different institutional arrangements and cultural traditions. Capitalist development is not, as macrodynamic growth models would have us believe, a cumulative process of mechanical dynamics where everything is determined by an unchanged set of initial conditions.

On the contrary, as anyone that has actually been involved in development policy knows, capitalist development takes place in interaction with precapitalist and/or earlier capitalist formations. Its expansion requires a thorough reorganization of society, with new social forces gathering the power and strength to challenge the existing dominant groups and to take over the institutions that regulate the generation, appropriation and utilization of economic surplus. Economic growth implies changes in social structure, a redistribution of political power, institutional and cultural transformation, and this is a dialectical process, full of conflict.

Not only must there be structural change, but this change takes place through confrontation. The state, the main legitimate instrument of power and force, is usually the crucial battle ground between the different social groups. It is a central factor in the process of development, playing a fundamental role in allocating the surplus generated by the export sector to new social groups. The poverty of the social sciences, and particularly of economics, including classical political economy, in terms of their treatment of the role of the state has undoubtedly been one of the greatest weaknesses of development thinking.

The failure to perceive development as capitalist development, the ignorance of its history and lack of recognition of its peculiar contemporary characteristics are some of the reasons why development specialists have been so surprised at the results of development: economic growth with increased unemployment, growing inequality and polarization, new forms of dependence, and authoritarian regimes. The ideological blinkers of the modernization paradigm put all the emphasis on the positive and ex-post aspects of capitalist development, treating its end products—high living standards, relative reductions in social inequality, urban-industrial life styles, political democracy—as the means of development. The real history of capitalist development is made to stand on its head.

Capitalist development, as Schumpeter so aptly put it a long time ago, is a process of creative destruction. It might perhaps be worth recalling that when Western Europe was becoming industrialized during the nineteenth century, a substantial proportion of its population not only had to leave the countryside, but had to emigrate overseas. Around 60 million people left Europe between 1840 and 1920, compared with a total population in 1900 of around 300 million. Under present day conditions of the world-wide expansion of a highly innovative and capital intensive oligopoly capitalism, the destructive effects of development are still more severe in the peripheral countries than they were in the central capitalist countries.

In the industrial countries themselves two decades of unprecedented growth in the capitalist economy during the 1950s and 1960s also had unanticipated effects: alienation, consumerism, waste, excessive concentration of power, destruction of the environment, bureaucratization, the loss of jobs due to industries moving abroad and so forth. The recent depression, coupled with inflation, the international monetary crisis, uncertain prospects for economic growth, the inefficacy of Keynesian policies, the decline in the industrial countries' control over the world's natural resources and increasing concern about their availability, the threat of socialim both in Europe and in the developing countries, indicate profound development problems in the so-called developed countries; problems which are not only national but global, not only economic but also social, cultural and political. As a consequence, social scientists in these countries are also beginning to focus again on the central concern of classical political economy in the nineteenth century and of development thinking in recent years: the development of capitalism.

NOTES

1 *The Development of Development Thinking,* Report of the First Inter-Regional Meeting on Development Research, Communication and Education, 12–16 September, 1976, organized jointly by the Institute of Development Studies, and the OECD Development Centre.

2

MODERNIZATION AND DEPENDENCE: ALTERNATIVE PERSPECTIVES IN THE STUDY OF LATIN AMERICAN UNDERDEVELOPMENT

J. Samuel Valenzuela, Arturo Valenzuela

The end of World War II marked the beginning of fundamental transformations in world affairs. The defeat of the Axis Powers and the devastating toll which the war had exacted on Britain and the European allies propelled the United States into a position of economic and military pre-eminence. However, United States power did not go unchallenged. The Soviet Union was able to influence the accession to power of socialist régimes throughout Eastern Europe. And, a few years later, Chinese communists defeated their Western backed adversaries to gain control of the most populous nation on earth. These events called for an urgent strategy to revitalize the economies of the Western nations. With massive U.S. public and private economic investment, Western Europe soon recovered from the ravages of war. However that recovery, and the dramatic progress made by West Germany and Japan, did not simply recreate the economic system of the pre-war years. Multinational corporations, mostly U.S. based, soon became the dominant force in international affairs changing the very character of the international economic system (Sunkel, 1971; Sunkel and Fuenzalida, in this volume).

But World War II ushered in another important change whose global implications would not be felt for some years. The weakening of the European powers and the logic of a war effort aimed at preserving freedom and self-determination, marked the final collapse of the vast colonial empires of the nineteenth century and the establishment of a multiplicity of states each claiming sovereign and independent status. These 'new nations' soon drew the attention of U.S. policy makers concerned with the claim that Marxism presented the best and most logical road to full incorporation into the modern world. They also captured the attention and imagination of U.S. scholars who, in the pursuit of knowledge as well as the desire to influence appropriate governmental policy, began to produce a vast body of literature on the 'developing' nations.

For many economists the solution to the problems of the 'Third World' was simply to turn to the same policies applied so successfully to Europe with a massive transfer of capital and technology to spur economic growth. But, other social scientists questioned the viability of such a strategy. Before appropriate policies could be elaborated they argued that a prior and more basic question needed answering: 'Why is there such a stark contrast in the developmental experience of a handful of 'Western' countries and the rest of the world? Why did the United States and Europe achieve high levels of economic and technological development while most of the nations of Africa, Asia and Latin America continue to live in the remote past?'

The answer to these questions led to the development of what will be called in this essay the 'modernization perspective'. Elaborated by a few economists (disillusioned with the assumptions of economic theory) and by anthropologists, sociologists and political scientists, this perspective argued that it was essential to consider the cultural characteristics of the 'new' nations in determining their potential for economic growth. The 'non-economic' factors in development became the cornerstone of a new conceptual framework with alternative policy implications which would soon influence the United States response to the 'Third World'.[1]

As with other world areas, the study of Latin America, which in the United States had been the province of a few historians, experienced dramatic growth. The expansion of academic departments and area studies programmes supported by the federal government and private foundations, created a whole new generation of social scientists exploring the sociological and political aspects of Latin American development. Though 'Latin Americanists' did not write the major theoretical or conceptual works of the modernization literature, that perspective soon became the dominant approach influencing the methodology and conclusions of the most important and trend setting studies.

United States scholars, however, were not the only ones preoccupied with the difficulties of applying neo-classical economic assumptions to the developmental problems of Latin America. In international agencies, notably the United Nations Economic Commission for Latin America, and university research centres, Latin American social scientists tried to come to grips with the widespread economic stagnation which affected Latin America in the post-war period. Working separately, often with little communication among each other, scholars in various disciplines began to widen the scope of their work to search for more basic explanations for the relative underdevelopment of their region in relationship to the rest of the Western world. Many of these intellectual strands came together in the 1960s, particularaly in Santiago, with the elaboration of a more general and comprehensive conceptual framework for the study of Latin America. The 'dependency perspective' differing sharply from its United States counterpart soon became the dominant approach in Latin American intellectual circles and continues to guide the research efforts of scholars of different disciplinary and political persuasions.

It is revealing that the most important writings of the 'dependency perspective' have still not been translated into English, over a decade after the first mimeographed drafts began to circulate in Santiago, despite the fact that Spanish and Portuguese versions have gone into repeated printings. Indeed, dependency analysis became known in the United States and Europe not through the writings of Latin Americans but through interpreters such as Andre Gunder Frank whose work differs substantially from that of the most important authors in the field such as Fernando Henrique Cardoso, Osvaldo Sunkel and Theotonio dos Santos.[2]

Modernization and dependency are two very different perspectives seeking to explain the same reality. They originated in different areas, with different evaluative judgements, different assumptions, different methodologies and different explanations.[3] The purpose of this essay is not to describe the sociological origins of the two perspectives, their 'extra scientific' elements, but to systematically compare their conceptual approaches to the study of Latin America. As such, it will be necessary to consider the two perspectives as 'ideal types', accentuating important characteristics of each framework in a manner not found in any particular author, and neglecting to fully develop the specific arguments of individual writers. There is a good deal of variety and several polemics (particularly in the dependency literature) stemming from disagreements over the operationalization of concepts, the way in which certain processes occur empirically, or even in the emphasis given to important elements of the conceptual framework. Though the essay will refer to some of the controversies within each perspective its purpose is to draw broad comparisons in order to provide some judgement as to the relative utility of the competing frameworks in explaining Latin American underdevelopment.

THE MODERNIZATION PERSPECTIVE

In discussing the modernization perspective this review will describe the assumptions of the literature drawing on the work of some of the most important writers. That discussion will be followed by some illustrations of the use of the modernization perspective in the study of Latin America. This format is dictated by the fact, noted earlier, that specialists on Latin America have for the most part, contributed few important theoretical efforts to the field. This is particularly true for sociology and political science, less so for anthropology and developmental economics.[4] Though there are many explanations for the failure of Latin Americanists to do pioneering work, one of the most compelling is that Latin America, in contrast with Africa or Asia, presented far greater ambiguities, making it much more difficult to point to obvious differences with the experience of the developed countries. Indeed, the early theorizing made a distinction between the Western and Non-Western experience, and, as John Martz has noted 'the Latin Americanist inevitably wondered if his own region was included' (Martz 71, p.78). That fact, however, did not prevent many students of Latin America from drawing extensively from the modernization literature once it became the dominant interpretation in the field.

Assumptions

The basic building block of the modernization perspective is the structuring of parallel ideal types of social organization and value systems at two polar ends of the evolutionary process. The use of the 'tradition-modernity' dichotomy implies that a qualitative change takes place as societies move from one end of the continuum to the other, though it is never clear at exactly what point societies become modern. Third world countries, including those of Latin America, are perceived to be below the threshold of modernity, with a preponderance of traditional features. The use of parallel ideal types was not an innovation in the literature. It was borrowed from several classic 19th and early twentieth century studies also preoccupied with accounting for the differences between European societies and the subject peoples of the colonial empires.[5]

The specific elements included in the two polarities varies substantially in the literature. The traditional society is variously understood as having a predominance of ascriptive, particularistic, diffuse and affective patterns of action, an extended kinship structure with a multiplicity of functions, a preponderance of primary groups, a relatively simple occupational system, little spatial and social mobility, low literacy rates, a deferential stratification system, mostly primary economic activities, a tendency toward autarchy of social units, little outside contact, almost no change, an undifferentiated political structure, with traditional elitist and hierarchical sources of authority, etc. By contrast, the modern society is characterized by a predominance of achievement, universalistic, specific and neutral orientations and patterns of action, a nuclear family structure serving limited functions, a preponderance of secondary groups and affiliations, a complex and highly differentiated occupational system, high rates of spatial and social mobility, universal literacy, a predominance of secondary economic activities and production for exchange, the institutionalization of change and self sustained growth, extensive communications networks, highly differentiated political structures with rational legal sources of authority etc.[6]

The literature assumes that the values, institutions and patterns of action of traditional society are both an expression and cause of underdevelopment and constitute the main obstacle in the way of modernization. To enter the modern world, underdeveloped societies have to overcome traditional norms and structures opening the way for social, economic and political transformations. Generally speaking, for some authors modernization derives from a greater differentiation of societal functions, institutions and role and the development of new sources of integration. (Smelser 1971; Parsons 1966). For others, modernization is based more on the actual transformation of individuals through their assimilation of modern values. (Mclelland, 1967; Hagen, 1962).[7] The primary source of change is discussed in terms of innovations, that is the rejection of procedures related to traditional institutions, together with the adoption of new ideas, techniques, values and organizations. Innovations are pursued by innovators and the group that assumes this role inevitably clashes with defenders of the old order. The struggle is over two different ways of life.[8]

In describing the assumptions of the modernization literature it is important to note that the modern pole of the parallel ideal types is the pivotal conceptual and analytical point, because it best approximates the characteristics that societies must attain in order to develop. The traditional end of the dichotomy is largely a residual category, established by logical opposition to the categories at the modern end. In turn, the basic features of the modern pole are derived from the history and imputed characteristics of those countries already considered modern, since in the process of modernization all societies will undergo by and large similar changes. That the societies considered modern are the source of universally useful conceptualization is explicitly recognized by many modernization writers. Historian Cyril Black notes, 'Although the problems raised by generalizations from a rather narrow base (the now modern countries) must be acknowledged, the definition of modernity takes the form of a set of characteristics believed to be applicable to all societies. This conception of modernity, when thought of as a model or ideal type, may be used as a yardstick with which to measure any society' (Black, 1966, pp.53–54). Political scientist Gabriel Almond expresses a similar view when he says that to study modernization in the non-Western areas the political scientist needs to 'master the model of the modern, which in turn can only be derived from the most careful empirical and formal analysis of the functions of the modern Western polities' (Almond, 1960, p.64). Sociologist Wilbert Moore adds that 'on the basis of what is known about the 'Western' experience, we can go rather far in predicting the course of social change in major parts of the social organization and value systems of societies which are now seeking to become part of the modern world' (Moore 1968, p.375).

For modernization theorists the previous assumptions are a logical extension of the view that the impetus to modernize in the now developed countries was the result of endogenous cultural and institutional transformations, while modernizing changes in the late developers results primarily from the exogenous process of diffusion of modern values and structural arrangements from the early modernizers. Modernizing elites are understood to be guided by the Western model adopting and adapting its technology, assimilating its values and patterns of action, importing its financial, industrial and educational institutions, etc. . . Western colonialism, foreign aid, foreign educational opportunities, overseas business investments, the mass media, etc. are all important channels for the transmission of modernity. For some writers this means that less developed countries will modernize in strikingly similar ways through acculturation into Western values and institutions. They see the world converging to a uniform and standarized culture resembling that of the United States and Western Europe.[9]

Though, as will be noted, there is disagreement on the extent to which traditional features will disappear or the extent to which only Western characteristics will serve the modernizing process, there is broad agreement on the notion that individual developing countries must in some way replicate the path followed by the early modernizers. The principal difference with already developed countries is not in the nature of the process but in its speed and intensity making it possible for the later modernizers to 'skip stages' or 'telescope time' (Silvert, 1966, p.261). Despite the fact that the modernization perspective stresses the importance of the worldwide context in its analysis of social change, the basic historical setting for modernization is the nation state, established at an early phase in the process. As Cyril Black notes, Societies in the process of modernization must ... be considered both as *independent* entities, the traditional institutions of which are being adapted to modern functions, and also as societies under the influence of many *outside* forces (Black, 1966, p.50, emphasis added). The world is fragmented, and yet bound by intersocietal communication. It is, in the words of Dankwart Rustow, a 'world of nations' (Rustow, 1967).

Finally, it is clear that the stress on values and the differences, in values from one context to another has some important implications for the modernization perspective's concept of human nature. The characteristic of developed societies, which has received the most attention in the literature as the key ingredient in the modernization process, is the presumed 'rationality' of both leaders and followers. Economic, social and political development in Western Europe and the United States is thought to be closely related to the widespread existence of values which allow for 'rational' decisions to maximize satisfactions, both individually and collectively. Indeed, Wilbert Moore has recently argued that modernization is best understood as 'the process of rationalization of social behaviour and social organization'. Rationalization or the 'institutionalization of rationality' is defined as the 'normative expectation that objective information and rational calculus of procedures will be applied in pursuit or achievement of any utilitarian goal ... It is exemplified but not exhausted in the use of sophisticated technology in construction and production' (Moore, 1977, pp.34–35). As such modernization theorists agree with the assumption of economic rationality implicit in the economic growth models of traditional economic theory. Where modernization theorists differ with traditional economics is in the assumption that rational behaviour is a universal human characteristic. As Wilbert Moore noted in an article written in the 1950s for 'traditional economic theory ... human attitudes and motives are simply assumed to be appropriate to rational choice ... human wants are thought to be essentially unlimited, and human nature pretty much the same wherever encountered' (Moore, 1964, p.291). Moore adds that the contribution of sociologists and anthropologists was to question this assumption of a 'similarity of human nature'. By contrast with the developed countries, in developing nations attitudes and values are such that individuals 'behave in ways that are 'irrational' or 'non-rational' as judged on economic grounds' (Moore, 1964 p.292). This explains why Bolivian business men will not take risks with their capital in an effort to maximize future profits, preferring to put money in Swiss banks. Or why Ecuadorians will study law rather than enter a more lucrative career in business or technology. Or why Colombian politicians will be driven by status considerations rather than by the progamatic outlook of their North American counterparts.

In concluding this section, it is necessary to note that from the very outset certain elements of the modernization perspective came into criticism from scholars who generally shared its basic assumptions. It is revealing that much of the criticism came from researchers who had done extensive field work in Third World areas and were experts in many of the features of individual 'traditional' societies. They were uncomfortable with the arbitrary designation of a wide variety of phenomena as 'traditional' with little concern for the rich, complex and often strikingly different characteristics subsumed under that vague concept. That in itself, however, was not a fundamental problem. Given the assumptions of the dual polarities, the particular characteristics of individual non-modern societies are important only in so far as they aid or hinder modernizing transformations. What turned out to be a more serious criticism was the argument put forward by various scholars that many belief systems and institutional arrangements with no common referent in the United States or Western Europe could have modernizing functions. Joseph Gusfield has conveniently summarized many of the relevant arguments adding that even in modern societies certain traditional characteristics may survive or gain renewed importance (Gusfield, 1967).[10] These arguments, however, do not constitute a rejection of the assumptions of the modernization perspective but an illustration of their use. Despite the title of his article, Gusfield does not argue that tradition and modernity are 'misplaced polarities'. Rather, he continues to accept the assumptions that tradition and modernity are valid theoretical polarities and that tradition in its many ramifications is the basic obstacle to modernization. Gusfield simply points to a confusion in the use of terms and the misapplication of the terms in concrete situations; not the appropriateness of the terms themselves. If a particular society or region experiences significant economic growth, what was thought to be an other wordly religion undermining rational economic behaviour may in fact be a creed capable of promoting the instrumental values conducive to modernization.

Recent amendments to the modernization perspective are extensions of the same internal critique and not fundamental challenges to its basic assumptions. Reflecting the sobering reality of the 1970s with many studies pointing to an ever increasing gap between rich nations and poor nations (Adelman and Morris, 1973; Sunkel, 1971) several of the most prominent modernization theorists have questioned the earlier optimism of an inevitable and uniform process of modernization leading to a convergence of socieities on economic as well as social and political grounds (Moore 1971: 31, Eisenstad, 1973). Others, while not questioning the inevitability of the process, point more forcefully than before to its disruptive and negative effects which affect the 'latecomers' much more seriously than the 'survivors' (Levy, 1972). It still remains the case, however, that to modernize, however good or inevitable that process is, it is necessary to overcome traditional values and institutions and substitute them for more modern ones.

Latin America and the Modernization Perspective

Mainstream United States scholarship on Latin American has implicitly or explicitly drawn on the modernization perspective to explain Latin American underdevelopment. Often contrasting the Latin American experience to that of the United States or Western Europe, it has argued that traditional attitudes and institutions stemming from the colonial past have proven to be serious, if not fatal, stumbling blocks to any indigenous effort to develop economically, socially or politically. The values of catholicism, of large Indian populations, or of aristocratic rural elites have contributed to 'irrational' patterns of behaviour highly detrimental to modernization.

One of the most influential statements of the modernization perspective applied to Latin America is Seymour Martin Lipset's 'Values, Education and Entrepreneurship', the introductory essay to the best-selling text *Elites in Latin America*. Lipset draws directly on modernization theorists such as Talcott Parsons and David McClelland in arguing that 'the relative failure of Latin American countries to develop on a scale comparable to those of North America or Australasia has been seen as, in some part, a consequence of variations in value systems dominating these two areas. The overseas offspring of Great Britain seemingly had the advantage of values derivative in part from the Protestant Ethic and from the formation of 'New Societies' in which feudal ascriptive elements were missing. Since Latin America, on the other hand is Catholic, it has been dominated for centuries by ruling elites who created a social structure congruent with feudal social values' (Lipset, 1966, p.3).[11]

In his article Lipset concentrates primarily on explaining economic underdevelopment as a function of the lack of adequate entrepreneurial activity. He notes that the lack of instrumental behaviour, weak achievement orientations and the disdain for the pragmatic and material have prevented the rise of a risk-taking business sector oriented toward rational, competitive and bureaucratic enterprise. The educational system has only served to perpetuate the problem by continuing to socialize the population with inappropriate attitudes. He notes that 'Even (in Argentina) the second most developed Latin American country . . . the traditional landed, aristocratic disdain for manual work, industry, and trading, continues to affect the educational orientations of many students' (Lipset, 1966, p. 19). Lipset cites a whole host of studies, many of which were based on survey research in Latin America, to conclude that 'the comparative evidence from the various nations of the Americas sustains the generalization that cultural values are among the major factors which affect the potentiality for economic development' (Lipset 1966, p. 30).[12] Recent textbooks on Latin America have clearly been influenced by such observations. Thus Robert Adie and Guy E. Poitras note that 'there is in Latin America a social climate in which the very rewards which have spurred on the entrepreneurs in, for example, North America, are consistently deemphasized . . . socioeconomic change dependent on business activities . . . cannot necessarily be expected to follow the same path as it has elsewhere' (Adie and Poitras, 1974, pp. 73, 74).[13]

K. H. Silvert, one of the leading authorities on Latin America until his death in 1976, wrote extensively on the impact of traditional values not only on Latin America's 'poor' economic performance but also on its 'poor' political performance. Silvert made it very clear that Latin America's experience had to be gauged against that of the more advanced countries. As he noted, in a recently reprinted article, development has to be 'defined with reference to the experience of Western Europe and its cultural spawn. What else is one to do other than define development by the selection of certain characteristics of the already developed states?' (Silvert, 1974, p. 160). On the basis of implicit comparisons with his own society, Silvert goes on to say that 'there is something in the quality of the Latin American man and his culture which has made it difficult for him to be truly modern. . . which has made this part of the Western world so prone to excesses of scoundrels, so politically irrational in seeking economic growth, and so ready to reach for gimmicks' (Silvert, 1974, p. 162). It is judgements such as those which, in turn, led Silvert to argue during the heyday of the Alliance for Progress, that the United States should make every effort to 'trip the domestic political scales' in the direction of 'modernizing groups'. 'Moneys spent (by the U.S.) on the kind of education, for instance, which will attract persons of a modern mentality can be confidently expected to assist the general move toward development. Moneys spent in bettering or certifying the positions of students of a traditional cast will make more robust the anti-development sectors . . . if help can be extended to the attitudinally developed in such countries, then it should be done. Otherwise assistance merely certifies non-development or invites unpredictable revolution' (Silvert, 1966, p. 271).[14]

Similar sentiments are expressed by Robert Scott, another prominent Latin Americanist. Scott notes that the 'inability of Latin America's political structures to act as efficient integrating mechanisms. . . . suggests that the only real solution in the long run is to alter the value system of the people. If both elites and followers can be modernized, the existing political institutions . . . will adjust themselves to changes, or new working structures will evolve to perform the function' (Scott, 1966, pp. 133–34). A recent text echoes that theme: 'A traditional psychocultural world does indeed predominate in Latin America . . . to depict collective attitudes and value traits as basically traditional does help to explain much of political life south of the Rio Grande. . .' (Duncan, 1976, pp. 102–103).[15]

The basic assumption that the key to Latin American society can be found in its cultural values is not only characteristic of the literature of the 1960s and of a rash of new textbooks aimed at the college market.[16] It has also found renewed currency in the writings of a number of United States historians and political scientists. In what has become known as the 'new corporatism' an effort is being made to explain economic, social and especially political, features of Latin American countries by stressing the durability of Catholic and 'Thomistic' values. Authoritarian political patterns, corporativist economic organizations and the disdain for democratic and liberal values are the results of a 'distinct tradition'. As a prominent representative of this 'new' intellectual fashion has argued 'largely untouched by the great revolutionary movements—social, economic, religious, political, intellectual—that we associate with the emergence of the modern order, the Iberic and Latin American nations remained locked in this traditional patterns of values of institutions that postponed and retarded development' (Wiarda, 1974, p. 269).[17]

Wiarda maintains that the focus on Latin American corporatism represents a significant departure from the modernization school. He bases his claim on the fact that he stresses the importance of studying Latin America on its 'own terms' without advocating the desirability or inevitability of change along United States or Western European lines. He questions the convergence thesis noting that 'many traditional societies, and particularly those of the Iberic Latin nations, have proved remarkably permeable and flexible, assimilating at various points more 'modern' and 'rational' elements, but without losing their characteristics' (Wiarda, 1973, p. 232). But this position differs little from the well established 'modernity of tradition' argument referred to earlier. Wiarda merely provides an example of the concrete application of the tradition-modernity dichotomy to the Latin American case; he does not question the basic assumptions of the perspective. The impressive examples of economic development, which have occurred from time to time in Latin America are simply due to the adaptability of some traditional values and institutions. He continues to assume that the modern and rational are assimilated from outside and constitute the necessary ingredients to induce change. However remarkable the flexibility and permeability of tradition in Latin America, it is implicit in Wiarda's argument that such flexibility and permeability have been the exception rather than the rule. Otherwise, Latin America would not have fallen behind in the road to development.[18]

THE DEPENDENCE PERSPECTIVE

Like the modernization perspective, the dependency perspective resulted from the work of many different scholars in different branches of the social sciences. Much of the work proceeded in an inductive fashion. This was particularly the case with economists working in ECLA who first sought to explain the underdevelopment of Latin America by focusing on the unequal terms of trade between exporters of raw materials and exporters of manufactured goods. ECLA 'doctrine' called for a concerted effort to diversify the export base of Latin American countries and accelerate industrialization efforts through import substitution. However, the continued difficulties with that model of development soon led to a focus on the internal constraints to industrialization, with an emphasis on factors such as distorting effects of unequal land tenure patterns and the corrosive results of an inflation best explained by structural rather than monetary variables. Soon these two trends came together with scholars such as Osvaldo Sunkel (1967) attempting to combine the early emphasis on external variables with the internal constraints to development (Girvan, 1973; Chilcote, 1974; O'Brien, 1975).

But this dependency perspective was also anticipated by many Latin American historians who had for many years been working on various aspects of economic history. The studies of Sergio Bagú and Luis Vitale on the colonial period, and works of historians such as Julio Cesar Jobet and Hernán Ramirez Necochea on the evolution of Chilean history, clearly stressed the close interrelation between domestic developments in Latin America and developments in metropolitan countries. And, particularly in Brazil sociologists such as Florestán Fernandez, Octavio Ianni, Fernando Henrique Cardoso and Theotonio dos Santos turned to broad structural analyses of the factors of underdevelopment, or focused on entrepreneurial elites with a primary focus on the context in which they behaved. The fact that so many of these scholars found themselves in Santiago in the 1960s only contributed to further development of the perspective.[11]

Dependency analysts deliberately part company with the assumptions of neo-classical economics and modernization because of the failure of that conceptual framework to provide explanations for important 'anomalies' and because of a deliberate rejection of many of its evaluative assumptions. In its emphasis on the expansive nature of capitalism and in its structural analysis of society, the dependence literature draws on Marxist insights and is related to the Marxist theory of imperialism. However, its examination of processes in Latin America imply important revisions in classical Leninist formulations both historically and in light of recent trends. The focus is on explaining Latin American underdevelopment, and not on the functioning of capitalism, though some authors argue that their efforts will contribute to an understanding of capitalism and its contradictions.

Assumptions

The dependency perspective rejects the key assumption made by modernization writers that the appropriate unit of analysis in studying development in Latin America is the national society. The domestic cultural and institutional features of those societies are simply not the key independent variables accounting for the relative backwardness of the area, though, as will be seen below, domestic factors are certainly critical intervening variables. The relative presence of traditional and modern features may, or may not, help to differentiate societies; but it does not in itself explain the origins of modernity in some contexts and the lack of modernity in others. As such the tradition-modernity polarity is of little value as a fundamental working concept. The dependency perspective assumes that the development of a national or regional unit can only be understood in connection with its historical insertion into the worldwide political-economic systems which emerged with the wave of European colonizations of the world. This global system is thought to be characterized by the unequal but combined development of its different components, some of which constitute its 'centre' and others its 'periphery'. According to Sunkel and Paz:

> A fundamental working hypothesis . . . for the explanation of the process of change in Latin America is to consider underdevelopment as part of the global historical process of development. Both underdevelopment and development are aspects of the same phenomenon, both are historically simultaneous, both are linked functionally and, therefore, interact and condition each other mutually. This results . . . in the division of the world between industrial, advanced or 'central' countries, and underdeveloped, backward or 'peripheral' countries. . . (Sunkel and Paz, 1970, p. 6).

The centre is viewed as capable of dynamic development responsive to internal needs, and as the main beneficiary of the global links. On the other hand, the periphery is seen as having a reflex type of development; one which is both constrained by its incorporation into the global system and which results from its adaptation to the requirements of the expansion of the centre. As Theotonio dos Santos indicates:

> Dependency is a situation in which a certain number of countries have their economy conditioned by the development and expansion of another. . . placing the dependent countries in a backward position exploited by the dominant countries. (Dos Santos, 1970, p. 180).

It is important to stress that the process can be understood only by reference to its historical dimension and by focussing on the total network of social relations as they evolve in different contexts over time. For this reason dependence is characterized as 'structural, historical and totalizing' (Sunkel and Paz, 1970, p. 39) or an 'integral analysis of development' (Cardoso and Faletto, 1971: Chapter II). It is meaningless to develop, as some social scientists have, a series of synchronic statistical indicators to establish relative levels of dependence or independence among different national units in order to test the 'validity' of the model (Kaufman, Chernotsky and Geller, 1975; Chase Dun, 1975).[19] The unequal development of the world goes back to the sixteenth century with the formation of a capitalist world economy in which some countries in the centre come to specialize in industrial production of manufactured goods precisely because peripheral areas of the world were able to provide the necessary primary goods, agricultural and mineral, for consumption in the centre. The world system was clearly interdependent, but different units performed different functions. Contrary to some assumptions in economic theory the international division of labour did not lead to parallel development through comparative advantages. The centre state accumulated capital at the expense of the periphery but just as significantly the different roles of centre and peripheral societies in the international economic system had a profound effect on the evolution of internal social and political structures. Those which evolved in the centre reenforced dynamic development, those which evolved in the periphery reenforced economies with a narrow range of primary exports (Sunkel and Paz, 1970, pp. 44–45). The interdependent nature of the world capitalist system and the qualitative transformations in that system over time make it inconceivable to think that individual nations on the periphery could somehow replicate the evolutionary experience of the now developed nations.[20]

It follows from an emphasis on global structural processes and variations in internal structural arrangements, that the dependency perspective assumes that contextual variables, at least in the long run, shape and guide the behaviour of groups and individuals. It is not inappropriate values and attitudes which contribute to the absence of entrepreneurial activities or to institutional arrangements reenforcing underdevelopment. Dependent, peripheral development produces an opportunity structure such that personal gain for dominant groups and entrepreneurial elements is not conducive to the collective gain of balanced development. This is a fundamental difference with much of the modernization literature. It implies that dependence analysts, though they do not articulate the point explicitly, share the classical economic theorists' view of human nature. They assume that individuals in widely different societies are capable of persuing rational patterns of behaviour, able to assess information objectively in the pursuit of utilitarian goals. What varies is not the degree of rationality, but the structural foundations of the incentive systems which, in turn, produce different forms of behaviour given the same process of rational calculus. It was not a change in values which contributed to incipient industrialization in a country such as Chile in the late 1800s, but the flow of resources and the demand for new products generated by the expansion of the nitrate industry, Likewise it was not attitudinal transformations which generated the rapid industrialization which developed after the great depression, but the need to replace imports with domestic products. Because of the war the former were in short supply and, more importantly, governments undertook a deliberate policy of curbing imports. Or, as Cardoso points out in his studies of entrepreneurs in Brazil, it is not the values of entrepreneurs which condition their behaviour but the problems of technological dependence, the intervention of the state in the economy and their political weakness *vis-à-vis* domestic and foreign actors (Cardoso, 1964, 1971). What appear as exceptions or anomalies in the modernization literature, can be easily explained by a focus on contextual processes in the dependence literature given the different view of human nature.

It is necessary to underscore the fact that dependence writers stress the importance of the 'way internal and external structural components are connected' (Cardoso and Faletto, 1971, p. 20) in any elaboration of the structural context of underdevelopment. As such underdevelopment is not simply the result of 'external constraints' on peripheral societies, nor can dependence be operationalized solely with reference to clusters of external variables.[21] Dependence in any given society is a complex set of associations in which the external dimensions are determinative in varying degrees of the internal ones and, indeed, internal variables may very well reinforce the pattern of external linkages. Historically it has been rare on the periphery for local interests to develop which are capable of charting a successful policy of self sustained development. This is the case because dominant local interests, given the nature of class arrangements emerging from the characteristics of peripheral economies, tend to be those which favour the preservation or rearticulation of patterns of dependency which are clearly in their interests.

It is also important to stress that while relations of dependence viewed in a historical perspective help to explain underdevelopment, it does not follow that dependent relations today necessarily perpetuate across the board underdevelopment. With the evolution of the world system, the impact of dependent relations can change in particular contexts. This is why Cardoso, in studying contemporary Brazil stresses the possibility of 'associated-dependent development', and Sunkel and Fuenzalida are able to envision sharp economic growth among countries most tied into the contemporary transnational system.[22] The point is that because external-internal relations are complex, and because changes in the world system over time introduce new realities, it is indispensable in the dependency perspective to study comparatively concrete national and historical situations. As Anibal Quijano states 'the relationships of dependency . . . take on many forms. The national societies in Latin America are dependent, as is the case with the majority of the Asian, African and some European countries. However, each case does not present identical dependency relations'. The dependency perspective has therefore concentrated on a careful historical evaluation of the similarities and differences in the 'situations of dependency' of the various Latin American countries over time (Cardoso and Faletto, 1971, p. 19–20). For Sunkel and Paz this implies careful attention to 'preexisting conditions' in different context (Sunkel and Paz, 1970, pp. 5, 9).

The descriptive categories used to characterize the various phases of the world system and the differing configurations of external-internal linkages, follow logically from the insistence on a diachronic analysis and its application to concrete cases. The dependency perspective is above all a historical model with no claim to 'universal validity'. This is why the dependence perspective has paid less attention so far to the formulation of precise theoretical constructs such as those found in some of the modernization literature. Its emphasis has not been on the elaboration of interrelationship between conceptual assumptions, but on providing guidelines through a specification of historical phases. The description of these phases is an integral part of the framework.

The dependence literature distinguishes between the 'mercantilistic' colonial period (1500–1750), the period of 'outward-growth' dependent on primary exports (1750–1914), the period of the crisis of the 'liberal model' (1914–1950), and the current period of 'transnational capitalism' (for example, Sunkel and Paz, 1970).

As already noted, because of the need for raw materials for the growing industrialization of England, Germany, the United States and France, the Latin American productive structures were aimed from the outset at the export market. During the colonial period, the specialization of the economy was imposed by the Iberian monarchies, which attempted to monopolize the export/import trade (Bagú, 1949; Vitale, 1967). As Bagú notes in his classic study, 'Colonial production was not directed by the needs of national consumers, and not even by the interests of local producers. The lines of production are structured and transformed as necessary in order to fit into an order determined by the imperial metropolis. The colonial economy was, therefore, shaped by its complementary character. The products that did not compete with those of Spain or Portugal in the metropolitan, international or colonial markets, found tolerance or stimulus. . .' (Bagú, 1949, pp. 122–23). During the nineteenth century, it became a policy actively pursued by the politically dominant export oriented entrepreneurial groups. The independence movement did not necessarily attempt to transform the internal productive structures; rather, it was aimed at eliminating Iberian interference in the commercialization of products to and from England and northern Europe. The logic of the productive system in this period of 'outwardly directed development', in ECLA's terms, was not conducive, to the creation of a large industrial sector: economic rationality—not only of individual entrepreneurs, but also of the system—dictated payments in kind and/or extremely low wages and/or the use of slavery. Thus the internal market was extremely limited. Furthermore, the accumulation of foreign exchange made the acquisition of industrial products abroad relatively easy. The expansion of the local economies depended more on political than on economic factors. Its success was guaranteed with a saleable export commodity, plenty of labour, and plenty of land for extensive use.

There were, however, important differences among the various regions and countries. During the colonial period, these are attributable to the variety of colonial administrations, the differences in natural resources and the types of production established. During the nineteenth century one of the principal differences between the various countries is attributed to the degree of control local elites had over various lines of productive activities for export. Although in all countries local elites controlled production in the export sector initially (external commercialization was mainly under foreign control), towards the end of the century this control (or significant parts of it) was relinquished in some countries to foreign capital. Where this occurred, the economic role of local elites was reduced considerably; though the importance of this reduction varied considerably, depending both on the degree to which the foreign enclave displaced the local elite from the export sector, and on the extent to which its economic activities were diversified. Concurrently, the state bureaucracy expanded significantly and acquired increasing importance due to its new regulatory functions on the enclave exploitation and its receipt of export taxation. The state thus became the principal intermediary between the local economy and the enclave, which in itself exerted little direct internal secondary effects. Other differences, especially at the turn of the century, can be seen in the varying importance of an incipient industrial sector (strongest in Argentina) (Dorfman, 1967), the size and importance of middle and working class groups (the latter being specially significant in countries, such as Chile, in which mining was a crucial sector for the economy and the state, the variations in export products, natural resources, etc.[23]

The World Wars and the depression produced a crisis in the export oriented economies through the collapse of external demand, and therefore of the capacity to import (Sunkel and Paz, 1970, p. 347). The adoption of fiscal and monetary policies aimed at supporting the internal market and avoiding the negative effects of the external disequilibrium, produced a favourable climate for the growth of the industrial sector under national auspices. The available foreign exchange was employed to acquire capital goods to substitute importation of consumer articles (Tavares, 1969). The early successes of the transition to what the ECLA calls 'inwardly directed development' depended to a large extent on the different political alliances which emerged in the various national settings, and on the characteristics of the social and political structures inherited from the pre-crisis period.

Thus in the enclave situations the earliest developments were attained in those countries, such as Mexico and Chile, where middle and lower class groups were allied in supporting state development policies, which ultimately lead to the strengthening of the urban bourgeoisie. These alliances were successful, in Chile, due to the importance of middle class groups and parties in the final period of export oriented development, and the early political and trade-unionist organization of the working class. The antecedents of the Mexican situation are to be found in the destruction of the power of traditional agricultural elites through the revolution that developed at the end of the *porfiriato*. These structural conditions were absent in other enclave situations (Bolivia, Perú, Venezuela and Central America), where the internal development phase began later under new conditions of dependence, although in some cases with similar political alliances (Bolivia, Venezuela, Guatemala, Costa Rica). Through the acute crisis period the agrarian based and largely non-exporting groups were able to remain in power, appealing in some cases to military governments, and preserving the political scheme that characterized the export oriented period.

In the non-enclave situations, considerable growth of the industrial sector was attained in Argentina and Brazil. In Argentina the export oriented agrarian entrepreneurs had also invested considerably in production for the internal market; the contraction of the export sector only accentuated this trend. In Brazil the export oriented agrarian groups collapsed with the crisis; the state, as in Chile and Mexico, assumed a major developmental role with the support of a complex alliance formed by urban entrepreneurs, non-export agrarian elites, popular sectors, and middle class groups. In Colombia the export oriented agrarian elites remained in power and did not foster significant internal industrialization until the fifties (Cardoso and Faletto, 1971: Chapters 4 and 5; Sunkel and Paz, 1970: Part IV, Chapter 2).

The import substituting industrialization attained greatest success in Argentina, Brazil and Mexico. It soon, however, reached its limits, given the parameters under which it was realized. Since capital goods for the establishment of industry were acquired in the central nations, the success of the policy ultimately depended on adequate foreign exchange supplies. After reaching maximum growth as a result of the accumulation of foreign exchange during the Second World War, the industrialization programs could only continue afterwards—given the available political options—on the basis of an increased external debt and further reliance on foreign investment. The accumulation of foreign reserves had permitted the success of the national-populist alliances in Argentina and Brazil, which gave the workers greater welfare while maintaining investment rates. The downfall of Perón and the suicide of Vargas symbolize the end of the period of relatively easy import substitution.

But the final blow to 'import substitution' industrialization came not from difficulties in the periphery but further transformations in the centre. With rapid economic recovery the multinational corporations sought new markets and cheaper production sites for their increasingly technological manufacturing process. Dependency consequently, acquired a 'new character' which would have a profound effect on Latin America. Several processes were involved resulting in (a) the investment of centrally based corporations in manufactures within the periphery for sales in its internal market or as Cardoso and Faletto call the process, the 'internationalization of the internal market'; (b) a new international division of labour in which the periphery imports capital goods, technology and raw materials from the central nations, 'exports' profits, and sells its traditional raw materials and a few manufactured items produced by multinational subsidiaries (although these, as indicated above, produce mainly for the internal and other peripheral markets); (c) a denationalization of the older import substituting industries established originally (Dos Santos, 1966; Cardoso and Faletto, 1970; Sunkel, 1970, 1971). Although productive structures throughout Latin America reveal 'new dependence' characteristics, the process has asserted itself to a greater extent in the largest internal markets. This has been particularly the case in Brazil, where the weakness of the trade-union movement (the comparison with Argentina in this respect is instructive), coupled with authoritarian political structures have created a singularly favourable investment climate. Brazil's (and to a lesser extent, Mexico's) 'situation of dependency' is thus understood to be best suited within Latin America to the present expansion of the centre.

In subsequent and more recent works writers within the dependency framework have pursued different strategies of research. Generally speaking, the early phases of the historical process have received less attention, though the contribution of Immanuel Wallerstein to an understanding of the origins of the World system is a major addition to the literature (Wallerstein, 1975). Most writers have preferred to focus on the current 'new situation' of dependence. Some have devoted more attention to an effort at elaborating the place of dependent capitalism as a contribution to the Marxist analysis of capitalist society. Scholars in this vein tend to argue more forcefully than others that dependent capitalism is impossible and that socialism provides the only historically possible alternative (Dos Santos, 1970; Bambirra, 1973). Others have focused more on the analysis of concrete cases of dependence, elaborating in some detail the various interconnections between domestic and foreign forces, and noting the possibility of different kinds of dependent development (Cardoso, 1973). Still others have turned their attention to characterizing the nature of the new capitalist system, with a particular emphasis on the emergence of a 'transnational system' which is rendering more complex and problematic the old distinctions of centre and periphery (Sunkel and Fuenzalida, this volume). Particularly for the last two tendencies in the literature, the emphasis is clearly on the design of new empirical studies while attempting to systematize further some of the propositions implicit in the general conceptual framework. But, the framework continues to be an 'approach' and is far from being conciously considered a 'theory' of development.

SUMMARY AND CONCLUSIONS

Modernization and dependence are two different perspectives each of which claims to provide conceptual and analytical tools capable of explaining the relative underdevelopment of Latin America. The object of inquiry is practically the only thing that these two competing 'visions' have in common, as they differ substantially not only on fundamental assumptions, but also on methodological implications and strategies for research.

Though there are variations in the literature, the *level of analysis* of a substantial tradition in the modernization perspective, and the one which informs most reflections on Latin America, is behavioural or micro-sociological. The primary focus is on individuals or aggregates of individuals, their values, attitudes and beliefs. The dependence perspective, by contrast, is structural or macrosciological. Its focus is on the mode of production, patterns of international trade, political and economic linkages between elites in peripheral and central countries, group and class alliances and conflicts, etc. . . . Both perspectives are concerned with the process of development in national societies. However, for the modernization writer the national society is the basic *unit of analysis*, while the writer in a dependence framework considers the global system and its various forms of interaction with national societies as the primary object of inquiry. For the dependency perspective, the *time dimension* is a crucial aspect of what is fundamentally a historical model.

Individual societies cannot be presumed to be able to replicate the evolution of other societies because the very transformation of an interrelated world system may preclude such an option. The potential modernization of individual societies must be seen in the light of changes over time in the interactions between external and internal variables. The modernization perspective is obviously concerned about the origins of traditional and modern values; but, the time dimension is not fundamental to the explanatory pretensions of the model because it claims 'universal validity'. Without knowing the source of modernity inhibiting characteristics, it is still possible to identify them by reference to their counterparts in developing contexts.

At the root of the differences between the two perspectives is a fundamentally different *perception of human nature*. The dependency perspective assumes that human behaviour in economic matters is a 'constant'. Individuals will behave differently in different context not because they are different but because the contexts are different. The insistence on structures and, in the final analysis on the broadest structural category of all, the world system, follows logically from the view that opportunity structures condition human behaviour. Modernizationists, on the other hand, attribute the lack of certain behavioural patterns to the 'relativity' of human behaviour; to the fact that cultural values and beliefs, regardless of opportunity structures underly the patterns of economic action. Thus, the *conception of change* in the modernization perspective is a product of innovations which result from the adoption of modern attitudes among elites, and eventually followers. Though some modernization theorists are now more pessimistic about the development potential of such changes, modernizing beliefs are a prerequisite for development. For dependency analysts the *conception of change* is different. Change results from the alignment of dependency relations over time. Whether or not development occurs and how it occurs is subject to controversy within the dependency perspective. Given the rapid evolution of the world system dependent development is possible in certain contexts, while not possible in others. Autonomy through a break in relations of dependency may not lead to development of the kind already arrived at in the developed countries because of the inability to recreate the same historical conditions. But, it might lead to a different kind of development stressing different types of values. Thus, the *prescription for change* varies substantially in the dependency perspective depending on the ideologival outlook of particular authors. It is not necessarily a logical consequence of the model. In the modernization perspective the prescription for change follows more automatically from the assumptions of the model, implying greater ideological consensus.

From a methodological point of view the modernization perspective is much more parsimonious, than the dependency perspective. And, the focus of much of the literature on the microsciological level clearly makes it amenable to the elaboration of more precise explanatory propositions such as those available in the works of David McClelland or Everett Hagen. Dependency, by contrast is more descriptive and its macrosciological formulations are much less subject to translation into a simple set of explanatory propositions with universal validity. Many aspects of the perspective, and particularly the linkages between external phenomena and internal class and power relations are unclear and need to be studied with more precision and care. For this reason the dependency perspective is an 'approach' to the study of underdevelopment rather than a 'theory'. And yet, precisely because modernization theory relies on a simple conceptual framework and a reductionist approach it is far less useful than the dependency perspective for the study of a complex phenomenon such as development or underdevelopment.

But the strengths of the dependency perspective lies not only in its consideration of a richer body of evidence and a broader range of phenomena. The dependency perspective is also more valuable because in the long run it should provide a set of propositions capable of providing a real test for the assumption that the evolution of international structural linkages over time have conditioned development. The modernization perspective, by contrast, has fundamental flaws in its assumptions and methodology which make it difficult to provide for a fair test of its own assumptions. It will be recalled that the modernization perspective draws on a model with 'universal validity' which assumes that traditional values are not conducive to modern behavioural patterns of action. As a logical inference from that assumption, a shift away from traditional values is necessary if a society is to replicate the experience of the now modern societies. The latter provide not only a rough approximation of the end point of the modernization process but a convenient source for the formulation of empirical referents. Given the fact that underdevelopment, on the basis of various economic and social indicators, is an objective datum, the research task becomes one of identifying modernizing values and searching for their opposites in underdeveloped contexts.

In actual research efforts, the modernity inhibiting characteristics are often 'deduced' from impressionistic observation. This is the case with much of the political science literature on Latin America. However, more 'rigorous' methods, such as survey research, have also been employed, particularly in studies of entrepreneurial activity. Invariably, whether through deduction or survey research, less appropriate values for modernization such as *arielismo* (a concern for transcendental as opposed to material values) or 'low-achievement' (lack of risk taking attitudes) have been identified in Latin America thus 'confirming' the hypothesis that traditional values contribute to underdevelopment. If by chance the use of control groups should establish little or no difference in attitudes in a developed and underdeveloped context, the research instrument can be considered to be either faulty or the characteristics tapped not the appropriate ones for identifying traditional attitudes. The latter alternative might very well lead to the 'discovery' of a new 'modernity of tradition' literature or of greater flexibility than anticipated in traditional norms or, conversely, of traditional residuals in the developed country.

The problem with the model and its behavioural level of analysis is obvious. The explanation for underdevelopment is part of the pre-established conceptual framework. It is already 'known' that in backward areas the modernity inhibiting characteristics play the dominant role, otherwise the areas would not be backward. As such, the test of the hypothesis involves a priori acceptance of the very hypothesis up for verification; with empirical evidence gathered in a solely illustrative manner. The focus on individuals does not permit consideration of a broader range of contextual variables which might lead to invalidating the assumptions. Indeed, the modernity of tradition literature, which has pointed to anomalies in the use of the tradition-modernity 'polarities' in particular contexts, is evidence of how such a perspective can fall victim to the 'and so' fallacy. Discrepancies are accounted for not by a reformulation, but by adding a new definition or a new corollary to the preexisting conceptual framework. For this reason, the ideological consensus on prescriptions derived from modernization theory is not a chance consensus. It is the logical product of an ideology disguised as theory.

NOTES

1 This summary draws on Manning Nash's foreword to the anniversary issue of *Economic Development and Cultural Change* published in honor of Bert Hoselitz (Nash, 1977). As Nash notes Hoselitz was one of the first economists to draw attention to the 'non-economic' factors in development and thus to stress the importance of considering sociological and anthropological perspectives. The journal he helped found became an influencial vehicle for the modernization perspective. It is instructive that, as the bibliography of Hoselitz' work included in this special issue notes, Hoselitz' principal book on the subject was translated into 25 languages by the United States Department of State (Hoselitz, 1960). The book edited by Myron Weiner (1966) consists of contributions by prominent 'modernizationists' originally prepared as lectures to be delivered by the 'Voice of America'.

2 The principal works in the dependency perspective are Cardoso and Faletto (1969) and Sunkel and Paz (1970). The former is scheduled for publication by a United States university press in 1978. There are no plans for an English translation of the Sunkel volume despite the fact that it has gone through nine printings in Spanish. Because of the language 'barrier' Frank is often thought of as the most important exponent of the dependence school and the initiator of a new 'paradigm' (see for example Foster-Carter who refers to him as the copernicus of the new paradigm (1976, p. 175)) when, in fact, Frank draws on works carried out by Latin American scholars years earlier. Both Frank and Bodenheimer (1971) often present oversimplified views of the Latin American contributions thus (unintentionally) distorting them for the consumption of English speaking audiences (Cardoso, 1977).

3 These two perspectives can be thought of as different paradigms in that they have differing constellations of beliefs conceptual assumptions, rely on different classical treatments, and employ different methodologies (Kuhn, 1970). We prefer to use the term 'perspective' because generally speaking the social sciences are 'pre-paradigmatic', only approximating a 'normal science' in Kuhn's terms.

4 The important works by economists such as Hoselitz (1960) and Hagen (1962) draw at least in part on some Latin American field research experience. Robert Redfield's anthropological work on Yucatan is considered one of the classic precursors of modernization (Redfield, 1941). Important theoretical contributions to the modernization field were made by Argentine sociologist Gino Germani drawing on his work on Latin America, but his most important

books were not published in English. Portuguese and French translations are available (Germani, 1963). Germani's work is without a doubt the most carefully articulated discussion of Latin America within a modernization framework. For a summary of Germani's work see Kahl (1976).

5 See the classic distinctions between status and contract (Maine, 1861); gemeinschaft and gesellschaft (Tonnies, 1887); mechanical and organic solidarity (Durkheim, 1893); traditional and rational-legal authority (Weber, 1922); folk and urban society (Redfield, 1941).

6 Surveys of the literature include Sutton (1963) and Lerner (1968).

7 See the excellent distinction made by Portes (1976) between 'development as social differentiation' and 'development as the enactment of values'. As Portes notes the first involves the description of evolutionary trends, while the second is explanatory.

8 See Black, 1966, pp. 68–75, in which he refers to a two staged process: the first, 'the challenge to modernity', in which innovators appear; and the second, 'the consolidation of modernizing leadership' in which they are victorious. Where there are important differences between the social system and psychological approaches, both place a heavy stress on normative and value dimensions. And, for both innovation is an important source of change.

9 For statements of the view that modernization is an exogenous process which will lead to convergence, see Black (1966), Lerner, Kerr *et al.* (1960), Blanksten (1960).

10 Important works in this vein are those of the Rudolphs (1967), who stress the 'modernity of tradition' in India and Ward and Rustow (1964) who stress the significance of 'reinforcing dualism' in Japan.

11 In his earlier study of the United States Lipset also stressed the difference between the two areas noting that Latin America was less developed because 'it retained many of the pre-industrial values of the Iberian peninsula. Latin America lacked a dynamic business class, a Protestant work ethos, and an ideological commitment to economic modernization'. (Lipset, 196, p. 59).

12 For similar views see Germani (1963:49). Some of the studies cited by Lipset include Cochran, 1960; Solari, 1964; Siegel, 1963; Fillol, 1961; Strassman, 1964; Hirschman, 1958. Though Albert Hirschman shared many of these views (1965, p. 170) his thinking has moved much closer to that of the dependency perpsective (1977).

13 See also Adie and Poitras, 1974, pp. 252–53; and Duncan, 1976, p. 240.

14 See Silvert, 1966, p. 265, for a fuller elboration of what he means by 'modern man'. In the preface to the volume, Arthur Whitacker, a noted historian, says that the book 'ought to be made required reading for anyone who wishes to express an opinion' on the Alliance for Progress, p. ix.

15 Scott retains this emphasis on cultural determinants in later writings, see Scott, 1973. The role of traditional features in explaining political as well as economic patterns in Latin America was stressed by many of the most important studies of the 1960s. For a sampling see the articles in the collections by Johnson, 1964; Maier and Weatherhead, 1964; Heath and Adams, 1965; Moreno and Mitraini, 1971 and Tomasek, 1967 and the studies such as those of Blanksten, 1960 and Needler, 1967. See also Andreski, 1967; Mander, 1969; Mercier Vega, 1969. One of the most self conscious attempts to apply a simplistic version of the modernization perpsective to a particular case study was Payne, 1968, who sought to explain Colombia's politics by the 'status orientations' of leaders in that country as opposed to the 'pragmatic orientations' of leaders in the United

States. A case study which attempts to explain the entire evolution of Chilean history on the basis of political culture and an 'authoritistic' mentality is Moreno, 1969. For a more sophisticated study which draws at times on cultural explanations see Powell, 1971. For an alternative perspective in another Latin American country see Valenzuela, 1977. It must be stressed that while the literature cited is representative of the main thrust of the Latin American field, some important authors took different approaches. Thus Kling (1956), Anderson (1967: Chapter I), Adams (1967) and Chalmers (1969) presented different overall interpretations of Latin American development, much closer in fact to what the dependence perspective was elaborating in the same period. Outstanding Latin Americanists such as Schmitter (1974) and Stepan (forthcoming) have consistently avoided some of the cultural assumptions. A good reader with an alternative focus published in the U.S. is Petras and Zeitlin (1968).

16 See Adie and Poitras, 1974; Duncan, 1976; Williams and Wright, 1976; Denton and Preston, 1975; Needler, 1977. One of the few 'alternative' texts is Petras (1970).

17 See also the contributions of Richard Morse and Ronald C. Newton to the Wiarda book. The book edited by Frederick Pike is another important contribution to this literature. See Pike, 1974.

18 Not all writers on corporatism in Latin America draw on cultural or attitudinal variables. Phillipe Schmitter, for one, explicitly rejects the circularity implicit in the cultural approach (Schmitter, 1974: 87).

19 It is interesting to note that some Marxist critics of dependence make a similar mistake. They point to many of the features of dependent countries such as unemployment, marginalization, etc. . . . arguing that they are indistinguishable from those features which characterize capitalism in general. Because these features, though in differing degrees, are not peculiar to underdeveloped areas, 'dependence' is said to have no explanatory value beyond Marxist theories of capitalism (Lall, 1975; Weicskopf, 1976). The point of dependency analysis is not the relative mix at one point in time of certain identifiable factors, but the evolution over time of structural relations which are intimately related and which help to explain the very different question as to why some forms of capitalism were more successful than others. The dependence perspective is a historical model which cannot be 'tested' by doing cross national research at one point in time. For an attempt to differentiate conceptually the contemporary capitalism of the core countries from those of the periphery (and thus more amenable to this type of criticism) see Amin (1974a, 1974b).

20 Some authors have criticized the literature's focus on the evolution of the capitalist world system as the key unit of analysis in explaining Latin American underdevelopment. Ray (1973) notes that 'soviet satellites' are in a dependent and unequal relationship *vis-à-vis* the Soviet Union and that the key variable should therefore not be capitalism but 'power'. Again, however, this argument misses the fundamental point. Dependence is a historical process in which the evolution of a mercantilistic and capitalist world system contributes to an international specialization more favourable to some than others. It is the importance of the evolution of world capital capitalism which has led to the preoccupation in the dependence literature with rejecting interpretations stressing the 'feudal' nature of colonial and post colonial rural relations. (Bagú, 1949; Vitale, 1966; Laclau, 1977; Kossok, 1973; Stavenhaven, 1968). As

Cardoso notes (1977, p. 22) this literature was well established not only in Spanish America but in Brazil well before the more simplistic arguments of Frank on the same subject (1967) were put forth. A brilliant recent exposition of the importance of studying the evolution of the capitalist world system in order to understand underdevelopment is Wallerstein (1975). Wallerstein's contribution to the dependence literature is to provide a persuasive explanation for the origins of the 'core' states in Europe, rather than in other areas such as China, and to provide rich new insights on internal development in the core which affected the periphery.

21 Indeed, Cardoso notes that the distinction between the external and the internal is 'metaphysical' (Cardoso, 1970; 404). The ontology implicit in such an analysis is the one of 'internal relations' (Ollman, 1971: Part I). The early ECLA literature on 'unequal terms of trade' tended to stress too much the external variables. The same criticism has been directed at the work of Gunder Frank because of his tendency to postulate an almost mechanicistic relationship between internal and external variables. Frank acknowledges this criticism (1972). Critics as well as those who have sought to 'test' 'dependence', have tended to overlook this important historical interplay between the external and the internal (Kaufman, *et al.*, 1975; Ray, 1973).

22 The argument that dependency necessarily exacerbates underdevelopment is found primarily in the work of Frank, though it is also stressed by some Latin American scholars such as Marini (1969, 1972) Bambirra (1973). Cardoso has criticized some of the 'fallacies' in this view (1974). Quantifyers have been quick to try to refute the entire perspective by pointing to cross national empirical evidence that degrees of dependence are not necessarily related to degrees of development (Weiscopf, 1976; Ray, 1973). Whether or not scholars believe that dependence today exacerbates underdevelopment is clearly related to prescription for change, which, given the historical dimensions of the model do not necessarily follow in a logical fashion. As will be noted below there is considerable disagreement on prescription despite a general agreement on the validity of the model.

23 For detailed discussions of the non-enclave versus enclave situations see Cardoso and Faletto, 1969, pp. 42–53; Sunkel and Paz, 1970, pp. 306–43.

BIBLIOGRAPHY

Adams, R. N., 1967, *The Second Sowing: Power and Secondary Development in Latin America*, San Francisco, Chandler Publishing Company.

Adelman, I. and C. T. Morris, 1973, *Economic Growth and Social Equity in Developing Countries*, Stanford, Cal., Stanford University Press.

Adie, R. F. and G. E. Poitras, 1974, *Latin America: The Politics of Immobility*, Englewood Cliffs, N.J., Prentice Hall, Inc.

Almond, G., 1960, 'Introduction: A Functional Approach to Comparative Politics' in G. Almond and J. Coleman, eds., *The Politics of the Developing Areas*, Princeton, N. J., Princeton University Press.

Amin, S., 1974, 'Accumulation and Development: A Theoretical Model', *Review of African Political Economy*, 1 (August–November).

1974, *Accumulation on a World Scale*, New York, Monthly Review.

Anderson, C., 1967, *Politics and Economic Change in Latin America*, Princeton, N.J., Van Nostrand.

Andreski, S., 1966, *Parasitism and Subversion: The Case in Latin America*, New York, Pantheon.

Bagú, S., 1949, *Economìa de la sociedad colonial*, Buenos Aires, El Ateneo.

1971, 'Industrialización, Sociedad y Dependencia en América Latina', *Revista Latinoamericana de Ciencias Sociales* 1 and 2 (June–December).

Bambirra, V., 1973, *Capitalismo Dependiente Latinoamericano*, Santiago, CESO-PLA.

Black, Cyril, 1966, *The Dynamics of Modernization*, New York, Harper and Row.

Blanksten, G., 1960, 'The Politics of Latin America' in *The Politics of the Developing Areas*, edited by Gabriel Almond and James Coleman. Princeton, N.J. Princeton University Press.

Bodenheimer, S. J., 1971, *The Ideology of Developmentalism: The American Paradigm Surrogate for Latin American Studies*, Beverly Hill, California, Sage Professional Papers.

Cardoso, F. H., 1964, *Empresario Industria e Desenvolvimento Economico no Brazil*, Sao Paulo, Difusao Europeia do Livro.

and Enzo Faletto, 1969, *Dependencia y Desarrollo en America Latina*, Mexico, Siglo XXI.

1970, 'Teoría de la Dependenciao Analisis de Situaciones Concretas de Dependencia?', *Revista Latinoamericana* de Ciencia Política, 1 (December).

1971, *Ideologías de la Burguesía Industrial en Sociedades Dependientes* (Argentina y Brasil), México, Siglo XXI.

1973, 'Associated-Dependent Development: Theoretical Implications', in *Authoritarian Brazil*, edited by Alfred Stepan, New Haven, Yale University Press.

1974, 'Las Contradicciones del Desarrollo Asociado', *Desarrollo Económico*, 4, (Abril–Junio).

1977, 'The Consumption of Dependency Theory in the United States', *Latin American Research Review*, XII (No. 3).

Chalmers, D. A., 1969, 'Developing on the Periphery: External Factors in Latin American Politics', In *Linkage Politics*, edited by J. Rosenau, New York, Free Press.

Chase-Dunn, C., 1975, 'The Effects of International Economic Dependence on Development and Inequality: A Cross-National Study', *American Sociological Review*, 40 (December).

Chilcote, R. H., 1974, 'A Critical Synthesis of the Dependency Literature', *Latin American Perspectives*, 1 (Spring).

Cochran, T. C., 1960, 'Cultural Factors in Economic Growth', *Journal of Economic History*, 20.

Denton, C. F., and L. L. Preston, 1972, *Latin American Politics: A Functional Approach*, San Francisco, Chandler Publications.

Dorfman, A., 1967, *La Industrialización en América Latina y las Políticas de Fomento*, México, Fondo de Cultura Económica.

Dos Santos, T., 1966, *El Nuevo carácter de la Dependencia*, Santiago, Centro de Estudios Socio-Económicos.
1970, 'La Crisis del Desarrollo y las Relaciones de Dependencia en América Latina', in *La Dependencia Político-Económica de América Latina*, edited by T, Jaguaribe *et al.*, Mexico, Siglo XXI.
1970, *Dependencia y Cambio Social*, Santiago, Centro de Estudios Socio-Económicos.
1972, *Socialismo o Fascismo: El Nuevo Carácter de la Dependencia y el Dilema Latinoamericano*, Buenos Aires, Ediciones Periferie.

Duncan, W. R., 1976, *Latin American Politics: A Developmental Approach*, New York, Praeger.

Durkheim, E., 1893, *De la División du Travail Social*, Paris, F. Alcan.

Eisenstadt, S. N., 1973, *Tradition, Change and Modernity*, New York, John Wiley and Sons.

Fillol, T. R., 1961, *Social Factors in Economic Development: The Argentine Case*, Cambridge, Mass., M.I.T. Press.

Fitzgibbon, R., 1967, 'The Party Potpourri in Latin America', in *Latin American Politics: 24 Studies of the Contemporary Scene*, edited by Robert Tomasek, Garden City, N.Y., Doubleday and Co.

Foster-Carter, A., 1976, 'From Rostow to Gunder Frank: Conflicting Paradigms in the Analysis of Underdevelopment', *World Development*, 4 (March).

Frank, A. G., 1967, *Capitalism and Underdevelopment in Latin America*, New York, Monthly Review.
1972, *Lumpenbourgeoisie and Lumpendevelopment*, New York, Monthly Review Press.

Germani, G., 1968, *Política y Sociedad en una Epoca de Transición*, Buenos Aires, Editorial Paidós.

Gillin, J., 1955, 'Ethos Components in Modern Latin American Culture', *American Anthropologist*, 57.

Girvan, N., 1973, 'the Development of Dependency Economics in the Caribbean and Latin America: Review and Comparison', *Social and Economic Studies*, 22 (March).

Gusfield, J. R., 1967, 'Tradition and Modernity: Misplaced Polarities in the Study of Social Change', *American Journal of Sociology*, 72 (January), pp. 351–62.

Hagen, E. E., 1962, *On the Theory of Social Change*, Homewood, Ill., Dorsey.

Heath, D. B. and R. N. Adams (eds.), 1965, *Contemporary Cultures and Societies in Latin America*, New York, Random House.

Hirschman, A., 1958, *The Strategy of Economic Development*, New Haven, Conn., Yale University Press.
1965, 'Ideologies of Economic Development in Latin America' in *The Dynamics of Change in Latin America*, edited by John D. Martz, Englewood Cliffs, N.J.
1977, 'A Generalized Linkage Approach to Development, with Special Reference to Staples', *Economic Development and Cultural Change*, 25 (Supplement).

Hoselitz, B. F., 1960, *Sociological Aspects of Economic Growth*, New York, The Free Press.

Jobet, J. C., 1955, *Ensayo Crítico del Desarrollo Económico-Social de Chile*, Santiago, Editorial Universitaria.

Johnson, J. J., 1964, *Continuity and Change in Latin America*, Stanford, Cal., Stanford University Press.

Kahl, J. A., 1976, *Modernization, Exploitation and Dependency in Latin America: Germani, Gonzalez Casanova and Cardoso*, New Brunswick, N.J., Transaction Books.

Kaufman, R. R., Daniel S. G. and H. I. Chernotsky, 1975, 'A Preliminary Test of the Theory of Dependency', *Comparative Politics*, 7 (April).

Kerr, C. *et al.*, 1960, *Industrialism and Industrial Man*, Cambridge, Mass, Harvard University Press.

Kling, M., 1956, 'Toward a theory of Power and Political Instability, in Latin America', *Western Political Quarterly*, 9, (March).

Kossok, M., 1973, 'Common and Distinctive Features in Colonial Latin America', *Science and Society*, 37 (Spring).

Kuhn, T., 1970, *The Structure of Scientific Revolutions*, Chicago, The University of Chicago Press.

Laclau, E., 1971, 'Feudalism and Capitalism in Latin America', *New Left Review*, 67 (May–July).

Lall, S., 1975, 'Is Dependence a Useful Concept in Analysing Underdevelopment?', *World Development*, 3 (November).

Lerner, D., 1968, 'Modernization: Social Aspects', in *International Encyclopedia of the Social Sciences*.

Levy, Jr., J. Marion, 1972, *Modernization: Latecomers and Survivors*, New York, Basic Books.

Lipset, S. M., 1963, 'Values, Education and Entrepreneurship' in *Elites in Latin America*, edited by S. M. Lipset and A. Solari, New York, Basic Books.

1963, *The First New Nation*, New York, Basic Books.

Maier, J. and R. W. Weatherhead, 1964, *Politics of Change in Latin America*, New York, Praeger.

Maine, Sir. H., 1861, *Ancient Law: Its Connection with the Early History of Society and its Relation to Modern Ideas*, London, J. Murray.

Mander, J., 1969, *The Unrevolutionary Society*, New York, Alfred Knopf.

Marini, R. M., 1969, *Subdesarrollo y Revolución*, Mexico, Siglo XXI.

1972, 'Brazilian Sub-Imperialism', *Monthly Review*, 9 (February).

Martz, J., 1971, 'Political Science and Latin American Studies: a Discipline in Search of a Region', *Latin American Research Review*, 6 (Spring).

McClelland, D., 1961, *The Achieving Society*, Princeton, N. J., Van Nostrand Co.

1977, 'The Psychological Causes and Consequences of Modernization: An Ethiopian Case Study', *Economic Development and Cultural Change*, 25 (supplement).

Mercier Vega, L., 1969, *Roads to Power in Latin America*, Praeger.

Moore, W. E., 1963, *Social Change*, Englewood Cliffs, N. J., Prentice Hall.

1964, 'Motivational Aspects of Development', in *Social Change*, edited by A. Etzioni and E. Etzioni, New York, Basic Books.

1968, 'Social Change', in *International Encyclopaedia of the Social Sciences*.

1977, 'Modernization and Rationalization: Processes and Restraints', *Economic Development and Cultural Change*, 25 (Supplement).

Moreno, F. J., 1969, *Legitimacy and Stability in Latin America: A Study of Chilean Political Culture*, New York University Press.

and B. Mitraini, 1971, *Conflict and Violence in Latin American Politics*, New York, Crowell.

Nash, M., 1977, 'Foreword', in *Economic Development and Cultural Change*, 25 (supplement).

Needler, M. C., 1967, *Latin American Politics in Perspective*, Princeton, N. J., Van Nostrand.

1977, *An Introduction to Latin America: The Structure of Conflict*,

Englewood Cliffs, N. J., Prentice Hall.

O'Brien, P., 1975, 'A Critique of Latin American Theories of Dependence', in *Beyond the Sociology of Development*, edited by I. Oxaal *et al.*, London, Routledge and Kegan Paul.

Ollman, B., 1971, *Alienation: Marx's Conception of Man in Capitalist Society*, Cambridge: Cambridge University Press.

Parsons, T., 1966, *Societies: Evolutionary and Comparative Perspectives*, Englewood Cliffs, N. J., Prentice Hall.

Payne, J., 1968, *Patterns of Conflict in Colombia*, New Heaven, Yale University Press.

Petras, J. and M. Zeitlin (eds.), 1968, *Latin America: Reform or Revolution?* New York, Fawcett.
1970, *Politics and Social Structure in Latin America*, New York, Monthly Review.

Pike, F. B., and T. Stritch, 1974, *The New Corporatism: Social-Political Structures in the Iberian World*, Notre Dame, Ind., University of Note Dame Press.

Portes, A., 1976, 'On the Sociology of National Development: Theories and Issues', *American Journal of Sociology*, 82 (July).

Powell, J. D., 1971, *Political Mobilization of the Venezuelan Peasant*, Cambridge, Mass., Harvard University Press.

Quijano, A., 1970, 'Dependencia, Cambio Social y Urbanización en América Latina', in *América Latina: Ensayos de Interpretación Sociológico-Político*, edited by F. T. Cardoso and F. Weffort, Santiago, Editorial Universitaria.

Ramirez Necochea, H., 1951, *La Guerra Civil de 1891: Antecedentes Económicos*, Santiago, n.p.

Ray, D., 1973, 'The Dependency Model of Latin American Underdevelopment: Three Basic Fallacies', *Journal of Inter American Studies and World Affairs*, 15 (February).

Redfield, R., 1941, *The Folk Culture of Yucatan*, Chicago, The University of Chicago Press.

Rudolph, L. I., and S. H. Rudolph, 1967, *The Modernity of Tradition: Political Development in India*, Chicago, Ill., University of Chicago Press.

Rustow, D., 1967, *A World of Nations*, Washington, D. C., The Brookins Institution.

Schmitter, P. C., 1974, 'Still the Century of Corporatism?' in *The New Corporatism: Social-Political Structures in the Iberian World*, edited by F. B. Pike, Notre Dame, Ind., University of Notre Dame Press.

Scott, R. E., 1973, *Latin American Modernization Problems*, Urbana, Ill., University of Illinois Press.

Siegal, B. J., 1955, 'Social Structure and Economic Change in Brazil', in *Economic Growth: Brazil, India, Japan*, edited by S. Kuznets, W. E. Moore and J. J. Spengler, Durham, N.C., Duke University Press.

Silvert, K. H., 1966, *The Conflict Scoeity: Reaction and Revolution in Latin America*, New York, American Universities Field Staff, Inc.

Smelser, N. J., 1966, 'The Modernization of Social Relations', in *Modernization: The Dynamics of Growth*, edited by M. Weiner, New York, Basic Books.

1971, 'Mechanisms of Change and Adjustment to Change', in *Political Development and Social Change*, edited by J. Finkle and R. Gable, New York, John Wiley and Sons.

Solari, A., 1964, *Estudios Sobre la Sociedad Uruguaya*, Montevideo, Arca.

Stavenhagen, R., 1968, 'Seven Erroneous Thesis Concerning Latin America', in *Latin America: Reform or Revolution?* Edited by J. Petras and M. Zeitlin.

Stepan, A., (forthcoming) *State and Society*, Princeton, N.J., Princeton University Press.

Strassman, W. P., 1964, 'The Industrialist', in *Continuity and Change in Latin America*, edited by J. J. Johnson, Stanford, Cal., Stanford University Press.

Sunkel, O., 1967, 'Política Nacional de Desarrollo y Dependencia Externa', *Estudios Internacionales*1 (April).

and Pedro Paz, 1970, *El Subdesarrollo Latinoamericano y la Teoría del Desarrollo*, Mexico, Siglo XXI.

1971, 'Capitalismo Transnacional y Desintegración Nacional en América Latina', *Estudios Internacionales*, 4 (January–March).

1972, 'Big Business and 'Dependencia': A Latin American View', *Foreign Affairs*, 50 (April).

and Edmundo Fuenzalida (this volume), 'Transnationalization and its National Consequences'.

Sutton, F., 1963, 'Social Theory and Comparative Politics', in *Comparative Politics: A Reader*, edited by H. Eckstein and D. Apter, New York, The Free Press.

Tannenbaum, F., 1962, *Ten Keys to Latin America*, New York, Random House.

Tavares, M. da C., 1969, 'El Proceso de Sustitución de Importaciones como Modelo de Desarrollo Reciente en América Latina', in *América Latina: Ensayos de Interpretación Económica*, edited by Andrés Bianchi, Santiago, Editorial Universitaria.

Tomasek, T., 1967, *Latin American Politics: 24 Studies of the Contemporary Scene*, Garden City, N. Y., Doubleday and Co.

Tonnies, F., 1887, *Gemeinschaft und Gesellschaft*, Leipzig.

Valenzuela, A., 1977, *Political Brokers in Chile: Local Government in a Centralized Polity*, Durham, N. C., Duke University Press.

Vitale, L., 1966, 'América Latina: Feudal o Capitalists', *Revista Estrategia*, 3.
1967, *Interpretación Marxista de la Historia de Chile*, Santiago, Prensa Latinoamericana.

Wallerstein, I., 1974, *The Modern World-system: Capitalist Agriculture and the Origins of the European World-Economy in the Sixteenth Century*, New York, Academic Press, Inc.

Ward, R. and D. Rustow, 1964, 'Conclusion', in *Political Modernization in Japan and Turkey*, edited by R. Ward and D. Rustow, Princeton, N. H., Princeton University Press.

Weber, M., 1922, *Wirtschaft und Gessellschaft*, Tubingen, Mohr (P. Siebeck).

Weiner, M. (ed.), 1966, *Modernization: The Dynamics of Growth*, New York, Basic Books.

Weisskopf, T. E., 1976, 'Dependence as an Explanation of Underdevelopment: A Critique'. Paper presented at the Sixth National Meeting of the Latin American Studies Association in Atlanta Georgia, March 25–28.

Wiarda, H. J., 1973, 'Toward a Framework for the Study of Political Change in the Iberic-Latin Tradition: The Corporative Model', *World Politics*, 25 (January).
1974, *Politics and Social Change in Latin America: The Distinct Tradition*, Amherst, Mass., The University of Massachussetts Press.

Williams, E. J., and F. J. Wright, 1975, *Latin American Politics: A Developmental Approach*, New York, Mayfield.

3

TRANSNATIONALIZATION AND ITS NATIONAL CONSEQUENCES[1]

Osvaldo Sunkel, Edmundo F. Fuenzalida

INTRODUCTION

During the last three decades most of the so-called underdeveloped or developing countries of the Third World have been undergoing intense processes of capitalist development. These processes have been heavily conditioned by the preexisting socio-cultural and geo-political characteristics of each country as well as by the uneven nature of capitalist development itself. Furthermore, they have been strongly influenced by the *new* characteristics that capitalist development has acquired in the postwar era in the industrial countries.

The Centre-Periphery approach has been used to explain earlier periods of capitalist development in the periphery in terms of the characteristics of the corresponding metropoli and their phases of expansion and crisis (Prebisch, 1949; CEPAL, 1951; Furtado, 1970; Sunkel and Paz, 1970; Emmanuel, 1972; Amin, 1973; Pinto and Kñakal, 1973; Pinto, 1976).[2] The spread of the Industrial Revolution and the imperial expansion of the central countries during the latter part of the 19th century, for instance, has been seen as the main element in the shaping of the peripheral countries as specialized primary commodity exporters. The period of crisis that capitalism underwent since the First World War until the 1940s, on the other hand, is seen as the fundamental factor in inducing and allowing the development of import-substituting industrialization in many underdeveloped countries. Nevertheless, except in the restricted sense of the importance of external primary commodity, technology, and capital markets, and of the postwar growth of the multinational corporation, which is stressed in the dependence literature, the analysis of the development process of the peripheral countries is done as if the global context had ceased to exist, remained basically unchanged or did not matter.[3]

This article suggests, on the contrary, that the development process of national societies during the last three decades has been to an important degree conditioned by the emergence of a new type of global system brought about by the worldwide expansion of techno-

67

industrial oligopoly capitalism in its new phase of transnational organization (Sunkel, 1971; Keohane and Nye, 1971; Amin, 1972; Meister, 1976; Michalet, 1976; Mennis and Sauvant, 1976; Fröbel, Heinrichs and Kreye, 1977). The context within which national development is to be seen in the past three decades is this global system. Yet, not only have the new centre-periphery relationships been largely overlooked in the more conventional analysis of recent national development, but also the changes that have taken place in the Centre, and their implications.

Partly as a consequence, national development policies have tended to underestimate the influence and strength of transnational capitalism. Higher average rates of economic growth and modernization than ever before have been achieved in most countries, but the peculiar nature of the highly dynamic technological innovation process which lies at the heart of the expansion of techno-industrial oligopoly capitalism has simultaneously had extremely negative consequences, *over and above* the characteristic unevenness of traditional capitalist development. In the underdeveloped countries, this new pattern of growth is highly dependent on the wholesale importation of consumption patterns, production processes, technology, institutions, material inputs and human resources, adding new *internal* economic, socio-cultural and political dimensions to the old patterns of external dependence, and aggravating the structural tendency towards increasing external imbalance (Sunkel, 1967; Furtado, 1973; Sauvant and Mennis, 1977). Given a high and increasing capital intensity, a very unequal income distribution and a relative shortage of savings and markets, capital accumulation tends to become highly concentrated and wasteful in the production of new consumption goods and services, creating very little new employment, while preexisting activities are starved of capital and stagnate or are seriously disrupted. This contributes to massive displacements of labour (Nun, 1969; Quijano, 1974; Godfrey, 1977), adding to the marginal and informal sectors, to unemployment, underemployment, poverty and inequality (Sunkel, 1971; Adelman and Morris, 1973; Chenery *et al.*, 1974; Foxley, 1974).

This paper is an attempt to outline in a highly synthetic and preliminary form the nature of this new global system, its main components and their interrelations, its historic roots in the crisis of a previous kind of global organization of industrial capitalism and, finally, how its presence conditions the development process of national societies.

Given the nature and objectives of this paper, it may overemphasize its systemic features, neglecting the analysis of its contradictions and limits. Furthermore, by focusing on the process of integration of underdeveloped countries into the transnational system, a phenomenon common to them all, the differences that do arise in each particular case will not be discussed. These are two important areas for further research.

THE CHARACTER OF TRANSNATIONAL CAPITALISM

The study of transnational capitalism requires that a number of concepts be defined which are considered to be useful for this purpose.[4]

To characterize transnational capitalism as a 'system', is to imply that although there are diverse component parts in contemporary capitalism – national, subnational and transnational – some of them in conflict and contradiction with others, they all operate on the basis of dominant parameters, criteria and objectives, and are highly interdependent, acting and reacting as an integrated whole. There are, of course, variations in the forms of insertion into the system, as well as in the characteristics of each component. There is some flexibility with respect to behaviour within the system, but there are limits beyond which a country, for example, either breaks away from the system or is subject to strong reactions from it.

This system is characterized as 'techno-industrial' to refer to the close structural interrelationship between scientific and applied research and development, and mass production and marketing, which is at the heart of its dynamic process of technological innovation in the production of an ever increasing and diversifying range of means of production, consumption and destruction (Galbraith, 1967; Touraine, 1976).

It is 'oligopolistic', because most economic activity is highly concentrated in a few very large enterprises, which occupy a dominant position *vis-à-vis* a large number of medium and small enterprises, that carry out a very small proportion of total economic activity (U. S. Senate, 1964 and 1977). Also, 'oligopolistic' competition tends to take the form of technological innovation and product differentiation thereby constituting the moving force behind the manipulation of consumption (Scherer, 1971; Schiller, 1976; Sauvant and Mennis, 1977).

To describe it as 'capitalist' denotes that production is organized on the basis of the private ownership of the means of production, profit maximization and the operation of (highly imperfect) markets, with the state playing a very crucial role in maintaining and expanding the capitalist system as well as in ensuring the integrity of the nation-state.

The expression 'global' calls attention to two facts. It has the more obvious and conventional meaning of the worldwide horizontal or geographical coverage of the system, what could be called the 'widening' of capitalism. But there is also a vertical dimension, the 'deepening' of capitalism. Transnational capitalism is not only a particular way of organizing capital and labour in production, and of appropriation and utilization of surplus. It is also a set of ideas and beliefs about the world (Sauvant, 1976a); the organizations and institutions that generate and develop them; a global community of men and women that subscribes to them; in brief, a socio-cultural system.[5] The 'widening' of capitalism does not preclude the fact that pre- and semi-capitalist situations survive to a larger or lesser extent in many countries, under the dominance of capitalistic relations of production. Similarly, the 'deepening' of capitalism does not mean that it has pervaded all aspects of social life everywhere.

Finally, the phrase 'in its new phase of transnational organization' tries to convey the idea that the main characteristic of techno-industrial oligopoly capitalism today is that production is organized at a transnational rather than a national or local level. Transnational corporations, for instance, which constitute a high proportion of the oligopolistic core of contemporary capitalist economies, have spread their production worldwide, locating subsidiaries in many countries (Magdoff, 1966; Levitt, 1970; Sunkel, 1971; Barnet and Müller, 1974; U. N. 1973, 1974). Their location preferences are now decided on a worldwide basis, comparing labour costs, government subsidies and taxes, exchange rates and political conditions of all countries. Profit maximization is also achieved at the global level and for the corporation as a whole. This has become possible because the transnational corporation transfers intermediate and capital goods, finance, technology, personnel and information across national frontiers – transnationally – within the boundaries of its organization, largely superseding the market, and therefore, having relative freedom in fixing prices, costs, fees and interest rates in such a way as to maximize net profits for the corporation as a whole. This is the practice known as transfer pricing (Ellis and Joekes, 1977). Prices, which used to be independent variables determined by market forces, have become dependent variables in an accounting model of global profit maximization.

The trend is away from the reliance on the functioning of markets as the means of relating independent production and consumption units, to an organization of these different units within a single enterprise and decision making structure, where planning for the entire organization replaces markets. Local producers and consumers in the different regions of a country used to relate to each other through markets, until national firms took over local firms and created a network of local subsidiaries of the national firm. National firms of one country used to relate to national firms of other countries through the international market, until transnational corporations of one country took over national firms of other countries converting them into subsidiaries. While in the international phase of capitalism national economies interacted basically through markets (except in the case of some international monopolies engaged in primary commodity extraction and processing), in the transnational phase international markets are increasingly superseded by transactions within the transnational corporation.

The same trend from decentralized to highly centralized organization is happening at other levels of international relations: the generalization of formal and informal transnational institutional structures in the realms of politics, defense, finance, culture, professions, mass media, information, education, science and technology (see the articles by Godfrey, Luckham, Fuenzalida and Cruise O'Brien in this volume).

THE MAIN COMPONENTS OF TRANSNATIONAL CAPITALISM

(a) *The transnational institutions*

The dominant institution of the global system is the transnational corporation (TNC); dominant because it is the focus of crucial decision-making with respect to what to produce, by whom, how, for whom, and where in the world market. Dominant also because, as a group, they are highly influential institutions with respect to national and global society, politics and culture.

But the TNCs are by no means the only important institutions in the global system. They may have more visibility because of their enormous economic and political power and influence, the conflicts and confrontations with states in which they have been involved (Vernon, 1971; UN, 1973, 74; Gilpin, 1976; Blair, 1977), and the huge amount of resources that they devote to promote their image (Sauvant, 1976a, 1976b), but there is a whole network of other institutions that support the operations of the TNCs. Some of them are intergovernmental institutions, such as the IMF (Wachtel, 1977), the World Bank or the OECD in the economic sphere, or

NATO and the Rio Pact in the military sphere, with as high a visibility as the one enjoyed by the TNCs. Others, public and private, operate at the national or subnational level and have less obvious links to the global system but in fact operate as parts of it. Those engaged in foreign aid, export promotion and finance activities, both civilian and military, fall in this category.

Particular importance should be given to those educational institutions that prepare the staff of the transnational institutions, usually outstanding universities and polytechnics in the richer countries and their 'subsidiaries' in the Third World (Fuenzalida, 1971a, b, c; Vasconi and Reca, 1971; Leite Lopes, 1972; Fagen, 1973; Alemann, 1974; Carnoy, 1974; Mazrui, 1975). These institutions share with the magazines, newspapers of worldwide circulation, news agencies, multinational advertising companies and television networks, the task of elaborating and diffusing the vision of the world that promotes the interests of the TNCs (Cruise O'Brien, 1974; Sauvant, 1976; Schiller, 1976; Smith, 1976; Somavía, 1976; Varis, 1976).

Finally, there are the transnational journals and the informal networks of scientists and professionals, with their periodical and highly publicized meetings and conferences which provide not only basic information but also the human inventory from which specialized staff is recruited (Ben-David, 1968; Crane, 1972; Alger and Lyons, 1974).

(b) The transnational community

The global system is operated by a stratum of society that appropriates most of the surplus produced by it. Their position in the productive structure ranges from that of owners of the means of production and the top managerial and financial positions, through the higher professional, technical and bureaucratic ones, both in private and public institutions.

The basis of their hegemony is the specialized knowledge they possess, and their indispensability in the process of creation and application of that knowledge to the production of new goods and services and to the process of innovation and product differentiation that is the main reason for the superiority of the TNCs.

As stated above, the activities of the TNCs are supported by the scientific and technological progress generated by the institutions of higher learning, as well as by the highly skilled personnel trained by them. The transnational community, therefore, has its base not only in the TNCs, and in all the economic sectors in which these operate

(industry, agriculture, mining, transportation, construction, marketing, information, mass media, banking and finance, tourism,
entertainment, etc.), but also in the other transnational institutions
(Field, 1971). On the basis of their specialized knowledge, professional organization and social prestige, these elites have a
measure of control over these institutions, and the power to capture
part of the economic surplus, which allows them to sustain relatively
high standards of living.

(c) *The transnational culture*

The stratum of society that we have called the transnational
community is made up of people that belong to different nations,
but who have similar values, beliefs, ideas (and a *lingua
franca*—English), as well as remarkably similar patterns of behaviour as regards career patterns, family structures, housing, dress,
consumption patterns and cultural orientations in general (Sunkel
and Fuenzalida, 1976). The transnational community, then, shares
what could be considered a transnational culture. As any other
culture, this transnational culture has two main components:
specialized and common culture.

The first emerges out of the specialized scientific-technological
activities carried out by the members of the transnational community— and is a necessary input for the expansion of industrial
capitalism. This segment of the culture is permeated by the
specialized knowledge possessed by its carriers, the one that has
allowed them to become members of the transnational community
in the first place. Since this knowledge is based on the progress
attained by the systematic application of the so-called 'scientific
method' to every aspect of reality, the transnationals approach to
the world and to themselves is heavily influenced by a belief in the
effectiveness of 'problem solving' through rational analysis and the
application of 'the scientific method' (Gehlen, 1963; Schelsky, 1965;
Ellul, 1967; Galbraith, 1967; Habermas, 1971; Berger and Kellner,
1973; Steger, 1977).

The second component of transnational culture is common
culture. Transnational capitalism has affected habits, ideas, beliefs,
values and behaviour in matters such as family life, housing,
consumption patterns, and other aspects of everyday life. One of the
most important effects has probably been on consumption patterns,
as the cultural feature of the dynamics of oligopoly capitalism has
been the creation of a homogeneous market for consumption goods
and services on a worldwide scale. The transnational community is

the best and most complete and coherent expression of these new consumption patterns, but they spread over wider sectors of the population as a consequence of the demonstration effect and the active and extensive use of the mass media (see the article by Villamil on Puerto Rico, in this volume). The consequence on the lower income classes is a partial adoption of these new consumption patterns and the distortion of the existing ones. This refers not only to the better known examples related to consumer durables, but to basic food, as when bread substitutes for maize or manioc (Barnet and Müller, 1974; Brown, 1974; Sauvant, 1976, a, b).

(d) The spatial organization of transnational capitalism

The recent technological revolutions in transportation and communications have drastically reduced the costs of distance and time. The application of electronic innovations to production processes has allowed further disaggregation of the labour process into distinct and simple tasks. Production processes can therefore be separated into specific stages, and these distributed all over the world on the basis of locational advantages such as cheap and disciplined labour, access to markets, government subsidies, access to strategic resources or inputs and the absence of environmental regulations. In other terms, the geographical decentralization of production facilities within and among countries can proceed much further than ever before, taking advantage of locational factors, while at the same time maintaining centralized control over planning, finance, manpower, marketing, production and innovation (Fröbel *et al.*, 1977).

Distinct types of spatial configurations tend to take place as a consequence: on the one hand, a functional separation of managerial, scientific and technological, and production activities, into downtown business districts, areas of concentration of academic establishments and peripheral industrial areas. On the other hand, a hierarchical decentralization between world headquarters in central countries, located in cities such as New York, London, Paris, Frankfurt and Tokyo; regional headquarters located in the cities of the more transnationalized countries of the various regions of the Third World, such as Mexico City, Sao Paulo, Nairobi and Singapore; and national headquarters, usually in the capitals of less important or strategic countries (Hymer, 1971). The scope for independent policy, planning and decision making becomes more restricted when moving from world to national or local levels, and some functions disappear altogether. Innovative scientific and technological activities, for instance, will take place almost entirely at world level, as will overall strategic planning, and financial and manpower management. This obviously implies increasing rigidity and declining autonomy as one moves towards the local production unit, and this is a source of friction and conflict with the national/local environment.

At all levels, the transnational institutions have to establish contacts and relationships with national and/or local governments, business firms, and the labour market, both for professional, technical and bureaucratic personnel as well as for skilled and unskilled labour. In time this process brings about the development of national and local counterpart institutions and communities, increasingly integrated into the transnational institutions and communities. These communities will tend to concentrate in suburban residential areas, which will reproduce the urban structure, housing and life styles of the transnational communities of the central countries. Local middle and higher income segments of the population will seek to extend these life styles to themselves, as a means of incorporation into the consumption patterns of the transnational sector.

Although the members of the transnational community that live in the central countries have much in common with those living in the peripheral ones, there is a division of labour between the two, and important differences between them. As regards the first aspect, high level personnel of the transnational corporations will remain in the central countries, as the functions of devising global strategy and planning are retained there; so will most of the personnel dealing with innovation, both in science and technology as well as in production and marketing. At the local level the highest functions will be those of administering and implementing global strategies.

As a consequence of these spatial patterns, national and local resources will be allocated preferentially to expanding the 'modern' sectors of towns and cities, while older quarters decay and slum areas proliferate, accentuating the characteristic heterogeneity of contemporary cities: modern residential, business, government, industrial and even working class areas intermingled with older and decaying residential, business, government, working class and industrial areas, all of it surrounded by growing slum areas.

In synthesis, the transnational institutions and communities are spatially scattered around the world in an archipelago of nuclei of 'modernity', linked among themselves through a number of centralized hierarchical structures that define dominant and dependent nuclei. These nuclei interact with national and local societies, parts of which have become more or less integrated into the transnational nuclei, while the rest is indirectly related or affected through the labour market, the exchange of goods and services, the socialization agencies of education and the mass media and the reallocation of resources brought about by transnational influences.

Since the size, importance and type of transnational nuclei varies from country to country, as do the socio-cultural and geo-political characteristics of national and local societies, each country will present the same generic similarity of the interaction between a new and expanding transnational nucleus and a pre-existing society, but will also show great differences according to the nature of the society in which this interaction takes place. Comparative studies of these different types of situations seem therefore crucial for a better understanding of the transnationalization process under different sets of national characteristics. (See country-case studies by Villamil on Puerto Rico, and Godfrey and Langdon on Kenya, in this volume).

(e) *The transnational system and the nation state*

The transnational system has developed an economic infrastructure of TNCs and related institutions, it has a population which constitutes the transnational communities, these communities share a common culture, and all of these elements are established in certain territories. But while these elements are components of the transnational system, they also happen to be under the jurisdiction of national states. In other words, the transnational system overlaps with a system of nation states. As a consequence there may be a coincidence with the objectives and procedures of the state and its sociopolitical base, but there are also bound to be conflicting situations when the aims and procedures of each system are different (United Nations, 1973 and 1974; U.S. Senate, 1977. See also the papers by Fortín and Langdon in this volume).

From the point of view of its global rationality, a TNC may want its subsidiary in a given country to produce a certain product for the local market, employing its own technology, imported inputs and capital goods, buying out or displacing local competitors, keeping full control of its capital, management and organization procedures, using its own public and labour relations practices and remitting the maximum amount of profits to headquarters. The national government may want to strengthen national capitalists, have the subsidiary produce for export, buy inputs locally, have nationals share in ownership, management and technological know-how, adapt to local organization, accounting and labour relation practices, minimize its remittances abroad, maximize reinvestment locally and pay taxes on profits. This is, of course, the traditional conflict over the conditions for foreign private investment, and it deals essentially with the sharing of the additional income generated by the subsidiaries.

A much more fundamental question is that related to the whole strategy of development, heavily influenced by the local transnational nucleus, seeking to reproduce the living standards, patterns of consumption and culture that characteize transnational nuclei elsewhere. The main instrument through which this aim can be achieved is the state, and access, control and influence over it becomes crucial. This was achieved in recent decades as a consequence of the expansion and transformation of the functions of the state brought about by the internal and external pressures for economic and social development. The new activities of the state were heavily promoted by international technical assistance, which introduced new approaches and methods in public administration and planning. A new and enlarged government bureaucracy emerged, both civilian and military, whose function was to modernize and rationalize the state in its promotion of economic and social development, as well as in its capacity to deal with internal conflicts and subversion (See the paper by Luckham in this volume). These new social sectors share to a very large extent the values, principles and methods of the transnational community, and have a direct interest in the transnationalization process. Through its global and local influence, as well as its strategic intcrnal presence within the state itself, the transnational community acquired significant influence over the process of resource allocation and policy making, quite out of proportion to its actual economic or political power. In their attempt to reproduce locally the methods and life styles of the developed countries, they have contributed significantly to a massive allocation of resources for the satisfaction of these 'needs', with extremely positive effects for the standards of living of a minority of the population, including themselves, and very negative consequences for the majority of the population.

Conventional development theory has argued that this conflict does not exist, at least in the longer term, because the expansion of the 'modern' (transnational) nucleus will increase the total product, and this will in turn bring about a 'spill over' that will improve the lot of the majority of the population in due time, as occurred in the now developed countries. Our argument, on the contrary, is that contemporary transnational capitalist growth has produced cumulative and increasing polarization, which in turn has affected relations between the nation state and transnational capitalism.

The conflicts between the nation state and transnational capitalism were overshadowed to some extent by the formidable expansion of transnational capitalism until the early 1970s. This expansion created the impression of a coincidence of interests between both. But the crisis and recession of recent years is pointing in the direction of increasing conflicts between national interests and transnational capitalism.

Indeed, one of the increasingly serious problems that the nation-state has had to confront since 1973 is the decline in economic growth rates, the tendencies to increasing external and fiscal imbalance, the consequent increased indebtedness and inflationary pressures, the continuous increase in unemployment, underemployment and poverty (Adelman and Morris, 1973) and the increasingly limited room for manoeuvre in its redistribution policies (Chenery *et al.*, 1974). This is particularly serious in the case of the so-called developing countries, but is also becoming a matter of concern in the developed countries (U.S. Senate, 1977), as TNCs increasingly invest abroad, establishing productive facilities for serving local markets or for reexport to the developed countries. Employment opportunities are thereby doubly threatened and political pressure is increasing for protectionist policies to be adopted.

This is one example of the contradictions between the expansion of the transnational system and its requirement of political stability, both in developed as well as in underdeveloped countries. In developed countries, where average levels of living are very high, and inequality is less acute, stabilization and 'incomes' policies have so far been able to deal with short term economic disequilibria. There are nevertheless very serious long-term structural problems as regards access to natural resources, the environment, growing structural unemployment and others which are not unrelated to the expansion and characteristics of transnational capitalism (Cole, 1977).

In underdeveloped countries, where the level of average income is low, inequality is severe, and poverty widespread, growing economic disequilibria and political tensions can only be contained by means of force. The spread of authoritarian and military regimes in the countries of the Third World in recent years is undoubtedly related to these tendencies (Nun, 1969; Sunkel, 1973; O'Donnell, 1972; Touraine, 1976).

Differences arise also because transnational elites in underdeveloped countries find themselves in a much more exposed and segregated position with respect to the rest of their society and because they have to perform the functions of articulating their country to the global system while preserving the integrity of their nation state. They tend to be more closely linked to the state and more explicitly political.

The objective pressures for adopting protectionist and nationalistic policies in developed and underdeveloped countries have been mounting, but the actual possibilities of disengaging to a greater extent internal processes from international phenomena have simultaneously become much more severely restricted. The transnational system has not only developed strong structural links across national frontiers, both economic, social, cultural and political, but a set of international organizations and institutions, such as the OECD, the IMF and the World Bank among others have been established, a semblance of a global state, with the aim of maintaining the transnational system and dealing with any threats to its functioning. Therefore, socio-political 'adjustments' tend to take place internally rather than internationally.

THE PROCESS OF TRANSNATIONALIZATION
OF THE GLOBAL SYSTEM

Techno-industrial capitalism, in its contemporary form as a global transnational system, is the product of a long historical process. Each of its components, and their interrelationships, are transformations of previous ones and coexist and are interrelated with elements corresponding to previous phases of capitalist development and/or of precapitalist systems, a review of which is necessary to understand the present phase of capitalist development. These few paragraphs are merely a sketch of the main periods of capitalist development; in addition to the classics others have recently analysed the evolution of global capitalism in great detail (Polanyi, 1957; Ashworth, 1962; Hobsbawm, 1965, 1968, 1975; Davis, 1973; Braudel, 1974; Wallerstein, 1974a, b). Some authors have related Latin American development to the evolution of global capitalism (Furtado, 1970; Stein and Stein, 1970; Sunkel and Paz, 1970; Cortés Conde, 1973).

The following main historical stages can be identified: a formative period of capitalism as a worldwide commercial system, from the last third of the fifteenth century to the last third of the eighteenth century (Trevor-Roper, 1959; Hobsbawm, 1965; Braudel, 1966; Davis, 1973; Wallerstein, 1974a); the emergence of the first historical instances of industrial capitalism and modern nation-states, during the last third of the eighteenth century and the first third of the nineteenth century (Dobb, 1946; Hobsbawm, 1968; Landes, 1969; Mathias, 1969); internal consolidation and external imperial expansion of the first industrial capitalist states, from about 1825 to the 1870s (Church, 1975; Hobsbawm, 1975); industrial capitalism as a global trading, financial and investment system, in its international-imperial organization phase, between 1870 and 1914 (Ashworth, 1962; Davies, 1973); crisis of international-imperial capitalism, the emergence of a socialist alternative and attempts at reorganization of industrial capitalism as a response to it, between 1914 and 1945 (Polanyi, 1957); techno-industrial capitalism as a global system in its transnational organization phase, as a response to the previous crisis period and the internal consolidation and external expansion of the socialist alternative, from about 1945 to the present.

The process of reorganization of the capitalist system after the long period of crisis from 1914 to 1945 evolved out of different national situations. The countries that had been liberated from German occupation by the U.S.S.R., or that had undergone a socialist revolution made up the socialist block under the leadership of the Soviet Union. The industrialized countries of Western Europe, whether defeated (Germany, Italy) or victorious (France, U.K., Holland, Belgium), were severely weakened by the war effort and confronted very serious internal political problems, with strong left wing parties of a reformist or revolutionary character. Japan's situation in Asia was similar to that of the former Western European countries. In the colonies of the industrialized countries of Western Europe and Japan in Africa, Asia and Latin America the nationalist struggle for independence became more intense, taking advantage of the crisis of the metropolitan powers and the presence of the socialist countries. The independent non-industrialized states on these continents, mostly those in Latin America, had embarked on protectionist policies of import substitution industrialization during the crisis and war years and were pressing for international acceptance and support for their policies.

The U.S.A. emerged as the single most powerful economic, political and military power from the period of crisis and war, and as the new centre of the capitalist system. In 1948, it launched a massive economic, diplomatic, military and ideological offensive in order to contain the expanding socialist block and the threat of left wing parties in many capitalist countries both in the Centre and in the Periphery. A global network of international treaties of mutual defense between the U.S. and countries on the borders of the socialist world was built up and U.S. military bases maintained or established in their territories.

The reconstruction of the economies of the industrialized countries of Western Europe and of Japan was promoted through a massive transfer of financial resources and technology (Marshall Plan) and the creation of the OECD and the EEC. Further industrialization and modernization of the independent states, especially in Latin America was also supported at a later stage through technical aid, financial cooperation and promotion of private foreign investment. Finally, a network of international, economic, financial and technical assistance organizations were created, aimed at reconstructing the international system that had broken down during the period of crisis, at dismantling the protectionist structures and policies that all countries had adopted during that period, and at promoting the reincorporation of underdeveloped countries into that system, once the reconstruction and revival of European capitalism was well underway.

These processes, and certain fundamental characteristics of the economy and society of the U.S.A., constitute the immediate origin of the emerging transnational system. The westward territorial expansion of the American economy and society took place in sparsely populated areas, at the expense of relatively primitive indigenous societies, and largely over the North American subcontinent, a vast contiguous territory richly endowed with natural resources. The continental dimension of the country and its vast internal market, as well as the relative scarcity of labour, favoured the development of capital intensive technology, mass production and very large oligopolistic business organizations, with wide geographical coverage (Chandler, 1961). Science, technology and business had become closely associated in the development of mass production. Moreover, as a consequence of the Great Depression and World War II, which brought about government intervention in the economy and a great war effort, a symbiosis of government, large corporations and science and technology took place.

This dynamic core of the American economy and society, which had remained relatively 'isolationist' until the Second World War—with the exception of the Caribbean and Central America—, penetrated throughout the world during the war, and remained and expanded afterwards, in the 1950s and 1960s during the period of the Cold War. This was instrumental in the worldwide expansion of American techno-industrial capitalism. It was also fundamental in the reconstruction and development of a similar 'style' of capitalist development in the former European and Japanese capitalist centres, where similar dynamic oligopolistic cores were formed or reconstructed, as well as in the underdeveloped countries, where expanding 'modern' sectors emerged.

Although the immediate origin of transnational capitalism is the oligopolistic corporate sector of the American economy, and the techno-scientific establishment of American society, as well as parts of its government apparatus, its American 'national' character has been gradually eroded as similar dynamic cores of business, science and technology and government have emerged in the revitalized industrial centres of Europe and Japan, and as their subsidiaries expand and penetrate the underdeveloped countries and even, to a more limited but growing extent, the socialist countries. The original American drive to reorganize capitalism has therefore been transformed, becoming a transnational drive, which is in turn penetrating and affecting American society itself, as well as others.

MECHANISMS OF INCORPORATION OF UNDER-DEVELOPED COUNTRIES INTO THE GLOBAL SYSTEM

Since this paper is mainly concerned with the process of capitalist development in the countries of the Third World, we will limit our discussion to the effects of transnationalization on these countries. As these effects are greatly influenced by the way in which the transnationalization process manifests itself in each particular case, we will first examine briefly the various means through which national societies interact with the global system: (a) foreign investment in the primary export sectors, tourism and/or in the manufacturing sector, usually by establishing subsidiaries of transnational corporations; with two main variations in the case of manufacturing: production for the internal market or for export, usually to the more advanced industrial societies; (b) systematic use of the mass media (newspapers, radio, television) to create a demand for new consumption goods and services, employing advanced techniques of advertising; in most cases this implies the creation or expansion and modernization of a national system of communications; (c) foreign public loans and technical assistance to rationalize, modernize and expand the state apparatus, with particular emphasis on economic and social infrastructure and military institutions; in recent years there has been increasing access to a new and rapidly expanding private international financial market; (d) scholarship programmes, both civilian and military, to train local personnel in the educational institutions of the core countries in the different branches of science and engineering and in the new disciplines of management, planning, national accounting, information processing, mass media, marketing, and 'national security' (Carnoy, 1974 and also Luckham in this volume); (e) reform of the educational institutions in order to educate locally human resources able to replace foreign technicians (Fuenzalida, 1971c; Vasconi and Reca, 1971; Carnoy, 1974; Mazrui, 1975); (f) generalization of the criteria, priorities and methods of the transnational style to all areas of social life, from economic activities to health, education, housing.

These various mechanisms have been in evidence in the different underdeveloped countries since the early 1950s. They did not all commence simultaneously, and they were promoted by different social and professional groups, economic interests and government departments, both from the underdeveloped as well as from the industrial countries. But even if they were not intended to operate simultaneously and coherently, it soon became apparent that they constituted a new kind of process of technological innovation in its widest sense, a whole package of mutually reinforcing innovations in production, consumption, organization, behaviour and values, both in the private and public sectors—in short, a new culture. During the international phase of industrial capitalism the mechanism of incorporation into the global system was primary-product exports and the main technological innovation was the railway. Furthermore, the social groups affected were highly restricted. As a consequence 'modernization' was an 'enclave' phenomenon. Transnational modernization, with its emphasis on developing a mass consumption market, its reliance on the mass media, on large-scale, capital intensive and technologically sophisticated local production units, on planned government and international action and on the local reproduction of the 'model' offered by the industrial countries, has had much more far reaching aggregate effects, both intended as well as unintended.

EFFECTS OF TRANSNATIONALIZATION ON UNDERDEVELOPED SOCIETIES

In general, these effects are threefold. The first one is the emergence of a dependent nucleus of the global system in the underdeveloped society, with its own institutions, culture and community, that differentiates itself sharply from the rest of the society, and that controls to a large extent the machinery of an increasingly repressive state.

The institutions that become integrated into this nucleus include the subsidiaries of the TNCs in the different sectors of the economy; the larger local firms that use advanced technology, both private and public; the specialized government agencies that deal with the planning and implementation of ambitious development projects and with the overall planning of 'areas' such as health, education, the cities, transportation and communication; the higher educational institutions, especially those that are involved in scientific research; the international organizations; the armed forces.

The aggregate of these institutions provides jobs, income and goods and services for a segment of the local population, that therefore may share similar patterns of behaviour with the inhabitants of the dominant nucleus of the global system in the developed countries. Among the patterns of behaviour that are particularly striking are the residential areas of the capital cities of underdeveloped countries that reproduce the layout and architectural styles of similar residential areas in the dominant nucleus and that tend to be physically separated from the rest of the city.

The second effect is the creation of a mass of unemployed or underemployed people that, having very precarious and unstable sources of income, are forced to survive in conditions of extreme poverty, whereas at the same time they are stimulated to aspire to the level of living enjoyed by the people in the dependent nucleus of the global system. This state of affairs is the direct consequence of the destruction, displacement and or stagnation of the traditional socio-economic institutions that offered them jobs, income and goods and services—however poor and primitive—by the more efficient ones brought in by the global system; the incapacity of the new capital-intensive activities to absorb the demographic increase of the work force and the un- and underemployment generated by trans-nationalization; the intense effort of the mass media to replace traditional goods and services by the products of the new economic activities that results in a change of the pattern of consumption in society; and the acceleration of the growth of the poorer population and of the labour force as a consequence of innovations, modernization and extension of the health services, which have reduced the mortality rates of the poor but not their birth rates.

As the process of transnationalization is basically urban, this mass of marginalized people concentrate in certain areas around the big cities, and mainly in the capital, where the aspired goods and services are on display, in dramatic contrast to the limited employment opportunities. There, they are physically segregated from the other segments of their own society. The glaring contrast between their own lot in life and that of their fellow countrymen that have found a place in the new system, and the objective scarcity of 'legitimate' ways to obtain the desired goods and services, leads them to react in various ways, both individually and collectively. The actions of the deprived bring in turn the reaction of the privileged, who turn to the state for protection. Since they, as a whole, control the state, its force is used against these masses, contributing to its authoritarian character.

As we have already indicated, the transnationalization and polarization effects described above, have a third effect: the accentuation of the authoritarian and repressive character of the state as the hegemonic social groups become increasingly threatened. But there are also other types of responses that attempt to deal with the causal forces rather than with its consequences. These are attempts at severing the links of the society with the global system and at reorganizing it internally in a less polarized way, both in terms of social action and in social thinking. These attempts are a second order effect of the two aforementioned ones and range from the re-discovery and reformulation of the values, symbols and art, to the founding of political movements that have as their main goal the disengagement of the society or of parts of it, from the global system (see the article by Oteiza in this volume).

One can then perceive three dimensions to the process of transnationalization: transnational integration, national disintegration and attempts at reintegration.

CONCLUDING REMARKS

The statements concerning the impacts of incorporation into world capitalism affect all countries, but the degree of permeability and the intensity with which the impacts are felt will vary. Each country's historical evolution, its mode of incorporation into the global system at present and in previous phases of capitalist development (including its colonial experience) will influence the degree and intensity of these effects. Similarly, one can point to a number of characteristics of countries which are relevant in this respect: size, location and natural resource endowment; extent of previous industrialization; the nature and organization of the labour foce; the degree of state control and the evolution and strength of a 'non-Western' cultural tradition and institutions.

Each individual country presents a different combination of these variables, but it should be possible to reduce this variety to some main types of countries. For example: (a) Relatively large countries with foreign and local capital exploiting its natural resources for export, located at a 'safe' distance from the hegemonic power; advanced process of import-substitution industrialization, with a well organized labour force, highly urbanized; interventionist state; advanced process of building a national culture with its cultural institutions (e.g. some South American countries like Argentina, Brazil, Chile, Colombia, Venezuela). (b) Small countries, scarce endowment of natural resources, near to the hegemonic power; weak process of import-substitution or export oriented industrialization, without a well organized labour force; some degree of urbanization, weak state; weak national culture (Puerto Rico and most of the Caribbean). (c) Medium sized countries, well endowed with natural resources, still to be fully exploited; beginnings of industrialization; low level of urbanization. Recent colonial and independence experience; weak state and national culture, but several strong tribal cultures (e.g. Kenya). (d) Big countries, scarce in natural resources, at a distance from the hegemonic power; some degree of industrialization; big cities, but basically rural; weak state and national culture, but a strong and rich pre-industrial culture, with its own institutions (e.g. India).

These categories are, of course, very crude. The point which it is necessary to emphasize is that work must be done on particular country experiences. Some of the articles in this book do precisely this, but it is necessary to extend this line of work.

NOTES

1 This paper is a highly synthetic *interim* report on our work on the transnationalization process. It builds upon work done previously and research in progress, and attempts to provide the outline of a coherent conceptual framework to which further work on the many and complex aspects of development can be related. Research of this kind cannot be carried out without the support of many colleagues and institutions. We are particularly grateful to the members of the 'Dependence Cluster' at IDS and the participants in the IDS Study Group on 'National Development and International Relations'. The cooperation of Stepanka Griffith-Jones, Rogelio Pérez Perdomo, Arturo Valenzuela and José Villamil in the preparation of this paper has not only been invaluable but also extremely pleasant. It is obvious that they do not necessarily subscribe to all of its contents. For institutional and financial support, we are most grateful to IDS, the Institut für Iberoamerika Kunde, the Ford Foundation, Stiftung Volkswagen and the Swedish Agency for Research Cooperation with Developing Countries (SAREC).

2 References are included to literature which represents some approaches to the topics covered in this article. No attempt has been made at developing a comprehensive and systematic bibliography. This is being done as part of the longer range research programme.

3 See, for instance, the well known textbooks by Higgins, Meier, and Baldwin, and G. Meier. The dependence literature is a reaction to this situation; see surveys by Girvan (1973), Cardoso (1974), O'Brien (1975), Cueva (1976) and the papers by Valenzuela and Sunkel in this volume. On the growth of TNCs and their effects see Sunkel (1967 and 1971), Vernon (1971), UN (1973 and 1974), Vaitsos (1974).
4 Alternative sets of concepts have been suggested by others for the analysis of world capitalism in its actual phase. Thus Murray (1971), Amin (1972), Palloix (1973), Fröbel *et al.* (1977), speak of the internationalization of capital and labour; Keohane and Nye (1971) and others speak of growing 'interdependence'.
5 The expression is used by Sorokin (1962 and 1974) as part of his frame of reference, but the concept is implicit in Polanyi (1944). See O. Sunkel and E. Fuenzalida, (1974).

REFERENCES

Adelman, I. and Taft Morris, C., 1973, *Economic Growth and Social Equity in Developing Countries*, Stanford University Press, Stanford, California.

Alemann, T. von, 1974, 'International Contacts of University Staff Members: Some Problems in the Internationality of Science', in *International Social Science Journal*, Vol. 26, No. 3, pp.445–457.

Alger, C. F. and Lyons, G. M., 1974, 'Social Science as a Transnational System', in *International Social Science Journal*, Vol. XXVI, No. 1.

Amin, S., 1972, *Accumulation on a World Scale*, Monthly Review Press, New York.
1973, *Le Développement Inégal. Essai sur less Formations Sociales du Capitalisme Péripherique*, Les Editions de Minuit, Paris, and English translation *Unequal Development*, Harvester Press, Hassocks, 1978.

Ashworth, W., 1962, *A Short History of the International Economy 1850–1950*, Longmans, London.

Aston, T. (ed.), 1965, *Crisis in Europe 1560–1660*, Routledge and Kegan Paul.

Blair, J. M., 1976, *The Control of Oil*, Macmillan, London.

Barnet, R. J. and Müller, R. E., 1974, *Global Reach: The Power of the Multinational Corporations*, Simon and Schuster, New York.

Ben-David, J., 1968, 'National and International Scientific Communities'. Unpublished paper, Hebrew University, Jerusalem, Israel.

Berger, P.; Berger, B. and Kellner, H., 1973, *The Homeless Mind*, New York, Vintage Books.

Bernstein, H. (ed.), 1973, *Underdevelopment and Development*, Harmondsworth, Penguin Books Ltd.

Braudel, F., 1966, *La Mediterranée et le Monde Méditerranéen à Epoque de Philippe II*, 2e éd., 2 Vol., Lib. Armand Colin, Paris, 1974, *Capitalism and Material Life, 1400–1800*, Fontana Collins, Great Britain.

Brown, L., 1974, *By Bread Alone*, Praeger, New York.

Cardoso, F. H. and Faletto, E., 1971, *Dependencia y Desarrollo en América Latina*, Siglo XXI, Mexico.

Cardoso, F. H., 1974, 'Notas Sobre el Estado Actual de los Estudios Sobre la Dependencia' in J. Serra (ed.) *Desarrollo Latinoamericano. Ensayos Críticos.* Fondo de Cultura Económica, México.

Carnoy, M., 1974, *Education as Cultural Imperialism*, New York, David Mckay.

CEPAL, 1951, *Economic Survey of Latin America, 1949*, United Nations, New York.

Chandler, A. D., 1961, *Strategy and Structure, Chapters in the History of the Industrial Enterprise*, Doubleday and Co., New York.

Chenery, H., *et al.*, 1974, *Redistribution with Growth*, Oxford University Press.

Church, R., 1975, *The Great Victorian Boom, 1850–1873*, Macmillan, London.

Cole, S., 1977, *Global Models and the International Economic Order*, Pergamon Press, Oxford.

Cortés Conde, R., 1973, *The First Stages of Modernization in Spanish America*, New York, Harper and Row.

Crane, D., 1972, *Invisible Colleges*, The University of Chicago Press, Chicago.

Cruise O'Brien, R., 1974, 'Dominance and Dependence in Mass Communications: Implications for the Use of Broadcasting in Developing Countries', IDS Discussion Paper, No. 64.

Cueva, A., 1976, 'A Summary of Problems and Perspectives of Dependency Theory', *Latin American Perspectives*, Issue 11, Fall, Vol. III, No. 4.

Davis, R., 1973, *The Rise of the Atlantic Economies*, Weidenfeld, London.

Dobb, M., 1946, *Studies in the Development of Capitalism*, Routledge and Kegan Paul, London.

Dos Santos, T., 1968, *El Nuevo Carácter de la Dependencia*, Cuadernos del Centro de Estudios Socio-Económicos de la Universidad de Chile, Santiago.
1969, 'The Crisis of Development Theory and the Problems of Dependence in Latin America', in Bernstein, H., 1973.

Ellis, F. and Joekes, S., 1977, *A Report of the Proceedings of the IDS-UNCTAD Conference: Intra-Firm Transactions and their Impact on Trade and Development*, IDS, 7th–11th November.

Ellul, J., 1967, *The Technological Society*, New York.

Emmanuel, A., 1972, *Unequal Exchange: A Study of the Imperialism of Trade*, Monthly Review Press, New York.

Fagen, P. W., 1973, *Chilean Universities: Problems of Autonomy and Dependence*, Sage Comparative Politics Series, Beverly Hills, California, Sage Publications.

Field, J. A. Jr., 1971, 'Transnationalism and the New Tribe' in Keohane, R. O. and Nye, J. S. (ed.), 1971.

Foxley, A. (ed.), 1974, *Distribución del Ingreso*, Fondo de Cultura Económica, México.

Frank, A. G., 1967, *Capitalism and Underdevelopment in Latin America*, Monthly Review Press, New York.

Fröbel, F., Heinrichs, H. and Kreye, O., 1977, *Die neue internationale Arbeitsteilung*, Rowohlt, Taschenbuch Verlag GmbH, Reinbek bei Hamburg, Germany.

Fuenzalida, E., 1971a, 'Problemas de Ciencia y Tecnologia en el Paso al Desarrollo', *Mensaje*, XX, September–October, pp. 444–451.

1971b, *Investigación Científica y Estratificación Internacional*, Santiago, Andrés Bello.

1971c, 'la Dependencia en el Ambito del Saber Superior y la Tranferencia de Modelos Universitarios Extranjeros en América Latina', *Modernización y Democratización en la Universiadad Latinoamericana*, Santiago, Corporación de Promoción Universitaria, pp. 3–27.

Furtado, C., 1970, *Economic Development of Latin America; A Survey from Colonial Times to the Cuban Revolution*, Cambridge University Press.

1973, 'The Concept of External Dependence in the Study of Underdevelopment' in Ch. K. Wilber (ed.) *The Political Economy of Development and Underdevelopment*, Random House, New York.

Galbraith, J. K., 1967, *The New Industrial State*, Boston, Houghton Mifflin.

Gehlen, A., 1963, 'Ueber Kulturelle Kristallisationen' in *Studien zur Anthropologie and Soziologie*, Berlin.

Gilpin, R., 1976, *U.S. Power and the Multinational corporation: the Political Economy of Foreign Direct Investment*, Macmillan, London.

Girvan, N., 1973, 'the Development of Dependency Economics in the Caribbean and Latin America: Review and Comparison' *Social and Economic Studies*, Vol. 22, No. 1, March (Special Issue on Dependence in the New World and the Old).

Godfrey, M., 1977, 'Surplus Population and Under-Development: Reserve Army or Marginal Mass?' *Manpower and Employment Research*, Vol. 10, No. 2, April, McGill University, Montreal.

Habermas, J., 1971, *Toward a Rational Society*, London, Heinemann.

Hobsbawm, E. J., 1965, 'The Crisis of the Seventeenth Century', in T. Aston (ed.), 1965.
1968, *Industry and Empire. An Economic History of Britain Since 1750*, Weidenfeld and Nicolson, London.
1975, *The Age of Capital, 1848–1875*, Weidenfeld and Nicolson, London.

Hymer, S., 1971, 'The Multinational Corporation and the Law of Uneven Development', in J. Bhagwati (ed.), *Economics and World Order*, Macmillan & Co., New York.

Inkeles, A., 1975, 'The Emerging Social Structure of the World', in *World Politics*, 27, July, pp. 467–495.

Keohane, R. O. and Nye, J. S. (eds.), 1971, *Transnational Relations and World Politics*, Harvard University Press, Cambridge, Mass.
1977, *Power and Interdependence*, Little, Brown & Co., Boston and Toronto.

Landes, D., 1969, *The Unbound Prometheus. Technological Change and Industrial Development in Western Europe from 1750 to the Present*, Cambridge University Press, Cambridge.

Leite Lopes, J., 1972, *La Ciencia y el Dilema de América Latina: Dependencia o Liberación*, Buenos Aires, Siglo XXI.

Levitt, K., 1970, *Silent Surrender, The Multinational Corporation in Canada*, Macmillan of Canada, Toronto.

Magdoff, H., 1966, *The Age of Imperialism*, Month Review Press, New York and London.

Mazrui, A., 1975, 'The African University as a Multi-National Corporation: Problems of Penetration and Dependency', *Harvard Educational Review*, Vol. 45, No. 2, May, pp. 191–210.

Meister, A., 1975, 'Le Système Transnational', *Civilisations*, Vol. XXV, No. 1/2, pp. 33–51.

Mennis, B. and Sauvant, K. P., 1976, *Emerging Forms of Transnational Community*, D. C. Heath and Company, Lexington, Mass.

Michalet, C. A., 1976, *Le Capitalisme Mondial*, Paris, Presses Universitaires de France.

Morse, E. L., 1976, *Modernization and the Transformation of*

International Relations, The Free Press, New York.

Murray, R., 1971, 'The Internationalization of Capital and the Nation State', *New Left Review*, No. 67, May–June.

Nun, J., 1969, 'Superpoblación Relativa, Ejército Industrial de Reserva y Masa Marginal', *Revista Latinoamericana de Sociología*, Vol. 5, No. 2.

O. Brien, P., 1975, 'A critique of Latin American Theories of Dependency', in I. Oxaal, T. Barnet and D. Booth (eds.), *Beyond the Sociology of Development*, Routledge and Kegan Paul Ltd.

O'Donnell, G. A., 1972, *Modernización y Autoritarismo*, Editorial Paidós, Buenos Aires.

Palloix, C., 1973, *Les Firmes Multinationales et le Procès d'Internationalisation*, Maspero, Paris.

Pinto, A., 1976, 'Styles of Development in Latin America', in *CEPAL Review*. First Semester.

and Knakal, J., 1973, 'The Center-Periphery System 20 years Later', *Social and Economic Studies*, March.

Polanyi, K., 1957, *The Great Transformation*, Boston, Beacon Press.

Prebisch, R., 1949, 'The Economic Development of Latin America and its Principal Problems', *Economic Bulletin for Latin America*, Vol. VII, No. 1, February 1962 (first published 1949).

1976, 'A Critique of Peripheral Capitalism', in *CEPAL Review*, First Semester.

Quijano, A., 1974, 'The Marginal Pole of the Economy and the Marginalized Labour Force', *Economy and Society*, Vol. 3, No. 4, November.

Sauvant, K., 1976 a, 'The Potential of Multinational Enterprises as Vehicles for the Transmission of Business Culture' in *Controlling Multinational Enterprises: Problems, Strategies, Counterstrategies*, K. Sauvant and F. Lavipour (eds.), Boulder. Colorado, Westview Press, 1976.

1976b, 'His Master's Voice', *CERES*, Vol. 9, No. 5, September–October, 1976, pp. 27–32.

and Mennis, B., 1977, 'Puzzling Over the Immaculate Conception of Indifference Curves: The Transnational Transfer and Creation of Socio-political and Economic Preferences'. Paper presented to the Second German Studies Conference, Indiana University, Bloomington, April.

Schelsky, H., 1965, 'Der mensch in der wissenschaftlichen Zivilisation', in *Auf der Suche nach Wirklichkeit*, Düss-Köln, Diederichs, 1965.

Scherer, F. M., 1971, *Industrial Market Structure and Economic Performance*, Rand McNally, Chicago.

Schiller, H., 1976, *Communication and Cultural Domination*, New York, International Arts and Sciences Press, 1976.

Smith, K., 1976, 'The Impact of Transnational Book Publishing on Intellectual Knowledge in Less Developed Countries'. Presented to a Meeting of Experts, UNESCO, Paris, 1st–5th June, 1976. SHc-76/Conf. 635/10.

Somavía, J., 1976, 'The Transnational Power Structure and International Information' in *Development Dialogue*, No. 2, pp. 15–28.

Sorokin, P., 1962, *Social and Cultural Dynamics*, New York, The Bedminster Press.

1947, *Society, Culture and Personality*, New York, Harper and Brothers.

Steger, H. A., 1977, 'Dominación Transnacional y De-cualificación Regional del Intelecto: La Vinculación Entre los Regímenes 'Consulares' y la Reforma Universitaria en América Latina', *papers*, No. 7, Barcelona.

Stein, S. and Stein, B., 1970, *The Colonial Heritage of Latin America*, New York, Oxford University Press.

Sunkel, O., 1967, 'Dependencia Externa y Política Nacional de Desarrollo', *Revista de Estudios Internacionales*, Vol. 1, No. 1, Santiago, Chile. (English translation in *Journal of Development Studies*, October 1969).

1971, 'Capitalismo Transnacional y Desintegración Nacional en América Latina', *El Trimestre Económico*, Abril-Junio. (English Translation in *Social and Economic Studies*, March, 1973).

1972, 'Big Business and Dependencia' in *Foreign Affairs*, April.

1974, 'External Economic Relationships and the Process of Development:Suggestions for an Alternative Framework', in Williamson, Glade and Schmitt (eds.), *Latin American–U.S. Economic Interactions*, American Enterprise Institute for Public Policy Research, Washington.

and Fuenzalida, E., 1974, 'Transnationalisation, National Disintegration and Reintegration in Contemporary Capitalism: an Area for Research', IDS Internal Working Paper No. 18, June 1974.

and Fuenzalida, E., 1976, 'The Effects of Transnational Corporations on Culture'. Paper presented to a Meeting of Experts, UNESCO, Paris, June. SHC-76/Conf. 635/6.

and Paz, 1970, *El Subdesarrollo Latinoamericano y la Teoría del Desarrollo*, Siglo XXI, Editores, México.

Tavares, M. C. and Serra, J., 1971, 'Más Allá del Estancamiento',

Revista Latinoamericana de Ciencias Sociales, June–December.

Touraine, A., 1976, *Les Societés Dependantes, Essais sur l' Amerique Latine*, Sociologie Nouvelle, Paris.

Trevor-Roper, H. R., 1965, 'The General Crisis of the Seventeenth Century', in T. Aston, 1965.

U.N. Dept. of Economic and Social Affairs, 1973, *Multinational Corporations in World Development*, (ST/ECA/190 and Con. 1), New York.

1974, *The Impact of Multinational Corporations on Development and on International Relations*(E/5500/Rev. 1, St/ESA/6), New York.

United States Senate, Committee on Foreign Relations, 1977, *International Debt, the Banks, and U.S. Foreign Policy*, A Staff Report, foreword by Senator Frank Church, U.S. Government Printing Office, Washington.

United States Senate, 88th Congress, 2nd Session, Pursuant to Resolution 262, 1964, *Economic Concentration: Hearings Before the Subcommittee on Antitrust and Monopoly of the Committee on the Judiciary*, in particular works by Mueller, W., Blair, J. and Adelman, M. A.

Vaitsos, C. V., 1974, *Intercountry Income Distribution and Transnational Enterprises*, Clarendon Press, Oxford.

Varis, T., 1976, 'The Impact of Transnational Corporations on Communication'. Paper presented to a Meeting of Experts, UNESCO, Paris, June, SHC-76/Conf. 635/7.

Vasconi, T. A., and Reca, I., 1971, *Modernización y Crisis en la Universidad Latinoamericana*, Santiago, Cuadernos del Centro de Estudios Socio-Económicos de la Universidad de Chile.

Vernon, R., 1971, *Sovereignty at Bay: The Multinational Spread of U.S. Enterprises*, Basic Books, Inc., New York.

Wachtel, H. M., 1977, *The New Gnomes: Multinational Banks in the Third World*, Transnational Institute Pamphlet No. 4, Washington, Amsterdam.

Wallerstein, I., 1974a, *The Modern World-System*, Academic Press, New York, San Francisco, London.

1974b, 'The Rise and Future Demise of the World Capitalist System: Concepts for Comparative Analysis', *Comparative Studies in Society and History*, XVI, No. 4, pp. 381–415.

1976, 'From Feudalism to Capitalism: Transition or Transitions?', *Social Forces*, LV, No. 2.

4

PATTERNS OF DEPENDENCE

Dudley Seers

One of the symptoms of the immaturity of the social sciences is a
lack of interest in taxonomy. Since the war, a three-part classification of 'centrally planned', 'developed', and a 'third world' of 'less
developed' or 'developing' countries[2], has held sway. This classification has helped to shape the way in which we all perceive and
interpret international trends and events and provided a set of
boundaries to academic subject areas (such as 'development economics'). But it emerged in response to political needs rather than
professional theorizing.

I am going to look briefly at the basis and implications of this
division, then at the way in which it has been eroded by political and
economic tendencies in the last two decades, and conclude by
suggesting a classification based on dependence, which seems more
appropriate for many purposes, especially professional research.

THE THREE-WORLD CLASSIFICATION AND
ITS IMPLICATIONS

The conventional classification has rested mainly on two criteria,
first on whether a country is or is not communist, and secondly—if
the answer to the first question is 'no'—on its *per capita* income. Its
widespread use has depended partly on the fact that it is convenient
to the parties concerned. Governments of 'developing' countries use
it as a means of pressure on the 'developed'. These categories have
also suited governments of 'centrally planned' economies because
the former colonies are encouraged to address their demands to the
former metropolitan countries. While the governments of 'developed' countries have found these demands irksome, they have
acknowledged some interest in helping the 'developing' countries to
'develop' and avoid communism.[3]

This classification suggested that a 'developing' country could, by
raising its *per capita* national income, join the 'developed' countries.
This could be done with an economic growth plan (generally but
misleadingly called a 'development plan'). Using national income

accounts, various income and expenditure targets, projections and constraints could be brought together and their joint implications drawn. Plans of this sort have played a big part in focussing the minds of decision-makers, planning officials and members of the public on global growth targets and their capital requirements, thus diverting attention from political and social problems.

Another implication was that the help of the 'developed' countries was needed to raise investment to adequate levels, and provide the necessary expertise. The 'Developed' countries had solved their economic and social problems; those of the Third World had an easier task because shelves were full of the necessary technologies, and they could simply choose what they wanted, with the assistance of the aid agencies.

If economies did not grow quickly enough, and poverty did not end, this must be due to 'obstacles'—trade controls, religion, traditional customs, extended family systems, linguistic barriers, illiteracy, etc.—which hindered the operation of the various factor and product markets. Marxists put the emphasis more on property rights, especially in land, and the resultant concentration of economic and political power. But there was little disagreement across the political spectrum on the basic objective; obstacles could and should be removed by 'modernization' and economic growth accelerated. One can in fact talk of a Chicago-Marxist paradigm.[4] What was important was to create productive capacity. In due course—whether by 'trickling down' or revolutionary change—the mass of the people would achieve a modern standard of living.

The task of international organizations such as UNCTAD was seen by the governments of 'developing' countries (and by their own secretariats) as primarily to arrange a sufficient transfer of resources to make this possible. Targets for growth rates implied targets for transfers of aid and private capital (e.g. in the UN 'Development Decade' strategies) and resolutions were drafted about tariff preferences, commodity prices, etc.[5]

THE GROWING IRRELEVANCE OF THE 'THIRD WORLD'

The heyday of this highly optimistic approach was the decade from about 1955 to 1965. This was, in retrospect, a rather simplistic era. Perhaps what did most to undermine it was that countries with sustained fast economic growth over more than two decades (for example Jamaica), as high as 3–4 per cent in *per capita* terms, did not by any means experience reductions in unemployment, inequality or poverty. One consequence was the extension of economic planning into the fields of distribution and employment (Chenery *et al.*, 1973).

Nor did fast-growing countries become economically more independent. Import-substituting industrialization turned out to reinforce imported styles of consumption (enjoyed by small minorities) and to create new sorts of dependence on technology, equipment and intermediate products from abroad. It also usually led to some neglect of the agricultural sector and therefore dependence on imported foodstuffs, especially wheat; many countries which had traditionally been cereal exporters became importers (Brown, 1975).

While these economic trends were undermining the growth-centred ideology that was the counterpart of the three-world system, it was also being made obsolete by other developments:—first, a partial fragmentation of the Communist world and a degree of 'convergence' with non-Communist countries. After the government of China broke its political alignment with the Soviet Union, Rumanian international policy showed increasing independence. There has been a general tendency in the Communist group to rely much more on market forces, while in Western Europe state intervention and nationalization have spread.

There has also been a growing fuzziness in the boundary between the 'developed' and 'developing' countries. The power of the word 'developed' to inspire emulation was weakened by none of the 'developed' any longer seeing themselves as paradigms. Several countries in Western Europe have been showing the characteristic chronic payment difficulties, chronic unemployment and chronic inflation of developing countries. More to the point, they have increasingly been importing technology and capital via trans-national companies (*IDS Communication* No 121, 1977).

The conventional model of world development (or rather growth) was further weakened by the combined oil and food crises of recent years. In the first place, this showed that a country need not rely on aid or private investment, but could get capital by bargaining with natural resources. Secondly, it exposed the vulnerability of growth strategies based on highly-mechanized industrialization, including those which has been adopted in the 'developed' and 'centrally planned' countries. Indeed it cast a considerable question mark against the possibility of the whole world population reaching a 'modern' standard of living within the next couple of generations—or ever. As at present, some people in some countries would enjoy this: the rest would not. The world suddenly became a much less benign place, and state bargaining capacity became much more important.

The question also now arose: how to classify Kuwait, a country with a *per capita* income of over $10,000? If we describe it as more 'developed' than the United States, this intuitively seems absurd. On social indicators such as life expectancy, it does not come very high in an international league table (mainly because of the poverty of its immigrant population). Its prosperity is also precarious. Although Kuwait exports a great deal of one saleable commodity, it has several important weaknesses. It is a town in the desert and produces practically no food except a few vegetables. The country's pattern of production totally fails to match its consumption structure. It has to import technology for all sectors, even to extract its main economic asset, oil; its government has nationalized the physical assets of the petroleum companies but cannot nationalize their technology for production or processing, or their access to world markets. It still needs expertise from abroad, and it may not have the professional capacity even to judge the best sources of such expertise. It is also a country with too small (and heterogeneous) a population to defend itself, especially in such a politically unstable area as the Gulf. The level of living of the Kuwaiti public has in fact become wholly dependent on foreign corporations and governments—though these in turn cannot exercise their full dominance with impunity, because of the importance of uninterrupted flows of oil.

SOME DETERMINANTS OF DEPENDENCE

I am now introducing facts which, though evidently important, have little place in the neo-classical texts in which the old classification (and its policy implications) were rooted Dependence theory does provide an alternative world 'model' that takes account of these. Let us look briefly at some of the sources of dependence. A clue to the nature and extent of a country's dependence can be obtained by simulating a situation in which its has been cut off from the outside world. This need not actually happen or even be a real possibility: the merely potential consequences of autarchy determine a government's freedom of action.

The first step is to simulate what would occur if the normal supplies of imports and markets for exports were cut. There are many economic inputs which it would be painful for almost any economy to do without—minerals, foodstuffs, etc. (I shall return to the significance of these later). A country is especially dependent if it relies on one or two foreign countries for foreign exchange to buy imports which are essential either as industrial inputs or consumer goods (especially spare parts), i.e. which depends ultimately on the goodwill of one or two particular governments. This raises questions about the geographical destination of its exports and their commodity composition, and about whether its customers could buy the same product elsewhere, obtain substitutes, or manage to do without.

The need for foreign exchange naturally raises questions about the large quantities pre-empted to service debts to foreign governments, banks or international agencies. Yet the very dependence on foreign supplies makes it impractical to default on such obligations (however strong the case for doing so, especially if the obligations were incurred under coercion). This applies even to revolutionary governments, if the countries concerned are heavily integrated into the world economy. The potential costs of retaliation may be too heavy. (Expropriation of foreign companies raises similar issues).

A government that tries to sever its links with dominant countries also faces the possibility of invasion, as happened to Cuba, Guatemala and Czechoslovakia. If its military strength is limited, it has therefore little room to manoeuvre in policy, including policy to reduce economic dependence.

An important determinant of economic and military autonomy is the extent to which a government can appeal to patriotism to justify reductions in the level of consumption and, if necessary, the sacrifice of life itself, when confronting another government. This patriotic capacity depends in part on cultural factors such as ethnic homogeneity and the extent to which language and religion are common and indigenous. These are rooted in history: the cultural base of patriotism may be fundamentally flawed in former colonies which were, as was often the case in Africa, artificially created by colonial governments without regard to ethnic patterns. It may also have been undermined by the immigration of settlers or slave (or indentured) labour.

Internal cultural disunity may also have been created or aggravated by the economic, political and cultural influences of dominant countries. The modern sector (not necessarily the same as the urban) may have come to rely heavily on foreign political and economic links (including arms) and developed loyalties primarily to imported value systems, fed to them by foreign travel, education overseas, imported television programmes and news agency material. Foreign fashions may be followed in, among other areas, consumption, architecture and economic theories. Where such influences are strong, members of the professional class fail to give due weight to national interest and are easily lured to jobs overseas in the TNCs; the political leadership and the bureaucracy may lack even the desire to reduce dependence.

A country's capacity to withstand external pressures is also affected by the size of its population. This determines the numbers available for military service and arms production. At a given level and distribution of income, it sets the size of the market, which is in turn closely related to the structure of production, especially the degree of self-sufficiency in capital goods. It also sets a limit to research capacity, and thus to the level of technology and the ability to select from techniques available overseas those appropriate to national needs.[6]

A big population is likely, however, to be vulnerable economically unless it has corresponding space, especially adequate arable land. Geographical size has other advantages. A large country is more capable (as Russia has often shown) of absorbing and defeating invading armies. Since oil and other natural resources appear to be scattered more or less at random (though not of course evenly), the larger the country, including its territorial waters, the more likely it is to have a diversified resource base and less need for trade—though much, naturally depends on climate, soil and technique as well.

Another factor determining in some degree economic, military and cultural dependence is location, especially distance from countries which are more powerful in these respects. Distance affects trade, military accessibility and the penetrating power of television and radio as well as personal contacts. Governments of countries with big and powerful neighbours, especially if there are common land frontiers, have to accept limits on their freedom of action, whatever their resources.[7]

A special case is that of small countries in a strategically important position, like Iceland or Malta. Similar limitations of freedom of action apply, but they are able—up to a point—to charge for exclusive rights for military use of harbours, airfields, and other facilities.

An important point about these last characteristics (area and location, population size) is that, like ethnic composition and natural resources, they are not changeables; they have to be taken wholly or largely as data by those formulating policy, even by hypothetical revolutionary governments of the future. This is worth stressing because many dependence theorists have been reluctant to accept that some countries are almost permanently highly dependent for geographical reasons, whatever the political changes at home or abroad (Best, 1966; Thomas, 1974). It has been underlined in the recent slowing down of investment in Cuba, and the appearance of open unemployment there (though on a small scale), due in part to the collapse of the world market price of sugar since 1975.

These aspects of dependence are hardly reflected at all in the original three-world classification. It is true that this still has a certain reality. Countries remain grouped into military alliances (NATO and the Warsaw Pact) and politico-economic organizations (OECD and COMECON). There is also obviously some life in the 'Third World' as a group, due to their common interests as buyers of technology and equipment and their common historic resentments against the leading countries of European stock (including the United States). In fact the diplomatic creation of 'the 77' has survived the rise in oil prices remarkably well (partly because of the financial aid programmes of oil exporters).

On the other hand, the growing irrelevance of the old categories, especially since the growth in the power of OPEC, implies that this way of looking at the world is becoming an increasingly obvious barrier to professional analysis, to the transfer of experience, and even in some countries (such as Britain) to the recognition of national interests.

One might well ask whether any classification would have much meaning in the present confused international scene. We do however need categories to handle information, whether as analysts or policy-makers, and to provide the basis for the organization of both professional work and international diplomacy. Without them, we would find difficulty in assessing the significance of new pieces of information—e.g. a major new oil find.

A CLASSIFICATION BASED ON ECONOMIC POWER

Any classification has to be manageable. We should select a few factors of key importance, preferably ones that can in some way be measured. Methodologists might claim that a classification should be derived empirically, e.g. by correlation analysis. This would no doubt be the correct approach for those who treat economic growth or concentration of income as crucial yardsticks of progress, and assume they can be properly measured. However, my analysis is designed to throw light on the behaviour of something even more difficult to define or measure, the room to manoeuvre of existing or potential governments. The influences on this are, moreover, too numerous and complex to be incorporated in an explanatory model. So, I shall begin by tentatively making an intuitive list of the most important determinants.

The first place to look is trade. One of the most crucial influences on a country's economic independence is the extent to which its demand structure matches its supply structure, particularly in energy and food, basically petroleum and cereals. Economic power depends very much on whether a country is a substantial net importer or exporter of these key inputs and they seem likely to be increasingly important in the future.

Oil is the more significant of the two. Its income elasticity of demand is much higher and its supply non-renewable. All countries produce some cereals and it might not be very difficult for many of them to make do with local supplies in a crisis, especially if these were supplemented with other foodstuffs: food output would automatically and quite quickly increase as prices rise. On the other hand, it is generally impossible to increase oil output significantly in the short period, and impossible in countries where no oil has so far been found: the time lag between exploration and commerical production is several years, especially for offshore output. There is no satisfactory substitute for oil in transportation systems nor in many sectors of industry, because it is also a feedstock. It is even the source of some the main fertilizers needed for cereal production. Its market is much less competitive: to be dependent on imports of oil probably means being dependent on two or three of the 'seven sisters'. Finally, whereas dependence on oil becomes a chronic charge on the balance of payments, fluctuations in cereal prices determine the economic consequences of being a net importer or exporter in any particular year, and this itself depends partly on climatic fluctuations (*viz* the experience of the Soviet Union). At times, cereal importers even find that gluts elsewhere due to weather or price policy provide them with a temporarily strong bargaining position. Still, to be dependent on imported cereals (due for example to consumption of wheat bread having become customary in a country which cannot produce wheat), can be politically and economically crippling, especially whenever cereal prices are high or the prices of the country's own exports low.

Yet resources themselves are by no means the main determinant of dependence. A country with plenty of subsoil petroleum and arable land in relation to its own needs, can hardly be considered truly self-sufficient if to exploit these resources it has to rely on foreign technology, i.e. what is embodied in exploration and mining equipment, tractors and harvesters, etc. Even the extent of mineral reserves or the acreage of potentially arable land depend partly on the technology available. Moreover, technological capacity of another sort is needed to plan the optimal development of oilfields and the agricultural sector (including decisions on what are the best sources of equipment and expertise).

Technological dependence is very closely related to other forms. Technology usually moves along the same channels as equipment and capital, which in turn flow most strongly to those countries where there are already large assets as a result of past investments. In most countries, a fairly high proportion of industrial capital is owned by foreign importers of technology and sometimes a significant proportion of land too. The government of countries where these companies are based will try to protect them, in extreme cases by military means.

Reliance on foreign investment and technology tends to sap a country's independence. Unless these are carefully screened (as in Japan), a Ministry will simply react to proposals, instead of conducting a strategy of industrialization that reflects national interests and draws the most appropriate technologies from the most appropriate sources. The pattern of industrial development in these countries may simply reflect the pattern of foreign business executive arrivals at the main airport. Moreover, a large role for foreign capital tends to limit drastically the flexibility of trade. Transnational corporations have their own interests: they may wish to import from their affiliated companies and to avoid making exports competitive with those of their subsidiaries. Less formal links via licensing arrangements may have similar effects.

Local technological capacity is also essential to genuine military independence. A government such as that of Iran cannot sustain a war which is not condoned by its military suppliers, since it relies on them for spare parts for aircraft and on foreign personnel, both operational and maintenance. It also has constantly to refresh its political alliances to keep militarily up-to-date *vis-à-vis* potential enemies.

Perhaps, therefore, technological dependence is the most basic form. It is, however, in contrast to natural resources and other factors mentioned above changeable to a significant degree within a generation. Moreover, it is heterogeneous—much more so than oil or even cereals: countries are often exporters of some types of technology, importers of others, and these are by no means substitutable. So 'dependence on technology' is rather an oversimplification. It is also hard to measure: imports of machinery and transport equipment are not entirely satisfactory as a proxy.

Still, it may be useful to classify countries according to whether they are chronically dependent on imports for one, two or three of these inputs—oil, cereals and technology. This has been done in the diagram which uses data for 1972–74 to show whether a country is a net importer. We should remember in interpreting it that the extent

Diagram

Illustrative profiles of dependence on key inputs

	(1) Oil	(2) Cereals	(3) Technology
A *Least-dependent countries* (net importers of only 1 key input)			
USA	X		
Soviet Union		X	
China			X
B *Some semi-dependent countries* (net importers of 2 key inputs)			
(i) *Net exporters of technology*			
Japan	X	X	
East Germany	X	X	
West Germany	X	X	
(ii) *Net exporters of oil*			
Iran		X	X
Kuwait		X	X
Nigeria		X	X
(iii) *Net exporters of cereals*			
Argentina	X		X
Thailand	X		X
C *Some dependent countries* (net importers of all 3 key inputs)			
Brazil	X	X	X
Cuba	X	X	X
Portugal	X	X	X

Sources: See Appendix.

and nature of dependence on each of these items are also important. We should also bear in mind that these are determined not only by supply availability but also by demand, reflecting in turn styles of living and productive structures. The paragraphs that follow contain some brief notes on the implications of this classification.

A. *The least dependent countries*

Certain features stand out. In the first place, the United States, the Soviet Union and China are each net importers of just one key input, and none of them lacks any of the three entirely. They would be the countries best able to withstand a breakdown of their trade with the rest of the world (as indeed they have each demonstrated during the second world war). They are also substantial net exporters of at least one key input (both cereals and technology for the United States; oil for the Soviet Union and China).[8]

But although they each have only one economic weakness, this is serious. For the United States, it is oil, and it is true that oil imports might in the long-term be eased by the combined development of coal, nuclear power and new types of energy, but these involve enormous capital and environmental costs, and nuclear power would require imports of uranium. The life styles which have become customary in the United States have also induced net imports of iron ore and many other industrially important metals. To round out the picture, we also need to mention its non-economic assets. It is a large country with a big population, bordered by two oceans and two relatively weak neighbours. Its ethnic diversity has been partially overcome by determined policies of assimilation.[9] Many would argue that another advantage of the United States is that its political system is flexible because there are relatively few constraints on the expression of dissent.

Cereals form the Achilles' heel of the Soviet Union and have required import contracts in several recent years. To eliminate these permanently would apparently require a difficult reorganization of the rural economy—though not as big a task as faces the United States over energy (for the reasons given above). It is, moreover, less independent in technology than the United States,[10] and is no longer able to meet the oil needs of Eastern Europe. (it has big reserves in Siberia, but these raise major problems of transportation, especially in view of limits on pipeline construction capacity).

The Chinese on the other hand are increasing their exports of oil, and their deficiency in technology, including military types, can—in contrast to dependence on key natural resources—be more easily made up.[11] Moreover, consumer aspirations can be more effectively restrained there than in the other two, even the Soviet Union. China may therefore become the least vulnerable country in a few decades.

Yet even these three can hardly afford autarchic or isolationist policies. Although they are, especially the United States and the Soviet Union, militarily very powerful (because of their large populations and high technology), their security requires neighbours which are at least neutral. The Soviet Union and China lack these: indeed precisely, their main weakness is that the two of them share a long common frontier. Either of them would be gravely threatened in the long run by an alliance between the other and the U.S.A.

So none of these three is truly independent. Some countries are currently termed the 'least developed': I have called these three the 'least dependent', to reflect their limited dependence.

B. The semi-dependent countries

Japan is often counted as a 'super power' and certainly its *per capita* income (even its national income) is far higher than that of China. It has other important assets, which do not appear on the table: a population which is large and more homogeneous, ethnically and linguistically, than that of most countries. Although its internal differences in income (and in access to social services) are severe, a common culture is deeply rooted in Japanese history: its people might well show considerable cohesion during a politico-economic crisis, even one involving major changes in patterns of consumption. It is a net exporter of technology (and thus capital equipment). However, because of restrictions imposed after the war of 1941–45, it is not a manufacturer of major military equipment such as warplanes. Yet its population needs imported oil to keep warm, to communicate, to move from one place to another, as well as to produce and distribute their necessities. It is also dependent on cereal imports, so it is significantly more dependent than any of the three 'least dependent' countries.

It also faces bigger environmental constraints and costs than other countries in expanding steel and other heavy industries, the products of which may therefore increasingly need to be imported (Japanese External Trade Organization, 1974). Political opposition is strong against conversion of power generation to nuclear sources. The dependence pattern of West Germany is strikingly similar and, with a few variations, this could be taken as broadly representative of some other West European countries.[12] They buy technology (and also arms and equipment) from transnational corporations based in the United States and Japan (as well as other European countries) but also sell these to the rest of the world in sufficient quantities, via their own transnational corporations, to be net exporters. Most are, however, to some degree dependent on imported cereals and all highly dependent on imported oil.[13]

It now seems useful for many purposes, not merely academic, to distinguish the basic interests of West European countries and Japan from those of the United States. This approach helps explain the observable growing policy difference among countries previously considered a single group. The relative bargaining strength of the United States has increased due to the emergence of a long-term seller's market in cereals, and the increasing importance of sophisticated armaments and other forms of high technology (especially off-shore and satellite exploration for minerals), in which the United States now has a clear lead.[14] It is not surprising that many European governments are less vehement in defending transnational corporations when these are under attack in international fora such as UNCTAD.

It therefore seems preferable, at least for some purposes, to treat the technologically advanced countries of Western Europe and Japan as a separate class. One might call them 'semi-dependent'. East Germany, and possibly one or two other East European countries, could also be put in the same group. Differences between their resource patterns and those of the Soviet Union have become increasingly important. As in Western Europe, international cultural influences create consumer aspirations which, in conjunction with resource deficiencies, limit the room to manoeuvre of governments. Just as the category 'developed market economies' is ceasing to be useful, so is the category 'centrally planned economies'.

Another class of country is also 'semi-dependent', but in a different sense, the petroleum exporters.[15] It is true that the members of OPEC differ sharply among themselves in several important respects, notably in the extent of their agricultural hinterland and their population base. But they also all have much in common—oil to trade for technology, arms, equipment, and the manufactures and foodstuffs needed to meet very high consumer expectations. They are also heavy creditors in international finance. They cannot now be usefully classified for many purposes as among the 'developing' countries.

A case can also be made for considering as a separate group countries which have export surpluses of cereals (usually wheat or rice) to trade for oil and equipment, technology, etc. Since cereals are, for the reasons given above, a good deal less valuable than oil as an export commodity, and they usually form a much small proportion of total exports, cereal exporters can hardly be treated on a par with exporters of oil or technology. However, they are in a distinctly different category from countries which import not only oil and technology, but also basic foodstuffs, as would be revealed in any serious crisis.

C. The dependent countries

The countries without any key input to market, form the largest group, though only a few examples are shown in the diagram. Nearly all countries in Africa, Asia and Latin America depend on imports of oil, cereals and technology. To buy these very necessary imports and to service foreign capital, they offer less essential commodities such as coffee, tea, bananas, cocoa, sugar and cotton and/or tourist facilities and migrant labour. They can therefore truly be termed 'dependent' countries.[16] So can Portugal, as well as other countries in Southern Europe: they have basically more in common with this group than with the 'developed market' economies, where they were placed in the old classification. (Seers, 1978b). Cuba also remains basically dependent on the world sugar market to buy its essential imports.[17]

This is therefore a very mixed bag. Some large countries with a varied resource base and indigenous technological research capacity, such as Brazil, have very much greater possibilities for autonomous action than (say) Cuba or even Portugal. They are essentially a residual group, as was the old category 'developing countries', which had however less in common.

CONCLUDING REMARKS

There are other ways of dividing up the world.[18] Some might prefer to use a political dimension, especially how 'socialist' a country is. Yet Cuba, like Vietnam, remains a small country dependent on capital, technology and energy needs which cannot be wholly satisfied by the Soviet Union or China. Moreover, to take an extreme case, if the United States were to undergo a social revolution, it would still need oil from the Middle East and Venezuela, as well as iron ore and various other metals (not to speak of coffee and tea) from the rest of the world. The hypothetical post-revolutionary government in Washington would still have to finance these essential imports and could hardly stop exporting technology and arms, or receiving payments of debt service and profit remittances; nor could it give up its military and diplomatic leverage. Any government is bound to be primarily concerned with its own survival, and use the bargaining power based on its fundamental assets to protect as best it can the consumption standards of its own population, especially of the classes that form the base of its power—even if this means perpetuating 'unequal exchange'. Indeed, continued exploitation (in this sense) of overseas countries would be *especially* necessary after a social upheaval, because these standards would be threatened by the disruption of economic activity: as the example of Cuba shows a new revolutionary government faces internal unrest and the potential emigration of technical and administrative personnel, as well as possible trade embargos and military intervention, apart from inevitable opposition from the former ruling class.

Another classification which appears to have some analytical potential, can be derived basically from one of the sources of dependence mentioned above, namely location. A series of regional core-periphery systems can be seen, the two most obvious and important being Western Europe and North America (Seers, 1978b). Characteristic linkages in such a system (though not so important as other forms of dependence) are migration and tourism. The foreign exchange receipts these generate can assume a predominant weight in the balance of payments (as in, say, Portugal or Mexico).

Enough has been said perhaps to indicate that classifications based on dependence theory may, in general, be the most useful, certainly for social scientists but perhaps increasingly for government officials and political leaders too. Such classifications provide starting points for studying what determines national room to manoeuvre, how this differs in the short and long term, and thus what polices are feasible or might become so, and how techniques of planning need to be altered.

The emphasis suggested by this approach would be to aim at greater national self-sufficiency, by policies directed at consumption as well as production, rather than maximizing economic growth, but above all to plan the creation of technological and negotiating capacity. It may even be worth developing 'uneconomic' sources of energy and food and 'wasteful duplication' of research facilities to increase bargaining strength. This may yield an economic return as well, partially or wholly offsetting any economic costs in such a policy. There is of course a limit to the extent to which it is worth trading income for autonomy and security; the position of this limit will vary according to the value judgements of the analyst and also local circumstances, especially the accessibility of hydrocarbons and other materials and the fertility of the soil. It would be a crucial area for research by a planning office.

NOTES

1 This paper is based on seminars given at the Universities of Harvard and Puerto Rico, and a contribution to a consultation meeting of the United Nations University in Tokyo. An earlier and much shorter version was printed in the IDS *Bulletin* (Vol. 7, No. 4) under the title 'A New Look at the Three-World Classification'. I am indebted to Marja Kiljunen for help with the basic research for this version.

2 In the odiously euphemistic language of the United Nations. The 'developed' countries are more formally known as 'developed market economies'.

3 See Seers, (1977) for a fuller discussion of this point.

4 Marxism is, of course, strictly a particular form of neo-classical doctrine. It shares with the Chicago school a common origin in the classical writers. Adam Smith and Ricardo. See Seers,(1978a).

5 Will the delegations to UNCTAD V in 1979 show yet again a degree of mindless euphoria when they get last-minute agreement to vague statements of aspiration?

6 Of course, to say that a large population is an asset to a country is not to imply that fast population growth necessarily strengthens it in any but the longest of long runs. For one thing, demands on resources are raised, reducing exportable surpluses, and increasing the need for imports and social infrastructure. But I do not propose to take up a Malthusians position. A citizen of a rich country could argue that slower population growth would be in the interest of mankind—if his government were actively adopting other policies in the interests of mankind as a whole (e.g. on armaments, energy, control of TNCs). It is unseemly (and suspect) for us to urge the advantages of population control on other countries in the absence of such policies.

7 The implications of proximity for dependence are discussed in Seers,(1978b).

8 France is, like the United States, self-sufficient in cereals and technology. However, it is a less significant exporter of both of these, and totally lacks oil. It has, moreover, a considerably smaller population, and its vulnerable strategic position makes it highly dependent on military alliances. So it can hardly be put in the same category.

9 But one of the potential vulnerabilities of the United States is its growing *chicano* population, especially in Texas (precisely its main source of oil), with some degree of allegiance to Mexico—due in part to exploitation by U.S. farmers and other employers.

10 It is in fact shown as a marginally net importer of goods of SITC category 7 for 1972–74, but this deficit would be outweighed by exports of arms if the data were available.

11 China is estimated by FAO to have been a net importer of cereals in 1972–74, but it would be misleading to classify her as a chronic importer (especially since even in those years imports were apparently low in relation to China's very large population).

12 It is true that Britain will shortly cease to be an oil importer, but the Government's capacity to exploit oil exports is inhibited by membership of EEC and it could cease to be a net exporter of equipment and technology, especially if its exchange rate becomes overvalued, as is typical for oil exporters.

13 These statements would be true of EEC as a whole. Of course it has a large population but, even if it were politically unified, it could not be considered in the same 'least dependent' class as the U.S.A., the Soviet Union or China. This is not merely because of deficiencies in the key inputs, cereals and especially oil, but also because of cultural heterogeneity and strategic vulnerability.

14 An additional reason for this divergence is the much greater weight of the Zionist political lobby in the United States.

15 In 1974, they were portrayed by some as almost another world power (e.g. in the doctrine of 'polycentricity'). However, euphoria has led to such a massive waste of resources that it is no longer even conceivable to depict them in this way.

16 There are a few very poor and isolated countries, such as Nepal, which do not export oil, cereals or technology, but have not developed imports of oil or cereals either. Some of them are classed as 'least developed', but from the point

of view developed here, they could also be considered a special sub-category of the 'least dependent'.
17 The 1975 agreement with the Soviet Union gave Cuba a guaranteed market for part of its crop at a relatively high price indexed to Soviet export prices (including oil)—though paid in inconvertible roubles. The Soviet Union now clearly lacks the finance, energy and technology (especially in consumer goods) to provide for a big 'sphere of influence'.
18 For some purposes, cultural factors mentioned above, such as degree of homogeneity, may be insignificant. I suggested earlier an economic classification based on stages of imported substitution (Seers, 1963). This corresponded to a 'structuralist' theoretical approach and, while I would still consider it more useful for many purposes than the 'three-world' classification, it no longer seems the most appropriate.

REFERENCES

Best, L., 1966, 'Size and Survival', *New World Quarterly*, Vol. 2, No. 3.

Brown, L., 1975, *The Politics and Responsibility of the North American Breadbasket*, Worldwatch Institute, Washington.

Chenery, H. *et. al.*, 1973, *Redistribution with Growth*, a World Bank-IDS study, Oxford University Press.

IDS Communication No. 121, 1977, 'North Sea Oil: the application of development theories', by a group of faculty and students on the M Phil course in development studies.

Japanese External Trade Organization, 1974, *Japan's Industrial Structure—A Long-Range Vision*, Tokyo.

Seers, D., 1963, 'The Stages of Economic Development of a Primary Producer in the Middle of the Twentieth Century', *Economic Bulletin of Ghana*, Vol. 7, No. 4.

Seers, D., 1977, 'Back to the Ivory Tower? The Professionalization of Development Studies and their Extension to Europe', *IDS Bulletin*, Vol. 9, No. 2.

Seers, D., 1978a, 'The Congruence of Marxism and other Neo-Classical Doctrines', (*IDS Discussion Paper*, No. 136).

Seers, D., 1978b (forthcoming), 'The Periphery of Europe', *Underdeveloped Europe: Studies in Core-Periphery Relations*, ed. Seers, Schaffer, Kiljunen, Harvester Press.

Thomas, C. Y., 1974, *Dependence and Transformation*, Monthly Review Press, New York.

Appendix

Dependence profiles of selected countries. Imports and Exports 1972–74 average (US $ billions)

Country	Machinery & Transport Equipment		Cereals		Crude Petroleum		Population (m) 1970
	Imports	Exports	Imports	Exports	Imports	Exports	
A. Least dependent countries							
USA	21.1	29.5	—	7.3	7.9	—	203
USSR	7.0	4.6	1.1	0.7	0.3	2.1	242
China	..	..	1.1	0.7	..	..	772
B. Semi-dependent countries							
Net exporters of technology							
Japan	3.3	19.0	2.1	0.1	9.6	—	105
GDR	0.4	3.4	0.3	—	..	—	17
FRG	9.2	30.6	1.0	0.2	4.9	—	61
Net exporters of petroleum							
Iran	1.5	—	0.2	—	—	7.9	29
Kuwait	0.4	0.1	—	—	—	4.9	1
Nigeria	0.8	—	0.1	—	—	4.4	58
Net exporters of cereals							
Argentina	0.7	0.2	—	0.9	0.2	—	23
Thailand	0.7	—	—	0.5	0.2	—	34
C. Dependent countries							
Brazil	2.6	0.4	0.4	0.1	1.4	—	92
Cuba	0.4[1]	—	0.2	—	0.1[1]	—	9
Portugal	1.0	0.2	0.2	—	0.2	—	9

Sources: FAO *Trade Yearbook*, 1975
UN *Statistical Yearbook*, 1975
UN *Yearbook of International Trade Statistics*, 1975

.. not available
— less than $50 million
[1] 1970–72 average

PART TWO

TRANSNATIONAL STRUCTURES

5

THE PROBLEM OF TECHNOLOGICAL INNOVATION IN LATIN AMERICA

Edmundo F. Fuenzalida

In recent years a small number of scholars have concerned themselves with the situation in Latin America regarding the systematic use of scientific research for its own development (Herrera, 1970; Fuenzalida *et al.*, 1974). This article surveys some of the relevant literature and offers an alternative interpretation of the situation in the field of technological innovation in Latin America.

A REVIEW OF THE LITERATURE

Herrera's work (1968) deals with an evaluation of scientific and technological research in Latin America, on which he asserts:

> . . . the greater part of scientific research being carried out has very little to do with the most pressing needs of the region. (p. 14)
> Technological research is very rare and is generally limited to the possibilities of using natural resources in the laboratory phase and does not reach the pilot plant stage; accordingly it does not consider the technical and economic aspects of the process of industrialization. (p. 14)
> As far as basic research is concerned, what is undertaken in the region is carried out mainly at universities or in institutions having links with them or in government organizations. With only rare exceptions, their research programmes bear no relationship to the needs of industry or the general problems of economic development of the region. (p. 15)
> The most important characteristic of the picture that has just been briefly sketched is the scant nature of the relationship between the scientific and technological activity of the region and the basic problems of development which it faces. This situation, just as much as or more than the actual amount of research being carried out is, in our opinion, a distinctive characteristic of underdevelopment in the field we are considering. (p. 15)

Herrera asserts that the causes of the scientific and technological backwardness of Latin America relate to inefficiency of the state and the absence of technologically progressive industry.

With respect to devising solutions to this problem, Herrera rejects two alternatives that are frequently put forth: the acquisition of technological know-how from the industrialized countries, through patents or other means, and the development of 'intermediate' science and technology. He considers it necessary for the Latin American countries to develop high-level scientific and technological capabilities of their own. But, he says:

> It is not simply a matter of starting scientific activity. It already exists and always has existed in every civilized society because, like art, it is one of the primary products of human activity. It is a matter of joining in what has come to be called the Scientific and Technological Revolution, that is to say, in that self-activating process in which the scientific activity is translated spontaneously and automatically into a better standard of living for society which, in turn, stimulates further scientific activity. This is the process which today enables the advanced countries to increase their standard of living at a rate never before attained in history. (pp. 29–30)

What are the conditions required for a society to be able to join in the Scientific and Technological Revolution? Herrera answers by reviewing the experience of those societies which managed to do so both in the past and recently, with particular reference to England, Japan, Russia and China, and concludes that a prerequisite is a transformation of their political and social structure.

Herrera's work is valuable for the description of the current state of scientific and technological research in Latin America and for its rejection of the alternatives to the creation of highlevel scientific and technological capabilities, which are frequently suggested.

However, his explanation of the current state of scientific and technological research in the region, does not appear to be satisfactory. In fact, if the impetus for scientific and technological research in Latin America were dependent, as he asserts, on the actions of the state and of those running large concerns, this ought to have led to a quite different situation in scientific and technological research from the one he outlines. Either there ought to be no scientific and technological research whatsoever (the way in which the state and the Latin American entrepreneur are portrayed in the article is sufficiently severe for this), or there ought to be some activity in areas of particular interest to the state or the business entrepreneurs. Nevertheless, Herrera himself states that there is some scientific and technological research, but that its most important characteristic is its scant relationship with the basic problems of the region.

Could it not be that the impulse for scientific and technological research in Latin America stems neither from the state nor the business entrepreneurs but from some other source which accounts for its irrelevance? Is it not the case that 20th century Latin America is faced with conditions which are different from those which confronted the advanced societies in the past? Sábato and Botana's work (1968) contains basically two ideas. The first is that in contemporary societies the social process which they call innovation is produced when a triangular system of relationships is established between three elements: the government, the productive structure and the scientific-technological infrastructure. This system can be represented by a triangle in which each of these elements is a vertex, and is defined by 'the relationships arising within each vertex, which we shall call internal relationships; by the relationships arising between the vertices of the triangle, which we shall label inter-relationships and, lastly, by the relationships arising between the triangle as a whole, or between each of the vertices and the surrounding space, which we shall call external relationships'. (p. 6)

The triangular relationships described should guarantee that a society has the capability to direct its scientific and technological work to the achievement of basic objectives. (p. 66) Also, the internal relationships should be structured so that each of the three actors carries out specific sets of activities: entrepreneurial in the case of the productive structure, innovative in the case of the scientific-technological structure and of implementation in the government's case. According to the authors, it is important that societies have the capability to counteract external influences which may disrupt the creation of the triangular relationships defined. This is what happens when, for example, one of the three vertices in a Latin American country links up with a fully integrated scientific-technological system in another country such as the United States. In effect this makes it impossible to develop the triangle as defined by Sábato and Botana.

The second idea developed in the article is that there is no system of relationships such as the one described, in Latin America, nor even an awareness of the need to establish it. The authors propose creating the scientific-technological system in specific sectors, such as in petroleum and related activities.

Their article demonstrates that scientific innovation in the developed countries has not been the result of chance but of the development of a system of relationships between elements of its social structure, and suggests ways to deal with the situation in Latin America. The concept of the triangle, however, is particularly related to North American experience and is of no use in describing the situation in Latin America, or in explaining how this situation came about. Without this knowledge, their suggestion that similar triangular relationships be established—albeit in specific sectors— in unrealistic for the same factors that are responsible for the non-existence of the triangular structure as a whole, could come into play. The authors have allowed themselves to be influenced too much by what happened in the United States and tend to see the experience of Latin American countries simply as new instances of this past experience. From an abstract description of the system of relationships which made innovation possible in a country such as the United States, they propose a strategy for establishing this system in Latin America, the only justification being that it is not found in this part of the world.

Referring to external relationships they argue that 'partial development of the vertices of the triangle have taken place in our continent, which show a tendency, which is more marked every day, to link themselves independently with the scientific-technological relationship triangles of the developed countries'. (p. 71) But, if there is no such system of relationships in existence anywhere in Latin America, this means that there is no triangle, and thus there is little point in even talking about partial development of the triangle and its external relationships.

Jaguaribe (1971) attempts to give a succinct general analysis of the situation in the field of science and technology in the socio-political context of Latin America. The first major aspect with which he is concerned is the backwardness of scientific-technological activities in Latin American countries, as compared with other parts of the world. The author maintains that the scientific-technological lag in Latin America, far from being due to chance or adverse external factors, was the inevitable result of the kinds of deficiencies which characterize Latin American culture and society, as a result of their Iberian origins. These kinds of deficiencies imply, as far as culture is concerned—especially with reference to the past—rational but non-operational concepts of the world; and, as far as the social institutions are concerned, concepts which are not favourable to relatively autonomous and endogenous scientific production and which are certainly not favourable to, and even inhibit, the use of any but imported technology. It would have been possible, argues Jaguaribe, to overcome these obstacles at one time, perhaps during the Enlightenment, when the traditional orientation of Iberian culture could have been transformed. To overcome this situation at a later time, would have entailed a complete modification of the socio-economic structure in Latin American countries, in order to make possible the increased use of scientific and technological approaches. The crisis of the thirties gave rise to the necessary conditions. The process of industrialization by import substitution from 1950 onwards provided the wherewithal so that scientific and technological production increased in the various countries. During the 1960s, and in connection with the crisis of populism, ideological neo-liberal dogmatism combined with powerful internal and external economic and political pressures led to the opportunities gained in the previous decade being lost. Control of the modern Latin American industries increasingly passed into the hands of the multinational firms, which were nearly always North American. Scientific and technological production thus increasingly came under the control of U.S. interests.

Jaguaribe is also concerned with the possibilities of making up the gap that confronts the Latin American countries in the scientific-technological field, by a self-sustained, autonomous and endogenous scientific-technological development. The author concludes that only through a major national plan oriented towards autonomous national development can any one country experience significant success. Only countries such as Brazil, Argentina or Mexico would be able to initiate a programme, alone or together, without prejudice to the need for them to be integrated in a regional system. The author says that to carry out a national programme related to scientific-technological development requires consistent and firm intervention by the state in the scientific, technological and economic fields. He argues that in Latin American countries only the state has the necessary resources, power and organization to take on the extremely heavy obligations entailed by scientific and technological development. Jaguaribe emphasizes the importance of the cultural factor in the development of science and technology, and focuses attention on the specific experience of Latin America. Nevertheless, he does not quite succeed in grasping the importance of the events in the past decade, to which he alludes, and, as a consequence, his proposals are not viable.

Evaluating the work of Herrera and Sábato and Botana as a whole it appears that the authors were too preoccupied with the experience of national societies which have been able to benefit from science and technology: Herrera appears to be influenced by the experience of England, Japan, Russia and China; and Sábato and Botana by the experience of the United States. This is not the case with Jaguaribe who particularly concerns himself with past experience in Latin America. However, his understanding of the most recent phase is limited.

What all these authors fail to note is the basic fact that the Latin American economic, social and cultural context has changed radically from 1950 onwards, and that, accordingly, their present situation is very different from that of countries which managed to integrate modern technology in their productive processes in the past. It is this new general situation that has to be taken into account in order to describe and explain the situation in the scientific and technological field in Latin America and to formulate policies for its development.

THE SOCIAL CONTEXT OF TECHNOLOGICAL INNOVATION

A second group of writers have emphasized the particular conditions facing Latin America. Leite Lopes (1967) provides valuable information on the organization of scientific and technological development in the United States and the Soviet Union. What is most interesting in the article, however, is the discussion of the relations of government and science, and scientists and industry in the developing countries, and his discussion of the Brazilian experience.

Referring to industrial concerns in Brazil linked to foreign firms, he states: 'These concerns have research laboratories or finance research in their home country, obtaining new inventions and new products as a result. They are accordingly not interested in providing a stimulus to the laboratories and universities in the countries in which they operate. . .'. (p. 53) And, '. . . it is more likely that these large companies will not duplicate the number of research laboratories they have by opening new ones in the developing countries, which could possibly limit expansion of the existing ones in the home country. And since no employment is available in their own country, scientists from the developing countries will end up by emigrating to the developed countries'. (p. 57)

These observations are interesting in that an aspect is introduced into the analysis of Latin American scientific and technological research which is not found in Herrera's article nor in that of Sábato and Botana, the link between multinational concerns and innovation and development of scientific and technological research in the region. This very obvious fact of life in Latin America, the multinational concern, is a factor of prime importance in the configuration of the present situation facing the countries in the region and one which countries like Japan, Russia and China did not have to concern themselves with.

According to Fajnzylber (1972) the process of industrialization in Latin America has pursued a course which can be termed 'internally oriented but externally dependent': 'internally oriented' because it has developed under the aegis of a protectionist policy practised by governments in the sphere of trade; 'externally dependent' because importance is given to foreign markets and economic aid administered from abroad. With this perpsective it appears essential to relate the protectionist policy practised by governments in trade, to the attitude adopted with respect to the import of technology. The presence of multinational firms and the use of unadapted imported technology are the central themes with which the study referred to is concerned.

Sunkel (1971) puts forward a comprehensive interpretation of the phenomena of underdevelopment, dependence, marginalization and spatial disequilibrium. According to him, these phenomena are manifestations of a unique process of transnational integration and national disintegration, in the context of a restructured world capitalist system. In this new phase of capitalism the multinational firm is the dominant institution. What are the implications of this new situation?

First, although multinational firms systematically apply the results of scientific research to develop new products or new ways of manufacturing those products, this scientific and technological activity is carried out at the parent company in the industrialized country.

> In the plants, laboratories, design and sales promotion departments, and corporate planning and finance sections which form the headquarters in an industrialized country, the large multinational corporation develops: (a) new products, (b) new ways of producing these products, (c) the machinery and equipment required to produce them, (d) the synthetic raw materials and intermediate products involved in manufacturing them and (e) the necessary sales promotion to create and vitalize the market for them. On the other hand, the final stages of manufacture of these products are carried out in the developing countries, giving rise to a process of industrialization through the establishment of subsidiaries, the import of new machinery and manufacturing supplies and the use of brands, licences and associated patents, by both state and private domestic firms, whether in association with or independently of foreign subsidiaries. All of this is backed by foreign private and state credit and even by international technical assistance which thus makes an efficient contribution to the expansion of the international markets of the large North American, European and Japanese multinational conglomerates'. (p. 15)
> Technological 'transfer' also has somewhat special characteristics since, as it mainly takes place within the framework of the multinational conglomerate, one cannot expect either any great effort at adaptation to the local situation or any stimulus to domestic scientifc and technological development; new techniques are learnt, but not the way to adapt them or to produce them. (p. 52)

Thus, the subsidiaries of the multinational conglomerates and the entire organization of the conglomerates do not generate any scientific demand on the domestic scientific infrastructure of the Latin American countries. In addition to not generating any demand on the scientific infrastructure of the Latin American countries, the multinational conglomerates are slowly absorbing and/or taking the place of those entrepreneurs who could be interested in applying the results of research to their production processes.

Sunkel's work goes a long way towards providing an understanding of the changing capitalist system and the impact that this reorganization has had in Latin America in general, and on scientific and technological activity in particular. However, it is insufficient with respect to the latter, and particularly in explaining the rapid growth in scientific activity in the region.

In a previous article (Fuenzalida, 1971) an exploration of the causes underlying the development of science and technology in Chile was attempted. Some of the findings of that particular study provide the basis for generalizing on the Latin American experience as a whole. A number of aspects related to the development process are singled out for special importance because of their relevance.

> One of these aspects is the so-called 'Revolution of growing aspirations'. Whatever else underdevelopment might mean, it signifies that vast sectors of the domestic society aspire to a much higher standard of living than they currently have and one which is similar to that found in societies they have taken as models. Such aspirations have principally been generated by the development of transport and mass communications which have made other societies aware of the standard of living enjoyed by a limited number of societies elsewhere. Naturally, this had a particularly great effect on the urban population which was even more marked in large cities. Another of the aspects of underdevelopment on which studies usually agree is the so-called 'fusion effect' according to which the new aspirations generated in the urban sectors, strengthened by the increase in real and/or symbolic contacts with societies having a high consumption, become fused with the attitudes and ideals of life found among the upper classes in traditional society. In particular these attitudes and ideals include disdain for gainful activity, the overvaluation of intellectual work compared with manual work, the emphasis on the freedom of the individual, etc.

The explanation for the development of scientific research activities in Chile proceeds then from the basic idea that it is a consequence of these characteristics of the urban sectors. Attempting now to go into this idea in more detail and to describe how these characteristics of the urban sectors have affected the upsurge in scientific research, the following may be put forward as a hypothesis. The urban sectors did not simply aspire to the standard of living in more developed societies but, in addition, to achieve this in occupations with certain specific characteristics such as being white collar, not being physically dangerous, providing individual freedom, and other similar ones. These aspirations were nurtured by political parties, whose social base was constituted by the educated sectors of the urban population, and transformed into demands on the political system. The political system, faced with the difficult objective of transforming the economic structure of the country in order to absorb these sectors of the population into a more broadly-based occupational structure, chose the easiest way out by creating new bureaucratic posts. These posts had the occupational characteristics to which the urban sectors aspired and, to begin with, provided their incumbents with sufficient income to achieve the standard of living they required.

Soon, however, this solution became impractical: the number of applicants for work of the kind referred to grew steadily and the financial ability of the state to create more and more jobs in the Civil Service began to reach a limit. This sparked off a two-fold process: on the one hand, the educational attainments required for a career in the Civil Service were made more demanding; on the other hand, the remuneration for employment in the Civil Service became insufficient to achieve the standard of living desired. The continuation of this two-pronged process caused the urban sector to become interested in higher-level education and to press for access to universities.

The possession of a university degree, however, did not assure its holder of obtaining a position with the desired characteristics due to the insufficient growth of the employment structure and because the Civil Service could not absorb further employment. Accordingly, the urban sectors began to look for a solution to their problem by studying for new careers and professions which would be, as far as possible, relatively independent of the country's situation and which, at the same time, would match certain values shared by large sectors of the population, so that they could be financed by public funds.

Among other possibilities, scientific research as a career fits the bill particularly well as a solution to the problem of these sectors of the urban population. In fact, in a way that few others careers do, it combines the characteristics sought by these sectors: it is clean, there is no physical danger, it is independent, and is characterized by intellectual rather than physical effort. Moreover, the value society places on science enables those who take it up as a career to obtain the necessary resources and to earn sufficient income to achieve a relatively high standard of living. Thirdly, as a career, scientific research has one attribute which makes it especially attractive to the urban sector—namely, it provides a good measure of international mobility for those involved in it. If an individual does not obtain the level of income to which he aspires in his country, he still has the option of emigrating to another country. For all these reasons, the urban sectors are interested in taking up scientific research as a career.

This social origin of scientific research activities in Chile, and, generally, in other Latin American countries is what leads them to link up with the scientific-technological vertex of the Sabato-Botana triangle of the highly developed countries, giving rise to a transnational social structure in scientific research.

In conclusion, then, it can be said that the presence of subsidiaries of international firms in Latin American countries represents one of the factors determining the situation in which these countries find themselves in the field of science and technology. It is not the only one, and perhaps not even the most important.

A second factor determining the situation of Latin American countries trying to integrate themselves into the Scientific-Technological Revolution is the fact that research is undertaken not in response to demands from the production sector or the state, but responds to a transnational social structure.

AN ALTERNATIVE FORMULATION OF TECHNOLOGICAL INNOVATION

In order to present the problem of technological innovation in Latin America in schematic form it is necessary to recall Sábato and Botana's assertion that in today's highly developed societies, technological innovation is brought about by the establishment of a system of relationships between three elements: the government, the productive structure and the scientific-technological infrastructure. But, in another part of their work, Sábato and Botana assert that in Latin America, only partial developments have taken place in this system, and these show an increasingly strong tendency to link up with the scientific-technological systems of the highly developed societies.

Leite, for his part, when referring to the industrial concerns established in Brazil, which are related to companies abroad, asserts that they receive the new inventions and the new products from the research laboratories of these companies or from research work financed by the companies in their country's universities. Sunkel (1971), asserts that the increasingly rapid development of the multinational corporations has given rise to a transnational nucleus of the global capitalist system made up of relatively large segments of society in the advanced countries of the centre, and smaller segments of society in the less advanced countries of the periphery.

These points provide a basis for explaining the particular character and problems of scientific and technological development in Latin America. However, if one wishes to explain the inability of these countries to develop an integrated scientific-technological system, and the tendency for the scientific-technological infrastructure in Latin America to link up with the corresponding systems in the industrialized countries, additional elements must be added.

It is necessary to add that, according to Sunkel, not only has the development of the multinationals given rise to a supra-national productive structure, but is also 'bringing about a radical change in the structures and functioning of the capitalist system, not only in the leading industrialized countries but throughout the entire world, ultimately creating a new model of civilization embodied in the high-consumption society, the most extreme example of which is the United States'. (p, 49)

The spread of this new model of civilization by means of mass communications from the industrialized countries to those on the periphery has given rise to the 'revolution of rising aspirations' which, alongside immediate consequences such as the creation of a demand for the consumer goods produced by the multinational conglomerates, has generated a host of side effects including, as was previously mentioned, an interest in certain social groups in scientific research as a career. This social origin of scientific research activities in Latin American countries is what explains their link to the scientific-technological infrastructure of the highly developed countries, giving rise to a transnational social structure in scientific research.

To sum up, both the productive and the scientific-technological structures of the Latin American countries are an integral part of transnational capitalism, of its cultural superstructure, of the high-consumption transnational civilization, and not part of national society. In both cases they are integrated with the corresponding structures in the advanced industrial countries, which precludes their behaviour as an integrated system in the country in which they are located.

This article has dealt with the issues presented at a very general level. Obviously much of the detail has to be filled in by empirical research. Differences among the Latin American countries must be taken into account with respect to many aspects of their development, not least of which is their degree of integration into the world capitalism system and the impacts which this may have had. There are, however, still two aspects which should be dealt with on this general level. One is that the productive structure of the Latin American countries encompasses far more than just the subsidiaries of the multinational conglomerates. It is necessary to mention at least two other groups of productive concerns: private domestic ones and state enterprises. Do the above conclusions also apply to them? The answer is in the affirmative, as far as new products or new ways of producing existing products are concerned. The difference between them and the subsidiaries is merely that instead of being an internal operation of the multinational conglomerate, the transfer of technology is a transaction between the multinational and the private or public domestic concern.

Why don't these concerns make use of the domestic scientific-technological infrastructure? Part of the reason is that the entrepreneurs who run them are also part of that transnational nucleus of the capitalist system to which Sunkel referred and act according to its values and norms. Production may respond to the demands of the domestic market (in fact, highly influenced by exogenous factors) but the technology of production will most likely be that used in the highly developed countries. There is, therefore, no need for them to innovate.

In conclusion, then, the problem of technological innovation in Latin American countries confronts conditions very different from those which faced countries such as Japan, Russia and China in their initial development. Thus, the experience of these countries in the development of a scientific-technological capability cannot be readily transferred to Latin America, however successful they may have been.

REFERENCES

Fajnzylber, F., 1972, 'La empresa internacional en la industria-lización de América Latina', *Comercio Exterior*, Banco Nacional de Comercio Exterior, S. A., México, D. F., April, pp. 324–338.

Fuenzalida, E. F., 1971, 'Problemas de ciencia y tecnología en el paso al desarrollo', *Mensaje*, Nos. 202–203, September-October. and Ramos, J., and Plaza, O., 1974, *Ciencia, Tecnología y Desarrollo en los países del Pacto Andino. Una Bibliografía Comentada*, Ediciones CINDA, Santiago.

Herrera, A. (ed.), 1970, *Ciencia y Tecnología en el Desarrollo de la Sociedad*, Editorial Universitaria, Santiago.

1971, 'La ciencia en el desarrollo de América Latina' *Estudios Internacionales*, Year 2, No. 1, April–June, 1968. Reproduced in *Ciencia y Tecnología* en el Desarrollo de la Sociedad, edited by Amílcar Herrera, Santiago, Editorial Universitaria, 1970, pp. 11–36. See also *Ciencia y Política en América Latina*, México, Siglo XXI, 1971.

Jaguaribe, H., 1971, 'Ciencia y tecnología en el contexto socio-político de América Latina'. Instituto Universitario de Investigaciones de Rio de Janeiro. Series: *Mensaje*, Universidad Nacional de Tucumán.

Leite Lópes, J., 1967, 'La ciencia, el desarrollo económico y el Tercer Mundo', *Revue Tiers Monde*, Vol. VIII, No. 29. Reproduced in Herrera, 1970.

Sábato J. and Botana N., 1968, 'La ciencia y la tecnología en el desarrollo en América Latina', *Revista de la Integración*, No. 3, November. Reproduced in Herrera, 1970.

Sunkel, O., 1971, 'Capitalismo transnacional y desintegración nacional en América Latina', *Estudios Internacionales*, Año IV, No. 16, January–March.

6

MASS COMMUNICATIONS: SOCIAL MECHANISMS OF INCORPORATION AND DEPENDENCE

Rita Cruise O'Brien

INTRODUCTION

The capacity of the world capitalist system to influence the rate and pattern of industrialization in developing countries is greater now than at any time in the past. The rapidity with which countries are incorporated into the system in economic terms is complemented by the socio-cultural influence of the flow of information throughout the world. The mass media in particular, as a techno-industrial mechanism for transmitting information and entertainment to a potential mass audience are an important element in this global process. Documenting the content of such flows is important. But it is equally important to understand the influences on media production in the periphery—in particular the socio-cultural features of transferred metropolitan models of professional training and the organization of communications structures. These concerns are based on an underlying, perhaps prejudicial, assumption that the maintenance of cultural identity (or identities) in developing countries is a means of containing transnational influence, and of supporting economic and social policies more relevant to the needs of developing countries.[1]

There is no simple unilinear process of global flows from centre to periphery in the mass media: there are rather considerable regional differences which it is useful to distinguish at the outset. The influence of the U.S.A. in Latin America is one of relatively unimpeded market forces transferred in the case of the media through commercial audience-maximizing systems built around advertising. One effect this has had is to encourage, through advertising in particular, high consumption patterns and the creation of expectations which can only be met by further incorporation into the world economy. This makes it more and more difficult to establish economic policies which correspond to the capacity of these countries to foster locally conceived and based development strategies.

In Asia and Africa, by contrast, there is a more limited

129

incorporation into the modern consumer economy. The model of institutional transfer in broadcasting is that of the state corporation, though this does not necessarily exclude the influence of the market. Although it is possible that a rise in living standards may mean greater incorporation—or the generalization of the Latin American model—the current influence of the European model of professionalism on the state corporations already reproduces certain important characteristics of dependence. This article tries to illustrate that there are a host of mechanisms contained in the socio-cultural system which not only support but reinforce and make more penetrating the narrowly defined economic features of dependence.

TECHNOLOGY, STRUCTURES AND MEDIA FLOWS

Few questions have been asked about the effects of the transfer of technology on socialization, role relationships and organization, as economists have mainly concerned themselves with the effects of different types of technology on employment and labour utilization. Consideration of broadcasting from this perspective raises a new series of questions. On the one hand the technology is very sophisticated and does not easily lend itself to experimentation in the development of appropriate technology. But the radio or television programme, in contrast, is a *cultural* product and its influence goes beyond the simple consumption of goods and services.

The organization of broadcasting in developing countries is bureaucratic, often as a consequence of the model imported from developed countries, although there is no necessity for this in terms either of technology or product. Yet, Third World broadcasting is not simply part of an international enclave. As a local institution, it contains many secondary characteristics of dependence expressed through choice and use of technology, organizational transfer, working methods and professional socialization. Structures and occupations are only partly shaped by transnational influence.

The transnational influences carried through the mass media operate at two distinct levels: first, the direct influence on consumption patterns and life styles of foreign programmes and advertising; second, the influence on standards and norms of training, professionalism, models of organization and media production which cause various occupations to identify with their metropolitan counterparts, and ultimately draw the media away from the cultural base and resources of a poor country. It is this secondary influence with which current research is concerned. The transfer of technology in any production process will have an effect on organization, labour utilization and output. But, in media production, such changes also have a critical influence on patterns of cultural expression. In contrast to transfers of technology in textiles or food processing, those in the mass media reproduce and make more penetrating the other forms of external influence.

As Schiller wrote in one of the first texts which shifted interest in the mass media to a consideration of transnational influences:

> Cultural patterns once established are endlessly persistent. The opportunity to freshly mould a new nation's outlook and behaviour is historically unique and merits most careful deliberation. Yet in modern mass communications hard and inflexible laws—economic and technological—operate. If these are not taken into account in the beginning and at least partially overcome, courses of development automatically unfold that soon become unquestioned 'natural patterns'.[2]

Media technology and systems 'can act as the chief cultural arm of the industrial order from which they originate'.[3]

It becomes apparent in considering the process of social differentiation in developing countries that occupational differentiation did not emerge in relation to the growth of industry and technology. The process was rather transferred from outside, often transmitted through training and reaffirmed through occupational 'ideologies'. Far from being a neutral feature in the process of industrialization or the transplantation of production processes, technology transfer necessitates certain types of social organization, role differentiation and training. The technical aspects of broadcasting and their organization reflect this most obviously.

For an electrical engineer trained in a metropolitan university and with close professional contacts with his counterparts throughout the world (through professional meetings, journals and, above all, a positive attitude towards the most sophisticated technology which is most important to his 'transnational community'), the system he would most like to have installed in his country reflects *not* necessarily local needs but reference to outside standards and norms. Engineers in broadcasting are as impressed as other members of the scientific and technical elite in developing countries with the ingenuity and sophistication of very expensive 'gadgets'. In addition, a source of their claim to authority as an occupation or profession may be based precisely on the sophistication of the equipment with which they work, and on which they have become dependent because of certain objectives of training or socialization in the wider sense. Considerations of this kind engender the choice of complex system design and costly equipment while placing a heavy burden on the local service, which may have originally been intended to achieve low cost national coverage. Such a problem is indicative of the fact that the reorientation of cognitive categories achieved in the process of socialization may be at odds with the realities of local economic capacity. This is most dramatic on the technical side of broadcasting. The technology of broadcasting, almost without exception imported by developing countries, is designed for production systems which emerged in relation to metropolitan needs and markets.

While the advanced and expensive technology of broadcasting is largely fixed, there is at least a possible choice of lightweight and heavy equipment which may be made. Unfortunately, like experimentation in terms of community participation in the mass media, the versatility and capacity of this lightweight equipment, which is cheaper and easier to use, is best known in international organizations (UNESCO seminars and FAO experiments on rural participation) or the leisure industries of developed countries. Even where it does come to the attention of engineers from developing countries, it is often resisted as being below 'professional' standard. This especially limits the capacity for outside broadcasting, which is potentially so important in developing countries, to cumbersome purpose-built units, particularly the outside broadcasting unit for television.[4]

This professional/non-professional distinction, a linchpin of the engineers stock in trade, has recently been called into question by experimental uses of broadcasting in major industrial countries.[5] Yet, news often travels slowly to the periphery. And it does so in relation to transnational features of socialization combined with local social differentiation. One problem is the extent to which social relations of production or working methods and organizational structure can be made more flexible, even given the necessarily advanced nature of the technology required for production (whether lightweight or not).

Very important work has been done in recent years which documents the control of global news flows by a few predominant Western news agencies[6] or the volume of television entertainment programmes sold through a carefully constructed marketing structure.[7] Documenting and analysing the flows are important, but equally worthy of consideration is *an understanding of the components of media production in the periphery and the transfer of the knowledge and organization necessary to communications, structure.*

Heads of Government and Ministers of Information from

developing countries have in recent years begun to make critical pronouncements on the effects of cultural imperialism, of which media has become an acknowledged component. These pronouncements have served to call attention to some of the apparent characteristics of dependence—television programme imports, dependence on a few western agencies for the circulation of news and information. More subtle processes which are essentially structural and technological, however, are hardly questioned. Such processes are, of course, less apparent, but no less penetrating. Thus, while the percentage of locally produced programmes in proportion to imported television series is improving in many countries, thus satisfying at least the ephemeral characteristics of the battle against cultural imperialism, the quality and relevance of local production remains heavily constrained by the organization, technology and professional assumptions which go into its production.

PROFESSIONALISM IN THE MEDIA[8]

The aims of recent research were to consider in a preliminary manner the influence of professionalism and organizational structures, transferred from industrialized to developing countries, in the field of broadcasting. In particular, what constraints have imported characteristics created, potentially impeding the use of electronic media to support local national development and cultural policies. This research considered the effects of socialization, training and the perpetuation of standards and norms of metropolitan derivation in three principal occupations of radio and television—engineers, managers and producers—in two African countries, Algeria and Senegal. It also examined problems of recruitment and methods of work in the local environment and considered these in relation to metropolitan influences. The influence of the state on broadcasting in developing countries is crucial and more attention had to be given to this than was anticipated in the original research design.

Individual and, in some cases, group interviews were made which sought information on training, local output, methods of work and changes in organization since independence. It is hoped that this preliminary enquiry will lead to a more systematic elaboration of research questions which can be applied to other broadcasting systems in developing countries. The four principal occupational groups in broadcasting were identified as: (1) technicians and engineers whose working methods and occupational identification are most closely linked to the transfer of technology; (2) journalists whose reference to professional independence based on investigative reporting often clashes with local political imperatives; (3) managers who are most often simply co-opted from the civil services in state-run broadcasting organizations; (4) producers/directors whose technico-artistic basis of work often provides the most challenging element for an examination of professional and cultural transfer.

Because of the ambiguity inherent in the dual nature of the occupational speciality of production, the technical aspects often become more important than the artistic ones. Owing to the lack of formalized training (in contrast to journalists and engineers, for example), and a lack of consideration for the important managerial aspects often contained in this role, producers become nothing more than technical operators or presenters. The design aspect is usually absent, except in certain circumstances where directors have been recruited from the film industry. The lack of latitude awarded to this occupation reflects both low status and the desire of management to control production, in keeping with state ideology. It allows for the possibility and likelihood of imitative production. Therefore, although there is a considerable increase in local production, it is altogether possible that given a host of constraints this local production remains a form of *cultural import substitution*.

THE PROBLEM OF PROFESSIONALISM

In an interesting book on the professions and their organization, Johnson defines professionalism as 'a particular form of institutionalized control of certain occupational activities in which an occupational community defines client needs and the manner in which these are catered for.'[9] His work focuses on the client-professional relationship, stressing not only variations in professional autonomy but also variations in the social characteristics of the consumer. Broadcasting in developing countries, however, presents some difficult problems for the analysis of professionalism. Among other things, the power and resources available to the different broadcasting occupations and their capacity to exercise control over their work are circumscribed directly by the state.

In traditional terms the client of a broadcasting organization is the audience. But in a system which is non-commercial and largely unconcerned with audience definition or maximization, but rather with the diffusion of a centrally-defined ideology, the principal client appears in some respect to be the government. While broadcasters do not define the needs of government, they decide (in collaboration with various ministries and parastatal organizations) which elements of policy are to be diffused, and the techniques and form in which they are to be presented. The state in the two countries examined is not only the major source of policy directives, but often takes a principal role in the definition of national cultural orientation as well as ideology. While lip service is paid to the audience, the two major influences on broadcasting are transnational and state control.

The stress on occupational autonomy is the ideology or professionalism transferred via metropolitan influences. While usually mediated through a common language and common social institutions, professionalism contains 'elements forcibly and clearly expressed by those occupational groups making claims for professional status and engaged in an ideological struggle. Such occupations lay great stress on the need for occupational and individual independence as a pre-condition of fulfilling obligations to consumers'.[10]

In a recent article on journalists in Nigeria, Peter Golding has considered professionalism as the transfer of an ideology which supports the transfer of technology.[11] Journalists are perhaps the most 'craft conscious' of all occupations in broadcasting, although their relationship to the technology transfer process is less direct than it is for engineers, technical and production staff. The defence of the 'Fourth Estate' and the freedom of the press is a statement of professional control usually used to protect the journalist from state censorship.

In certain respects, the transnational features of professionalism , which are closely related to the transfer of technology, and provide its social structural component, might be seen as a counterveiling force to state control and its ideological requirements. In practice the contrasting forces of transnational ideology and state control only come into conflict at certain points in the organization. Control of the recruitment of senior managers from the civil service incorporates them into the state system. Technical and production staff have been discussed previosuly. Journalists have perhaps the most apparent source of conflict with the state in the elucidation of their professional codes: rejecting the possibility of carrying out investigative reporting in the Western tradition, the term 'development journalism'—or reporting within the limits of broadly defined government policy—is as yet only a controversial and tentative solution.

BROADCASTING IN ALGERIA AND SENEGAL

The two countries examined in case studies done in 1975 on the development of broadcasting have sharply contrasting socio-political systems, development strategies and measures of in-corporation into the world economy. They share at the very least, significant French influence maintained from the period before independence but which is manifested very differently in each system, and a Muslim population, the socio-cultural features of which are however differently apparent. They are a challenge to compare. Yet, one can trace in each similar tendencies in broadcast-ing, which may be inevitable and which permit one to generalize. Many optimistic studies and experiments on broadcasting[12] have pointed out the great potential it may have in countries, like those studied, which still have significant rates of illiteracy and a majority of the population living in rural areas. This apparent 'vocation' of broadcasting to serve as an instrument of mass education or information has hardly been exploited. In most African countries, radio is a mass instrument of entertainment and diffusion of state ideology. Many radio broadcasts use vernacular languages to reach the greatest number of people. Television, an expensive medium with considerable technological constraints, is confined mainly to urban groups of sufficient income to purchase a receiver, those who would most likely be already open to other influences on buying patterns and life style which would be merely reinforced by television viewing and additional exposure to advertising. The content of these media and their use reflects and reinforces not only economic patterns of differentiation but accentuates a differential exposure to entertainment or culture, information and education.

Both Algeria and Senegal exhibit vigorous state control of broadcasting, although Algeria uses the media to diffuse a more coherent ideology. Metropolitan influences based mainly on French models of organization and training remain important but interact differently with local social and ideological structures. The following schematic presentation of some of the principal differences between Algeria and Senegal may help to establish the context in which broadcasting in those two countries has developed.[13]

General policy

Algeria is a leading oil-rich country with an important Third World strategy in external relations and an internal strategy of heavy industrialization based on state ownership. Senegal has only barely emerged from colonial status economically and politically and remains heavily dependent on the franc zone, French aid and French private investment. It has only limited industrialization based on import substitution and relies heavily on two primary exports—groundnuts and, more recently, phosphates.

Cultural features

Algeria is making a sustained and self-conscious attempt to redefine its indigenous culture after more than one hundred years of French domination. It is based on arabisation and Islam. One of the principal ideological supports of the current Algerian system is its cultural policy which contains consistency in direction but a series of contradictions in application.

In Senegal, the educated urban elite remains heavily influenced by French culture while the rural cultural and social structures are relatively unaffected by that culture. The spread of the Wolof language with the marketing system for the cash cropping of groundnuts has produced something of a national culture in social and linguistic terms. Official cultural policies often find defintion in the works of President Senghor based on negritude and a version of African socialism, while they have relatively little local impact.

French influence

In Senegal, French influence is dominant in all features of modern life since modernization is defined as the improvement of performance within basically French institutions. In Algeria an important sector of the educated elite remains influenced by French intellectual and cultural life. Structural features based on French patterns of administration, fiscal policy and legality often exhibit a major constraint on the current socialist strategy. France is only one among many sources from which Algeria purchases the advanced technology and expertise on which its programme of industrialization is based.

Education

Algeria has had a remarkable growth of universal primary education since independence, designed to eradicate illiteracy and spread a knowledge of written Arabic. Considerable achievement has been made in the field of technical education serving the manpower needs of industry. Senegal has been marked by the French tradition of classical education and its institutions remained almost unreformed, including a disdain for technical and practical education. Attempts to reform the system or make it more relevant come from non-French donors and international agencies.

Broadcasting policy

In Algeria this policy is highly articulated in keeping with the definition of the ideological and cultural priorities. Broadcasting is

used as a main vehicle for disseminating official ideology and the
officially defined cultural strategy. It is also being used to teach
Arabic, and has contributed with the educational system a considerable effort towards the aim of eradicating illiteracy. In Senegal, there
is no definition of the priorities for broadcasting, and a distinct lack
of purpose in the organization. Without its recognition officially,
however, radio serves (and has served) as an important vehicle for
the spread of the Wolof language.

Coverage

Algeria has total national coverage in radio and television via
satellite since 1975. Senegal has moderate national radio coverage
through transmitters largely provided through French aid and
based in the regions. There is a single television transmitter which
covers the capital city and up to 60 kilometres beyond.

Decentralization of Broadcasting

Little autonomy is awarded to regional stations either in Algeria or
Senegal. In Senegal there is some more latitude since the officially
diffused ideology from the centre is less well defined than in Algeria
but, on the other hand, Algeria's regional stations have a much greater
technical capacity than the small regional radio stations in Senegal.

Participation in Broadcasting

While Algeria recently attained total national coverage via satellite,
no consideration was given to the differing cultural origins of the
people in the southern or Sahara regions of the country, in
particular, who will receive a diet of imported programmes from
France, the United States, and other Arab countries, as well as local
programmes which are designed mainly for a sophisticated urban
audience. Algeria has a state centralizing regime largely unconcerned with participation and discussion until 1976, when there was
an exceptional series of discussions on state ideology and policy,
some of which were diffused by radio and television. Attempts to
experiment with different types of media, with community viewing
or listening groups, or with an attempt to incorporate different
audiences into the programming structure, have been largely
ignored in Algeria. Discussions like those surrounding the National
Charter of 1976 are rather carefully orchestrated elements of
participation within the main lines of government policy.

An interesting but short-lived rural educational radio experiment in Senegal gave some potential indication of participation. The experience was best known for the voice it gave to the peasants in elaborating their grievances against state control and exploitation through the state marketing system. Started as a UNESCO experiment,[14] it coincided with a particularly acute phase of peasant hardship (the Sahel drought) and was kept going largely on the basis of the initiative of local broadcasters, but importantly with the approval of the President of the country who apparently used it for political ends against certain highly placed government officials. It was later altered in form and content by state intervention, but while it lasted served as one of the most interesting examples of the potential importance and power of radio in the rural as well as the national context.[15]

CONCLUSION: A NECESSARY RE-ASSESSMENT OF SCHOLARSHIP

In contrast with the complicated set of global influences on the development of the media in developing countries, studies of mass communication and development have until very recently ignored this international dimension. Scholarly research which was mainly American based was concerned to focus narrowly on the relationship between communications and other 'factors of modernization',[16] on the diffusion of innovation within a given system[17], or on individual participation in the modernization process and its psychic effects.[18] Such work concentrated on monitoring individual or group response to the new stimulus of the mass media, regarding the process itself as an unquestioned catalyst of social change and therefore development. Looking at the media institutions themselves in this idiom went no further than reaffirming occupational differentation familiar in other fields.[19] The tenacity of this line of research deliberately myopic to internationalization through the media is striking. It reflects cogently the implicit ideological bias in studies based on modernization and development which were pervasive in the Sixties. This literature was designed to illustrate how rapidly the socio-cultural or socio-political systems were exhibiting the qualities necessary to make less developed countries more like the industrial countries which preceded them (and perhaps most explicitly in the image of the United States). In the field of mass communications, such orthodoxies persisted alongside the most extraordinary growth of the power of transnational corporations marketing the technical capability, the growth of advertising and the volume of sale of U.S. entertainment programmes. And yet the studies continued to document and analyse development problems as if each country or process of social change existed in isolation from the obvious processes of external influence and incorporation, perhaps most obvious in the mass media. No less dramatic was the influence on sociologists, in particular, from developing countries who studied at the major centres of graduate study of mass communications in the United States.[20] Socialization into the scholarly tradition of modernization and media studies has left an indelible mark on the emergent institutes of mass communication research in developing countries in the past decade.

Those working on modernization as an aspect of communications growth or diffusion of innovation have recently made a rather disappointed reassessment of its progress, but continue to ignore the features of domination and dependence implied in media growth, or attempt to relegate them to a separate field of study.[21] At the very best, the somewhat more enlightened scholars have begun to concern themselves with the *distribution* of communications *within* developing societies noting, quite accurately, its tendency to inequality of access and its potential for reinforcing already existing social and economic inequalities.[22] But this reformulation as well is achieved without reference to the manifold importance of external influences on this process. It seems impossible to consider features of social differentiation in the periphery in isolation from such influences.

A shift of interest and a much more comprehensive approach to the role of the media which incorporates the global influences, comes from two principal sources. In the political arena the concern for 'cultural imperialism' and in particular the dominance of major news agencies placed information as an item on the agenda of the New International Economic Order in 1976.[23] Used to redress the balance of power in terms of information, one must remain somewhat sceptical of ideological pronouncements of government spokesmen of developing countries on this issue while more subtle and penetrating forces of dependence in the media and in other fields may be ignored.

The second source of reinterpretation of the impact of the media in developing countries comes from academic or para-academic research. The demand for a reinterpretation of media and develpment thinking[24] is complemented by a serious reconsideration of the role of largely American-influenced media development in Latin America. Certain analyses focus on the interlocking power of transnational corporations to the information and entertainment industries[25] and others link this to the source of American business culture and advertising.[26] A documentation of flows of news and television programmes responds not only to the needs of developing countries but also to small European countries like Finland which are also major importers. The importance of this work cannot be denied, especially as it has begun to situate media marketing and the imitation of media forms in a global context. It will be most encouraging if more studies are done on the *effects* of this process in peripheral countries, through the consideration of not only marketing forces and technological transfer but the more subtle and complicated features associated with organizational transfer and socialization, the transfer of knowledge and the organization of media production. Emerging from sectoral studies on the development and use of the media in various countries may be rich and fruitful material which will provide a more complete understanding of socio-cultural processes in the international context.

NOTES

1 The analysis contained in this article is part of a research programme on the mass media. An original statement of research questions can be found in R. Cruise O'Brien, *Domination and Dependence in Mass Communications: Implications for the Use of Broadcasting in Developing Countries*, IDS Discussion Paper No. 64, 1974 and IDS *Bulletin*, March 1975. The research problems include flows of information, institutional transfers, sources of aid, technology and private investment, and the activities of transnational firms in mass communications. To date, work has been done on *Professionalism in Broadcasting*, IDS Discussion Papers Nos. 100, 101 and U.K. firms which export equipment and programmes to developing countries (with Richard Stanton, forthcoming). Current work on *The Social Structural Implications of the Transfer of Technology in Mass Communications* (with Drummon Hislop) will be partially completed for UNESCO in 1977. At every stage of the formulation of this research programme, I have benefitted from suggestions and criticisms from the group of colleagues who have contributed to this volume.
2 H. Schiller, *Mass Communications and American Empire*, New York: Kelley, 1970.
3 George Gerbner, 'Institutional Pressures Upon Mass Communications,' in P. Halmost, ed., *The Sociology of Mass Media Communications*, Sociological Review Monographs No. 13 (Keele), 1969.
4 A striking example is drawn from empirical research. Senegal's recently established television station has an outside broadcasting unit supplied by Thomson-C.S.F. through a French aid award. It was practically never used because it required eleven people to staff the unit, and the entire technical staff of the newly founded television service was only twenty-two! When I enquired as to why that number of people were required, it became obvious after much

probing that it was O.R.T.F. Union requirements which demanded a certain number of assistant video and sound staff per unit. This was justified as 'good professionalism'! The few local programmes which are made are done in inadequate studios, while the sun shines outside the buildings of the television station, and the O.B. van, which provides a latent function as a symbol of technological modernity, remains parked in front.

5 Much of the most advanced technology used for broadcasting in developed countries has begun to imply a *deprofessionalisation* among staff, interestingly considered in M. Gurevitch and P. Elliot, 'Communication Technologies and the Future of Broadcasting Professions', in G. Gerbner *et al.* (eds.) *Communication Technology & Social Policy*, New York, Wiley, 1973.

6 See Juan Somavía in *Development Dialogue* (The Dag Hamarskjold Foundation), 1976, or P. Harris, 'International News Media and Underdevelopment', M.Phil. Thesis, University of Leicester, 1975.

7 K. Nordenstreng and T. Varis, *Television Traffic: A One-Way Street?* UNESCO Reports and Papers on Mass Communications, 1970.

8 The introduction to the research problem described here is an adaptation of IDS Discussion Papers No. 100, *Professionalism in Broadcasting: Issues of International Dependence*, and No. 101, *Professionalism in Broadcasting: Case Studies of Algeria and Senegal.* Fieldwork was carried out during January–June, 1975 on a grant from the Social Science Research Council.

9 In contrast to the traditional literature on the sociology of the professions his emphasis is on the exclusiveness and social control exhibited by professions. See T. J. Johnson, *Professions and Power*, London, Macmillan 1972. Subsequent work by Johnson seeks to link his approach to professionalism with the Marxist analysis of modes of production: 'The Professions in the Class Structure', unpublished paper, University of Leicester, March 1975.

10 *Ibid*, 1972, p. 57.

11 P. Golding 'Media Professionalism in the Third World: The Transfer of an Ideology' in James Curran *et al.*, (eds.) *Mass Communication and Society*, London, The Open University 1977.

12 See conclusion for more precise reference.

13 Detailed data on the development of professionalism in broadcasting in each of these countries can be obtained from R. Cruise O'Brien, IDS Discussion Paper, No. 101, *Professionalism in Broadcasting: Case Studies of Algeria and Senegal*, 1976.

14 UNESCO Reports and Papers on Mass Communications, No. 69, *Mass Media in an African Context: An Evaluation of Senegal's Pilot Project*, 1973.

15 The Rural Educational Radio programme in Senegal was listened to as 'a voice of opposition' by urban residents as well and had an important national following. See R. Cruise O'Brien, 'An Experiment of Rural Radio in Senegal', *CERES*, 1977.

16 D. Lerner and W. Schramm *Communication and Change in Developing Societies*, Honolulu, University of Hawaii Press, 1962.

17 E. M. Rogers and L. Svenning, *Modernisation Among Peasants: the Impact of Communication*, New York, Holt, Rinehart and Winston, 1969.

18 D. Lerner, *The Passing of Traditional Society*, N.Y., The Free Press, 1969.

19 L. Pye ed., *Communication and Political Development*, Princeton, Princeton University Press, 1962.

20 For example, the Institute of Communication Research, Stanford University and the East-West Centre at the University of Hawaii.

21 W. Schramm and D. Lerner, *Communication and Change: The Last Ten Years and the Next*, Honolulu, the University of Hawaii Press, 1976.
22 Notably the work of E. Rogers and others at Stanford.
23 For a summary of political discussions on this theme, see Juan Somavia, 'Third World Participation in International Communications', unpublished conference paper, Instituto Latinoamericano de Estudios Transnacionales, 1977.
24 See P. Golding and P. Elliot, 'Mass Communications and Social Change: the Imagery of Development and the Development of Imagery', in E. J. de Kadt and G. Williams, *Sociology and Development*, London, Tavistock, 1974 and P. Golding, 'Media Role in National Development', *Journal of Communication*, Vol. 27, No. 3, 1974.
25 A. Mattelart, *Multinationales et Systems de Communication*, Paris, Eds. Anthropos, 1976, and T. Varis, *The Transnational Corporation and Communications*, Tampere Peach Research Institute Reports, No. 10, 1976.
26 H. Schiller, *Mass Communication and the American Empire*, New York, Kelly, 1970 and *Cultural Domination and Communications*, New York, 1976.

7

MILITARISM AND INTERNATIONAL DEPENDENCE: A FRAMEWORK FOR ANALYSIS

Robin Luckham

THE FRAMEWORK

Some of the salient features of militarism in peripheral countries are brilliantly described in Leon Trotsky's analysis of the pre-revolutionary Russian army:

> 'In as much as every army is considered unconquerable in the national mythology, the ruling classes of Russia saw no reason for making an exception of the army of the Czar. In reality, however, this army was a serious force only against semibarbaric peoples, small neighbours and disintegrating states; in the matter of defence it could fulfil its task only by the help of the vastness of spaces, the sparsity of population and the impassibility of the roads. The virtuoso of this army of serfs had been Suvarov. The French revolution in breaking open the doors to the new society and the new military art, had pronounced a death-sentence on the Suvarov type of army. The semi-annulment of serfdom and the introduction of universal military service had modernized the army only insofar as it had modernized the country—that is, it introduced into the army all the contradictions proper to a nation which still has its bourgeois revolution to accomplish. It is true that the Czar's army was constructed and armed upon Western models; but this was more form than essence. There was no correspondence between the cultural level of the peasant-soldier and modern military technique. In the commanding staff, the ignorance, light-mindedness, and thievery of the ruling classes found their expression. . . . In the matter of military supplies and finances, Russia at war suddenly finds herself in slavish dependence upon her allies. This is merely a military expression of her general dependence upon advanced capitalist countries. But help from the allies does not save the situation. The lack of munitions, the small number of factories for their production, the sparseness of railroad lines for their transportation, soon translated the backwardness of Russia into the familiar language of defeat—which served to remind the Russian national liberals that their ancestors had not accomplished the bourgeois revolution and that their descendants therefore, owed a debt to history'. (Trotsky, 1900, Vol. 1, pp. 33–34)

This passage summarizes many of the important features of military dependence: purchases of weapons supporting accumulation in the central capitalist countries rather than in Russia; superimposition of contradictions proper to a capitalist society on those of a pre-capitalist one; the borrowing of Western models of military organization which had little relationship to the Russian class structure; the accumulation within the army of all the contradictions of the nation; the weakness of the Russian state despite its highly centralized and authoritarian form; and the unreliability of its military forces for the purpose of either external defence and or domestic repression.

Nevertheless Trotsky paints on a very broad canvas. There are a number of features of his analysis which are peculiar to Russia in the particular stage of imperialist expansion prior to World War I that he was talking about. A more detailed analysis would have to take into account the considerable variation in the impact and timing of the economic and military expansion of the advanced capitalist countries in the different regions of the world. One major difference is between the countries in which the creation of modern military organizations was part and parcel of the wholesale imposition of colonial state superstructures; and those (like Turkey, Ethiopia and Thailand) in which armies were professionalized with the aid of the military instructors and mass produced weapons which, from the mid-nineteenth century, flowed in increasing quantities from Western Europe towards the remainder of the world. Yet such historical differences are increasingly blurred by international transactions—investment, trade, arms and military training etc.—which cut across the historical links forged in the heyday of imperialism. These of course reflect a fundamental shift in the accumulation of wealth and military power from Western Europe to new world centres, the U.S.A. and the U.S.S.R.

Yet such linkages between militarism and international dependence are hardly dealt with at all in the existing literature on the military in developing countries. This largely concentrates on epiphenomena such as coups, military regimes, the ideology of soldiers, spending on arms and its relation to GNP growth rates; and thus tends to leave aside more fundamental questions about the role of military force in the state and international relations, in the accumulation of flow of economic surpluses and in the determination of patterns of development and underdevelopment.

A more adequate treatment of the subject would require analysis at least three distinct but interrelated levels: (i) *The military relations of force*, that is the particular characteristics and internal contradictions of armies as organizations which control and reproduce the means of violence. (ii) *The national relations of force*, that is the role of military institutions as a basis of state power; the part played by violence in class formation and class conflict; and the way particular forms of force integrate (or destroy) modes of economic production and development or underdevelopment. (iii) *The international relations of force* which result from the historical legacy of imperialism. These link military institutions closely to the international system because military violence or threats thereof have been crucial in maintaining or changing the distribution of international wealth and power; and in supporting the state institutions which are the building blocks of the existing international order. One may in turn subdivide the international relations of force into at least two distinct levels, namely (a) the pressures associated with armament and conflict at a *regional* level, such as regional arms races or the sub-imperialism of the more powerful countries in each region, and (b) those which arise at the global scale, such as the effect on the Third World of cold war politics, of technological progress in the industrial countries or of the international arms economy.

Such an analysis would, secondly, involve a consideration of the military, the national and the international relations of force, in terms of four further groups of factors, by which they are interlinked, namely: (i) *The technology of force*, the dominant feature of which is the dependence (established through international arms transfers) of the developing countries on the technology of force of the advanced industrial powers. The latters' technological progress and military R and D tends thereby to have far-reaching consequences for the military organization, economy, social structure and conflict patterns of the former. (ii) *The capital relations of force*, the accumulation of armaments in developing countries being directly linked—through international arms purchases—to the accumulation of capital in industrial countries, with profound effects on arms races, resource distribution and underdevelopment. (iii) *The class structures of force,* the professional training of soldiers and transfer of models of military organization representing, in certain respects, a transnationalization of the class structure of industrial countries to the Third World, with important consequences for the way force is used and by whom in situations of class and of international conflict. (iv) *The political relations of force*, global conflict between the major powers encouraging them either to intervene directly in the Third World in pursuit of their competing interests or to stabilize national ruling classes through military and other connections. The fact that these ruling classes are so often able to sustain their state structures, expand their military establishments or pursue ideologies of national military power by relying on great power support, has profound implications for the way power is distributed nationally and for the armed conflict and international relations they engage in.

Analysis cannot be confined to any one of these dimensions of analysis, but rather must provide some understanding of the way they interpenetrate. Accordingly in Table 1, a model is put forward as an *aide memoire*, to indicate the range of inter-relationships to be considered, rather than as a rigorous theoretical statement. Insofar as the dynamism of the whole process is created by technological progress and the accumulation of capital in the advanced capitalist countries, the causal direction of the relationships set forth in the Table is from right to left (from core to periphery of the international system) and from top to bottom (from accumulation and technological progress to class formation and political relations).

In reality, however, the situation is far more complex, for one cannot assume that the Third World is merely the passive recipient of the trade, capital, arms, military missions and political directives of the major capitalist powers. In reality there is a chain of reciprocal causation, not least because uneven development creates classes, nations and states at the periphery which have sometimes resisted incorporation by world capitalism or opposed great power dominance. Because the military is at the interstice of nation states and the international system, it expresses such contradictions particularly clearly: being *both* the instrument of national aspirations and of international penetration.

Militarism is indeed only one part of a broad process of historical change creating an interdependent (but highly unstable) world order, which should not be seen in terms of static or undimensional categories, but rather as a series of dialectically-evolving transformations (the expansion of capitalism on a world scale, imperialism and colonial conquest, nationalism, alterations in the nature of capitalism itself which have been brought about by technological change and the increasing scale of operations, the partial reintegration of socialist countries into international circuits of capital and state relations, and emergence of inter-imperialist and inter-socialist rivalries) which have generated uneven development, class struggle and international military conflict.

WEAPONS, ARMIES AND THE
MILITARY RELATIONS OF FORCE

There is no more eloquent testimony to the internationalization of the military relations of force than the uniformity of certain

Table 1

Militarism and dependence: a framework

	Military Relations of Force	National Relations of Force	International Relations of Force (a) Regional	International Relations of Force (b) Global
Technology of Force	Effects on military hierarchies of change in technology of force	Effects of importing technology of force on the economy, social structure and conflict of the recipient countries	Distribution of technology of force (and of capacity to export/re-export it) among the countries of the region	Dependence on the technology of force and technological progress of the advanced industrial powers
Capital Relations of Force	Transformation of economic surpluses into armaments	Relationship between armaments and the pattern of accumulation (or under-development)	Linkage between international flow of resources and regional arms races	Linkage to world economy and to accumulation in arms producing countries through international arms purchases
Class Structures of Force	Positions in military hierarchy as basis for structuring class and corporate commitments of soldiers	Role of military in class formation and conflict and in the conflict arising from uneven development between regions ethnic groups etc.	Effects on intra-regional stratification and conflict of variations in military professionalism and effectiveness	Transnationalization of class structure via professionalization of Third World military establishments
Political Relations of Force	Maintenance (or strengthening) of military hierarchy and its capacity to coerce	Use of military force to uphold or replace dominant classes and groups, as an instrument of domestic repression	Effects of variation in military power (and external military support) on regional conflict	Exposure to great power intervention and attempts to influence composition and stability of Third World ruling groups and classes

characteristics of professional armies—the similarity in the weapons and techniques of coercion employed, the hierarchy of ranks, the exclusiveness of the military brotherhood, the emphasis on rituals of rank, the class distinctions between officers and ordinary soldiers—be they the armies of advanced capitalist, Third World or (in many cases) socialist countries.

One explanation of this uniformity is the concentration of technical progress in the advanced industrial countries, from which both weapons systems and models of military organization have been diffused to the Third World. This technical progress has accelerated significantly since World War II, military Research and Development having increased to around 10 to 15 per cent of total world military spending, compared with only one per cent before the War. For the developing countries the critical fact is that virtually all of this R and D takes place in the advanced industrial countries, 85 per cent in the U.S.A. and the U.S.S.R. alone and a further 10 per cent in the four other most important arms producers, Britain, France, West Germany and China. It is true to be sure that increasingly the more industrialized Third World countries manufacture arms, one or two like Brazil or India even having a certain amount of design capability of their own. Yet the greater part of this manufacture takes places under licence, makes use of components available only from the major arms suppliers, and is closely tied in with their other economic and military links.

The implications of this technological dependence for the way Third World military organizations are structured and the role they play in their national societies are far-reaching. For over the past one or two hundred years the peripheral countries have imported with their weapons a military division of labour shaped by the technology and class structures of the advanced industrial countries from which the weapons were obtained.

The countries of the Third World are not necessarily obliged to adopt the division of labour established in the professional armies of the central countries in order to make use of their imported weapons. But as a historical pattern the links between military professionalism and the absorption of external technology is extremely powerful. Professional soldiers identify themselves with the organizations they control and accordingly choose weapons which the latter can assimilate. Once set in motion, this process of professionalization on the one hand and absorption of external technology on the other tends to be self generating.

There are, moreover, structural similiarities between armies and the large scale economic enterprises of advanced industrial countries. Military organizations are established around a large physical plant of capital equipment, employ a numerous paid labour force of men in uniform and coordinate their activities in a hierarchical structure controlled by military managers of violence (Lasswell, 1941), the members of the officer corps. Yet there are certain critical differences. In the first place it is hard to say just what the 'output' is: fighting wars; preparing for wars they never fight; acting as the armoured fist of the ruling class; guaranteeing national security, or violence and insecurity; intervening when the police and civilian authorities are unable to deal with internal disturbances; making and breaking regimes by military coups; or symbolizing national sovereignty and independence? And whatever this output is, it does not enter the circuits of economic exchange, to which the military is connected only through the inputs it purchases.

The fixed capital of an army thus does not directly contribute to accumulation, despite the backward linkages of military spending to accumulation in the national economy or (in most peripheral countries) to the economies of the main producers and suppliers of arms. Since the surpluses which pay for weapons are not generated by exploiting the labour power of soldiers, they are extracted from production elsewhere. Furthermore, although soldiers are employees whose services are paid for, they cannot enter and leave military employment as they please. In spite of the fact that officers manage large scale organizations, they are as much concerned with command and power relations as with efficiency in the cost-benefit sense. And whereas the major capitalist enterprises are increasingly independent of territorial limitations, armies are nationally based by virtue of their function as they protectors of the territories of nation states.

The social relations of force in sum differ significantly from the social relations of production. Yet the analogy drawn between them calls attention to the close links between the structures of military power and the structures of economic production in any modern society. And it helps to explain how arms races are sustained, because military effectiveness is so often measured in terms of investment in increasingly sophisticated military hardware, on the analogy with the capital equipment of any production organization. Such pressure is indeed even greater than in production organizations because of the difficulty of applying criteria of economic cost-effectiveness to military spending in a conflict-ridden nation or a volatile international situation. And it is made almost overwhelming because of the way technical progress tends to make weapons systems obsolete almost as soon as they are introduced.

Because the military generates no surpluses of its own, it depends on those who control the means of production to provide them. At the same time its power to coerce and ability (in most countries of the Third World) to overthrow regimes, mean it is particularly well placed to divert surpluses on its behalf. Not only does this have significant implications for resource allocation in the national economy, discussed further below. But it also shapes the class commitments of soldiers in at least two ways: firstly through the corporate interests surrounding the military establishment as a whole; and secondly through the distinctive cleavages that tend to emerge within military hierarchies.

Members of military hierarchies tend to have a shared interest in ensuring that these hierarchies acquire the material and political resources that are considered to be needed for their reproduction or continued expansion. Corporate grievances are a standard item in the litany of excuses that soldiers recite for staging coups: be it the complaint as in Ghana's 1966 coup the holes in soldiers' boots and the lack of spare parts for their vehicles; or be it the Peruvian government's acquiescence in the U.S. embargo on the purchases of advanced weapons which helped to precipitate the coup of 1968. Transfers of military technology and the military assistance programmes of the large powers consolidate the professional and corporate commitments of increasing numbers of Third World establishments. The effects are most visible in the larger Latin American and Asian countries, like Brazil, Chile, Peru, Argentina or Indonesia; and have often been associated with the assertion of control over the state apparatus by the military institution itself, rather than by any of the individual groups of officers of which it is composed. In Indonesia, for example, a military establishment which was previously fragmented into regionally based fiefdoms which even engaged in production and foreign trade on their own account, has been transformed (with considerable foreign assistance) into a relatively cohesive force maintaining a firm grip over the machinery of state.

Nevertheless the corporate facade of national military establishments is often shattered by their tendency to fissure along the gradations of the military hierarchy. Coups are frequently associated with particular officer peer groups of similar rank, such as the Free Officers who brought the military into power in Egypt; the Eighth Graduating Class prominent in the Korean coup of 1961; the Majors and Captains and Lieutenants who staged coup and countercup in Nigeria in 1966; the Lieutenants who belonged to the *Tenentismo* movement in Brazil in the 1920s and 1930s; and the

Captains and Majors who organized the Portuguese and Ethiopian military revolutions of 1974. Such fissures tend to occur precisely because military organizations are at the same time hierarchies in which rank and career create shared interest and experience between officers of similar rank; and power structures in which the tension between upper and lower levels of command is difficult to contain.

Most armies reproduce the two class division of capitalist societies in the cleavage between officers and the men over whom they exercise command. Again there are numerous examples of military revolts from the ranks, often with the standard motives of any strike, namely better pay and conditions of service for the military labour force. Such revolts frequently have had momentous political consequences: the sergeants' revolt and naval mutiny which precipitated the assumption of power by the officer corps in Brazil in 1964; the East African mutinies of 1964 which almost (but for British intervention) destroyed the newly independent regimes in Kenya, Tanzania and Uganda and contributed directly to the rise to power in the latter of Amin; the coup of July 1966 in Nigeria which was as much a revolt of NCOs against the military command as it was a coup of Northerners against Ibo control of army and State; the revolt by ordinary soldiers in Sierra Leone who in 1968 locked up their entire officer corps and handed power back to civilians; and the Portuguese and Ethiopian military revolutions of 1974, the organizers of which acted under strong pressure from their own rank and file (in Ethiopia ordinary soldiers even put their officers under guard until they agreed to act on their behalf).

Military structures, in sum, generate cleavages that resemble class conflict in that they are generated in a systematic way through the military relations of force;[2] by the way men are fitted together in large-scale organizations around a weapons system designed to produce a certain 'output' of violence.

Such cleavages make it impossible to assume that the military is a monolithic institution or that its role is always conservative. Groups of middle-level and junior officers have sometimes developed radical political programmes: (the *Tenentismo* movement in Brazil, the Free Officers in Egypt in the 1950s, the Armed Forces Movement in Portugal and the Derg in Ethiopia in the 1970s).

Revolts from the ranks can be still more revolutionary in their potential than peer groups interventions. The turning point in the Russian Revolution of 1917 was when the ordinary soldiers refused to turn their guns on the striking workers and joined them. The movements initiated by the Derg in Ethiopia and the Armed Forces Movement in Portugal would probably have been less sweeping without the active pressure and participation of the military rank and file.

Although the military relations of force themselves thus generate impetus both for military radicalism and for military reaction they are nevertheless by no means a sufficient condition of either. The Russian Revolution was a revolution because soldiers joined the workers and peasants they were brought out to suppress and not the other way round. In some circumstances army revolt may amount to little more than narrow trades unionism: being easily suppressed because of the absence of wide social support or, like the East African Mutinies of 1964, as a result of external intervention; bought off by better pay conditions of service; or (if successful) turning the army into a machine for the extortion of tribute by the new lumpen-militariat as in Amin's Uganda or Batista's Cuba. For soldiers and officers who rebel against the hierarchy always have the option of expropriating the latter for their own benefit as a kind of military labour aristocracy; rather than seeking to transform society. They are unlikely to choose (or indeed think of) the latter unless external class forces also impel them to do so.

The centrality of military organizations in struggles for power reflects, to conclude, three of their most central characteristics. First that they are bureaucracies, giving rise to bureaucratic interests and cleavages, much as any other complex organization. Second, that they are arenas of power with internal dynamics of command and control that may sometimes conflict with their formal bureaucratic structure.[3] And third, that they are intimately connected with the exercise of state power, such that it is seldom possible to keep struggles for control in the military separate from struggles for control over the state machinery.

The contradictions which are thus inherent in military structures are perhaps more acute in peripheral countries where reliance on foreign models of military organization and behaviour has often resulted in excessive bureaucratization, so that actual power-relations by-pass the formal hierarchy, undermining the latter rather than supporting it. Hence the disconcerting mixture of ritual, spit and polish on the one hand and chronic internal intrigue and conflict on the other which is so often present in Third World armies, particularly in post-colonial situations (Luckham 1971a, Decalo 1976). Such tendencies are increased by the use of the army as an instrument of domestic repression on behalf of those who control the state machinery. This aligns it more closely with the other major state bureaucracies—particularly the police, the intelligence services and the high level civil service. But at the same time, however, it increasingly shifts the arena of conflict inside the armed forces themselves, accentuating their internal power struggles and weakening their hierarchies. Coups, murderous struggles between groups of military colleagues and the wide-scale use of military force as an instrument of repression are not simply the pathology of political decay in the periphery; but arise at least in part from contradictions inherent in the social relations of force in professional military formations, made more acute by endemic conditions of crisis in the peripheral countries. Let us now turn to a broader analysis of the role of military force in shaping development or underdevelopment, class formation and state power.

MILITARISM AND NATIONAL DEVELOPMENT

It has sometimes been contended that it is precisely its training in the use of advanced technology which gives the military a special role to play in the 'modernization' of the less developed countries. (Pye 1962: 78). But training in the use of sophisticated weapons does not mean that army officers are more skilled or progressive in their attitudes than any other elite groups. The military has a special place in Third World societies not because its technology is 'modern', but because it is particular kind of technology, that of force. And force is never used in the abstract, but in the struggle between different classes and groups. The functions of military force are different where it is used by an imperial power to secure its interests in the periphery directly (as by Britain or France in nineteenth century Africa, the USA in Vietnam) or indirectly (as through US supplies of counter-insurgency technology to Latin American governments); in situations of revolutionary change (as in Cuba, Mozambique or China); of broad social reform imposed by the military and other elite groups from above (as in Peru from 1968 to 1975 or Nasser's Egypt); yet again where it is used mainly to reproduce the existing regime and class structure (as in Iran); to change the regime in the interests of local or international economically dominant classes (as in Chile); or merely to secure (as in Uganda) the dominance of a parasitic military clique.

What is certainly true is that armies are in a unique position to extract the resources they want by blackmailing, coercing or taking over governments. And, spending on arms has a number of significant implications for the patterns of national development—or underdevelopment—which prevail in the Third World. Armies do not on the whole create the surplus value which sustains their own expansion. The resources have to be provided from taxation or by subsidies from international patrons and suppliers of arms. In the first place this puts the military in a special position relative to the remainder of the state machinery through which the necessary resources have to be raised internally or negotiated externally. Second, it implies a degree of integration with the international economy from which internationally negotiable purchasing power has to be obtained in order to acquire military hardware.

Yet the implications of this interrelation between military spending, state appropriation of surpluses and the international economy are little touched on in existing discussions, which for the most part attempt to measure the overall effect of military spending and of military regimes[4] on aggregate measures of economic performance. From one of the most comprehensive crossnational studies of the effects of arms spending (Benoit, 1973), we learn that levels of military spending in developing countries are (contrary to expectation) *positively* associated with non-military growth rates (i.e. rates of GNP growth, taking out the military expenditure component of GNP). But the causal direction of this correlation is not established. It could occur merely because countries with high GNP growth rates have more to spend on arms. Or the relationship could be spurious in the sense that military spending and high measured growth in non-military GNP may both be the product of other influences, such as the tendency of the major powers to pump economic development assistance as well as military aid into countries in which they have strategic interests.

Such discussions presuppose, furthermore, that we are mainly interested in growth rates rather than development defined in terms of broader criteria including how GNP is distributed. An explanation sometimes offered for the association between arms spending and growth—or rather for why there is not a *negative* association between them—is that the resources for armaments are typically diverted from social welfare spending rather than from productive investment. Statistical comparisons of developing countries (e.g. Schmitter, 1971) on the whole support this explanation. But it is a serious matter to divert resources from schools, hospitals and welfare services to guns, tanks and jet aircraft, and most probably can only be done by governments which are prepared in the final analysis to repress the discontent it brings about.

Even if one were to accept at face value the evidence that arms spending promotes growth it is difficult to find a sensible explanation for it. Military spending, to be sure, has some spin-offs, but it is hard to see how these could offset more than a small proportion of the cost of maintaining a large military establishment, except in those few countries like Brazil, Argentina or India which have arms industries of their own, backed by a relatively diversified industrial base. Even in the latter, many of the multiplier effects of military equipment purchases are felt by the arms industries of international suppliers rather than in the domestic economy, with consequent pressure on the balance of payments.

Nevertheless there is a certain logic to military spending because it plays a role in reproducing certain structural patterns commonly found in peripheral economies. Armaments may facilitate growth *within* the constraints established by such patterns, though at the same time tying up resources that could be put to much better use under alternative structural arrangements. What are the patterns that military spending supports and how does it do so? The main ingredients are as follows, though it should be emphasized that different developing countries share in them to a different extent, and what is described is very much a paradigm case:

(1)   Role of military spending in concentrating the capital and resources required for fast GNP growth in peripheral capitalist economies. Put simply, growth under these conditions requires forced saving, increased social inequality and the diversion of government spending from welfare to production and/or subsidies for capital. There are strong inflationary pressures and recurrent crises in the balance of payments. These pressures can only be dealt with, or so it is suggested, by governments which are prepared to hold down wages and rural incomes and to use military force to put down trades unions, strikes and peasant protest. This results in higher military expenditure which in turn requires further forced saving and increased inflationary pressure and public unrest.

(2)   Role of the military in strengthening the state structure and its control over the process of economic growth. The military establishment itself has a direct interest in a powerful and centralized state, since it can extract through it the resources for its own expansion. Even in countries such as Brazil where the military elite has explicitly embraced a capitalist strategy for development, the predilection of soldiers for state management of that development—for planning, for establishing enterprises under state or mixed ownership, for licensing and controlling economic activity—has made itself felt.

(3)   A built-in alliance between the military and the representatives of international capital. This arises because dependent capitalist development has created a disjuncture between the national ruling elites and the economically dominant classes with their commanding heights in the boardrooms of international firms. This has retarded

the formation of national bourgeoisies functioning as effective ruling classes able, through their policies, to exert control over the national economy. But, at the same time, it has created a problem for the representatives of international capital who have to find ways of influencing policy in developing countries, despite their inability to act directly as a fraction of the national ruling class. On the face of it the military seems to meet the political requirements of foreign capital under these circumstances almost better than any other institution. A powerful, relatively autonomous state apparatus—buttressed by military coercion—provides a framework of stability and predictability (or so it might seem) within which it is relatively easier for international capital to operate.

(4) The military, too, usually has its own interests at stake in the alliance with foreign capital, because arms spending adds to the pressure to increase or conserve hard currency earnings and to attract foreign investment. The military's preference for state-managed development may actually strengthen such tendencies rather than detract from them. The alliance of state and international capital, created through central planning, licensing and import control, joint ventures and management agreements, is a well-documented feature of many Third World countries.

In sum, the military's institutional interests and its particular character as an instrument of state power shape its *class commitments* in a number of distinctive ways that influence the pattern of production and of national development. Nevertheless there is considerable variation in the way these class commitments are actualized in different Third World countries.

(1) In the first place, different patterns of incorporation in the world economy create different constraints and crises to which the military must respond, some of which are depicted schematically in Table 2. The first two patterns set forth in the Table arise in economies which are based on the production of raw materials for the world market, though it makes a considerable difference whether these are produced (like many agricultural commodities) by numerous indigenous petty producers; or are extracted (like most minerals) through large investments of foreign capital. The third and fourth patterns are determined by the nature of a country's process of industrialization—whether by import-substitution or by the export of cheap manufactures produced by low-cost labour.

Few countries fit fair and square into any one of the categories in the Table. Indeed, the military often plays a critical role in the transition from one pattern to another. The crisis which led first to the rise to power of the Allende regime in Chile and then to its overthrow by the military in 1973 was, for example, brought on by the exhaustion of the process of import-substitution and the international forces set in motion by the government's expropriation of the foreign copper monopolies. In response to these external forces the military government has adopted economic policies—economic liberalization, sale of state enterprises, the curtailment of import-substitution, withdrawal from the Andean Pact—which virtually amount to a reassertion of its traditional position in the international division of labour as a raw material producer.

(2) Not all developing countries are so dependent on their links with the international economy that they have no room within which to manoeuvre. In the first place, some countries are less constrained by their foreign earnings than others. Indeed in the oil-rich countries military spending is about the fastest way of realising surplus hard currency earnings. A cynic would say that the availability of such earnings in countries such as Iran, Saudi Arabia and more debatedly Nigeria, merely removes all obstacles to the expansion of the state apparatus and makes it easier to buy off or suppress internal contradictions, without fundamental change in the structure of the economy or links with the international economic system. Nevertheless, oil surpluses also give radical regimes like those of Algeria or Libya more room in which to manoeuvre, even if they expose them to the same temptations to buy arms and proliferate soldiers and bureaucrats as in the more conservative countries.

Second, contradictions in the international system alleviate some of the obstacles to national development strategies created by international capital. Peru has been able to play the major capitalist powers off against each other, buying arms from Britain, France, and even the U.S.S.R. while never completely breaking with the U.S.A.

Most important of all there are several Third World countries (such as Iraq, Syria, Algeria, Somalia, Angola, Uganda, Tanzania, India) which are or have been supplied very largely or entirely by countries within the socialist bloc. Not all these countries are socialist themselves, by any stretch of the imagination. Yet there is no doubt that socialist arms sales and assistance make a real difference to the recipient countries, enabling them to arm themselves without having to earn large amounts of hard currency in the world market (though some of them find the economic conditions laid down by their socialist suppliers almost as onerous). In some the only effect of socialist, like Western, arms and military assistance is to allow an oppressive regime to survive (like Amin's in Uganda,

Table 2

Variations in Military's class commitments in dependent capitalist countries

Structure of Economy	Nature of State Functions	Nature of Crises	Nature of Military Commitments
1. Petty capitalist commodity production Agricultural and natural resource based commodities produced for export and/or local sale by indigenous producers under petty capitalist or pre-capitalist relations of production. Examples: most countries of sub-Saharan Africa, Bangladesh.	1. Minimum conditions of law and order. 2. Mediation between petty producers and world market, either (i) via foreign merchant capital, or (ii) directly via state marketing monopolies. 3. Extraction of surplus from export-import trade and conversion into (i) increases in size, power and military spending of state apparatus or (ii) industrialization programmes.	1. Political crises brought on by reinvigoration of pre-capitalist formations and loyalties (tribe, religion, language, region etc.) in response to competition for state power, jobs, economic resources and benefits. 2. Instability induced by fluctuations in commodity prices in world market, undermining regimes and their long-term economic plans.	1. (a) Holding fragile nation-state together and/or (b) using state machinery to establish hegemony of the particular tribal, religious, linguistic or regional groups who happen to control the military hierarchy. 2. Intervention to secure changes of regime in response to externally-induced economic and political crisis. 3. Reinforcement (through arms purchases) of pressure to earn foreign exchange in world market or to save it by engaging in import-substituting industrialization.

2. Enclave commodity production			
Agricultural commodities produced or natural resources extracted on large-scale (a) by international capital or (b) by state capital incorporated in circuits of international capital through export of commodities and imports of technology. Examples: most oil-producing (OPEC) countries and copper-producing (CIPEC) countries.	1. Minimum conditions of law and order. 2. Mediation between capital and labour in enclave enterprises; ensuring stability and quiescence of labour, in the last resort by physical repression. 3. Either (a) State is directly coopted by foreign capital and serves its interests (e.g. Gabon, Central American banana republics) Or (b) State expropriates foreign capital. The latter reorganizes itself and appropriates its share of mineral rents by sales of technology, management agreements, military sales etc. 4. (Where State not mouthpiece of foreign capital) promotion of natural resource ideologies; maximization of mineral rents and of state's share therein; conversion of these surpluses into expansion of state apparatus and/or industrialization.	1. Conflicts between central regions/groups/towns sharing the benefits of economic activity and employment created by enclave and peripheral regions/groups/rural areas. 2. Conflicts between capital and labour in enclave. 3. (a) Instability induced by fluctuations in commodity prices in world market, undermining regimes and their long-term plans, precipitating conflict between states and foreign capitalists except (b) when associations of producers (especially OPEC) exercise monopoly control in world market, minimizing direct effect of externally induced crises on state machinery.	1. Establishment of physical control by centre over peripheral regions. 2. Intervention in conflicts between foreign or state capital and labour. 3. (a) Direct physical repression on behalf of foreign capital, particularly in times of economic and political crisis (e.g. Chile) or (b) Intervention against foreign capital on behalf of nationalist projects to assure state control over natural resources (or support for such interventions by other groups or governments). 4. Reinforcement (through arms purchases) of pressures to maximize natural resource rents and to participate in transnational arms economy.

Table 2—(*Contd.*)

Variations in Military's class commitments in dependent capitalist countries

Structure of Economy	Nature of State Functions	Nature of Crises	Nature of Military Commitments
3. Import-substituting industrialization Development of industrial base through either (a) foreign investment or (b) state investment or both, replacing goods previously imported. Examples: Brazil, Mexico, Argentina, Philippines and (combined with 2. above) Indonesia, Iran, Venezuela, Chile and Nigeria.	1. Maintenance of political stability to assure smooth process of industrialization and to prevent flight of foreign capital. 2. Mediation between capital and labour; repression of latter to subsidize investment by the former. 3. State promotion of industrialization, bringing about symbiosis of state, local and international capital. Variations in extent of penetration by international capital, in the mechanisms (e.g. direct investment versus sales of technology) by which it is achieved and in extent of state control over the process.	1. Conflicts between industrial urban centres and rural/agricultural peripheries, intensified to extent that the latter subsidized process of industrialization. 2. Conflicts between capital and labour in industrial sector, intensified to the extent that profits and investment subsidized by low wages. 3. Marginalization, creation of 'reserve army of unemployed' by industrialization/urbanization process. 4. Crisis created by exhaustion of process of import-substitution. Cycle of foreign exchange shortages, inflation, unrest, repression, military spending and more shortages, inflation etc.	1. Establishment of physical control by centre over periphery. Repression of peasant movements, rural guerrillas etc. 2. Intervention in conflict between foreign or state capital and labour, usually to repress the latter on behalf of the former, but not always (e.g. the Peronist alliance between the military and unions in Argentina). 3. Establishment of physical 'security' in restive urban areas. Repression of crime, squatters, demonstrations, urban guerrillas etc. 4. Reinforcement (through arms purchases and sometimes arms manufacture) of import-substitution and of the crises induced by it.

4. **Export-promoting industri-alization** Examples: South Korea, Taiwan, Singapore and (combined with 3, above) Philippines.	As above except foreign capital (a) more footloose because not tied to domestic resources or markets (b) tends to an even greater extent to be vertically integrated with production and markets in central countries. For these reasons (a) political stability (and organized physical repression) are even more vital, and (b) the bargaining power of the state is weaker relative to that of international capital.	As above except (a) low wages often essential to attract foreign capital and hence greater repression of labour force (b) vulnerability to crises in international markets for manufactures rather than to constraints of narrowness of domestic market.	As above, except military involved to an even greater extent in establishment of physical security (particularly in urban centres), repression and counter-revolution.

now heavily dependent on Soviet military support). The tendency in most of them is toward state capitalism and military-bureaucratic control of the development process rather than full-scale socialist transformation, for which socialist military assistance is probably a necessary but not a sufficient condition.

(3) Armies and military regimes are seldom *directly* subservient to the interests of national or of foreign capital. The factors shaping soldiers' class allegiances are complex. The existing literature on the military in the Third World fails almost completely to establish the connections between the military's position in the class structure, its institutional characteristics and its international dimensions. Insofar as it deals with the subject of class at all it does so in terms of the alleged consequences of the recruitment and social origins of the officer corps. Officers are either said to be conservative because they originate from the upper levels of the class structure—an argument that was popular in the past with radical critics of the military—or they are said to be part of the 'new middle class', which brings about modernization.

A sophisticated attempt by Huntington (1968, chapter 4) to synthesize these arguments in terms of different stages in modernization postulates that when middle-class groups begin to challenge traditional landed oligarchies, the military plays a progressive role in dislodging the latter; but when lower class groups begin to organize, the military increasingly plays a repressive role in defence of established class interests. The military supports bourgeois revolutions but opposes socialist ones (although this is not how Huntington himself puts it).

No really convincing explanation, however, is given why the military should be located at some fixed 'middle point' in the class structure. Empirical studies of the class origins of army officers in the Third World on the whole confirm that officers are neither recruited from the ruling or upper classes—even in countries like Brazil where the class structure is relatively well developed—nor are many of them sons of peasants and workers. Few of these studies demonstrate, however, that class origins have a significant effect on political behaviour. The important differences between the military juntas of Brazil and of Peru, would for example, be impossible to predict from their class origins, which are strikingly similar (Stepan, 1973, chapter 2).

Nor do class origins provide an explanation of the nationalism which is so often a powerful theme in military ideology and behaviour. This arises directly from the military's institutional interests, from the military relations of force discussed earlier in this chapter. For the military is riven by the contradictions between those forces which hold together the national class structure and those which link classes together internationally. Armies are kept in operation by the international arms trade. Yet the surpluses with which arms are purchased are appropriated nationally. Soldiers fight external wars or at the very least keep themselves in a state of preparation for them. Yet they are also the agents of internal repression; indeed in some countries that is virtually their only function. Professionalism is an international ideology disseminated by the military assistance programmes of the advanced countries. Yet army officers play out their careers in national military establishments and are not as internationally mobile as the managers of multinational corporations. Their interstitial position between the nation state and the international system is critical in reproducing both.

Thus the military is seldom a completely stable ally, whether of the national or of the international bourgeoisie. Even military elites committed—like that of Brazil—to an orthodox strategy of capitalist development in close association with foreign investment face internal struggles against officers who advocate economic nationalism and greater state control over the economy. In countries like Peru, Ethiopia, Libya and Egypt (under Nasser) it is the military radicals who have prevailed and have effected quite sweeping changes, including nationalizations of key sectors of the economy. Nevertheless military nationalism itself often results in little more than new kinds of integration in the circuits of the international economy, even when the major means of production have been removed from foreign hands: because foreign exchange still has to be earned to pay for armaments, technology and the expansion of the state and military bureaucracy.

(4) Finally there are variations among different Third World countries in the relationship between military coercion and the exercise of state power; although it may well be that the basic functions of military repression vary much less than the political forms under which they take place.

Almost half of the countries of Africa, Asia, the Middle East and Latin America are under military rule. Still more of them have experienced military intervention or periods of military rule at some point or other during the past 30 years. And if one adopts broader criteria there are scarcely anywhere organized military force has *not* been used to keep in office or to change the regime or ruling class during the past three decades. Yet much of the existing literature takes as its starting point the problem of assuring 'civilian control' over the military establishment; looking at this over a whole continuum of military participation in politics, ranging from gentlemanly bargaining over strategy or appropriations, outright blackmail of the regime, participation in the reshuffling of ruling elites right through to direct military control of all the major political institutions of a society (Finer, 1962).

The absence of civilian control is only a 'problem' however, when contrasted with an idealized view of the relationship between soldiers and governments in the advanced bourgeois democracies. It is not an especially useful way of looking at the political institutions of Africa, Asia, the Middle East and Latin America, where military participation rather than civilian control might be viewed as the 'normal' state of affairs. Nor does the idea of a continuum from civilian to military take use very far. To be sure, the difference between a military establishment which intervenes as a 'moderating power' to resolve conflicts between civilian factions as in Brazil before 1964 and one which attempts permanently to substitute itself for parts of the state superstructure, to become the state as it were, as in the same country after 1967, is important. Yet to view this as just a change from less to more military participation in political life is superficial, for the military's formal participation in politics is less important than the question of how far the state superstructure is or is not held together by organized coercion.

The distinction between civilian and military regimes may well be less important than the similarities in the way they govern. Take a country like the Philippines where, under a civilian regime civil liberties have been curtailed, the media browbeaten, trade unions deprived of the right to strike, opponents of the regime repressed. There is intensive surveillance by the police and military intelligence networks, internal warfare is waged against dissident Moslem minority groups, the military is frequently consulted about major government decisions, martial law is in operation and political offences are tried before military rather than civilian tribunals. The extent of repression and its methods differ only in detail from that practised in other Third World countries such as South Korea, Indonesia, Taiwan, or Pakistan; Brazil, Argentina, Peru or Uruguay; Iran, Iraq, Egypt, Syria or Jordan; Senegal, Ghana, Zaire or Ethiopia; be they formally under civilian governments or under the military and whether the regime is of a conservative or progressive political tendency.

Coups and military régimes are, to be sure, the prevailing trend in the Third World, and this is hardly surprising. For when organized coercion is the main basis of state power, coups are to be expected merely because more 'democratic' methods of transferring power between different fractions of the ruling classes cease to operate. But struggles to gain or to remain in power can also be waged by assassination, mob violence, surveillance and terror by the secret police, bribery and the skilful dispensation of political patronage. Frequent coups *may* betoken instability in the framework of the state—but not necessarily more so than votes of no confidence, reshufflings of cabinets and frequent elections in bourgeois democracies. Like the latter they speed the circulation of elites and the realignment of fractions of the ruling classes more often than they bring about fundamental change in the organization of state power and its allocation between (rather than within) social classes.

In Karl Marx's classic analysis of Bonapartism it was recognized that in periods of acute crisis or of historical transition between modes of production members of the ruling class would often be prepared to accept authoritarian government by a state machine over which it had relatively little direct control: the bourgeoisie would sometimes sacrifice its own class rule in order to secure the political stability on which the smooth functioning of a capitalist economy and its own class interests depend.

Bonapartism however is not a magical category into which the analysis of the military can be hammered. The historical circumstances of the present-day Third World bring together a different combination of elements from that which prevailed in nincteenth century France. The crisis of hegemony suffered by ruling classes is permanent and endemic rather than temporary and expectional; and is given a particular nco-colonial twist because a significant portion of the economically dominant class is outside the country. Uneven development superimposes all the contradictions between centre and periphery, capitalist and pre-capitalist social formations, class and tribe, region, religion and nation; and makes it all the more difficult for any single ruling class or fraction thereof to establish its ideological claims to rule.[5]

Although particular fractions of the military elite may intervene on behalf of peripheral or excluded classes and groups in such conditions of crisis—as in some African states where the recruitment base of the army has traditionally been in the less developed parts of the country or as in the alliance between sections of the army and organized labour in Peronist Argentina in the 1940s—the military establishment *as a whole* has a vested interest in what military ideologists call 'national security' and what its opponents call repression on behalf of the dominant classes. For the natural response of professional soldiers is to suppress class struggle when it appears, because it divides the nation, undermines the international economic standing of the economy—causing flights of foreign capital—and imposes certain real costs—casualties, disruption of routine, threats to its structure and its monopoly of organized force—upon the military establishment itself.

Yet military repression by no means guarantees that stability will be secured. Sometimes the military's weapons have simply turned conflict into more bloody conflict: witness, for example, the effect of military violence in Uruguay or in Bangladesh just before its war of liberation from Pakistan. Or the military itself has become deeply divided—as in Nigeria and the Lebanon before and during their respective civil wars—and thus unable to stand above the conflict. Nevertheless the fact that military force settles things in the last resort is critical, particularly in societies in permanent crisis, where the last resort is always close at hand.

THE INSERTION OF THE THIRD WORLD IN THE INTERNATIONAL RELATIONS OF FORCE

A central argument of the two preceding sections was that neither military institutions themselves nor their role in national development can be understood in isolation from the international relations between industrial countries and the Third World.

Broadly speaking, the accumulation of armaments in peripheral countries is linked to the accumulation of capital in the central capitalist countries: both directly, in that military spending in the Third World creates markets for the arms industries of the industrial countries; and indirectly in that it increases pressures on Third World countries to earn the hard currency for their military purchases by trading in the world market or encouraging the inflow of foreign investment. Nevertheless this international arms economy is itself given by contradictory pressures which make its analysis extremely complex:

(1) In the first place the flow of armaments internationally is partly determined by the logic of accumulation and arms production in the major capitalist arms producing countries, especially the U.S.A., Britain, France, West Germany, Canada and in recent years Japan. The impetus comes from three sources:

(a) the logic of arms production itself. Because R and D is a high proportion of total production costs, long production runs are required to justify the initial outlay, creating strong pressures to market armaments abroad. Such pressures have increased because of the escalation in the cost of major items of military equipment and have affected the European arms producers the most, because their national military forces absorb a smaller proportion of the total weapons output than those of the U.S.A. or U.S.S.R. (Kaldor, 1973).

(b) pressures from the interrelation between arms production and the process of capital accumulation in the central capitalist countries. Here we are on more controversial ground, the issue having been debated with particular bitterness in the U.S.A. as a result of the Vietnam War.[6] There are those on the one hand who argue that the enormous increases of arms production have helped the U.S. economy overcome the crises of over-production to which capitalist economies are prone. The Vietnam war in sum was good for American capitalism. But others argue that the military-industrial alliance between the arms producing firms and the Pentagon has to the contrary diverted resources away from the productive investment and brought about inflation. Although the Vietnam War was good for the U.S. arms producers, it is argued, it put great strain on the productive capacity and international viability of American capitalism. Whichever is correct, however, they both imply pressure to market arms to the Third World, be it because of the search for markets to make use of spare industrial capacity or to alleviate balance of payments difficulties arising from America's own military spending.

(c) pressures arising from the relation between armaments and the international economy. In a general way capital will be invested in arms production so long as there is an international market for weapons. Arms exports, furthermore, play a critical role in resolving crises in the international economy such as that created by the redistribution of international purchasing power towards the oil producing countries. One of the major ironies of recent history is the way the crisis in the international economy precipitated by oil price increases has been partly bought off by the escalation of the arms race in the Middle East.

The pressures arising at these different levels—the specific requirements of capital invested in arms production, the logic of capital accumulation in the central capitalist economies, and the logic of world-wide capital accumulation—may be in conflict, though it is likely their overall effect is to increase the pressure on the industrial countries to export arms to the Third World.

(2) The economic forces sustaining the arms trade are modified by the fact that it is also an instrument of the states and ruling classes of the powers which exercise or aspire to hegemony within the international system. Just as the main importers of arms are the

governments and military establishments of developing countries, so the suppliers are either the governments of the supplying countries themselves or large firms closely inter-linked with these governments. The governments of the industrial countries either negotiate arms exports directly themselves, take a direct part in the promotion efforts of their main domestic arms producers, or push them indirectly through arms exporting firms which sometimes act (like certain British arms suppliers) in all respects as cover for the governments' own arms sales. Exports are usually licensed to ensure they reach the 'approved' recipient and are not diverted elsewhere, and above all, the supply of arms is consciously used by governments to enlarge their spheres of political influence and to promote their non-military trade and investment. Finally (at least in the past), a large proportion of the trade has been subsidized, increasing the ability of Third World governments to absorb huge quantities of armaments. Much of the arms sales and military assistance provided by the countries of the socialist bloc is subsidized and some is given free. In the 1950s and 1960s the greater part of arms transfers from the U.S.A. were also subsidized under the Military Assistance Program; though cash and credit sales now predominate.

(3) The competition in the world market for arms between societies based on antagonistic—socialist and capitalist—modes of production has a distinctive impact on both the economics and the politcs of the arms trade. Even if the overall effect of the cold war is to reduce the price of the arms supplied to developing countries, it undoubtedly increases their volume and total value. This has three major implications. First it increases the flow of resources towards the arms *industries* of the arms suppliers and increases the power and resources of their respective military-industrial complexes. Second, in so doing it helps to maintain the pace of technological innovation, increasing the complexity and cost of weapons in the long run. Third, subsidized arms supplies often increase rather than decrease the military outlays of developing countries: both directly through added local costs such as wages and accommodation and through imports of non-military supplies required to support larger military forces; and indirectly by increasing the power of the military establishment's claim on national resources. Finally, to the extent that hegemonic powers like the U.S.A. or France are actually successful in using military links to keep particular countries like Chile or Gabon within their respective spheres of influence, the economic benefits they hope for may well exceed the costs of the subsidy.

(4) The expansion in the international market for arms is greatly accentuated by the presence in the Third World itself of nodal points of international political conflict such as the Arab-Israeli conflict; the disputes between India and Pakistan and India and China; the border conflicts between Ethiopia, Somalia and Kenya; and the struggle for black rule in Southern Africa. Trends in the international arms trade can to some extent be explained in terms of the 'demand' for armaments created by such conflicts, though competition between the major suppliers reacts back upon the political situation, tending to accelerate local arms races.

The effect of this complex interaction between the arms trade and struggles for political hegemony on the flow of armaments from the major suppliers to the different regions of the Third World can be seen in Table 3. By far the biggest recipients of arms from 1965 to 1974 were the countries of East Asia and the Middle East, the dozen leading importers being (in descending order of magnitude): South Vietnam, Israel, Iran, Egypt, South Korea, Syria, India, Taiwan, Pakistan, North Korea and Saudi Arabia.

The nexus between militarism and international capitalism is found in its pure form only in Latin America and in those countries in Africa, the Middle East and East Asia which buy all their arms from the West. Even so, many of them have diversified in order to escape the influence of a single previously dominant supplier, be it the U.S.A. in Latin America or the former colonial powers in the Caribbean or Africa. Yet their military expansion is still connected to the *system* of international capitalism inasmuch as they rely on international purchasing power earned in the world market to finance their armies.

Competition among the capitalist arms suppliers and the struggle for hegemony between them and socialist suppliers are both responsible for an increased transfer of military resources to the Third World. The powerful socialist presence in the Middle East and Asia is thus two edged, permitting disengagement from the West to an extent that is seldom possible in Latin America; but simultaneously raising the stakes in local conflicts, reinforcing military and bureaucratic control over the state apparatus; increasing military outlays; and expanding the market for the arms of the capitalist countries in equal measure to the inflow of socialist-provided weapons.

The final outcome depends very much on the nature of the struggle and of the groups to which the support of the socialist countries is given. Socialist support for liberation movements with a genuine prospect of socialist transformation and disengagement

Table 3

Total arms transfers, by suppliers and recipient regions 1965–1974
($ million)

Recipient Regions	Major Capitalist Suppliers					Major Socialist Suppliers			Other Suppliers	Total
	U.S.A.	France	U.K.	West Germany	Canada	U.S.S.R.	Czechoslovakia and Poland	China		
World Total	31,563	2,826	2,089	1,221	1,187	18,793	2,481	2,119	2,125	64,404
NATO	8,447	770	505	724	893	—	—	—	515	11,854
Warsaw Pact	—	—	—	—	—	5,674	1,888	5	35	7,602
OPEC	2,374	668	662	154	89	2,152	136	—	570	6,825
East Asia	14,640	40	145	23	32	4,049	15	1,616	321	20,881
South Asia	139	271	98	36	10	1,706	159	335	36	2,922
Middle East	5,628	461	603	181	45	5,733	337	2	465	13,455
Africa	341	669	258	73	17	711	48	81	263	2,481
Latin America	811	463	269	137	172	323	2	—	229	2,406

Source: World Military Expenditure and the Arms Trade 1964–1974
U.S. Arms Control and Disarmament Agency, 1976.

from the capitalist world economy, as in the wars of Indo-China and in former Portuguese Africa, is one thing. But military assistance given by socialist countries to authoritarian military or one-party regimes for reasons of international power politics is quite another. The paradox is that the latter supports a superstructure of political links with Third World countries, while at the same time permitting many of them to remain internationally dependent on the world economy and to repress socialism internally. Such a situation is inherently unstable, for client states which do not have strong internal reasons for associating with the socialist bloc can, like Egypt, go elsewhere for arms if they do not like the conditions laid down for them.

This is but one aspect of a pervasive contradiction between the economic logic and the political functions of the arms trade. Socialist arms suppliers face it because they transfer arms to peripheral countries incorporated in a world market, which, both in general and for arms in particular, is still mainly organized on capitalist principles. For capitalist countries, on the other hand, the contradiction arises even more directly because of the link between the international arms trade and their own capital accumulation. When an arms producer is obliged to sell arms abroad to absorb high R & D expenditures, to sustain capital accumulation and to solve balance-of-payments difficulties, it is that much harder to use the promise of arms supplies or the threat of withholding them to influence the political behaviour of purchasers. At the same time competition between the main arms suppliers—socialist and capitalist alike—has made it difficult for any one of them to secure a lasting monopoly over transfers to any particular country or region, of the type which the U.S.A. previously enjoyed in Latin America.

The events of the past ten years have seen a strengthening of the economic forces increasing the arms trade including: accelerated technological progress in arms production; strong economic pressure within capitalist arms producing countries to sell abroad; an international shift in purchasing power to the OPEC countries: and the concentration of production in and greater competition between large arms-producing conglomerates like Lockheed, Dassault or the British Aircraft Corporation. The growth of the international market for arms has helped the major capitalist powers to avert the present crisis in the international economy. But this has been achieved at some cost to their ability to guarantee the political conditions for the expansion of capital at the periphery, except in particular regions or sub-regions like Latin America or the Persian Gulf relatively less open to socialist diplomacy and military assistance.

Besides the arms trade, however, there are two other main ways the advanced capitalist countries have used armaments to secure their political position in the developing countries. First, by helping to professionalize the latters' armed forces. And second, by direct participation in national or regional conflict in the Third World, whether by open armed intervention, by the use of diplomacy and threats, or by covert action CIA-style. (The same methods have been used by socialist powers, though the latter have also been able to encourage the establishment of revolutionary movements where the crises of dependent capitalist development are favourable to them.)

Military training makes professional soldiers peculiary susceptible to international influences. They often attend courses abroad at some stage in their military career; Latin American officers for the most part in the U.S.A. or in U.S.-sponsored institutes such as the inter-American counter-insurgency school in Panama; English speaking African officers in Britain and other countries of the Commonwealth like Canada, Australia, India or Pakistan, but also in the U.S.A.; French speaking Africans in France. Military academies and training schools are often modelled on the metropolis, sometimes indirectly as in Nigeria, where the Military Academy was set up with Indian advice and technical assistance, thus passing on British professional values and modes of military organization at second remove. The socialist countries have likewise recognized the importance of military training for transmitting their international influence; not only in countries where it supports an ongoing transition to socialism (Chinese assistance in the reorganization of the Tanzanian military or Cuban training missions in Angola) but also in countries where such a transition is more remote (Russian assistance to Uganda and Chinese to Zaire).

The implications of military training and assistance programmes for external dependence are easy to see. They train soldiers in the use of the technologies of the donor countries. They give sustenance to the military relations of force around which the professional armies of both metropolis and periphery are organized. They create networks of professional contacts both with metropolitan military institutions and among coursemates in different peripheral countries. And they are often explicitly intended, like U.S. counterinsurgency courses (or indeed Chinese guerrilla instruction) to promote the political philosophy and interests of the country which provides the training.

The effects of international military links can sometimes, however, be quite the opposite of that intended by their sponsors. For example, in the counterinsurgency training organized by Western powers military intellectuals often read and transmit to their colleagues the doctrine of the 'enemy'—Mao, Guevara, Giap or Fanon. When the military role is redefined in the direction of domestic repression rather than external security the contradictions to which these authors call attention begin to emerge. Doctrines of 'revolutionary war' politicize officers both in the direction of the radical right and of the radical left.

The contradiction between the two variants of professionalism—that of conventional warfare and that of counter-insurgency—corresponds to an important tension in the class-structure of a dependent social formation. On the one hand the techniques and organizational blueprints of advanced countries are transferred to the Third World, interlinked with arms sales and industrialization. On the other the armies and class structures of peripheral countries do not just become those of the advanced countries writ small, as they have been profoundly distorted by their contact with the latter.

Domination at the periphery requires different relations of force from those in use in the metropolis. Yet this sometimes conflicts with the vested interests of professional soldiers in more conventional military functions. Thus the Peruvian junta which took power in 1968 at the same time that it increased national control over the economy also reasserted the military's role in external defence by buying foreign military hardware of a kind which the civilian regime (under U.S. government pressure) had denied the soldiers.

One may, in conclusion, see two contrapuntal themes in military professionalism in the Third World: on the one hand, military nationalism directed towards the creation of an internationally effective nation-state supported by a well developed conventional army, increasingly linked through its arms purchases to the international economy; on the other, international pressure for political 'stability' at the periphery, requiring an internally powerful state machinery and enlisting military commitment to doctrines of 'national security'. legitimizing its role in internal repression. These themes are interlinked and contradictory. Both are present in military ideology and tend to be associated with the conflicts between opposed groups of army officers, which are so common in Third World armies.

As for the direct participation of large powers in conflict at the periphery, there is a whole continuum: from diplomatic pressure, economic aid and military assistance programmes; various forms of blackmail such as threats to withdraw economic and military assistance; covert subversion and the destabilization of regimes;

reassurances of recognition and support to coup-makers if successful; actual material support for a coup, or alternatively support in putting one down; military assistance and advice in counter-revolutionary operations; taking direct part in such operations (the U.S. in the early stages of the Vietnam conflict); direct participation in the revolutionary war (the Chinese in Korea or the Cubans in Angola); through to actual invasion by troops of the intervening power (the U.S. in the Dominican Republic and in Vietnam, or France and Britain in the Suez Crisis).

Yet one cannot measure the effect of external pressures on the military, the class structure or the political system as a whole solely by the level to which overt foreign interference has *actually* been pushed. In some countries, like Chile, intervention may have taken place precisely because the contradictions are sharper than elsewhere and the hegemony of imperialist powers less secure. In others the class structure and internal political forces may be self-sustaining and direct intervention unnecessary. The arms trade and discreet military assistance programmes are often all that is required to keep the professional military establishment in operation and the stability of the political system within tolerable limits. And in others again, like Iran, Indonesia or Zaire external penetration may be massive but multifaceted, so that to take one aspect alone such as support for a coup, covert CIA activities, foreign aid and investment, military assistance, or diplomatic pressure, may give an incomplete picture of foreign influence because all are important together.

Conversely, however, direct intervention has sometimes created more contradictions than those it represses. The Suez crisis, the American intervention in Vietnam and the South African invasion of Angola are perhaps the most glaring examples, but there are several others. Failure to examine abortive as well as successful interventions might lead one to underestimate the *limits* imperialism faces, the contradictions it creates for itself and the strength of the forces opposed to it on the periphery. These limits arise at a number of different levels.

First, the strength and disposition of anti-imperialist forces themselves: in Vietnam for example, the military effectiveness of the liberation armies and the presence of the Russian nuclear deterrent to discourage escalation of the conflict by the Americans; in Angola the extremely prompt and effective assistance provided by the Cubans and Russians and the reluctance of the U.S.A. to risk a diplomatic showdown in Africa by openly intervening.

Second, differences among the major Western powers, as during the Suez crisis, when the disapproval of the Americans and their refusal to support British borrowing from the IMF to halt the run on the pound caused by the crisis, brought the Anglo-French invasion of Egypt to a grinding halt.

Third the internal contradictions by which imperialist powers are sometimes weakened: the bitter opposition to the Suez invasion by the Labour Party; or the economic burden of arms spending by the U.S. government in Vietnam and the gathering strength of the anti-war movement. There are strong pressures impelling the major capitalist powers to intervene in their interest at the periphery. But it would be a mistake to regard them as monolithic and to under-estimate the constraints according to which they operate.

Intervention, furthermore, is not exclusive to capitalist powers but has also been an integral part of the struggle against them. External support has been a crucial element in most contemporary revolutions: Russian support (however grudging) for the Chinese revolution; Russian and Chinese assistance in Vietnam; Arab and communist bloc help to the Algerians in their war of national liberation from France; the assistance of the Russians and Chinese and of neighbouring African countries to the armed struggle in Guinea-Bissau, Angola and Mozambique.

Nevertheless such assistance is not without its own con-tradictions. External aid cannot overcome unfavourable objective conditions; witness for example the failure of Che Guevara to bring revolution to Bolivia. It all too easily triggers off nationalist responses and accusations of 'social imperialism' against the donor: visible already, for instance, in the ambivalence of the Angolans about the continued presence in their country of their Cuban and Russian liberators. Recipients of socialist assistance—however worthy according to revolutionary criteria—are vulnerable to changes in the interests of the donors. The revolutions in Laos and Cambodia were delayed because the Vietnamese gave and withdrew assistance in accordance with the progress of their own struggle. Socialist rivalries—for example Chinese support for the FNLA and Cuban and Soviet for the MPLA in Angola—have sometimes helped to create divisions in liberation movements.

In a very real sense the intervention of socialist countries is also limited and shaped by the constraints of balance of power politics. In several Latin American countries the Moscow-controlled com-munist parties have been ambivalent toward armed struggle: fluctuating between support for insurrection and for more 'legi-timate' activity in accord with the turns and swings of international politics. The support of socialist countries for the revolutions in former Portuguese Africa was covert and limited in quantity until the international political conjuncture became favourable to larger-scale involvement after the invasion of Angola by South Africa.

Countries in the Third World tend, in sum, to be pulled into the global conflicts between the major super-powers; and the latter, too to become deeply involved in struggles occurring at the periphery. The instability at the heart of international relations between developing and industrial countries accentuates the fact that, despite the expansion of capital on a world scale there is little semblance of an international superstructure comparable to the national state. There are instead only *partial* international superstructures; some based on region (the EEC, ASEAN etc.); some constituting military alliances between states (NATO, the Warsaw Pact and the moribund SEATO and CENTO) and some with specialized functions (the UN agencies, IMF, World Bank etc.). These do relatively little to bind the world system together. Indeed military alliances and regional pacts on the whole deepen the main fractures between blocs.

Rather than superstructure it might be more apposite to talk of a 'superstruggle': but for the integrating mechanisms of both of the international economy, which incorporates enterprises and states alike in the circuits of capital, and of balance of power politics which (at least for the time being) prevents the war of all against all.

Although most statesmen and military leaders subscribe to the concept of a balance of power—and thus make it take on the character of self-fulfilling prophecy—it is thoroughly ambiguous. The nature of the nuclear means of mass destruction on which the balance between the central world powers is based is such that balances computed merely in terms of the numbers of missiles, aircraft and nuclear warheads available to each side make little sense. Further, the very ability to participate depends on a very advanced technology and industrial base. The balance thus expresses the competing interests of the ruling classes of advanced industrial countries and the clientage of those of the Third World.

Such an international system does not even succeed in providing a political basis for the orderly expansion of capital on an international level; the tools of international economic management having proved woefully inadequate to deal with the current international economic crisis. Still less does it provide a reasonable prospect of peace and of a more just distribution of resources internationally.

Balance of power politics, furthermore, provides only temporary and largely inadequate solutions to the international crises which beset the Third World. Typically, it is devoted to stabilizing the *existing* situation without getting to grips with the substantive issues, the very real contradictions which underline conflicts such as the Middle East crisis or the wars of national liberation in Southern Africa.

The very severity of the present international crisis in some ways, however, provides favourable opportunities for the modification or destruction of existing relations of international domination: a nuclear stalemate in which great powers can be played off against each other; internal dissent within the large capitalist powers which makes it more difficult for their governments to pursue expansionist foreign policies; economic crisis which fuels this discontent inside capitalist countries, and, further, makes it difficult for them to finance external military ventures or to subsidize arms sales in order to gain political influence. The same crisis also brings things to a head in the periphery, concentrating economic grievances and mobilizing popular forces (but also increasing the repression by dominant classes).

This is a real dilemma for those who wish to change the existing pattern of international domination. On the one hand increasingly dangerous forms of armed struggle and international conflict. And on the other the severe limits of negotiated settlements which start from the existing distribution of power. To the extent that attempts to stabilize the existing pattern of international arrangements merely buy time, in which lines of conflict harden and the international production and diffusion of destructive weapons continues, they may *actually increase* the ultimate danger. Weapons and military organizations—the means of force—are in the international domain, in that their deployment and or use is a matter of common danger and common social concern for all mankind. Yet they are still appropriated and controlled by national ruling classes which use or threaten to use them to reproduce their national power and international interests. This makes social control over their use and conditions of lasting peace almost impossible to bring about without major transformation in the structures of international production, power and force.

NOTES

1 This article is a condensation and rearrangement of two articles which originally appeared in the IDS Bulletin (Luckham 1977a and 1977b), with some extension of the theoretical framework put forward in these articles. The word militarism is

not used here in its classical meaning of the pursuit of national territorial expansion by military means, but rather to indicate a somewhat broader phenomenon, namely increasing reliance on force and the means of force to maintain the existing social structures and international relations of modern societies, in particular those of the Third World.

2 Though they do not, strictly speaking, arise from the exploitation of soldiers as a workforce from which surplus value is extracted; but from their domination in a hierarchy of power relationships controlled by their superiors.

3 For a fuller analysis of the contradictions inherent in military bureaucratic structures see Luckham, 1971a, chapters 5–7.

4 Statistical studies on the whole provide *no* evidence of significant relationships (one way or the other) between military regimes and indicators of economic growth or social change (see particularly Jackman, 1976). These studies are, however, subject to most of the methodological criticisms made above in relation to statistical studies of the relationship between arms spending and economic performance.

5 The interaction between the military's institutional and class interests on the one hand and social conflicts based on tribe, region and nation are discussed more fully in Luckham 1977b.

6 The literature on this debate is too large to cite in detail here. There are useful summaries in Rosen, 1970.

REFERENCES

Astiz, A., 1972, 'The Peruvian Military', *Western Political Quarterly* No. 4.

Benoit, E., 1973, *Defence and Economic Growth in Developing Countries*, Lexington Books, D. C. Heath and Co., Lexingtonton (Mass).

Decalo, S., 196, *Coups and Military Rule in Africa*, Yale, University Press, New Haven.

Finer, S. E., 1962, *The man on Horseback*, Pall Mall Press, London.

Huntington, S. P., 1968, *Political Order in Changing Societies*, Yale University Press, New Haven.

Jackman, R. W., 1962, 'Politicians in Uniform', *American Political Science Review*, December 1976.

Janowitz, M., 1960, *The Professional Soldier*, Free Press, New York.

Kaldor, Mary, 1972, *European Defence Industries: National and International Implications*, Institute for the Study of International Organisations, Sussex.

Lasswell, H., 1941, 'The Garrison State', *American Journal of Sociology*, XLVI, January.

Luckham, R., 1971a, *The Nigerian Military: A Case Study in Authority and Revolt 1960–67*, Cambridge University Press, Cambridge.

Luckham, A. R., 1971b, 'A Comparative Typology of Civil-Military Relations' *Government and Opposition*, Vol. 6, No. 1.

Luckham, R., 1977a, 'Militarism: Arms and the Internationalisation of Capital', *IDS Bulletin*, March 1977.

Luckham, R., 1977b, 'Militarism: Force, Class and International Conflict', *IDS Bulletin*, August, 1977.

Marx, Karl 'The Eighteenth Brumaire of Louis Bonaparte' in Karl Marx and Frederick Engels, *Selected Works* Moscow: Foreign Languages Publishing House, 1958 Vol. 1, pp. 243–344.

McKinlay, R. D., and A. S. Cohan, 1975, 'A Comparative Analysis of the Political and Economic Performance of Military and Civilian Regimes, *Comparative Politics*, October.

Pye, L. W., 1962, 'Armies in the Process of Political Modernisation in J. J. Johnson (ed.), *The Role of the Military in Underdeveloped countries,* Princeton University Press, Princeton (NJ).

Rosen, S. (ed.), 1970, *Testing the Theory of Military-Industrial Complex*, Lexington Books, D.C. Heath and Co., Lexington (Mass.).

Schmitter, P. C., 1971, 'Military Intervention, Political Competitivenes and Public Policy in Latin America, 1950–67' in M. Janowitz and J. Van Doorn (eds.), *On Military Intervention*, Rotterdam University Press, Rotterdam.

Stepan, A. K., 1971, *The Military in Politics: Changing Patterns in Brazil*, Princeton University Press, Princeton.

Stepan, A. K., (ed.), 1973, *Authoritarian Brazil*, Yale University Press, New Haven.

Stockholm International Peace Research Institute, 1975 and 1976, *World Armaments and Disarmament, SIPRI Yearbooks 1975 and 1976.*

Trotsky, L., 1967, Vol. 1, *History of the Russian Revolution*, Sphere Books, London.

U.S. Arms Control and Disarmament Agency, 1976 *World Military Expenditure and the Arms Trade 1964–1974*, Bureau of Economic Affairs, Washington.

8

THE INTERNATIONAL MARKET IN SKILLS AND THE TRANSMISSION OF INEQUALITY

Martin Godfrey

In 1966, in a paper read to a conference in Addis Ababa, Dudley Seers (in Seers, 1970) drew attention to the way in which the emergence of an international market in professional skills was preventing the narrowing of the gap between the highly paid salariat and the remainder of the population in poor countries. At the time he expressed surprise that so little official and academic attention had been paid to 'this central problem of development'. Since then there has been some discussion of the ideas raised in his paper[1] but little or no empirical research in this area, apart from attempts to measure and 'explain' brain drain,[2] the symptom rather than the real problem.

The time seems ripe for a further exploration of these issues, for at least two reasons. One is the recent shift in the dependence debate towards questions of class characteristics and class formation. In particular, the Sunkel/Fuenzalida suggestion that a community has emerged which 'incarnates transnational capitalism and [is]. . . integrated at the worldwide level, in spite of the fact that its members live in geographically separate territories' (Sunkel and Fuenzalida, 1974) raises the questions, among many others, of whether such a community can be partly identified by the level of its rewards and of how that level is determined. A second reason for re-opening the discussion is the new interest of policy-prescribers, in the wake of the ILO employment reports (ILO, 1970, 1971 and 1972)[3], in questions of income distribution. A redistributive package is emerging which usually includes a freeze in money or real terms on top salaries. In Kenya's case, for instance, the ILO mission recommended that those earning K£700 or more should have no salary increase for five years. The chances of such recommendations being carried out might be better understood if we knew more about the forces which influence salary levels.

As a very early step in what would be a complex and detailed investigation it may be useful to put together some highly aggregated data for a number of African countries.[4] Ghana, Kenya,

Malawi, Nigeria, Sierra Leone, Tanzania, Uganda and Zambia have at least one common factor—their experience of British colonial rule, from which they gained independence between 1957 and 1964. Thus they inherited not only the administrative organization and practice of the British civil service but also civil service salary scales comparably distorted by the payment of British expatriates' international transfer earnings to the holders of top jobs. How successful have African bureaucrats been in maintaining the inherited differentials? And what are the reasons for the varying degrees of 'success' in different countries? These are the questions on which, it is hoped, our data will throw some tentative light.

First we need to have some idea of how salary differentials have moved in recent years. Table 4 shows the ratio of (a) the top of the civil service scale and of the graduate entry point to (b) the lowest point on the scale and to GDP per head. These figures are offered as indicators of changes not in overall distribution of income but in the range of personal incomes received. Even for this purpose they are not ideal. Wages and salaries are not the only source of income. Moreover, in Africa more than elsewhere a secure and well-remunerated job, which gives power to manipulate the state machine as well as surplus for investment, is the main route to the acquisition of other assets. Thus the ratios in the Table are likely to understate the range of personal incomes; and, since the extent to which civil servants earn secondary incomes varies from country to country,[5] the validity of international comparisons is also affected. The extent to which salary scales are skewed towards the top and to which the actual distribution of salary-earners on the scale is similarly skewed will also vary from country to country. Moreover, civil service salary increases take place at discrete intervals, so that the choice of period may affect the comparison. The improvement in the position of top Kenyan civil servants, for example, reflects the recommendations of a single commission of enquiry in 1970–1971. A later cut-off point would improve the relative position of their Nigerian counterparts, who are on the brink of a huge increase, in contrast to those in Tanzania where more recent changes have further improved the relative position of the lower paid. Also, our figures exclude fringe benefits,[6] relating to pensions, housing, transport, leave and family allowances etc., inclusion of which would considerably widen the differential between the higher and the lower paid. Finally, the figures are gross, before tax. The extent to which after-tax differentials would be narrower will also vary.[7]

Nevertheless, if these qualifications are borne in mind, the figures in Table 4 are of some interest. Only in the case of Kenya has there

Table 4

Civil service salary scales: ratio of top to bottom and to GDP per head, 1963–64 and 1971–72

	Top of scale		Graduate entry point		Top of scale		Graduate entry point	
	Bottom of scale*		Bottom of scale*		GDP per head		GDP per head	
	1963–64	1971–72	1963–64	1971–72	1963–64	1971–72	1963–64	1971–72
Ghana	36	35	6	6	40	34	7	6
Kenya	27	34	7	8	82	82	20	20
Malawi	44	40	11	11	145	90	35	24
Nigeria	37	30	7	5	118	98	23	19
Sierra Leone	26	29	6	6	54	44	13	9
Tanzania	24	16	7	5	96	70	26	21
Uganda	33	32	9	7	130	71	35	16
Zambia	44	44	11	14	49	32	13	10

* Lowest point on civil-service scale or minimum wage in the capital city, whichever is higher. For the actual figures on which this Table is based see Table 10.

Sources: National civil service salary scales, reports of commissions of enquiry; U.N. *Yearbooks of National Accounts;* U.N. *Demographic Yearbooks.*

been a substantial increase in the ratio between the top and bottom of the civil service salary scale. In Sierra Leone the ratio has increased slightly while in Zambia[8] and Ghana the ratio has shown little or no change. In the remainder the ratio has fallen, by a third in the case of Tanzania. In all cases the ratio of top salary to GDP per head has shown no rise and in many cases it has fallen substantially. The contrast between the ways in which the two sets of ratios have moved reflects differences between the relative gains of the lowest paid wage earners and of the population as a whole; only in Nigeria and Tanzania have the lowest-paid wage earners improved their relative position.[9] As for the ratio between graduate entrants and the bottom Zambia and Kenya show the largest increases. For Ghana, Malawi and Sierra Leone the ratio is unchanged and for the remainder it has fallen. In all cases except Kenya the ratio of the graduate-entry salary to GDP per head has fallen.

How is the difference in the experience of, say, Kenya and Zambia on the one hand, and Tanzania on the other, to be explained? To the unadulterated economist it would be merely a matter of supply and demand in the local market for high-level manpower. The premium earned by the top civil servant and the new graduate is in the nature of a 'scarcity rent', to be gradually reduced as the supply of qualified manpower increases.[10] It is almost impossible to test such a hypothesis satisfactorily but, in general, one might derive from it a cautious prediction that economies which experience similar rates of growth in demand and similar rates of growth in stock of qualified manpower might also see comparable movements in salary differentials. An attempt to set out the relevant data is made in Table 5.

Whether the considerable effort expended to estimate the indicators in this Table was worthwhile must be open to doubt. To aggregate demand and supply for 'graduates' into a single market is crude and the quality of some of the data used in the estimates is poor. In particular, the numbers studying overseas 'at third level' may include some who would not be regarded as graduate-equivalent by manpower planners and employers and the rate at which they become available for jobs at home may have been overestimated. Then there is the problem of estimating expatriate participation in the market. In the absence of firm data the assumption underlying the table is that the numbers of expatriates holding graduate jobs remained constant during the period. In fact such data as are available suggest that in the case of Kenya and Nigeria the number of such expatriates employed increased so that the growth rates in supply shown for these two countries may be under-estimates. On the other hand, Tanzania, Uganda and Malawi

Table 5

Some indicators of rates of increase in supply of and demand for high-level manpower

| | Supply Indicators | | | Demand Indicators | |
| | | | | Annual average rates of growth over same period at constant prices of: | |
	Stocks of graduate job-holders (at date shown)	Estimated addition to stock net of wastage[1] (in period shown)	Implied annual average rate of growth[2] (%)	GDP (%)	Government revenue (%)
Ghana	6,654 (1960)	9,583 (1960–70)	8	3	2
Kenya	6,279 (1964)	6,624 (1964–71)	9	6	12
Malawi	1,513[3] (1966)	1,373 (1966–71)	11	5	2
Nigeria	18,691 (1963)	18,965 (1963–71)	8	3	2
Sierra Leone	2,230 (1964)	1,197 (1964–70)	6	5	7
Tanzania	2,801 (1964/5)	3,586 (1965–71)	13	5	12
Uganda	3,000 (1963)	4,741 (1963–71)	13	4	1
Zambia	3,300 (1965)	756 (1965–71)	3	6	10

[1] Estimated output of graduates and diplomats from national universities plus graduates of overseas third-level courses, less wastage due to death and retirement estimated at 0.005 of initial stock per annum.

[2] On the assumption that the number of expatriates holding graduate jobs has remained constant.

[3] Actual number with university degress and professional qualifications.

Sources: UNESCO *Statistical Yearbooks*, supplemented by national manpower surveys and national sources of educational statistics.

seem to have experienced a fall in the number of expatriates so that their growth rates may be overestimates, while for Ghana the assumption of the table seems to hold, and for Zambia and Sierra Leone no information is available.

Moreover, no satisfactory procedure for estimating the demand for high-level manpower has yet been devised. Rather than attempt such an estimate we merely show the growth rates of GDP and government revenue at constant prices. Manpower planners, it is now clear, have tended grossly to overestimate elasticities of educated manpower in employment with respect to GDP. As Jolly and Colclough (Jolly and Colclough, 1972), summarizing the results of the OECD international comparisons exercise, report, 'the general picture that emerges from the cross-sectional regression studies is that [such elasticities] . . . tend to range around 0.9 to 1 rather than higher or lower'. As they recognize, it is a big leap from elasticities based on observed cross-section relationships to elasticities of future demand for particular countries. But until time series data become available the best guess we can make is that the GDP growth rates in our table may set a maximum above which the growth in demand for educated manpower is unlikely to rise.[11] The growth rates for government revenue are included to indicate the varying capacity of the civil service in each country to absorb additional manpower.

Given all these qualifications, the impression that Table 6 gives of most of these countries experiencing a faster growth of supply of graduates than of demand is probably not a false one.[12] The only countries for which a general 'scarcity-rent' explanation of widening differentials looks plausible on the strength of these data alone are Zambia and perhaps Sierra Leone. The similarity of the experience of Kenya and Tanzania is striking. Both enjoyed growth in their stock of graduates at a faster rate than that of GDP but both also experienced a particularly fast rate of increase in government revenue. Other explanations than changes in local supply-and-demand conditions will clearly have to be found for their differing patterns of change in wage and salary structure.

In a sense we do not have to took far for such an explanation. A cornerstone of the Tanzanian government's policy, after all, has been the prevention of the formation of a privileged bureaucratic class, whereas the Kenyan authorities have been concerned to shape a functionalist ideology to justify increasing the rewards of the already privileged.[13] Ideologies do not, however, emerge from and flourish in a vacuum. This is not the place to try to explain the emergence of differing ideologies in different countries[14] but we may at least be able to suggest how conditions are created which reinforce or undermine a prevailing ideology.

The force to which Seers drew attention in his 1966 paper (Seers, 1970), the existence of an international market in professional skills, is one of which those responsible for advising on African civil service salaries have long been conscious. For instance, the Ani commission, recommending a salary increase for higher civil servants in Uganda in 1963 (Kampala, 1963, p. 25), emphasized 'the fact that even local members of the service in these ranges of employment are to some extent affected by changed in the world market rates for qualified men and women'. The Mills-Odoi report for Ghana in 1967 (Accra, 1967, p. 28) frankly recognized that 'the criteria which effectively apply in determining the remuneration of the higher income groups with their international markets and scarcity values are very different from those that apply at the lower levels'. And the Elwood report for Nigeria in 1966 (Lagos, 1966, p. 9) referred to the pressure that had been put on it.

> particularly in respect of the more senior ranks and especially as regards professional staff to recommend that salaries should be very substantially increased and brought more into line with 'world market values'. . . A reasonable inference would be that Nigeria should enter into competition with wealthier countries in order to secure and retain the services of its own people.

The international mobility of the educated and their access to 'world market values' derives from the 'non-indigenous' nature of the education and training system. This usually prepares students for foreign (or foreign-oriented) qualifications, employs many foreign teachers and sends many students abroad, uses an international rather than a local language as a medium of instruction and is geared neither to the needs of the economy as a whole (which would imply equity in provision[15] as well as orientation towards employment and productivity) nor to its resources (which would imply low current and capital cost). Those who emerge from the apex of such a system have acquired, to a varying extent, international mobility.

Few make use of this mobility but all benefit financially from having acquired it, through the working of the principle of comparability. For instance, the Mayanja report for Uganda in 1966 (Kampala, 1966, p. 7) referred to:

> the great discontent that can be generated if substantial increases are granted to particular groups. . . if these cannot readily be seen by other groups of similar initial qualifications and period of training to be clearly justified.

And the rhetoric of the Ndegwa report of 1970-1971 for Kenya (Nairobi, 1971, p. 49), which implicitly invokes this principle, is worth quoting at some length:

> Can the country afford *not* to pay?... The technicians, the staff with professional qualifications and the senior administrators... are the people upon whom successful Government and development depends; it is their skill, resourcefulness and dedication which will shape the future of the country... There is a need for rededication to the tasks ahead, while this is obviously not just a question of money, it is difficult for even the most dedicated man to meet his commitments without it. If he is to give of his best he must feel that he is being fairly treated and that his worth is recognized.

Thus, in the name of fairness, the willingness of a few categories to make use of their mobility is prevented from disturbing traditional differentials within the upper echelons but not from widening the gap between the top and the bottom of the salary scale.[16]

In these circumstances one of the conditions of success of an egalitarian policy might be to insulate the local market for professional skills from the international market—by indigenizing education and evolving local qualifications which are 'at the same time highly suitable to the needs of the local economy and completely unacceptable to overseas employers' (Godfrey, 1970). Few African governments regard this as a desirable objective. In this they are encouraged by the transnational educational and professional establishment. As Johnson and Caygill (Johnson and Caygill, 1972, p. 90) report:

> at a time when the professional associations of the Commonwealth are combining to agree on common standards of training and entry it is unlikely that they would support attempts to introduce diversity in the system of professional training based upon local conditions and national requirements.[17]

Even those who call for 'localization' of qualifications do not necessarily have indigenization in mind. Dr. Robert Gardiner in a lecture at the University of Nairobi in 1973 (Gardiner, 1973) drew attention to the

> advantage in establishing relations and equivalents with world-wide recognized professional associations... In practice... a localization policy does not necessarily mean a radical break with established links with counterpart institutes overseas nor a complete abandonment of existing curricula, syllabuses and instructional material.

Significantly, in the context of our discussion of differing patterns of change in wage and salary structure, the only country which has made even gestures in the direction of indigenizing its education and training system is Tanzania. Swahili has been introduced as the medium of instruction in primary schools, academic qualifications and curricula have been indigenized as well as localized, and while the university might still be described as the most conservative institution in the country it has done more to adapt itself to the needs and resources of the economy than other African universities.[18] All this falls far short of insulating the Tanzanian market for high-level manpower from the international market, but it is at least a step towards resolving the emerging contradictions between government policy and international pressures.

There is in any case another aspect of the international market in skills, rather neglected in earlier papers on this subject.[19] The operations of multi-national corporations (MNCs), and to a lesser extent international organizations,[20] have in effect made it possible for the educated to take part in the brain drain without leaving their country, giving further support to bureaucrats' salaries. Different African countries are affected to varying degrees by this. The data needed to illustrate the differences—perhaps the MNCs employment of qualified manpower as a proportion of the total—are not available. The best we can do is to show net foreign direct investment as a proportion of gross fixed capital formation in recent years, as in Table 6.

The figures, although they hide a multitude of variations in composition (Nigeria's oil, Sierra Leone's diamonds, Zambia's copper, etc.), probably do give a fair picture of the extent to which these African countries have differed in their ability or desire to

Table 6

*Net foreign private direct investment as a
proportion of gross fixed
capital formation*

Ghana*	(1967–70)	7
Kenya	(1967–72)	14
Malawi	(1967–72)	13
Nigeria	(1967–70)	20
Sierra Leone	(1967–70)	16
Tanzania*	(1967–72)	0.02
Uganda*	(1967–69)	1
Zambia	(1967–69)	3

* Net private long-term capital inflow.
Sources: IMF, *Balance of Payments Yearbooks*; UN, *Yearbooks of National Accounts*, supplemented by national sources.

attract transnational capital. Thus Nigeria, Sierra Leone, Kenya and Malawi can be said to have followed a particularly MNC-based strategy, while Zambia is a special case, with the domination of the copper mining industry over the economy in general and the market in high-level manpower in particular not being reflected in recent investment figures.[21]

The predicted effect of a heavy MNC presence on changes in salary differentials will depend on what procedure foreign companies follow in setting their salaries. There is no argument about the fact that the private sector, and MNCs in particular, pay higher salaries for equivalent qualifications and experience than does the public sector. For instance, the median salary of a general manager in twenty-seven private firms surveyed by the Nigerian National Manpower Board in 1972 (Lagos, 1973) was £N4,500 compared with the top of the civil service salary scale at that time of £N3,850. Moreover, salaries in the larger firms which would include most of the MNCs were even higher, and fringe benefits were greater in the private than in the public sector. Langdon (Langdon, 1974, pp. 69–71) quotes similar evidence for Kenya and even suggests that 'in some cases African managers in Kenya receive more for their work than MNC managers doing the same job in the U.K. or Europe'. Nor is there any doubt that civil servants are very much aware of rates of pay in the private sector. Leys (Leys, 1975, p. 196) reports, for instance, that the submissions made to the Nidegwa commission by Kenyan civil servants 'were notable for their constant repetition of a single theme, namely that unless civil servants were paid as much as private sector personnel, they would join the private sector'. He quotes, as summing up all of them, the view of the Senior Civil Servants Association that:

> if civil servant salaries do not keep in line with those in the private sector, the result will be that the Government will be unable to retain the services of its qualified and experienced staff who would drift away from their posts,[22] and the country as a whole would suffer.

The question remains, however, as to whether the MNCs base their salary policy on paying just what is necessary to bid away the required talent from the public sector or on paying an international rate for the job to a large extent regardless of local circumstances—or, as a third possibility, on the need under pressure of indigenization policy to compete *with each other* for scarce managers. The answer to this question is obviously crucial to the power of a government to implement a policy of restraint on top salaries.

The conventional wisdom among salary commissioners has usually been in favour of the first hypothesis that it is the public sector which sets the pace. For instance, the Millar-Craig commission for Kenya in 1967 (Nairobi, 1967, p. 24) felt that:

> the loss of some high-level manpower to the private sector because of higher salary levels there is inevitable; since Government is the largest employer of such manpower, the private sector will always pay a higher salary in order to bid the needed personnel away from Government. If Government raises the salaries of these people the private sector will follow, and the result will be a general movement upward in the level of their salaries without much change in the pattern of allocation.

Similarly the Ani commission for Uganda in 1963 (Kampala, 1963, p. 27) quoted 'evidence to show that it is the level of salaries in Government Service that determines the general salary pattern,' a view endorsed by Knight (Knight, 1967, p. 249) who suggested that:

> firms probably pay whatever corresponding civil servants receive plus an addition to attract staff of high calibre. Therefore a cut in civil service salaries would lead to a corresponding cut in private sector salaries.

However, in recent years not only has MNC penetration of African countries increased[23] but there is evidence to suggest that they have designed their salary policy with a view to creating a world-wide cadre of company men. Business International, which might be called the house journal of the MNCs, reported on May 18, 1973 the general emergence of 'a unified salary structure, the gradual elimination of multiple allowances and the concept that any given job is 'worth' a given amount regardless of the nationality of the incumbent'. That this might be an emergent trend is supported by Langdon's work in Kenya. He found that '25 of the 81 firms surveyed—including 13 of the 31 large subsidiaries (with over £1 million cap. emp. in Kenya)—clearly followed a policy of equating salary levels for similar managerial jobs throughout the world firm—regardless of local labour market conditions. Some subsidiaries without such an explicit policy sometimes nevertheless paid Kenyan managers the same—or even more—than similar managers in a home-base country' (Langdon, 1974, footnote 46).

We are not here really concerned with the argument as to whether high salaries are 'justified' on productivity grounds. Such arguments are usually circular. From the point of view of the MNCs' objectives such salaries are obviously justified. But from the host country's point of view alternative non-MNC means of achieving its own objectives are available which would not need to involve creating a cadre of managers paid at international rates. Moreover, while the assumption that MNCs are profit-maximizers is plausible, their profits are usually highly protected. In effect governments by protecting MNCs are contributing to their ability to pay high salaries.

At any rate if it is the case that MNCs are pace setters in the process of salary determination we might expect that those countries which follow a particularly MNC-based strategy would also be those where top civil servants can argue their way to particularly large salary increases; or, to put it the other way round, that it would be particularly difficult in such countries for a government to implement a policy of salary restraint. A comparison of Tables 4 and 6 is far from constituting a test of such a hypothesis but the fact that Kenya, Zambia and Sierra Leone show the largest increase in the ratio between top and bottom salaries and Tanzania by far the smallest suggests that further investigation along these lines might be worthwhile.

The crude aggregate data of our tables can perhaps be more easily assessed if they are summarized in a single table. Table 7 accordingly ranks the eight countries by size of increase recorded in the ratios between graduate-entry salary and the lowest point on the scale between 1963–1964 and 1971–1972 and summarizes the relevant information in each case.

The pattern is not perfect (among other things, Nigeria is perhaps ranked surprisingly low)[24] but our hypotheses seem to retain sufficient plausibility to be worth carrying into further investigation.

Table 7
Summary of data

	Graduate entrants' premium 1963–64/1971–72	Demand growing faster than supply?	Progress towards indigenization of education and training?	Extent of MNC presence
Zambia	Large increase	Yes	None	Heavy*
Kenya	Large increase	No	None	Heavy
Sierra Leone	No change	Possibly	None	Heavy
Malawi	No change	No	None	Heavy
Ghana	No change	No	None	Moderate
Uganda	Fall	No	None	Small
Nigeria	Fall	No	None	Heavy
Tanzania	Large fall	No	Some	Negligible

* but not reflected in capital inflow data of Table 6.

To summarize, the suggestion is: that the extent to which top civil servants are able to argue successfully for salary increases depends less on changes in the local supply and demand situation than on the extent to which the educated are tied into the international market for professional skills by a non-indigenous education and training system and by a large MNC presence.

In any further investigation, rather than indulge in cross-country comparisons, it would seem to be useful to look in detail at the historical experience[25] of one or two countries, with Tanzania as the obvious yardstick. It would be necessary also to set the study in a wider framework than the one that has been presented so far. In such a framework[26] changes in salaries would be important not only for their effect on income distribution but as part of the process of class formation. We seem to be witnessing a syndrome in which the 'bourgeoisie of the civil service' (Fanon's (Fanon, 1965) phrase to make Marxists wince) gain support for their high rewards from the new bureaucrats of the MNCs, aided by the foreign orientation of the education and training system. The resulting polarization of income distribution confirms the orientation of consumer demand towards the products of the MNC-led sector. These products are not just import substitutes but 'import reproductions', which imply the use of a protected capital-intensive technology and the creation of a privileged salariat in the way already outlined. The high rewards of the few (and the use of qualifications as criteria for access to those rewards) encourage an explosive expansion in schooling[27] and a high rate of rural-urban migration, intensified by the urban-MNC-oriented infrastructural expenditure of the state and the aid agencies. The ranks of the urban 'informal sector' (seen in Sunkel (Sunkel, 1973) terms as the disintegrative consequence of MNC-based modernization favoured by the state) are swelled, and the sector is further depressed by direct state harassment.

The protection of the 'formal' import-reproducing sector, implying negative effective protection of local capital-goods and exporting industries, build in, firstly, a chronic tendency towards balance-of-payments crises; and, secondly, continued dependence on the export of primary products (often an MNC-penetrated activity), from which the surplus for the support of the bureaucrats, the education system, etc. is derived. There is a symbiosis between MNCs and bureaucrats, based on the MNCs' need for political protection and the benefits, direct and indirect, which the bureaucrats derive from an MNC-based strategy. Moreover, within such a framework the vital connection between the process of income distribution and class formation and the pattern of capital accumulation becomes clearer. As part of their symbiotic relationship with the MNC, bureaucrats take measures to protect its profits, back it up with infrastructural investment, allow it access to local private and public finance and provide a market for the goods it produces. This both supports the MNC's ability to pay high salaries (to the benefit of the bureaucrats) and increases the return on MNC investment. The high salaries of the bureaucrats are not entirely consumed, but provide scope for 'investment' in land, property and retail and wholesale trade. They also act as signals diverting surplus from capital accumulation to schooling. And, of course, the payment of high salaries in itself represents a diversion of surplus from accumulation. Thus a study of inequality of personal incomes, far from drawing attention away from capital accumulation, becomes central to an explanation of its pattern.

At any rate, while further investigation of the international transmission of inequality would concentrate on the relationships emphasized in the earlier part of this paper, the hypothesized links with the remainder of the framework would need to be borne in mind. In this respect the use of the word 'syndrome' is not accidental. Even on such a cursory inspection as has been possible here, Tanzania's experience vis-à-vis the other African countries raises the suggestion that a move towards on egalitarian policy may be a matter not so much of manipulating a number of continuous variables as of moving from one structure to another. If it is indeed the case that inequality and dependence reinforce each other in the way outlined above then it is a situation which will not be amenable to piecemeal reform.

NOTES

1 e. g., Jolly and Seers (1971), Bienefeld (1972–3), Godfrey (1970).
2 Of which Glaser's (1973) is the latest and most ambitious.
3 The World Bank, in particular, is pursuing this interest, to the extent of participating in the preparation of a book entitled *Redistribution with Growth* (1974).
4 With thanks to Sarah Fildes who assisted with data collection.
5 In Tanzania, for instance, all 'leaders' are required to renounce all secondary sources of income. See Bienefeld (1972–3).
6 Fringe benefits for senior civil servants are still exceedingly generous. The most striking example comes from a country not in our sample, Mauritius, where a salary commissioner noted in 1967 that the provision of nine weeks' overseas leave with free passages for civil servants was costing the country $0.8 million a year and cutting the average working week to three days. He recommended the retention of overseas leave for 'senior officers' however! (1967).

7 Bienefeld writing in 1971 (1972–3) calculated that the ratio between the top salary and the lowest point in Tanzania would be reduced by over a third if income tax were taken into account. Since then Tanzanian income tax has been made even more progressive. In other countries after-tax and before-tax differentials would be closer together. See Westiake (1971) on Kenya.

8 In Zambia the 1971 salary increase for top civil servants was accompanied by a reduction in fringe benefits, which affects comparability with other countries.

9 This may seem to contradict the myth of the 'too high' wage but should be interpreted with caution since we are talking about the lowest point on a scale rather than average wage.

10 See Knight (1967) for a useful discussion of these issues and King (1973) for a strong statement of the scarcity-rent hypothesis.

11 Assuming that substitution of educated manpower for other factors of production as a result of changes in relative prices has not been significant.

12 All this is not to deny that there is an overall shortage of indigenous graduates nor that there are particularly acute shortages of particular categories of educated persons. But in a 'scarcity' rent theory the employment of expatriates presumably serves to reduce excess demand. And non-specialist civil servants are not one of the categories of which there is an acute shortage.

13 See Prewitt (1972).

14 For an interesting attempt at such an explanation for Kenya and Tanzania see Cliffe (1973).

15 i.e. provision which gives no advantage to one class over another or to one region over another (e.g. through the more effective schools being available only to those able to pay higher fees or through the concentration of schools in particular areas).

16 Slightly more complicated is the existence in many African countries of a lucrative local market for private professional services. The high incomes available in private practice have something to do with the international negotiability of professional qualifications, but also with the combination of a sizeable number of people and firms able to pay for such services at international rates and a limited number of practitioners. They are, therefore, in the nature of feedback mechanism, since they both derive from and support the high incomes of the state salariat.

17 A desire for transnational uniformity of standards is, however, often combined with a desire for national control of institutions, e.g. the break-up of the University of East Africa.

18 This has inevitably brought complaints of a lowering of academic standards. For instance, the *Standard* (Nairobi) of 5 September 1974, describes a report of a joint committee of university authorities and students, in which 'eleven departments are listed which are short of staff' and which 'gives instances of a drop in academic standards partly caused by low calibre teaching'.

19 Seers (1970) mentions the fact that 'local employees of foreign companies who are promoted as part of 'localization policies also receive these [expatriates'] salaries' as 'another type of link' but does not give it central importance.

20 The movement of African bureaucrats to overseas-based jobs in international organizations has long been familiar. In some countries this has been supplemented by a significant drain to locally-based jobs. For instance, the Permanent Secretary in Kenya's Ministry of Finance has recently been seconded to the Nairobi headquarters of the UN Environment Programme as economic adviser. In Tanzania a similar role is played by the East African Community.

21 See the 1969 Turner Report (1969), particularly Ch. XII, for a discussion of this point.
22 In fact, 230 higher level civil servants, including two Permanent Secretaries and a number of planning officers, resigned from the Kenyan Civil Service to join private firms in 1965–1970 (1971, pp. 35–36).
23 Certainly in, at least, the cases of Kenya, Nigeria and Malawi of the countries in our sample.
24 Perhaps because of the period chosen for the comparison.
25 'Historical experience' here would include experience of colonial penetration. The 'colonial heritage' is more than just a starting-point since it shapes post-independence responses and possibilities.
26 The obvious debt of this framework to the work of others, particularly Weeks (1973) and Langdon (forthcoming), is acknowledged.
27 The important role of the education system in all this should be noted. By its foreign orientation it helps to stretch out salary distribution and its qualifications determine position in that distribution. Bureaucrats, who are in a position to ensure differential benefit to their families from this process, may be unwilling to change it even though it results in the diversion of a large proportion of the economy's surplus towards the education system.

REFERENCES

Bienefeld, M. A., 1972–3, 'Planning People', *Development and Change*, IV, 1.

Chenery, H., *et al.*, 1974, *Redistribution with Growth*, Oxford.

Cliffe, Lionel, 1973, 'Underdevelopment or Socialism? A Comparative Analysis of Kenya and Tanzania', *IDS (Sussex) Discussion Paper No. 33*, October.

Fanon, Frantz, 1965, *The Wretched of the Earth*, London.

Gardiner, Robert, 1973, 'Local Professional Qualifications', *East African Management Journal*, 7, 4, September.

Ghana (Mills-Odoi), 1967, *Report of the Commission on the Structure and Remuneration of the Public Services in Ghana*, Accra.

Glaser, William A., 1973, *The Migration and Return of Professionals*, Colombia University Bureau of Applied Social Research.

Godfrey, E. M., 1970, 'The Brain Drain from Low-Income Countries', *The Journal of Development Studies*, April.

International Labour Office, 1970, *Towards Full Employment*, Geneva.

International Labour Office, 1971, *Matching Employment Opportunities and Expectations*, Geneva.

International Labour Office, 1972, *Employment, Incomes and Equality, a Strategy for Increasing Productive Employment in Kenya*, Geneva.

Johnson, Terence J. and Marjorie Caygill, 1972, *Community in the Making: Aspects of Britain's Role in the Development of Professional Education in the Commonwealth*, University of London, Institute of Commonwealth Studies, December.

Jolly, Richard and Christopher Colclough, 1972, 'African Manpower Plans: and Evaluation', *International Labour Review*, 106, 2–3, August-September.

Jolly, Richard and Dudley Seers, 1971, 'The Brain Drain and the Development Process', *IDS (Sussex) Discussion Paper No. 3.*

Kenya, Ministry of Finance (Millar-Craig), 1967, *Report of the Salaries Review Commission*, Nairobi.

Kenya (Ndegwa), 1971, *Report of the Commission of Inquiry, Public Service Structure and Remuneration Commission*, Nairobi.

King, John, 1973, 'Fiscal and Incomes Policy for Employment, Incomes and Equality', paper for Study Seminar on Strategies for Increasing Productive Employment in African Countries.

Knight, J. B., 1967, 'The Determination of Wages and Salaries in Uganda', *Bulletin of the Oxford University Institute of Economics and Statistics*, August.

Langdon, Steven, 1974, 'The Multinational Corporation (MNC) Sector in the Kenyan Political Economy, Carlcton University, mimeo.

Langdon, Steven, 'The Political Economy of Dependence: Notes Towards an Analysis of Multinational Corporations in Kenya', *Journal of East African Research and Development*, forthcoming.

Leys, Colin, 1975, *Underdevelopment in Kenya: the Political Economy of Neo-Colonialism*, London.

Mauritius (Gardner-Brown), 1967, *Report of the Salaries Commission*.

Nigeria (Elwood), 1966, *Report of the Grading Team on the Grading of Posts in the Public Services of the Federation of Nigeria*, Lagos.

Nigeria, National Manpower Board, 1973, *The Remuneration of Management in the Private Sector, 1972*, Manpower Studies No. 12, Lagos.

Prewitt, Kenneth, 1972, 'The Functional Justification of Inequality and the Ndegwa Report: Shaping an Ideology', paper for East African Universities Social Science Conference, Nairobi.

Seers, Dudley, 1970, 'The Transmission of Inequality', in Robert K. A. Gardiner *et al.*, *Africa and the World*, Addis Ababa.

Sunkel, Osvaldo, 1973, 'Transnational Capitalism and National Disintegration in Latin America', *Social and Economic Studies*, 22, 1 March.

Sunkel, Osvaldo and Edmundo Fuenzalida, 1974, 'Transnationa-

lization, National Disintegration and Reintegration in
Contemporary Capitalism: an Area for Research', *IDS (Sussex)
Internal Working Paper No. 18.*

Uganda, Ministry of State (Ani), 1963, *Report of the Uganda Civil
Service Salaries Commission*, Kampala.

Uganda (Mayanja), 1966, *Report of the Board of Inquiry into a Claim
for a Rise in Salaries of 'E' Scale Public Officers*, Kampala.

Weeks, John, 1973, 'Imbalance between the Centre and the
Periphery and the 'Employment Crisis' in Kenya', unpublished
paper.

Westlake, M. J., 1971, 'Kenya's Extraneous and Irrational System
of Personal Income Taxation', *IDS (Nairobi) Discussion Paper
No. 101.*

Zambia (Turner), 1969, *ILO Report to the Government of Zambia on
Incomes, Wages and Prices in Zambia: Policy and Machinery*,
Lusaka.

Table 8

Actual civil service salaries and GDP per head, 1963–64 and 1971–72

	Top of Scale		Graduate entry point		Bottom of scale*		GDP per head	
	1963–64	1971–72	1963–64	1971–72	1963–64	1971–72	1963–64	1971–72
Ghana (N ¢)	7,600	8,820	1,360	1,608	214	252	188	262
Kenya (K £)	3,200	4,584	798	1,128	120	135	39	56
Malawi (M £)	2,900	2,800	700	749	132	141	40	62
Nigeria (N £)	3,900	3,900	762	762	105	129	33	40
Sierra Leone (Le.)	5,700	6,500	1,368	1,368	216	228	105	147
Tanzania (T £)	2,600	2,520	702	739	108	162	27	36
Uganda (U £)	3,000	3,500	798	798	90	111	23	49
Zambia (Z £)	3,400	4,500	875	1,386	78	102	70	142

* or minimum wage in the capital city, whichever is the higher.

Sources: as for Tables 6 and 7.

PART THREE

THE NATION STATE: IMPACT AND RESPONSE

9

THE STATE, MULTINATIONAL CORPORATIONS AND NATURAL RESOURCES IN LATIN AMERICA

Carlos Fortín

A good deal of the current discussion on the relationship between multinational corporations and the peripheral state in the area of natural resources[1] is framed in terms of models of bargaining. Such models identify two actors—the MNC and the 'host country'— whose behaviour is assumed to be utility-maximizing and whose interests, while conflicting, are seen as not necessarily incompatible. They then proceed to ask questions such as, What are the possible joint-maximization outcomes in the interaction? What is the bargaining strength of the actors? and How do different bargaining strategies affect the outcome? Two main strands within this approach can be identified: one, which has been labelled 'static', is based on game theory and the theory of bilateral monopoly (Moran, 1974, pp. 158ff; Mikesell, 1971, pp. 40ff); another, which is dynamic and more influential, is discussed in this article.

The basic variables in the dynamic bargaining model of foreign investor-host country relations in natural resources are: the bargaining assets of both actors; their perceptions of goals and possibilities of achieving them; their knowledge of the substantive elements of the relationship—i.e. the operation of the extractive industry in question—and of the bargaining process itself; and the way in which all three—power, perspectives and knowledge— change in a more or less predictable manner.

Whether applied to the operation through time of a single concession, or to the various relationships between the host government and foreign investors, or to general trends in the terms of new concessions, the model suggests that at the beginning of the relationship it is the foreign investor who is in a position of strength through his control over capital, technology and markets; he is also keen to use his advantage in order to get maximum privileges in view of the risk involved in committing substantial capital to a venture that he perceives uncertain both in terms of its economic profitability and its political life expectancy. On the other hand, the host government's eagerness to put the country's natural riches to good

205

use is matched only by its acute awareness of its inability to do so without the foreign investor. Hence the 75-year concession, with no serious obligations for the investor. However, as soon as operations start—as soon as the prospective deposit is confirmed as economically valuable, oil starts to flow or minerals to surface, and profits begin to show—then the bargaining strength position is reversed and the perspectives change. It is now the investor, who has sunk his capital, who is more or less at the mercy of the host government: he can be taxed, subjected to regulations of various kinds and in the last resort expropriated. The risk has, furthermore, either disappeared or been considerably reduced, and the government begins to find the original terms of the concession excessive. It is at this point that the government will request and, if necessary, impose a revision of the terms. When next time round the same or another investor is called upon to expand the operation, or to extend it downstream into more processing, or to introduce new technology, the relative power positions and the corresponding perspectives are reversed again, only to swing back once more when the investment is sunk and profitable.

The process, however, is not simply cyclical. For one thing, the advantages of the international firms generally have a tendency to be eroded through time, as technology becomes standardized and disseminated, patents expire, capital markets develop and become more competitive—including 'aid' markets—and production and marketing know-how becomes available on a for-hire basis. For another, each host government undergoes a cumulative learning process on the basis of its own experience in successive negotiations, of diffusion of relevant knowledge generally and, perhaps less commonly, of sharing bargaining experience with other host governments. The government becomes increasingly capable of handling the foreign investor and indeed the industry itself, and its bargaining strength is commensurately higher. Finally, cumulative trends affect the perspectives of the host government in the direction of emphasizing the need to change to its advantage the terms of the relationship with the foreign investor; the inevitable growth of contact between the foreign enclave and the economy and the legal system of the country makes for difficulties and tensions that require adjustment; fiscal budgetary needs associated with development call for an evergrowing claim on the proceeds of the foreign operation; and the sense of dependency that the latter creates fosters feelings of nationalism.

So, the model predicts that the cyclical and reciprocal pattern of strength and weakness for the foreign investor and the host government will be reflected in the changing terms of their relationship through time, but within an overall cumulative trend for the host government to increase its share of benefit from the relationship (Moran, 1974, pp. 157 – 69; Vernon, 1967, pp. 81 – 90, 1971; Mikesell, 1971, pp. 35ff; Smith and Wells, 1975).

The preceding explanation is valuable in that it helps demystify the notion of the sanctity of the concession contracts: by emphasizing the power context in which they are initially entered into and in which they operate, it exposes their fallacious claim to moral and legal immutability. This assessment is especially significant considering that the main exponents of this approach are committed supporters of capitalism and, on the whole, of the multinational enterprise as a vehicle of progress and development.

Further, it goes some way in helping to understand the changes that are taking place in the international political economy of natural resources in the 1970s. Its weakness lies in its failure to relate the abstract power and learning processes it describes to the concrete contemporary development of the world capitalist system and its implications for the natural resource industries. It does not place the relations between foreign investors and host governments within the context of the changing relations between the centre and the periphery of the capitalist system, and their 'internal' expression in the latter. Thus, the objectives and interests of the foreign investors appear unrelated to those of the larger system of which they are a part, as well as to the particular national objectives and interests of their individual home economies and governments. Conversely, it assumes—*qua* model, i.e. as far as the generalizable and predictable behaviour of the actors is concerned—that the host countries are homogeneous actors trying to maximize through time the benefits to the local economy deriving from foreign investment, and progressively achieving this goal through a strengthening of their bargaining power and their knowledge. Such an assumption, while rightly pointing to the bargaining assets available to, and the learning process undergone by, the governmental decision-makers involved as significant variables, impoverishes the analysis by excluding systematic reference to the internal structure and development in those countries; the changes in the economic infrastructure, in the class structure and in the political forces of the periphery of capitalism as they relate to the development of the capitalist system worldwide.[2]

It can, however, be argued that the basic elements for understanding the contemporary international political economy of natural resources in terms of the emergence of nationalism in the underdeveloped world and the responses of international capital are given by understanding the structural changes that have taken place both in the centre and in the periphery of the world capitalist system after World War II. To these we shall now turn our attention.

A HISTORICO-STRUCTURAL APPROACH

It is, of course, well known that the world capitalist system experienced a major restructuring after the Second World War, in response both to tendencies that had appeared before the conflict and to developments resulting from it. Several of those major changes have a direct impact on the international political economy of natural resources.

To begin with, the trend towards increased dependence of the industrialized world on industrial raw materials from the underdeveloped countries is being countered by another trend inherent in the capitalist mode of production: that towards the development of the productive forces and technical progress which was further accelerated by the requirements of the war economy. This has resulted in a tendency for the raw material content of the finished products of the industrialized economies to decline, as the technological content tends to increase; it has also made possible a massive expansion in the use of synthetic substitutes, most notably plastics, thus further reducing the need for natural resources generally (in relative terms). Technical progress has, moreover, contributed to reducing the need for industrial raw materials from the underdeveloped world by increasing the availability of them in the developed countries. Advances in the techniques of exploitation of low-grade ores have transformed hitherto neglected areas of the industrialized world into economically viable conventional mineral deposits, as is the case with copper reserves in the United States, Canada and Australia, for instance. Unconventional sources of minerals and metals are being explored, such as seabed manganese nodules, that appear to be a potentially important source of nickel, among other materials, and high-aluminia clays, that can replace bauxite as a source of aluminium and are abundant in the United States. Significant improvement has also been achieved in the recovery and re-cycling of used metal; the great bulk of the potentially reusable metal of the world is, of course, in the industrialized countries. The general trend has been reinforced by the emergence of the United States as the centre of the capitalist system. The U.S. is comparatively more self-sufficient in natural resources than the European countries and, although its net requirements of natural resource imports seem to have grown as a percentage of domestic consumption, for a number of materials the opposite is actually the case.

This is not meant to suggest that the developed world no longer needs primary products from Africa, Asia and Latin America; a substantial part of the industrial raw material requirements of the developed economies still come from the so called Third World, and in one crucial area—that of energy—the degree of dependency has, if anything, increased in recent years.[3] The point is that we are assuming that the concrete behaviour of various agents in the capitalist system (firms, governments) is determined in the last analysis by the logic of the system as a whole, and that the latter will express itself not in spite of, but rather, through the contradictions, counter-tendencies and circumstantial determinations that the process will exhibit at any given point in time. The relative reduction of the dependence of the industrialized world as a whole on underdeveloped countries' raw materials, points to a trend in the logic of operation of capitalism in the period under consideration and is therefore a necessary part of the explanation of concrete empirical phenomena which does not exclude major variations in the degree of self-sufficiency of various developed economies (Japan, for instance, is singularly lacking in most industrial raw materials), and periods of intense competition for privileged access among governments and firms.

One of its expressions is a shift in the locus of capital accumulation away from the extractive industries and towards the technology intensive sectors of manufacturing and service industries, a point illustrated in Table 9 which shows the relative decrease in U.S. domestic expenditure in new plant and equipment in the mining industry in the period 1950–74, and compares it with the spectacular increase of expenditure in the communications industry for the same period. A parallel decrease is shown by available figures on capital

Table 9

*United States: Expenditure in new plant and equipment
in the mining and the communication industries
as percentages of total expenditure*
(five-year averages)

	1950–54	1955–59	1960–64	1965–69	1970–74
Mining	4.5	4.4	3.3	2.5	2.6
Communications	6.0	8.0	9.6	10.0	12.9

Source: Survey of Current Business.

Table 10
*Value of United States direct investment abroad in
mining and smelting*
(percentages, selected years)

	1950	1955	1960	1965	1970	1974
Developed countries	31.4	45.5	48.4	53.8	59.1	65.7
Underdeveloped countries	68.6	54.5	51.6	46.2	40.9	34.3

Source: Survey of Current Business.

expenditure in mining and smelting by U.S. firms in the underdeveloped countries.[4] This reflects not only the well-known general shift of U.S. foreign investment from mining and smelting towards manufactures, but also the decrease in U.S. investment in mining in underdeveloped countries as compared to investment in mining in other developed countries (Tables 10 & 11). For capitalism as a whole, therefore, the mining and smelting industries in the underdeveloped world have lost their primary interests as outlets for capital accumulation, while retaining importance as physical sources of industrial raw materials. This points to possible conflicts between central governments, interested primarily in access to supplies, and individual capitalists, interested in a continuous flow of profits.

The development of contemporary capitalism has also created the conditions for a redefinition of centre-periphery relations in natural resources that can satisfy the individual capitalist. As the contemporary agent of world capitalist expansion is the vertically integrated multinational corporation, the individual capitalist has acquired the ability to transfer the locus of profits from one stage of the productive process to another, and to recapture the capacity to derive monopoly rents by concentrating on the stages where it retains monopoly control over technology. In addition, new forms of surplus extraction have been developed that can satisfy national-

Table 11
*US direct investment abroad: distribution of
net capital outflows and undistributed subsidiary
earnings in mining and smelting*
(percentages, ten-year averages)

	1950–59	1960–69	(1970–74)
Developed countries	50.6	72.3	(90.1)
Underdeveloped countries	49.4	27.7	(9.9)

Source: Survey of Current Business.

istic feelings in the underdeveloped world without effecting any significant changes in the international sharing of surpluses or in the effective control over the industry internationally. The most important of these are:

(1) Joint ventures with the host state, with varying proportions of equity distribution. Irrespective of the percentage owned by the host state, such joint ventures often incorporate the feature that the partner in charge of the management of the operation, as well as the marketing of the product, is the foreign corporation. The distribution of profits on the basis of the shared equity is often offset by the privileged tax and duty regime accorded the joint venture, where the foreign partner would normally also have special rights in terms of repatriation of profits and income tax on distributed dividends.[5]

(2) The emergence of service contracts with foreign companies, even in the absence of any equity participation. These may refer to the management of the operation, or the procuring of inputs from abroad, or the international sales of the product, or the provision of technology, engineering, etc., or combinations of these. Through these arrangements the MNC can retain control over the industry and secure for itself a flow of surplus which is not necessarily less than what its profits would have been had it been the owner of the operation. In fact, it is becoming apparent that these are the preferred formats for the operation of MNCs in the field of natural resources in the underdeveloped world. (*Proceedings of the American Society for International Law*, 1973, pp. 227–45; Smith & Wells, 1975).

(3) Packages of finance and technology for new investments linked to sales of the future products of the venture at privileged prices. This is a particularly good solution for MNCs that are integrated downstream, such as U.S. oil companies. Agreements for the privileged supply of products to former owners also feature prominently in contemporary nationalizations of natural resource industries.

THE STATE AND NATIONALISM IN NATURAL RESOURCES

This analysis suggests that the underlying trends of the operation and expansion of capitalism after the Second World War appear to favour the emergence of forms of nationalism in natural resources in the underdeveloped world. This is not to imply that conflict will not take place whenever such nationalism asserts itself, as those MNCs involved, whose activity may be directly curtailed as a result, will no doubt derive little comfort from learning that the process is in line with deeper trends in the development of capitalism, and will on the contrary fight against nationalistic attempts. As suggested above, however, the basic trends help understand and predict the reaction of capitalism as a whole and of the governments of the central countries, as representatives of national capitalist classes. Equally crucial for the assessment of the conflicts that may occur and their likely resolution is the real meaning of nationalist resource policies in terms of the politico-economic projects and structures of political and social domination with which they are associated.

The most general framework in which to approach the latter is by looking at the reasons for the emergence of a 'natural resource ideology' throughout the Third World in the 1960s and 1970s. This has expressed itself in international declarations such as the 1962 U.N. General Assembly Resolution 1803 on Permanent Sovereignty over Natural Resources (proposed by Chile and supported by most developing countries at the time) and the initiatives of the Group of Non-Aligned Countries that resulted in the Declaration and Programme of Action on the New International Economic Order (U.N. General Assembly Resolutions 3201 (S-VI) and 3202 (S-VI), May 1, 1974) and the Charter of Economic Rights and Duties of States (U.N. General Assembly Resolution 3281 (XXIX), December 12, 1974). A curious feature of this phenomenon is the fact that it cuts across enormous differences in the economic social and political structures of the countries of Asia, Africa and Latin America, in the political projects advanced by their ruling sectors and in the political alignment of their governments in the world arena. Aside from the fact that at least some of this unanimity is explainable in terms of the intellectualness of the initiatives so far, other factors are also in operation. The development of the productive forces in the periphery of world capitalism and their corresponding effects in the level of the class struggle and in the political superstructure have given impulse to the emergence of anti-system movements that represent truly nationalistic projects and that cannot be completely ignored even in contexts in which the domination of groups co-opted by international capitalism is well established. Some of those sectors were constituted and/or strengthened in the struggle for colonial independence in Africa and Asia in the 1960s. From the viewpoint of the dominant classes, particularly in countries where natural resource industries represent a substantial sector of the economy, the needs of capital accumulation call for an increasing share of the surplus generated by the industries to be captured by the state; this process is not contradictory, indeed it is functional, with the insertion of the peripheral economy in the international circuit of capital through direct investment in the manufacturing industries. The role of the state in such cases may range from that of simply providing the essential infrastructure and supporting local capital that performs a subsidiary role to the dynamic expansion of the manufacturing MNCs, to a more direct participation in the process of capital accumulation, including the area of natural resources. The experience of the OPEC countries has no doubt strengthened the resolve of dominant sectors in the periphery whose purpose is not to break the ties with world capitalism but rather to increase their share in the distribution of surplus coming from natural resources among others, and to tighten the integration of their economies to world capitalism through foreign investment in other areas. A whole range of possibilities thus appear as concerns the policies of peripheral states towards natural resource MNCs, from those that are designed only marginally to alter the international sharing of surplus—irrespective of the rhetoric with which they may be presented—to truly revolutionary attempts to break away from dependency in natural resources.

Any concrete analysis of the relationship between the state in Latin America and the natural resource MNCs must therefore incorporate an examination of the nature of the state in the various countries considered, with a view to illuminating its concrete class character and the social project that the dominant sectors are putting forward. More specifically, the following elements may help to clarify the real significance of various government policies for natural resource MNCs and the limits that such policies have:

(1) Role, actual and/or potential, played by natural resource industries in the generation of surplus value that can be profitably capitalized. How dynamic is or can be the natural resource sector in the process of capital accumulation? Indicators would be the export *v.* domestic importance of the natural resource industries and their exchange revenue earning importance; the size of resource reserves; the linkages with the local economy; and the possibilities of downstream integration at the national level.

(2) Degree of differentiation of the productive structure and the corresponding differentiation of the class structure. What is the nature of the dominant classes? Are they agrarian oligarchies, financial, commercial or industrial bourgeoisies, or combinations thereof? What is the degree of autonomy of state bureaucracies? Conversely, what is the class composition of the popular sectors, and what their political expression(s)?

(3) What is the nature of the societal project of the dominant class?

Is it an attempt to break away from dependency ties with the world capitalist system, or to redefine a convenient form of insertion in it along the lines offered by the contemporary process of internationalization of capital? What is the role assigned to the state in the process of accumulation?

The following paragraphs will offer a very tentative first approximation to applying this type of analysis to the question of the relationship between the state in Latin America and the MNCs in natural resources.

SOME LATIN AMERICAN ILLUSTRATIONS

Many of the major initiatives to redefine the relationship between the state and natural resource MNCs in Latin America in the 1960s originated in countries undergoing a process of industrialization essentially activated by direct foreign investment but also with a substantial element of local capital accumulation and the consequent emergence of a national industrial capitalist sector, linked to the foreign sector; with a state with a certain degree of autonomy, given by the presence of a strong bureaucracy that can in some instances arbitrate among the various fractions of the dominant class; and with popular movements with a strong nationalistic ideological content. Given that the basic politico-economic project of the dominant sectors was one of reinsertion in the world capitalist system, rather than of adopting a non-capitalist path, the extent of the redefinition of the relationship with natural resource MNCs becomes a question of balancing the need to increase the local share of surplus and satisfy nationalistic sentiment with the need not to break away from the international capital circuit. The results range all the way from purely formal changes with minimal effect on either surplus sharing or control, to somewhat deeper restructurings.

Mexico, 1961

An early instance in the decade was the Mexican mining law of 1961. This essentially restricts the granting of mining concessions to companies the majority of whose capital is in the hands of Mexicans. While no provision was included to alter the ownership status of current concessions (which could have continued in foreign hands for up to 25 years after the law) extraordinary tax privileges were granted to Mexican controlled companies, amounting to a reduction of 50 per cent of the net federal portion of production and export taxes, and the right to request further reductions under special agreements. In view of the amount of the tax concessions most foreign-owned companies proceeded quickly to negotiate sales of majority interests to Mexican investors. By 1965, control of all major companies (except two sulphur companies) had been acquired by Mexicans (Wright, 1971, pp. 139–40).

Several elements are worth noting in this instance. First, in 1961 the Mexican mining industry was producing for the domestic market to a much larger extent than usual in Latin America. In fact, demands for Mexicanization grew apace with the growth of domestic demand as industrialization began in the late 1940s. By the end of the 1950s between one-fifth and one-fourth of production was being consumed by Mexican industry; it was the large Mexican industrial sector that pressed for Mexicanization in order both to have a share in the growth of the mineral industry and, most importantly, to be able to integrate upstream (Brothers, 1970, p. 16). While one manifest aim of the measure was to attract many small Mexican investors into the industry, as one observer notes 'finding Mexican buyers for their shares (was) extremely difficult for foreign companies trying to comply with the Mexicanization requirements, and with very few exceptions, control of the important mining companies has passed from a large number of foreign investors into the hands of a small group of Mexican owners' (Wright, 1971, p. 140). The true meaning of the new regime was, therefore, to transfer surpluses to the local large capitalists, not at the expense of the MNCs but rather of the state. 'Earnings on the minority interests received by the foreign companies appear to be at least as large as those realized before Mexicanization, reflecting not only tax benefit but also various fees charged the new joint ventures under management and technical assistance contracts with the former parent companies. Moreover, the funds received from Mexican investors have generally been invested in highly profitable industrial enterprises . . . presumably considerable dividends to the new domestic entrants into mining have been realized by integrating their industrial activities with raw material sources' (Brothers, 1970, p. 17). The mining law of February 1976 has not substantially changed the situation, which is one in which mining MNCs can operate without significant restrictions and with a highly privileged tax, profit- remittance and autonomy regime, provided a part of the surplus generated is transferred to the local capitalist sector (LAER, 1976).

Not surprisingly, Industrial Minera Mexicana—formerly American Smelting and Refining Company—announced, after the law became effective, that it would invest $300m in expanding its silver, copper, zinc and coal operations in Mexico (LAER, 1976).

Chile, 1967

The other major attempt at redefining the relationship between natural resource MNCs and the state in Latin America in the 1960s was the 'Chileanization' of the copper industry carried out by the Frei Government in Chile in 1967–69.[8] The context here was, of course, entirely different from the Mexican experience. In 1964, when negotiations with the American MNCs started, the Chilean economy was stagnating, after the exhaustion of the import substituting process had led to a halt in investments both by local capital and, despite the generous terms offered by the conservative Alessandri administration, also of foreign investment. In particular, the U.S. copper companies refused to embark on any major new projects as they felt their tax regime was excessively onerous. Copper, on the other hand, was a crucial sector for capital accumulation; 95 per cent of production was exported, generating about 75 per cent of foreign exchange. The Frei Government wanted capitalist development for Chile based on the modernization of agriculture and the transfer of surpluses from agriculture to industry; strong participation of the state both in creating the conditions for industrial capitalist accumulation and in the accumulation process in the basic industries; and attracting private foreign investment particularly in the manufacturing sector, as well as massive U.S. aid and credit under the Alliance for Progress. Further, it had redistributive aims, in line with the fact that the support for Frei's Christian Democratic Party included important sectors of the peasantry, the urban proletariat and the 'marginal' sectors. To this one must add the presence of a strong Marxist opposition pressing for both redistributive and nationalistic measures. Both the project, therefore, and the ideological context required an effective increase in the state share of copper revenue.

This, however, was to be accomplished not so much by means of increasing the share of the state in the existing levels of revenue but rather by means of a major investment programme that would increase production and revenue substantially over a five-year period. The presence of American MNCs was regarded as essential to the securing of finance for the programme and to its implementation, as was the necessity to offer adequate incentives for their continuing involvement. The solution was to set up joint ventures by means of the purchase by the state of a 51 per cent interest in the existing operations,[7] and to grant the new joint companies a very favourable tax regime, that would compensate the American MNCs for their divestment of a majority of the equity. The American companies would, furthermore, be in charge of the management of the operations, the procuring of imported inputs and the sales of copper in the world market, although the state would retain a supervisory role through its majority presence on the Boards, and would gradually increase its participation in the operational functions. In practice, therefore, the American MNCs retained effective control over the industry, and their share of the surplus remained basically unaltered in relative terms, while in absolute terms (due to a large increase in the world price of copper in 1967–69) it increased dramatically. This, in turn, led to a resurgence of nationalistic feeling in various sectors, including within the government party, which in the last months of the Frei Government pressed for a further redistribution of profits in favour of the state (through a preferential dividend in its favour when the price exceeds a certain level). If we relate this experience to some of the concepts suggested above and compare it with the Mexican case, the differences become apparent. In the Chilean case, the attempt was aimed at gaining for the state a quantum of participation (more apparent than real at the beginning but with a potential for growth) in an industry of crucial importance for the process of capital accumulation in the economy generally, and at increasing its share of the surpluses through an acceleration of that process in the industry (as well as satisfying nationalistic aspirations among popular sectors both in the government party and in the opposition). All this without antagonizing—in fact to a large extent at the request of—the American MNCs who would remain crucial actors in the process for some time to come. Full-scale nationalization of the copper industry by the Allende Government in 1971 impeded, of course, the consolidation of this particular form of restructuring of state-MNC relations.

THE 1970s

This model of interlocking relations between the state and MNCs in natural resource industries has become the prevailing one in the 1970s in those Latin American countries whose dominant sectors are bent on introducing a kind of dependent capitalist model of development. The forms this interlocking takes and the extent of actual state participation in the control and the surplus absorption vary. When, in Venezuela, the political project of the dominant sectors includes an element of popular mobilization in a context of democratic politics, and where mineral resources constitute by far the most crucial and dynamic sector for capital accumulation, the policy is one of nationalization, aimed at satisfying nationalistic sentiments and at increasing in real terms both state control and surplus extraction. However, in the case of the oil industry both concrete technical limitations in the ability to operate and expand the industry and to market the product, and the more general limits imposed by the need to remain in the international circuit of capital call for service agreements with the MNCs, whereby marketing of the oil is in the hands of the former owners (Exxon. Shell and Gulf); they furthermore provide technology to the nationalized companies, for which they are paid a flat fee per barrel of production. The compensation bonds are redeemable only in oil; the nationalization law also allows for the creation of joint ventures, both in new and in existing operations, a provision that was bitterly fought against by the united opposition in Congress (LEAR, 1976A). The regime of the nationalized iron industry is essentially similar to that of oil in these respects. In the case of the military authoritarian regimes, the approach towards MNCs in natural resources varies according to the political project of the power bloc, and in particular, in terms of the role assigned to the state in the process of capital accumulation. Brazil, the most consolidated of such regimes and whose hegemonic power bloc includes what has been called a 'state bourgeoisie' (Cardoso, 1975), seems to be a case in which the state will retain a significant degree of participation, and in some cases, control over natural resource industries. Thus, the normal format offered to foreign investors in minerals is that of joint ventures with state majority participation (*Business Latin America*, 1976, p. 366). In the case of oil, while exploration has been opened to foreign concerns, the draft contracts offered seem to safeguard the formal ownership of Petrobras over the fields and installations, while allowing for the signing of service contracts and the existence of production-sharing along lines similar to the Indonesian oil contracts (LAER, 1976B, p.76).

At the other extreme, the Chilean military regime, whose view of development involves a much more secondary role for the state, has apparently reverted to an open door policy for new ventures in copper, and has also opened oil exploration (until 1974 a state monopoly) to MNCs. This may well simply express the temporary predominance within the dominant sectors of the thinking of the Chicago school of economics, and may conceivably be reversed towards a more assertive role for the state in the process of capital accumulation when the limitations of the present economic project become intolerable. Significantly, the military have maintained the nationalization of the existing large scale copper industry effected by Allende, although they have paid substantial compensation to the former owners (Fortín, 1975, pp. 23–29).

A word is needed about the Allende experience with natural resource MNCs. The *Unidad Popular* model entailed a break with the American MNCs within an attempt to introduce structural changes in a socialist direction. Thus, copper was nationalized without compensation; control over both production, sales and purchases of imported inputs and over surpluses was assumed in full.[8]

The American MNCs embarked thereupon on an international offensive of legal and commercial sabotage, but one that was largely ineffective in disrupting the production or marketing of Chilean copper. It is difficult, of course, to assess the degree of success of the companies' offensive independently from the effects of the U.S. government's blockade of the Chilean economy and its 'destabilization' action, which were instrumental in determining the overthrow of Allende. It is now clear, though, that the decision of the Nixon administration to prevent the success of the Allende experiment in Chile by whatever means necessary was adopted independently of the conflict between Allende and the U.S. copper companies, such that a solution to the latter would probably not have altered the basic resolve of the U.S. government to work for the overthrow of the Popular Unity government. (United States Senate, 1976). In a number of respects, furthermore, the Chilean case was unique, in that it was always clear that the industry did not require the presence of the American MNCs either for the operation of the mines, or for marketing the copper. Even so, the policy of the Allende government was one of regarding the copper sector as the generator of surpluses that would finance the rest of the experiment; therefore the line taken was a cautious one, in which no dramatic changes were introduced either in the way in which the operation was run or in its system of external relations: the marketing arrangements under the nationalized regime remained essentially the same as when the American MNCs acted as sales agents. New ventures were invited internationally, both in copper and in other natural resources, but with arrangements that did not involve direct foreign investment or foreign control; the preferred arrangement was the kind that linked finance for a project to the future sales of the product in normal commercial terms. Despite the bad publicity that the expropriated American copper MNCs were able to create for the

Allende government, capitalists in both Western Europe and Japan—and indeed, to some extent in the United States—were prepared to come to Chile and invest under the terms offered by the Allende government.

The Allende experience with the American copper companies shows, therefore, that at least under certain assumptions regarding ability to operate the industry, a peripheral government can effect a break with natural resource MNCs without disrupting the industry concerned. The distinguishing feature here was, of course, the nature of the political project for Chile that *Unidad Popular* was trying to implement. And it is also the nature of that project—more than the conflict with Anaconda and Kennecott—that explains the ultimate destruction of the experiment by the combined forces of internal reaction and U.S. intervention.

NOTES

1 For purposes of the present discussion, 'natural resources' refers to petroleum, hard minerals and other non-renewable resources.
2 Not that the internal structures of the host countries are ignored; it is, though, that they seem to be regarded as unsusceptible of theoretical treatment, i.e. of systematic inclusion in the model in a way that will allow some predictability of behaviour. The references to these factors in the best analyses are, therefore, more or less casual as in Vernon 1967, pp. 193–201, or explicitly relegated to the empirical description of specific cases, as in Moran (1974, pp. 170). To include these elements in a theoretically meaningful way would require adopting some sort of general theory of the origins, dynamics and development of modern capitalist society. This fundamental epistemological choice is an intellectually risky step that most non-Marxist analysts of capitalism do not seem prepared to take.
3 Oil is, however, in many respects an exceptional case, because of the distribution of world reserves, the absence of substitutes, its perishable character and the fact that many of the technological innovations that save in other materials require more energy than traditional technologies or are themselves based on petrochemical derivates; even in oil, of course, the search is already on for new sources and substitutes, and there is little doubt of the likelihood of important oil-saving technological innovations in the long-run.
4 The time series of percentages of U.S. net capital outflows plus undistributed subsidiary earnings corresponding to mining and smelting in underdeveloped countries for the period 1950–74 shows a declining trend as measured by a least square regression line. The regression constant is 6.8709 and the regression coefficient is −0.2860. The original data was obtained from the *Survey of Current Business*.
5 There is wealth of literature on joint ventures in underdeveloped countries. See W. Friedmann *et al.* 1971 and Wells Jnr., 1970.

6 The best comprehensive discussion of the Frei copper policies in English is Moran, (1974), which further includes a useful bibliography.
7 For an analysis of the form of the joint venture arrangements, see Novoa, (1972) chas. 1–9.
8 For a general discussion of the nationalization of copper by the Allende Government, see Novoa, (1972). On the international aspect, C. Fortín, forthcoming.

REFERENCES

Brothers, D. S., 1970, 'Mexican Policy Towards Foreign Investment', Harvard Development Advisory Service.

Business Latin America, 1976, 'Brazilian Mining Sector appears capable of sustaining growth pace', November 17.

Cardoso, F. E., 1975, *Autoritarismo e Democratizacao,* Paz e Terra, Rio de Janeiro.

Fortín, C., 1975, 'Compensating the Multinationals: Chile and the United States Copper Companies', *IDS Bulletin*, Vol. 7 No. 1.

Friedman, W. *et al.*, 1971, *Joint International Business Ventures in Developing Countries: Case Studies and Analysis of Recent Trends,* Columbia University Press, New York.

Fortín, C., forthcoming, 'The Nationalization of Copper in Chile and its International Dynamics', in S. Sideri and B. Evers (eds)., *Chile: Structural Change in a Dependent Economy*, Nijhoff, The Hague.

Latin America Economic Report (LAER), 1976, 'Weak Mining Law in Mexico', Vol. IV No. 18, February 20.

1976A, 'Successful six months for Venezuelan oil industry', Vol. IV No. 32, August 13.

1976B, 'Questions remain on Brazilian oil contracts', Vol. X No. 19, May 14.

Mikesell, R. F., (ed.), 1971, *Foreign Investment in the Petroleum and Mineral Industries: Case Studies in Investor-Host Country Relations*, Johns Hopkins Press, Baltimore.

Moran, Theodore H., 1974, *Multinational Corporations and the Politics of Dependence: Copper in Chile*, Princeton University Press, Princeton.

Novoa, E., 1972, *La batalla por el cobre*, Editorial Quimantu, Santiago.

Proceedings of the American Society for International Law, 1973, 'Mining the Resources of the Third World: from Concession Agreements to Service Contracts', November.

Smith, N. D., and L. T. Wells Jr., 1975, *Negotiating Third World*

Mineral Agreements: Promises as Prologue, Ballinger Press, Cambridge (Mass.).

United States Senate, 1976, *Hearings before the Select Committee to Study Governmental Operations with Respect to Intelligence Activities, Vol. 7: Covert Action*, U.S. Government Printing Office, Washington, DC.

Vernon, R., 1967, 'Long-Run Trends in Concession Contracts', *Proceedings of the American Society for International Law*, April 1971, *Sovereignty at Bay*, Longmans, London.

Wells, L. T. Jr., 1970, 'Foreign Investments in Joint Ventures: Some Effects of Government Policies in Less Developed Countries', Harvard Center for International Affairs, Economic Development Report No. 167.

Wright, H. K., 1971, *Foreign Enterprise in Mexico: Laws and Policies*, University of North Carolina Press, Chapel Hill.

10

MULTINATIONAL CORPORATIONS AND THE STATE IN AFRICA

Steven Langdon

Dependency analysis in Latin America has not devoted much attention to state institutions in explaining the underdevelopment of periphery countries. In the context of Africa, however, such analytical attention is clearly essential. Under colonialism the state in Africa was an important agency by which the economic priorities of metropolitan mother-countries were implemented in African colonies; the very colonial basis of that state made it, almost by definition, an institution somewhat independent of the indigenous social structure, and oriented toward the function of connecting periphery economic activity into the wider international capitalist economy. In the post-colonial era, the African state has often maintained a rather special role, reflecting this colonial past. And this has made the state a key element in shaping African change.

This article analyses the African state role in relation to a particular aspect of the changing international economy—the growing penetration of multinational corporations (MNCs) into the manufacturing and resource-extraction sectors of periphery economies. Such penetration has been accelerating in post-colonial Africa, as in other parts of the Third World; this article analyses the long-run political impact of this trend. It is suggested that the nature of this impact is shaped by the relations evolving between MNCs and African state institutions. Indeed, the article identifies a mutual symbiosis between such institutions and the MNCs in given African nations as one critical basis of dependency in the continent.

The first section of the analysis reviews the recent debate on the role of the post-colonial state in Africa. Section two then explores the notion of MNC-state symbiosis, drawing especially on Kenyan research. Section three considers the longer-run dialectics of such symbiosis. And section four draws out the implications of this discussion for dependency approaches to African political economy.

THE STATE ROLE IN POST-COLONIAL AFRICA

In recent years, a school of thought has emerged that, drawing on a Marxian perspective, has attempted to define certain specific characteristics of state institutions in post-colonial Third World societies. Such analysts as Saul, Murray and Alavi have advanced a three-fold argument:[1] (a) that the post-colonial state is 'overdeveloped', because of its colonial role of dominating *all* indigenous social forces; (b) that this post-colonial state is now controlled by an indigenous social force, whether it be Murray's 'political class' or Saul's fraction of a petty bourgeoisie; and (c) that the particular ideological perspectives of the regimes that result are indeterminate because of the traditional ambiguity of such petty bourgeois elements toward the process of capitalist accumulation.

Colin Leys has now reviewed this analysis in skeptical terms,[2] stressing three detailed criticisms of the argument, and a wider critique of the overall approach. First, Leys attacks the idea of the 'overdeveloped' state as 'empty'; neither in terms of administrative apparatus nor of financial resources, Leys stresses, can the colonial state itself be considered 'strong' (a point particularly true, he says, in East Africa). Indeed, if the bureaucracies of post-colonial states are extensive, Leys adds, this is largely a result of post-colonial expansion, not a matter of historical inheritance. Second, Leys points out that the origins of the new African bureaucrats and politicians cannot in themselves establish that petty bourgeois elements now control the post-colonial state. Drawing on Poulantzas,[3] Leys notes that 'it is a mistake to think that the class origins, class ties or class ambitions of the individuals who compose the apparatus of the state need be the same as those of the dominant class . . .'. This reality, Leys adds, is illustrated by the African context where 'there can be little doubt that the *dominant* class is still the foreign bourgeoisie'. Petty bourgeois elements may indeed compose the bureaucracy, but the state *qua* state—in its institutional actions—may still be dominated by foreign capital. Third, Leys questions whether the elements generally included in the African petty bourgeoisie for analytical purposes (small capitalists, rich peasants and the white collar salariat) all have the same ambiguity toward capitalist accumulation as the traditional petty bourgeoisie of Marxian class analysis.

The first criticism is of most importance for purposes of this article, and so is the broad critique of the approach that Leys makes: 'this whole way of approaching the question of the significance of any state, i.e. of starting out from its structure or scope, whether inherited from an earlier situation or not, is a mistake. In order to understand the significance of any state for the class struggle we must start out from the class struggle, not the state'.

This insight is characteristically apt. Yet to start where Leys suggests, in fact, has the effect of resuscitating much of the theoretical framework which Leys seeks to demolish. To understand why this is so, consider as an example the colonial social dynamics of Kenya. There were certain ongoing conflicts evident there between a settler class and foreign capital (coming to a head most obviously in the transition to independence). But more important, basic conflict accelerated throughout Kenyan colonial history between those settlers and an indigenous population enmeshed primarily in a peasant mode of production. The former had to squeeze and destabilize that peasant mode of production to assure themselves the inputs of low-wage labour and fertile land they needed in order to accumulate capital in agriculture.[4] This critical settler ambition required that the *state* function in such a way as to assure these inputs. Similarly, the state had to fill other functions to assure the viability of the settler economy—including heavy infrastructure provision (of railways), organization of monopolistic, settler-controlled marketing co-operatives, and establishment of adjacent markets for settler output in Tanganyika and Uganda.[5] One could add that, throughout colonial history, the state had also to play a role in mitigating and managing the potential conflicts between settler and metropolitan capital.

Kenya was exceptional in the *degree* to which the state was active in structuring the economy to assure surplus appropriation from the indigenous population. But the same state organizing role was evident in other African colonies. Classic examples include the use of agricultural marketing boards to shift surplus from the peasant production sector into industry in Nigeria,[6] state coercion in French colonies like Senegal and the Ivory Coast to push subsistence agriculturalists into growing cash crops,[7] state pressure in the Belgian Congo to generate recruits for the palm-oil plantation sector,[8] and strict state agricultural regulations in Tanganyika to maintain food *and* cash crop production among the peasantry there.[9] On a formal or an informal level, it was also very common for the colonial African state to co-operate closely with the metropolitan trading companies of the respective mother-country to maintain their trade dominance in export and import flows.[10]

It is possible to subsume all of these economic functions the colonial state performed under what Lamb has called the state's 'general function of maintaining cohesion and domination (in capitalist society)'.[11] But it is more analytically useful to recognize that a *particularly wide range* of state functions was exercised in most colonial African economies. This is the point which Lamb makes in his analysis, by stressing the complexities associated with meshing

226 *The Nation State: Impact and Response*

together different modes of production in periphery economies. 'The essential point', he concludes, 'is that the state takes on the central role of managing and representing the myriad encounters and struggles between classes and agents of the different modes. The state provides economic, social and political services for capitalist penetration, orchestrates the de- and re-structuring of elements of the precapitalist mode . . ., and 'copes', so to speak, at the level of cohesion of the whole formation, with the dislocative consequences of the expansion of the capitalist mode.'

This is surely what Saul and others identify in discussing the 'centrality' of the state in colonial and post-colonial economies. To give this centrality a structural description, by using the term 'overdeveloped', *is* incorrect. But Leys is surely guilty of some oversimplification in rejecting the idea of centrality itself as an 'empty' word; 'the state', Leys says, 'is equally *important* in all class societies'. Certainly the state has a critical *general* function in all class societies—maintaining of cohesion and domination; but it would appear to have a rather particular *further* function in periphery economies, that of managing the meshing of capitalist and pre-capitalist modes of production. And that further function makes the colonial and post-colonial state more central in the direct process of surplus appropriation and capital accumulation than in advanced capitalist economies. It is in terms of state *functions*, then, not of state structures, that Saul and Murray (and Lamb) are accurate in their emphasis on the state's particularly key role in the dynamics of African political economy.

This meshing together of different modes of production has been further complicated in the post-independence period by the process of indigenous embourgeoisement taking place across Africa. Saul, Murray and others appear to be correct in seeing African nationalist movements as being led by indigenous traders, lower-level civil servants, teachers and other educated elements that are best described as a petty bourgeoisie.[12] And the post-independence period across the continent has been marked almost everywhere by a strengthening of state regulations and restrictions designed to give this petty bourgeoisie a more prominent economic position. Typically, African states have tried to funnel import trade through indigenous businessmen, to force greater use of indigenous staff in foreign-owned firms, and to promote indigenous shareholdings in new and existing enterprises.[13] This embourgeoisement process has generally made for considerable maintenance of pre-independence trade patterns with the rest of the international economy, but in an even more state-administered form than in the past. The process also *has* generated the emergence of an indigenous bourgeoisie throughout Africa.

This emerging state-dependent bourgeoisie, however, has commonly found that the same retarded class formation, which explained the relative state autonomy which permitted its embourgeoisement,[14] in turn left it highly vulnerable to attack from other petty bourgeois factions hurt by the state regulation that was taking place. This was particularly true if such opposing factions had some base in the military forces of the new states. No powerful bourgeoisie could develop to a position of socio-economic dominance; instead, coups, counter-coups and regionalized civil wars have marked the conflicts among petty bourgeois elements vying for state power. Such countries as Uganda and Benin have seen such conflict become particularly bitter or unstable, but the tendency has been there in many African political economies.

In a few African countries, the pattern has been somewhat different. In Tanzania, it would appear that the petty bourgeoisie used its post-independence autonomy to limit embourgeoisement to some degree, and to initiate relatively progressive development strategies. More significantly for purposes of this analysis, in certain other countries, a marked MNC role seems to have provided more viability to the embourgeoisement option—permitting more petty-bourgeois elements to share in the benefits of state manipulation, and neutralizing opposition from many African wage workers; at the same time, the larger MNC stake in such economies undoubtedly encouraged other metropolitan efforts to maintain and protect such regimes (via aid, military assistance, etc.). In such countries as Zambia, Gabon and Mauretania, such a marked MNC role has rested in the resource extraction sector; in other countries—Kenya, Ivory Coast and Senegal—MNC investment has been part of a change in economic structure focused around import-substituting industrialization.

In these cases, then, the successful indigenous embourgeoisement that is taking place seems to have been dependent on the heavy MNC investment that marks these countries. But what are the longer run implications of this process? Three important position can be cited, each suggesting a different answer. Warren would appear to argue that this emerging bourgeoisie is essentially independent, and will, as its capital accumulation accelerates and its bargaining skill grows, come to squeeze foreign capital more and more—generating capitalist development in the periphery.[15] Leys, on the contrary, sees the emerging bourgeoisie as 'auxiliary' to foreign capital, and expects contradictions to appear; particularly in the face of a succession crisis, these contradictions are likely to set repressed class forces in motion and could lead to overthrow of the (Kenyan) regime.[16] Sunkel, however, insofar as his analysis is applicable to Africa, would imply a much more comprehensive alliance between the emerging bourgeoisie and the MNC sector, with a 'transnational integration' that incorporates the periphery bourgeoisie more fully into international capitalism, at the expense of non-integrated majorities in the periphery.[17] Neither independent development nor immediate contradictions can be expected from the close relationship with foreign capital.

Clearly, this question of longer-run effects is a key issue in analysing ongoing class relations in periphery areas—what is the impact of MNC penetration on class dynamics? Yet, if the thrust of this section has been relevant, the state role in this context is likely to be critical—just as it is in the meshing together of different modes of production in periphery countries. This critical role is indeed suggested in the notion of symbiosis discussed in the next section.

THE MNC-STATE SYMBIOSIS

The previous section has stressed the centrality of the state role in post-independence Africa, seeing that role as crucial both in meshing differing modes of production and in regulating economic opportunities to promote indigenous embourgeoisement. This section examines the relationship between state institutions and the MNCs.

In the post-independence 1960s and early 1970s, foreign direct investment in Africa has accelerated. British direct investments, in Commonwealth Africa for instance, rose from a net asset book value of £252 million in 1966 to some £395.9 million in 1971, and have continued to increase to African countries in the statistics available for the 1972–74 period.[18] U.S. investment has also become more important in Africa, reaching a book value of close to $2.4 billion in 1975;[19] most of this investment has gone into petroleum, mining and smelting. Taking overall stocks of direct foreign investment, these increased over 1967–72 by 49 per cent in independent anglophone Africa and by 15 per cent in francophone Africa. Investments were concentrated, however, and took stocks to levels of more than $200 million in book value, in such countries as Nigeria (up 89 per cent), Ivory Coast (up 69 per cent), Gabon (up 41 per cent), Cameroon (up 40 per cent), Ghana (up 38 per cent), Kenya (up 37 per cent) and Senegal (up 37 per cent).[20] It is notable that, though new resource extraction projects have spurred increased investment flows to countries like Botswana, Guinea and Mauretania, foreign manufacturing investment has become distinctly more important across much of the continent during this period.[21] This is reflected in details of MNC dominance in the manufacturing sectors of such countries as Nigeria, Senegal, Kenya and Ethiopia.[22]

There is evidence that state actions have been crucial in many African countries in encouraging and permitting this accelerated MNC penetration. This is obvious in the case of countries in which the state has taken a leading role in negotiating conditions with companies sufficiently favourable for them to spur exploitation of a new resource deposit (as with bauxite in Guinea, or iron ore in Mauretania).[23] The same key state role has also been evident, on two levels, in the wider context of MNC manufacturing projects. First, African states have been prepared to provide the extensive import protection which MNC manufacturers have almost invariably made their priority demand; Kenyan research, for instance, showed 76% of manufacturing subsidiaries surveyed in 1972–73 having such protection, and indicated investors sought such protection more than any other privilege in entry negotiations over 1965–73.[25] Second, in their efforts to Africanize commerce, African states have pushed the traditional European trading companies on the continent into much new manufacturing investment; faced with restrictions on their trade role, these companies have often used their local knowledge and managerial expertise to diversify into manufacturing as a source of ongoing profitability.[26]

The notion of a symbiotic MNC-state relationship, though, involves more than this growing MNC role, and the contribution of the state to establishing that role. The suggestion is that in a number of African countries, MNCs have entered into a more intimate set of links with state agencies, such as to establish a mutual dependence between the two sets of institutions.

Research on MNC-state relations in Kenya has provided an outline of the defining characteristics of such symbiosis there; these include:[27] (i) considerable MNC ability to bargain out regulatory advantages for its subsidiaries, including protection from import competition from abroad, and (often) tax advantages over locally-owned Kenyan firms; (ii) close informal channels which MNC executives can use to approach state officials in the face of problems in regulation or competition; (iii) considerable state ability to bargain out accelerated managerial Africanization, African participation in product distribution, and increased local African shareholding in MNC enterprises; (iv) heavy tax revenues for the state from particular MNC subsidiaries (for example, one cigarette subsidiary alone contributed taxes in 1971/72 equal to 4.6% of the Kenyan government's entire recurrent revenues); (v) a degree of informal, illicit flow of financial favours to state personnel; and (vi) increasingly widespread state shareholding in MNC subsidiaries, often being negotiated on the initiative of the subsidiaries.

The state-MNC symbiosis in Kenya seems to involve mutual dependence; it is not the same as conventional *comprador* relationships, in which certain local officials become agents of foreign capital. The many regulatory instruments the Kenyan state can use, its other sources of resources (such as foreign aid), and the influence on it of the emerging African bourgeoisie all mean that the state has some independence *vis-à-vis* the MNC sector, and can insist on a growing African share in MNC privileges. The MNC sector, in turn, has an interest in close, co-operative relations with the Kenyan state, because of the many ways in which that state can provide subsidiaries with advantages in the local economy.

There is more involved, too, than close state-MNC ties in what is emerging in Kenya. The state is also proving to be the instrument by which the African petty bourgeoisie is being meshed into the structure of MNC enterprise—as executives, agent, directors, shareholders and suppliers. Indeed, there is evidence in many examples from this research of close links being institutionalized among subsidiaries, state institutions and local African capitalists.[28] The symbiosis emerging in Kenya integrates together the state, foreign capital and elements of local African capital in a set of increasingly important manufacturing and resource enterprises.

What is the economic and social basis of this symbiosis? Why are the multinationals able to carve out so prominent a role for themselves? And why does the Kenyan State play the role it seems to? Answers could be suggested at many levels of analysis; but two deserve emphasis in the present context.

At the level of straightforward economics of industrialization, reliance on multinationals in Kenya has resulted in high rates of profitability in Kenyan manufacturing. Subsidiaries have transferred technology from abroad in the form of differentiated, trademarked products and of fairly sophisticated processes to manufacture these; and this kind of technology transfer, especially with the state helping to offset foreign and local competition, lends itself to the accumulation of high profit, or 'monopoly rents' based on the technology and trade marks. In the 29 Kenyan manufacturing subsidiaries from which profit details were obtained in 1972/73, the after tax rates of return reached 21 per cent of capital employed (compared to overall rates in the parent firms of 9 per cent after tax). Such high profitability is a powerful incentive to the state and the local bourgeoisie to co-operate with the multinationals—insofar as those profits can be shared through the intermeshing described above. Similarly the multinationals appear to rely on local co-operation to maximize the long-run and secure profitability of technology transfer through their subsidiaries to the peripheral economy. Technology transfer and the local surplus appropriation it permits are, in short, the main focus of local-multinational bargaining. Their control of technological innovation on a world scale, plus the efficiency of the head-office-to-subsidiary channels of technology transfer,[29] are the key levers which give the multi-nationals such bargaining strength in Kenya, as in other less developed countries.

There is also a second, deeper level at which this transfer of technology by multinationals provides the basis for symbiosis. Multinational technology transfer has shaped the wider process of class formation and income determination in Kenya in such a way as to facilitate and sustain a highly unequal socio-political structure. At the same time, the income distribution associated with this structure has provided the market required for the multinationals' transfer of their consumption technology (an egalitarian income distribution would generate little demand for private automobiles where per capita income is £100 per year!). Sharing in subsidiary profits, of course, financially strengthens the emerging bourgeoisie. But the multinationals' socio-political impact goes much further than this. Multinational profits and taxes raise state revenues—which can be used to defuse periodic political protest through minimal gestures (like eliminating lower-level school fees in Kenya). More important, Kenyan evidence suggests that the highly-mechanized nature of multinational production technology helps to generate a small, relatively well-paid labour aristocracy in the country, making working-class political protest less likely.[30]

This whole process, in fact, looks very much like the pattern of 'transnational integration' that Sunkel discusses: a segment of Kenyan society is being integrated more fully into transnational capitalist production through multinational technology transfer, while most Kenyans remain excluded from the benefits of the transfer. The integration of that minority into the transnational system, though, serves to perpetuate the existing socio-political structure, through the benefits the minority clearly does enjoy.

It is possible to argue this case for symbiosis rather strongly in the Kenyan context, given the research results from there. Evidence is less specific from elsewhere. But such evidence certainly does exist.

Campbell, for instance, has carefully traced the intimate in-termeshing of state institutions and French corporations in the development of textile manufacturing in the Ivory Coast.[31] Sklar has illustrated the establishment of joint shareholding, state-organized localization of personnel, but ongoing MNC decision-making authority, in the copper sector in Zambia.[32] Evidence from the resource sector in Zaire shows growing state shareholding too, in a form which has given Belgian corporations dominant managerial control based on their monopolization of technology.[33] In Senegal, state action has also given local capitalists more participation in MNC enterprises, but appears in the process to have generated considerable bargaining advantages for the MNC sector.[34] Nigerian evidence shows even more explicit signs of developing symbiosis, particularly in the context of the Nigerian Enterprises Promotions Decree with its objective of arranging Nigerian share-holding in foreign-owned enterprises; Forrest has recently assessed the meaning of this decree:[35]

> on the whole the decree has accommodated the interests of foreign capital. It will strengthen the transnational component of the bourgeoisie, though effective control will not pass to this managerial group. . . where the state has participated with foreign capital in joint venture (oil, vehicle assembly, construction, fertilizers, cement, agro-industry), it is less indicative of a strong, productive state capitalism than the performance of a support role for foreign capital.

Symbiosis, then, seems more than a Kenyan phenomenon. State-MNC relations have emerged as the key to accelerated MNC penetration in a number of parts of Africa. This means that the state in Africa is coming to play a central role not just in the meshing together of different modes of production, and in the post-colonial embourgeoisement process—but also in the transnationalization process by which MNCs are incorporating segments of periphery economies more fully into international capitalist production. The next section examines the dynamics of this ongoing process in Africa.

THE DIALECTICS OF SYMBIOSIS

The patterns of political economic change in post-colonial Africa are far from stable. There are clearly inherent contradictions in the combined processes taking place, and these contradictions have generated social conflict that has overthrown regimes, led to civil wars, and, more rarely, shaped fairly radical change. The drive for African embourgeoisement, for instance, has complicated the difficult task of meshing together peasant and capitalist modes of production; sometimes excessive pressures from an emerging bourgeoisie have pushed the state to increase surplus appropriation from the peasantry, spurring peasant rebellions in such areas as Western Nigeria and Ghana, and peasant retreats from cash crop production in areas like Senegal. The central role of the state in organizing embourgeoisement has generated other contradictions, too, as often no petty bourgeois faction was clearly dominant in such a context, and yet the superior access of one faction to the state structure promised dominance for it in the future; under such conditions, factional conflict could escalate, often drawing on ethnic differences and pulling military factions into the fight. The resulting instability of regimes could also clash with the close state-MNC ties required for continuing MNC penetration.

In these circumstances, the state's financial basis for ongoing embourgeoisement could be eroded, and a direct clash could occur between the embourgeoisement and transnationalization processes. A frustrated petty bourgeois faction that had grabbed state power could then be forced to turn on foreign investments already in the country to try to find some ongoing basis for capital accumulation. This seems the best way to understand what has happened in Uganda, for instance.

A broad hypothesis may be applied to the analysis of these ongoing dynamics of change in black Africa. At the risk of considerable oversimplification, one can suggest that the ongoing processes of MNC penetration, African embourgeoisement and meshing modes of production have become mutually interdependent. The relatively stable and ongoing perpetuation of any one of these processes is dependent on the perpetuation of the others. Low MNC penetration, for instance, will make extensive petty bourgeois conflict more likely, thereby disrupting the meshing of modes of production. Similarly, some shock that disrupts the meshing of modes of production (as with drought in Ethiopia) can in turn be expected to disrupt embourgeoisement and MNC penetration.

It may also be suggested that a relatively strong state, somewhat independent of domestic social forces (and of foreign social forces) is critical to the successful management of these interdependent processes. The argument is: (a) that indigenous embourgeoisement, and some surplus sources from non-capitalist modes of production, can give the African state enough authority and independence *vis-à-vis*

MNCs to enforce on foreign capital a fair sharing of financial benefits with the emerging African bourgeoisie; (b) that MNC penetration can in turn give the state enough independence *vis-à-vis* this emerging African bourgeoisie to prevent the latter's destabilizing the peasant mode of production through excessive surplus appropriation; (c) that MNC penetration and sharing of revenues can provide enough extra surplus to limit factional fighting in the embourgeoisement process; and (d) that the state role in managing the mechanics of embourgeoisement and of meshed production modes can be sufficiently crucial to foreign capital's interests that MNCs are prepared to accept such a context of MNC-state co-operation rather than clear MNC dominance.

Research from Kenya suggests several further facets of such a crucial state role. Various examples were evident in that country of domestic firms entering into successful competition with the MNC sector (in the soap and shoe industries, for instance); but these successful firms appeared to require close support from the Kenyan state, through various subsidies, long-term state loans and purchase contracts from government ministries.[36] This dependence on the state has limited the likelihood of such domestic firms moving to challenge in any fundamental way the MNC-state symbiosis. The Kenyan state also seems to play an explicit role in managing and resolving MNC-bourgeoisie conflicts when they do emerge.[37] Overall, then, the somewhat independent base of the state in Kenya, and the dependence of the emerging bourgeoisie on that state, combine to limit the development of contradictions between MNC penetration and domestic embourgeoisement processes.

This effect also suggests why MNCs are willing to establish such a symbiotic relationship with various African states. In the end, the MNC sector seems able to count on the Kenyan state playing an overriding role in the political economy, managing relations between local and foreign capital, and thereby defending the long-term role of the MNCs in Kenya.

It is this that undercuts Warren's perspective on the dynamic of MNC-African business relations: it is not an independent bourgeoisie which is emerging in Kenya and *itself* manipulating the state apparatus. Rather, the state's symbiosis with the multinational sector gives it an institutional independence *vis-à-vis* that emerging local bourgeoisie, allowing the state to enforce the overriding symbiosis with foreign capital, disciplining local businessmen who move too strongly against MNC interests. Such a key state role as conflict regulator also questions the likelihood that the contradictions pointed to by Leys could emerge significantly. His 'auxiliary bourgeoisie' remains too state-dependent to extend opposition to MNCs of a kind that would create serious instabilities, while the strength of the state also guarantees that this bourgeoisie can obtain a rising share in the profits of MNC subsidiaries over time.

To return to the speculations in section one, then, the stable, ongoing embourgeoisement process in countries like Kenya, Ivory Coast, and Senegal *can* be explained by the heavy MNC penetration of those areas. In effect, as in Sunkel's model, MNC penetration has drawn the emerging bourgeoisie in those countries into partici- pation in the transnational capitalist economy, thereby generating extra benefits for that bourgeoisie—though excluding the majorities of people in those countries from such benefits.[38] The state-MNC symbiosis in those countries can be seen as critical to this process.

It seems clear that this symbiosis can be most stable in a particular context: where embourgeoisement pressure on foreign trading companies can be resolved through an import-substituting in- dustrialization process, by which manufacturing MNCs penetrate an African economy and foreign trading firms restructure their activities to become partners in that industrialization (as in Kenya or the Ivory Coast). Where resource extraction is involved, clearly any symbiosis may be less stable. In Nigeria, for instance, MNC penetration in the oil sector has become *so* extensive that it can destabilize regimes because the bourgeoisies begin to fight over the massive revenues being generated.[39] Where resource MNCs are not vertically integrated, and therefore base their corporate profitability directly on local surplus appropriation in Africa, considerable tensions can emerge in the symbiosis, with direct conflict between states and MNCs over respective shares in local resources revenues (the Zambian copper case illustrates this). The dynamics of state- MNC interaction in such situations are clearly more open to emerging contradictions in the future (perhaps in the way that symbiosis turned to conflict in the Chilean copper sector).[40]

What about the form of MNC penetration that is becoming more common in Southeast Asia and elsewhere—that involving export- oriented manufacturing?[41] Such manufacturing may lend itself even less to ongoing symbiotic stability in Africa. First, the state often has much less bargaining power against such MNCs, given competition among possible host countries, and MNC control abroad of the market channels for what is produced; thus, emerging African bourgeoisies will likely win a lower proportion of the surplus generated by such enterprises. Second, MNC export manufacturing may often depend on low-wage labour inputs; that limits the degree to which wage gains to unionized workers can be used to maintain their political acquiescence in the symbiosis, as in the import-substituting context. At the same time, export manufacturing may offset these factors to a degree, by being less likely than import-substituting to spur periodic balance-of-payments crises. Detailed research in such countries as Senegal, where MNC export manufacturing is growing, will be necessary to probe these dynamics satisfactorily.

CONCLUSION

This analysis has argued that three processes have commonly marked the changing political economy of post-colonial Africa: MNC penetration, African embourgeoisement, and the ongoing meshing of capitalist and non-capitalist modes of production. These processes have been interpreted here as mutually interdependent; and the potential contradictions among them have been identified as the cause of much of the political and economic instability that has marked the continent.

The argument has also suggested, however, that in various countries an MNC-state symbiosis has emerged, facilitating and accelerating MNC penetration in such areas as Kenya, Ivory Coast and Nigeria. This notion of symbiosis has been examined mainly in the Kenyan context, and describes the close negotiating relations, intimate informal links and widespread joint shareholdings that exist between the state and the MNC sector in Kenya; this relationship is seen to establish MNC economic privileges, which are shared with an emerging, state-dependent African bourgeoisie. The basis of this symbiosis rests on the technology transfer capacity of the MNCs, and on the Kenyan state's regulatory ability to shape domestic economic conditions so as to assure the profitability of such transfers.

This symbiosis has been seen as essential to MNC penetration in Africa. The agument is that these close MNC-state links have established a certain independence for the state structure, permitting it to manage and avoid potential conflicts between local and foreign capital.

In turn, MNC penetration can be seen as crucial to perpetuating the overall post-colonial change pattern in Africa. Such penetration provides expanding revenue possibilities for African embourgeoisement, making factional conflict somewhat less prevalent, and also allowing embourgeoisement to proceed with less heavy pressuring of the peasant mode of production.

But the socio-economic consequences of this change process do *not* conform to any notion of 'development', encompassing re-distribution with growth, the elimination of poverty or structural change toward an internally-integrated economy. These change patterns can, instead, be seen to generate trends that are counter-productive to all these goals. Rapid embourgeoisement efforts are widening inequalities in Africa; policies to improve living standards for peasant majorities are *not* becoming a development priority; and segmentation among economic sectors is becoming more pro-nounced, as some Africans are drawn into transnational capitalist production, while most remain enmeshed in non-capitalist pro-duction relations.

Thus the post-colonial changes in such countries as Kenya are resulting in *underdevelopment*, in the sense of ongoing movement away from the objectives of a more valid definition of development. MNC penetration, and the MNC-state symbiosis that supports it, can be seen as the basis of this underdevelopment.

The implication of this analysis can be examined at a number of levels. In terms of the theoretical debate over the post-colonial state, the argument tends to support Saul's position rather than Leys', by confirming the centrality of the state role in post-colonial social dynamics—but seeing the state as somewhat independent of an emerging bourgeoisie, and playing a key role in MNC penetration of the continent. This latter role, moreover, forces questioning of the arguments of both Warren and Leys on the relationship between foreign and local capital. While local capital clearly *can* move against foreign capital when state incapacity sets off some of the contradictions discussed above (as in Uganda), the more common pattern where MNC penetration concentrates seems to be a state-MNC symbiosis that counters and manages conflict between local and foreign capital.

This does not imply that the grossly unequal social polarization within countries like Kenya, Ivory Coast and Nigeria will not spark protests and political challenges in the medium-term future. The implication is simply that such challenges will, contrary to Warren, *not* be rooted in contradictions between local and foreign capital.[42]

What, finally, are the implications of this argument for de-pendency analysis? The thrust of the argument certainly supports a dependency perspective. MNC penetration and technology transfer are seen to be pulling the African state and the emerging African bourgeoisie more fully into the transnational capitalist economy, increasingly segmenting them from the majority of Africans who remain enmeshed in another mode of production. Sunkel's notion of transnational integration and national disintegration *is* reflected in what is occurring in black Africa. But the argument refines the dependence framework of analysis somewhat. The suggestion is that dependency approaches in Africa must focus explicitly on the role of the state, as a key organizing element in the symbiosis which marks post-colonial MNC penetration of parts of the continent.

NOTES

1 See J. Saul, 'The State in Post-Colonial Societies—Tanzania', *Socialist Register 1974*, (London, 1974); J. Saul, 'The Unsteady State; Uganda, Obote and General Amin', *Review of African Political Economy*, No. 5, 1976; R. Murray, 'Second Thoughts on Ghana ', *New Left Review*, 42, 1967; H. Alavi, 'The State in Post-Colonial Societies—Pakistan and Bangladesh', *New Left Review*, 74, 1972.

2 C. Leys, 'The 'Overdeveloped' Post Colonial State: A Re-evaluation', *Review of African Political Economy*, No. 5, 1976. I have presented some of the following analysis and critique of Leys previously, in 'The State and Capitalism in Kenya', *Review of African Political Economy*, No. 8, 1977.

3 See, for example, N. Poulantzas, *Classes in Contemporary Capitalism*, (London, 1975).

4 For evidence, see R. van Zwanenburg, *The Agricultural History of Kenya*, (Nairobi, 1972).

5 For evidence, see E. A. Brett, *Underdevelopment in East Africa*, (London, 1973); R. D. Wolff, *The Economics of Colonialism: Britain and Kenya, 1870–1930*, (New Haven and London, 1974).

6 See G. K. Helleiner, *Peasant Agriculture, Government and Economic Growth in Nigeria*, (Homewood, 1966).

7 See, for example, B. Campbell, 'Neocolonialism, Economic Dependence and Political Change', *Review of African Political Economy*, No. 2, 1975.

8 See M. K. K. Kabala Kabunda, 'Multinational Corporations and the Installation of Externally-oriented Economic Structures in Contemporary Africa: The Example of the Unilever-Zaire Group', in C. Widstrand, ed., *Multinational Firms in Africa*, (Uppsala, 1975), p. 311.

9 See, for example, L. Cliffe, 'Nationalism and the Reaction to Enforced Agricultural Change', in L. Cliffe and J. S. Saul, ed., *Socialism in Tanzania, Vol. 1*, (Nairobi, 1972).

10 For evidence from the Gold Coast, for instance, see R. E. Howard, 'Development and Underdevelopment in the Gold Coast: Foreign Business and the African Response, 1886–1939', *Ufahamu*, 1977.

11 G. Lamb, 'Marixism, Access and the State', *Development and Change*, VI: 2, 1975.

12 On the nationalist movement in Kenya, see C. G. Roseberg Jnr. and J. Nottingham, *The Myth of 'Mau Mau'—Nationalism in Kenya*, (Nairobi, 1966).

13 For evidence, see C. Leys, *Underdevelopment in Kenya*, (London, 1975); R. L. Sklar, *Corporate Power in an African State*, (Berkeley, 1975); T. Forrest, 'Notes on the Political Economy of State Intervention in Nigeria', *IDS Bulletin*,

9:1, 1977; World Bank, *Senegal: Tradition, Diversification and Economic Development*, (Washington, 1974), pp. 161ff; E. Siggel, Economic Development and Independence—Development Policy in Zaire', paper prepared for the conference of the Canadian Association of African Studies, 1975.

14 The notion here is borrowed from Marx and *The Eighteenth Brumaire of Louis Napoleon*; the absence of a dominant capitalist bourgeoisie, reflecting the incomplete development of capitalist production in nineteenth century France, gave the state an autonomy that left it open to capture and use by one or other emerging bourgeois factions. Leys applies this motion of 'Bonapartism' to postcolonial Kenya in *Underdevelopment in Kenya*.

15 B. Warren, 'Imperialism and Capitalist Industrialization', *New Left Review*, 81, 1973.

16 Leys, *Underdevelopment in Kenya*, chap. 8.

17 O. Sunkel, 'Transnational Capitalism and National Dinsintegration in Latin America', *Social and Economic Studies*, 22:1, 1973; O. Sunkel, 'External Economic Relations and the Process of Development: Suggestions for an Alternative Analytical Framework', in R. B. Williamson *et al.*, ed., *Latin American—U.S. Economic Interactions*, (Washington, 1974).

18 'Book Value of Overseas Direct Investments', *Trade and Industry*, Nov. 15, 1973; "Overseas Direct Investment in 1974', *Trade and Industry*, June 25, 1976.

19 O. G. Whichard and J. N. Freidling 'U.S. Direct Investment Abroad in 1975', *Survey of Current Business*, 56:8, 1976. It should be noted that this total includes large direct U.S. investments in Libya.

20 H. Hveem, 'The Extent and Type of Direct Foreign Investment in Africa', in Widstrand, *op. cit.*, p. 83.

21 See L. L. Rood, 'Foreign Investment in African Manufacturing', *Journal of Modern African Studies*, 13:1, 1975.

22 For evidence, see M. Berger, *Industrialisation Policies in Nigeria*, (Munich, 1975), pp. 161–163, R. Cruise O'Brien, *White Society in Black Africa: The French of Senegal*, (London, 1971), p. 197; L. Needleman *et al.*, *Balance of Payments Effects of Private Foreign Investment: Case Studies of Jamaica and Kenya*, UNCTAD, TD/B/C.3/79/Add. 2, 1970; UNCTAD, *Major Issues in Transfer of Technology to Developing Countries: A Case Study of Ethiopia*, TD/B/AC.11/21, 1974, pp. 31–36.

23 On the latter, see P. Bonté, 'Multinational Corporations and National Development: MIFERMA and Mauretania', *Review of African Political Economy*, No. 2, 1975.

24 For evidence of this priority, see Cruise O'Brien, *op. cit.*, p. 197; S. R. Dixon-Fyle, 'Economic Inducements to Private Foreign Investment in Africa', *Journal of Development Studies*, IV:1, 1967.

25 Reported in S. W. Langdon, 'Multinational Corporations in the Kenya Political Economy', in R. Kaplinsky, ed., *Readings on the Multinational Corporation in Kenya*, (Nairobi, 1978), Tables 12 and 17, pp. 170, 188.

26 See evidence for one of the largest such companies, Unilever's United Africa Company, in C. Wilson, *Unilever, 1945–65*, (london, 1968).

27 The details of this symbiosis are reported in full in the analysis of my research results forthcoming in Kaplinsky, *op. cit.* Examples illustrating this symbiosis are outlined in S. W. Langdon, 'Multinationals and the State in Kenya', *IDS Bulletin*, 9:1, 1977, pp. 36–41.

28 See *Ibid.*, pp. 37–38.

29 On concentrated MNC control of the research and development process, see R.

Kaplinsky, 'Technology for Development', *Scienza e Technica*, April, 1974: on the greater efficiency of MNC—subsidiary technology transfer channels, see R. E. Baldwin, 'International Trade in Inputs and Outputs', *American Economic Review*, 60:2, 1970.

30 For evidence, see A. Amsden, *International Firms and Labour in Kenya, 1945–1970*, (London, 1971).

31 Campbell, *op. cit.*

32 Sklar, *op. cit.*

33 See I. Ilunkamba, 'Conventions de Gestions et Tranfert de Technologie au Zaire: Le Cas du Cuivre', *Africa Development*, II:2, 1977.

34 See Cruise O'Brien, *op. cit.*, 'The political representation of economic influence is the principal political activity of French company directors in Senegal'.

35 Forrest, *op. cit.*, pp. 44–45.

36 See Langdon, *IDS Bulletin*, p. 38.

37 As exemplified in a conflict over inputs to the MNC shoe subsidiary in Kenya, reported in *Ibid.*, p. 38.

38 This polarization effect is discussed further in E. M. Godfrey and S. W. Langdon, 'Partners in Underdevelopment? The Transnationalization Thesis in a Kenyan Context', reprinted in this volume.

39 That such extensive MNC penetration *destabilizes* the Nigerian state is argued by T. Turner, 'Multinational Corporations and the Instability of the Nigerian State', *Review of African Political Economy*, No. 5, 1976.

40 On the Chilean dynamic, see T. Moran, *Multinational Corporations and the Politics of Dependence*: Copper in Chille, (Princeton, 1974).

41 See B. I. Cohen, *Multinational Firms and Asian Exports*, (Yale, 1975).

42 The potential basis of class and regional conflict more likely to challenge growing Kenyan inequalities is explored in S. W. Langdon, 'Kenya and African Development Patterns', *Canadian Journal of African Studies*, 9:4, 1975.

11

PUERTO RICO 1948–1976: THE LIMITS OF DEPENDENT GROWTH

José J. Villamil

INTRODUCTION

For many years Puerto Rico had been the model proposed for the rest of the underdeveloped world by the United States and some of the international agencies.[1] Many well known economists and social scientists had also referred to the Puerto Rican development experience in positive terms, some equating it with the Chinese Revolution in importance (Boulding, 1961). Others have utilized the experience of Puerto Rico as the basis for making more general statements on development policy and planning (Meier, 1965; Baer, 1959; Galbraith, J. and Solo, C., 1953; Chenery, 1961). It is not difficult to see why the Puerto Rican experience has enjoyed such admiration not only from government and international organizations, but also from academic observers. To a large extent it seemed to prove correct all the prescriptions of orthodox economics for achieving very rapid rates of growth: (1) Development was based on the postulates of free enterprise Capitalism, including free trade between countries. There are no restrictions on trade between the United States and Puerto Rico, and neither are there obstacles to the mobility of factors of production. In effect, Puerto Rico, could almost be considered a region of the United States. (2) There are no restrictions on foreign investment, direct or indirect. On the contrary, the development process has relied on foreign capital and technology, as well as foreign markets and imported inputs. (3) The state has acted as a catalytic agent to private enterprise, by providing tax incentives, building infrastructure and providing subsidies of various types. By stimulating emigration and providing social services it also kept social tensions within tolerable limits. (4) The process of social change was defined on the basis of achieving the consumption patterns, culture and technology of the industrialized capitalist economies, particularly the United States. (5) Development policy was growth oriented, the assumption being that a high enough rate of growth in income would, in time, resolve the distribution problem.

Given the above, and the fact that Puerto Rico exhibited many

241

characteristics of a politically democratic system in which elections were held every four years, and in which a number of parties participated, it is not surprising that Puerto Rico became the model not only for the United States government, but also for academics educated in the neo-classical and modernization traditions (Wells, 1969).

But, as of the early seventies, the image has been tarnished. The rates of growth have fallen drastically; unemployment, which never fell below 10 per cent increased to 23 per cent in 1977, and the government faced very serious fiscal conditions. Puerto Rico became known, not so much as a model of neo-classical success, but rather as the extreme example of dependent growth. The criteria which had been used to characterize Puerto Rico as an example of successful development were increasingly recognized as being insufficient. GNP growth was not enough (Seers, 1972). Also, it became clear that the political and social implications of having adopted a strategy such as Puerto Rico's were, indeed, rather negative. The works of a number of Latin American writers such as Tavares and Serra (1972), Cardoso (1974), Furtado (1969 and 1973) and Sunkel (1973) provided a different perspective from which to evaluate the Puerto Rican experience.

Among the points which arose from this literature were the following: (1) The need to distinguish between growth of the capitalist sector and national development. The first can very well be taking place independently of or to the detriment of the second. (2) The process of dependent capitalist growth fosters the marginalization of large numbers of the population. In order to deal with the consequences of this exclusion, the state has to recur to repression to handle social tensions. (3) Both the state and the local bourgeoisie remain active economic actors, but in supporting roles to foreign capital. (4) High and increasing external debt burdens become endemic in countries adopting this model. (5) The process of integration into the world capitalist system leads to increasing disintegration in national, social, economic and cultural structures.

Implicit in this body of work is a very different definition of development from that which had permeated much of the work done on development in the fifties and sixties. Among the components of this new definition of development was the need for countries to have a significant degree of control over their development process, their resources and capital; a restructuring of society's class structure so that not only income and wealth but also power is more equally distributed; that the development process itself generate the conditions for further development and increases the country's options or 'room for manouvre'. Obviously, economic growth is not enough, and the nature of the indicators utilized to evaluate development policies must be quite different (Seers, 1972; Dasgupta and Seers, 1975).

PUERTO RICO 1940–1975: AN OVERVIEW

1940 provides a convenient bench mark from which to begin this brief survey of the Puerto Rican experience, for it was in that year that the Partido Popular Democrático (PPD) started its political hegemony which lasted until 1976, with the exception of the 1968–1972 period. This is an arbitrary demarcation for the PPD arose as a result of conditions internal and external to the island which had been developing since the early years of the century, and particularly in the thirties (Herrero, 1970). Among them, one can mention the crisis of capitalism in the thirties and its impact on the island, the economic and social programmes set up by the Roosevelt Administration and the role of a previously dominant, land owning class, seeking to establish a new base from which to continue its hegemony (Quintero, 1975). All of these conditions to which must be added the increasingly strong Nationalist Party, set the stage for the establishment of a new, mildly nationalist and reformist political party, the PPD.

The party won the 1940 elections on a programme of independence, and deep social and economic transformations. It won the elections and governed with the support of the Roosevelt Administration in the United States. During the early years of the PPD Administration a number of innovations and reforms were carried out: an agrarian reform, nationalization of various public utilities, centralization of government activities, the establishment of a Planning Board and, perhaps most significant, the establishment by the government of state owned factories. By the end of 1945, practically all of the modern industrial sector was government owned, the agrarian reform had achieved some important changes in the organization of agriculture and the state apparatus had been transformed.

The picture is somewhat confused, however. Throughout the period, the PPD continued to enjoy the support of the United States government and, in fact, in some instances the United States appointed Governor of Puerto Rico appeared to be somewhat more radical than the Popular Party. The period has been mythologized into one of almost revolutionary dimensions, yet it appears that the reforms in public administration had more to do with the New Deal than with anything else. The Planning Board resembled more a town planning body than a national planning organization. In fact, its actions were mostly related to land controls and capital budgeting, and not with overall coordination and control (Villamil, 1967). Most important of all, by 1944 the PPD was beginning to abandon its pro-independence position in favour of one which gave priority to achieving high rates of economic growth and modernization as pre-requisites of any political change (Nieves Falcon, 1970).

Evaluations of the evolution of the PPD must recognize that the Party was not a monolithic bloc in terms of its class composition. There were serious conflicts among the various groups in the Party, particularly between the young technocrats and the older, more traditional and nationalist groups, which had much to do with its evolution. The group of young technocrats, trained mostly in United States universities in modern professions, triumphed and became responsible for the government's programmes and the party's orientation (Quintero, 1975). By 1948, the PPD had completely modified its position of only eight years earlier. All the government owned plants had been sold to the private sector, the pro-independence sectors in the PPD had been thrown out of the party, and the previously, if mildly, nationalist and redistributive orientation had been abandoned in favour of the attraction of foreign capital and a strong growth orientation (Herrero and Castañeda, 1965; Gutierrez and Villamil, 1975). The 1948 re-orientation cannot be characterized as an abrupt change in policy; in fact these changes had been evolving for a number of years, and important changes in the economic and social policies of the government had been under discussion for at least two years.[2] Obviously, much of the change had to do with the beginning of the Cold War and the renewed expansion of United States capitalism. Strong pressures were put on Puerto Rico to abandon its 'socialist' orientation.

The government shifted from being a direct producer of goods, to being an intermediary for private, foreign capital. Thus began the programme for which Puerto Rico received much publicity and because of which it became the example for the rest of the developing world, the tax holiday programme known as 'Operation Bootstrap'. Initially, the objective was to attract labour intensive industry, as Puerto Rico had a large unemployed and underemployed population. This initial attempt had some success if looked at from the point of view of numbers of plants established. However, the net employment generated was insignificant. This was due to the fact that this new employment merely compensated for losses in agriculture and in the home needlework industry (Gutierrez and Villamil, 1972). It is interesting to note that between 1950 and 1965, the labour force did not grow at all, despite an increase in population of close to 15 per cent. This was due primarily to two things: a falling labour force participation rate and massive out migration of the population. Between 1945 and 1953, close to 250,000 Puerto Ricans left the island, and between 1954 and 1964, that figure was approximately 500,000 (Nieves Falcon, 1975; Vazques Calzada, 1966).

The attractiveness of Puerto Rico as a low wage location became less and by the mid-sixties it was apparent that a different strategy should be pursued. This was due to a number of factors, but mostly because wages had increased substantially by the partial application of U.S. minimum wage legislation. This legislation was applied to Puerto Rico because of pressure from United States labour unions. This implied the loss of most of Puerto Rico's comparative advantage *vis-à-vis* the United States, at the same time that increasing competition was being felt from a number of other low wage countries.

Faced with this situation a new strategy was initiated based on the construction of large petrochemical complexes which, utilizing imported petroleum, would it was assumed, provide inputs for an extensive range of industrial processes. This strategy was based on the belief that the availability of industrial inputs would generate a series of forward linkages which would lead to the establishment of more labour intensive industries. This did not occur, or at least not in Puerto Rico. The products of the complexes were exported to be processed near the markets, which were in the United States (Gutierrez and Villamil, 1975). Total investment in the petrochemicals industry in Puerto Rico between 1965 and 1976 exceeded $1400 million but the number of direct jobs created has only been approximately 6,000.

It became evident that with a light industry which had reached its limits, and a heavy industry sector which was not creating employment, policies had to be initiated in order to ameliorate the conditions generated. Large scale emigration was no longer a possibility after 1965, due to conditions in the United States, although it continued at a reduced level. The government became the leading employer, and between 1969 and 1973, total government employment increased by 50 per cent. By the latter year, direct government employment represented 28 per cent of total employment, and government spending on infrastructure accounted for a substantial proportion of employment in the construction sector.

The other change which took place was the massive increase in welfare payments. Approximately 30 per cent of total income is now made up of transfer payments and close to 70 per cent of all families receive government assistance in the form of food coupons (Oficina del Gobernador, 1976).

This is a very brief and synthetic description of a much more complex process. However, for the purposes of this article it points out the basic elements which define the Puerto Rican Model, and its evolution: (1) The change from a redistributive, internally oriented strategy to a growth oriented, export dependent model of industrialization. (2) The shift from local, government control of the means of production to predominance of foreign capital. (3) A changed role for the state, from direct producer to an intermediary for foreign investment. (4) A change from an attitude of political and cultural separation, to one of incorporation into the United States economy and society.

THE IMPACTS OF DEPENDENT GROWTH

It is interesting to consider what the impacts have been of the strategy adopted, particularly in view of the fact that Puerto Rico has, for so long, been the accepted model. For these purposes, the framework elaborated by Osvaldo Sunkel (1973) is quite useful. Briefly, the basic idea in the Sunkel hypothesis is that integration into the world capitalist economy has disintegrative effects on the peripheral countries. These are reflected in various ways: polarization, increasing marginalization of large segments of the population, disintegration of national, cultural and social structures. At the same time those segments of the population which are directly linked to the transnational economy adopt the patterns of consumption and a style of living not very different from that of their counterparts in the central countries.[3]

The means through which Puerto Rico was incorporated into the economy of the United States experienced a transformation which in many ways is similar to that of many other countries in the periphery. From 1898 to the late forties, most U.S. investment in Puerto Rico was in the sugar cane industry. There was little manufacturing, except handicrafts and that related to sugar processing. After 1948, direct investment in manufacturing for export became the principal mode of incorporation and, beginning in the late fifties, an increasingly important role for U.S. firms becomes evident in retail trade (Sears, Woolworths, Grand Union, Barker's have all established various stores in Puerto Rico), in advertising (where the two largest companies, both American controlled, accounted for approximately $20 millions in billings), and in communications (Moreno Plaza, 1976).

In many ways, the same pattern can be seen as in many other countries which have become increasingly incorporated into the world capitalist economy, with the same types of distortions. In Puerto Rico, for example, the consumption patterns have changed dramatically over the past twenty five years. This reflects in part '. . . that the concentrated effort on an export-oriented manufacturing sector brought increased dependence on imported goods, the design, appeal, and promotion of which originated in the industrialized society from which they came' (Daubon, R. and Robinson, W., 1975). An example is provided by the fact that 96 per cent of the families have TV sets, but 60 per cent are considered to be indigent, with incomes below that level which is deemed necessary to cover basic needs, and thus must receive health and various other services from the public sector, as well as welfare payments.

Table 12 provides data on income growth and the modifications which have taken place in the industrial structure over the past three decades. Undoubtedly, growth has been rapid, despite the decreases in income in the past two years. Similarly, progress was achieved in

Table 12
Income and product
(current prices)

	1950	1960	1965	1970	1975
*Gross National Product	754.5	1,676.4	2,763.9	4,621.9	7,492.9
Gross National Product (per capita)	343.0	716.0	1,076.0	1,702.0	2,362.0
*Personal Income	653.4	1,373.6	2,222.6	3,795.8	7,682.1
Personal Income (per capita)	297.0	587.0	866.0	1,398.0	2,422.0
*Net Income	614.0	1,349.0	2,230.0	3,749.0	6,308.9
*Agriculture	149.0	180.0	191.0	178.0	329.5
*Manufacturing	89.0	289.0	553.0	955.0	1,963.4
*Government	70.0	175.0	307.0	611.0	1,392.4
*Rest of the World	31.0	− 16.0	− 118.0	− 368.0	−1,241.8
**Others	275.0	721.0	1,297.0	2,373.0	3,865.5

* Millions of Dollars.
** Commerce, Services, Construction, Finance (millions of dollars).
Source: Junta de Planificación, Estado Libre Asociado de Puerto Rico, *Informe Económico al Gobernador*, 1976.

the indicators related to health, education and housing. This side of
the Puerto Rican experience has been well chronicled. It is, however,
to the disintegrative impacts of the process that attention has not
been given, and to which this article refers.

Distribution and employment

The economic growth experienced over the past three decades has
not resolved the problems related to the distribution of income and
wealth and may, in fact, have worsened them (Herrero and
Castañeda, 1965). Although statistics on income distribution are
unreliable, there is sufficient evidence to sustain a rather pessimistic
conclusion. On the basis of the 1970 *Census of Population*, the
poorest 40 per cent of the families received only 8 per cent of total
income, whereas the wealthiest 10 per cent received 35 per cent.
These figures have not changed substantially over the past two
decades and may even underestimate the distribution problem.[4]

Distribution of income is closely related to the problem of
unemployment and underemployment. As Table 13 shows, unemployment has never been lower than 10.3 per cent and, in 1977,
reached close to 23 per cent. This very high figure, particularly in the
context of high rates of growth, becomes more significant when the

Table 13
Population and employment
(thousands)

	1950	1960	1965	1970	1975	Percent Increase 1950–1970
Population	2,200.0	2,340.0	2,564.0	2,710.0	3,075.0	39.8
Population, 14 years plus	1,284.0	1,383.0	1,518.0	1,718.0	2,060.0	60.4
Labour Force	684.0	625.0	680.0	765.0	872.0	27.5
Employed	596.0	543.0	604.0	686.0	738.0	23.8
Agriculture	214.0	124.0	107.0	68.0	49.0	—77.1
Manufacturing	106.0	91.0	112.0	132.0	133.0	25.5
Government	15.0	70.0	74.0	118.0	171.0	1,040.0
Other	261.0	258.0	311.0	368.0	385.0	47.5
Unemployed	88.0	82.0	76.0	79.0	134.0	52.3
(Percent)	12.9	13.2	11.2	10.3	15.4	19.4
Participation Rate (Percent)	53.0	45.2	44.8	44.5	42.3	—20.2

Source: Junta de Planificación, Estado Libre Asociado de Puerto Rico, *Informe
Económico al Gobernador*, 1976.

declining and quite low participation rates are considered. In this aspect the experience of Puerto Rico appears to be almost unique. The labour force participation rate, which in 1950 was 53 per cent decreased throughout the period to become 41.6 per cent by 1976. Notwithstanding the massive migrations, about which more will be said, the fact is that the process of marginalization of the population from productive activities became severe. This meant that, as mentioned, an increasing proportion of the population was subsisting on transfer payments. Income and production were progressively to become divorced.

Migration

Between 1954 and 1976, close to one million Puerto Ricans left the island. Although the government's position has always been that it neither favoured nor opposed emigration, the evidence has now become overwhelming that the government of Puerto Rico stimulated outmigration all throughout the period. Proposals were made for sending young women to the United States as domestics, as this would relieve the unemployment problem as well as have a positive effect on rates of growth of population (Hibben and Pico, 1948); for stimulating an out migration of 60,000 annually in order to prevent unemployment from becoming worse (Planning Board, 1955); and in 1974, when the economy in both Puerto Rico and the United States was deteriorating and some migrants were returning, measures aimed at making their return more difficult were considered (Oficina del Gobernador, 1974). Migration cannot only be looked upon as a result of a particular strategy of development, it was also very much a policy for controlling social tensions; it acted as an 'escape valve'. Of course, at least during parts of the period, the massive migration of Puerto Ricans was entirely compatible with the needs of sectors of the United States economy, particularly agriculture in some Eastern and Mid-Western states and the clothing industry.[5]

But, of course, when such massive population movements take place, questions concerning the beneficiaries of the development process arise. In Puerto Rico, the situation is made more complex by the fact that by 1970 (according to Census figures for that year), the number of Cuban, United States and other immigrants, had reached approximately 250,000. Unfortunately, the government has not collected statistics on migration since the early sixties, and thus information is very limited. However, it has become clear that the problem of population substitution is becoming a serious one.

External dependence

The measurement of external dependence can be done in many ways. Table 14 includes figures on the Balance of Payments and Table 15 on the external debt of the government. But, perhaps, the worst manifestation of external dependence has been the loss of control since 1948 over many areas of activity related to development policy.[6] Although Puerto Rico's political relationship with the United States is partly responsible for this, much of the blame must be placed on the particular development strategy adopted and its impacts. Once the need is established for increasing reliance on transfer payments from the United States to finance the welfare system and maintain the capacity of the public sector to generate employment, it becomes difficult if not impossible to resist increasing control over the decision-making process. Thus, in Puerto Rico this has meant that government programmes in health, housing, urban development and others, function on the basis of U.S. government criteria, that minimum wage legislation is determined to a significant extent by that country and that, in effect, Puerto Rico's room for manouvre has continually shrunk (Arbona and Ramirez de Arellano, 1977; Villamil, 1972).

One can define the extent of external control and dependency

Table 14
Balance of payments
(millions of dollars)

	1950	1960	1965	1970	1975
Exports	329.0	863.0	1,357.0	2.394.0	4,293.0
Imports	435.0	1,198.0	2,072.0	3,681.0	7,364.0
Balance	− 105.0	− 336.0	− 715.0	− 1,287.0	− 3,071.0
Unilateral transfers	75.0	121.0	215.0	376.0	1,845.0
Capital Movements, Net	38.0	207.0	488.0	920.0	1,571.0
Payments to Rest of the World Factors of Production	22.0	116.0	259.0	613.0	1,618.0
Exports as percentage of imports	75.6	72.0	65.5	65.0	58.3
Unilateral transfers as percentage of imports	17.2	10.1	10.4	10.2	25.1

Source: Junta de Planificación Estado Libre Asociado de Puerto Rico, *Informe Económico al Gobernador*, 1976.

Table 15
Public debt

	Millions of dollars	Index 1962 = 100
1962	615.6	100
1963	711.3	115.5
1964	801.8	130.2
1965	909.9	147.8
1966	983.2	159.7
1967	1,132.7	184.0
1968	1,308.8	212.6
1969	1,473.1	239.3
1970	1,656.6	269.1
1971	2,082.3	338.3
1972	2,555.0	415.0
1973	3,035.2	493.0
1974	3,705.1	601.9
1975	5,300.0	860.9
1976	5,749.4	934.0

Source:Banco Gubernamental de Fomento, Estado Libre Asociado de Puerto Rico.

through three measures. The first is the importance of direct transfers from the United States to Puerto Rico. These have grown from around 10 per cent of total income in 1960 to over 30 per cent in 1975 (office of the Governor of Puerto Rico, 1976). The external debt has grown almost tenfold, from $615 million in 1962 to $5,750 million in 1976. Finally, the ratio of external debt to total capital increased from 21 per cent in 1950 to 39 per cent in 1960 and 57 per cent in 1974 (Tobin, 1976; Gutierrez, 1976). Roughly 75 per cent of investment in manufacturing has been made by United States firms.

Notwithstanding the increasingly obvious difficulties which became apparent in the mid-sixties, the continuation of the development strategy adopted was feasible due to the massive increases in the external debt (Table 15), increased transfer payments and, for part of the period, emigration of a substantial proportion of the population. There was, however, no crisis of capitalism in Puerto Rico. In fact, return to capital remained exceedingly high, between 35 per cent and 60 per cent annually (Tobin, 1976), and the economy had continued to grow at satisfactory rates.

In late 1973 the situation changes, and 1974 and 1975 are both years in which the rate of growth is negative (– 2.4 per cent in constant prices), and in which total employment fell from 775,000 in 1974 to 718,000 in 1976. Unemployment increased from 109,000

(12.3 per cent) in 1974 to 172,000 (20 per cent) in 1976. The situation arose for a number of reasons which coincided: the recession in the United States economy, tightness in the money markets, the very high levels of the external debt of Puerto Rico, increased costs of petroleum and competition from abroad. Still, the crisis of the economy in terms of reduced rates of growth and increased unemployment did not affect the bourgeoisie, except for those in the construction sector which had been heavily affected by the inability of government to continue its expenditures in infrastructure. This was so, because at the same time transfer payments from the United States increased substantially. In 1975, payments on the food stamp programme alone totalled $500 million. This large inflow of funds did not stimulate local production, but rather lead to a massive increase in imports from the United States. Between 1973 and 1976, total imports of non-durables increased from $1.04 billion to $1.44 billion, of which foodstuffs increased from $.6 billion to $.9 billion (Junta de Planificación, 1976). It is precisely in the import sector in which the local bourgeoisie is concentrated (together with others such as financial and professional services). The import sector is not only important in terms of aggregate figures, but is also highly concentrated and monopolistic. Thus, in 1974, 76.5 per cent of cereals were imported by one firm, 71.3 per cent of all rice, 73.4 per cent of tooth paste, 51.6 per cent of powdered milk and 53.5 per cent of all malt beverages. In other products such as cigarettes, tyres, paper and a few others, the market is totally controlled by three or four firms. In most cases these companies are locally owned, although there are some which are subsidiaries of U.S. corporations. There is little work done on the import sector, but there is no doubt that it provides the economic base for much of the local bourgeoisie (Gutierrez and Villamil, 1974).

One consequence of the fiscal crisis confronting the government in 1974, was the appointment of a Committee to Study Puerto Rico's Finances, chaired by James Tobin. In large measure the Committee was appointed due to the concern of U.S. lending syndicates about Puerto Rico's solvency (Tobin, 1976). Thus, among the members of the Committee was the President of the First Boston Corporation which, together with the Chase Manhattan Bank, are perhaps the two most important financial institutions through which the government sells its bonds. Its findings reflected the fact that the government of Puerto Rico was utilizing deficit financing (made possible by increasing external indebtedness) in much the same way Keynesian economics suggests, with the difference that the situation was a chronic one, and that the financing was external. Its recommendations are similar to those one associates with IMF missions: reduce government spending, freeze public sector wages, increase taxes on property and durables, make certain that government corporations operate profitably, increase incentives to investment, restrict increases in wages in the private sector and adopt measures, such as the exemption of youths from minimum wage legislation, which will decrease labour costs to industry and others along similar lines. What is remarkable about the Report is that it recognizes that even these recommendations will not really bring about a substantial change in the situation. The crisis is not cyclical, it is structural.

CONCLUSIONS

Puerto Rico represents in many ways the most extreme example of the dependent growth model. It reflects many of the same characteristics, processes and effects which have been mentioned by Furtado, Pinto, Cardoso and Sunkel: high rates of growth of production with very unequal distribution of its benefits; the definition of the role of the state in terms of providing support for foreign investment; an active and economically important local bourgeoisie, but a dependent one; denationalization of the economy; marginalization of a large proportion of the population and growing external indebtedness.

There are, of course, differences. These are due to, among other things, the manifestations of direct colonial rule on Puerto Rico, particularly up to 1940, its size and the fact that foreign investment in manufacturing has been for export markets. In a way, the experience of Puerto Rico has less resemblance to that of the larger Latin American countries and somewhat more to that of Hong Kong or some of the other 'export platforms'. Also, in Puerto Rico's case, the instruments of social domination are different from those which have prevailed in Latin America, military governments and repression. In Puerto Rico, the tensions arising from its model of growth have been dealt with by increasing transfer payments and through stimulating migration. Thus, so far, there has been no need to resort to repression. What then is the lesson of the Puerto Rican experience? It seems that the lesson which must be drawn from Puerto Rico's experience is that once adopted, the strategy of growth maximization through foreign investment undoubtedly leads to greater dependence and reduced room for manouvre. Where there is also dependence on foreign markets, the problem could be worse. One can attempt a brief synthesis of what is entailed:

(1)   The decision to attract foreign investment implies that the appropriate investment 'climate' has to exist. Where the reason for investment is not the extraction of some natural resource, but rather as in Puerto Rico, production for export, the investment climate refers not only to guarantees, but special incentives. In Puerto Rico it became evident very early on that the model of industrialization was incompatible with both a pro-independence position and a social strategy aimed at achieving some measure of equality.

(2)   Direct foreign investment means importing technology which reflects factor proportions in the country in which it is developed. Typically it means highly capital intensive production processes. In Puerto Rico this has meant high levels of unemployment, the consequent need for government to act as an employer of last resort, the need for massive dependence on transfer payments and emigration.

(3)   Given the tendencies for an increasingly global framework for decision-making on the part of multinationals, the countries have to be constantly alert to slipping comparative advantage, competition from other locations and, thus, to the opening up of new areas of economic activity in the country which provide some advantage. In Puerto Rico, the limits reached by the labour intensive industries meant a shift to highly capital intensive industries such as petroleum refining and petrochemicals. This aggravated the problems of unemployment and added an additional one. The infrastructure requirements of these industries were much higher,[7] thus contributing to an increasing external debt and the ensuing fiscal/financial crisis. Since these industries are tax exempt and generate few jobs, the possibility of recuperating some of the infrastructure investment through taxes is very small indeed. In a small open economy, the forward linkages do not develop due to restrictions on the size of the market, and the inputs are in most cases imported.[8]

(4)   Thus, the costs of maintaining the model are constantly increasing to counteract the impacts of competition and slipping comparative advantage. The greater the possibilities for alternative locations, the higher the costs for each of the competing countries and the weaker their bargaining position. In the Puerto Rican experience this has meant increasing the tax holiday period, increased government investment in infrastructure, subsidizing labour and energy costs, and reducing environmental controls.

(5)   All of this invariably leads to an increasingly more irreversible condition of dependence and absorption into the dominant economies through various mechanisms: increasing external debt, dependence on markets, weakened bargaining position, and others.

In the case of Puerto Rico it meant losing much of the existing room for manouvre which it had and restricting its options for future development.

What then lies in store for Puerto Rico? It is difficult to visualize a return to the high growth years of the 1950s and 1960s. There could be an important industrial component mainly in pharmaceuticals and, perhaps, some sectors related to copper processing, if the mines are exploited. These developments will depend on the incentives offered but in large measure on maintaining less restrictive environmental regulations *vis-à-vis* the U.S. In fact, weak environmental regulations are becoming an important locational factor (Morales, 1976) and will become an increasingly important aspect of future development.

Assuming that massive emigration is no longer feasible, there will be even higher levels of unemployment, although undoubtedly, the government will continue to stimulate emigration.[9] Government and services will be important sources of employment, but there will be a substantial proportion of the population which is marginal to the economic processes. Transfer payments will continue to supply a large share of total income, certainly higher than the present 30 per cent.

The viability of this scenario depends on many factors. One of these is whether the United States will continue to finance transfer payments at present or even higher levels. At the moment, it seems that this presents no particular problem. There have been protests in that country concerning the size of payments to Puerto Rico, but these have had little impact. One could state that Puerto Rico is still good business for U.S. capitalism; after all, payments to factors of production in the U.S. were $1.6 billion in 1976.

The second factor is the approval of the local dominant groups. As mentioned, the local bourgeoisie has its economic base in the import sector, in finance and services. To them the objective of any economic strategy is not the maximization of industrial production (something which they realize is now not feasible) but the maintenance of high consumption levels. Thus, this group is perfectly at ease with an economy which is so dependent on transfers from abroad. Their aim is to assure that these transfers are maintained and even increased. Politically, this shift from a production oriented bourgeoisie to one dependent on consumption, partly explains the defeat of the PPD in the 1976 elections. The PPD had been, after all, the party of industrialization. The winner of the 1976 election (although still a minority), the New Progressive Party, offers higher transfer payments by seeking full association with the United States.

Obviously, adjustments will have to be made by some sectors (for example, the construction industry) but, in general, the local ruling class is confronted with no serious problems in this scenario.

There are aspects of the Puerto Rican experience which are particular to it. Certainly, its political relationship with the United States makes it different. But how different? The process of industrialization adopted resembles that in many others countries and the impacts, if less dramatic due to a shorter elapsed time, are quite similar: high unemployment, emigration, skewed income distributions, increasing denationalization, cultural disintegration, etc. The experience of the Dominican Republic, which has recently embarked on a Puerto Rican type of industrialization strategy, will be worth watching.

NOTES

1 For example, Teodoro Moscoso, who was the first Administrator of the Alliance for Progress, and who was later to be the United States Ambassador to Venezuela, had been the creator and, for many years, the head of Puerto Rico's industrial development agency. Thousands of government officials from Latin America, Africa and Asia visited Puerto Rico, particularly during the fifties and early sixties, as part of the U.S. Government's Point IV programme (International Cooperation Administration, 1960).

2 By 1946 a committee had been set up to consider the means to stimulate emigration by Puerto Ricans to, not only the U.S., but also South America and even Africa (*Revista Puertorriqueña de Investigaciones Sociales*, 1977). Within the PPD, divisions on the industrial development policy had arisen by 1945, and its future was already the subject of much debate.

3 A fuller statement of this framework is included in the article by Sunkel and Fuenzalida in this volume.

4 Herrero and Castañeda (1965), provide figures for income distribution in 1953 and 1963. In the former year, the poorest 25% of the families received less than 5% of total income, in 1963 somewhat less.

5 In a 1951 publication (Chase, 1951), the National Planning Association of the United States, an association of leading businessmen one of whose aims is, paradoxically, to 'avoid a 'planned economy'. . .', included the following among the benefits provided to the U.S. by Puerto Rico: '1. A market of some $350 million annually for American goods. 2. An outlet for U.S. venture capital. If you make a killing you can keep it—or most of it. 3. A winter playground. 4. A contingent of fighting men who can climb mountains in Korea, or anywhere else . . . 5. *A labor pool for shortages which are developing in the cold war's defense program.* 6. A laboratory for racial agreement and reform. 7. A cultural contrast within our country which can off-set many criticisms by Latins and others.'

6 Puerto Rico became a possession of the United States in 1898, prior to which date it had belonged to Spain. In 1952, it became a commonwealth or, as the literal translation of the Spanish title reads, a Free Associated State. This was brought

about by Public Law 600 of the U.S. Congress, although in fact, the creation of the commonwealth changed nothing (Serrano Geyls, 1974). In 1973 a committee was created to consider the relationship between Puerto Rico and the United States, but nothing has come of it. The committee, composed of an equal number of Puerto Ricans and Americans, submitted a Report which has still to be considered by the Congress. In fact, one can argue that the capacity for self-government was higher in the forties than at any other time since.

7 Three plants—Pittsburgh Plate Glass, Union Carbide (Peñuelas) and Union Carbide (Yabucoa)—absorbed 30% of the increased power generating capacity in Puerto Rico since 1967 (Escuela Graduada de Planificación, 1974).

8 Location in Puerto Rico was attractive to these petroleum refineries and petrochemicals for a number of reasons: (1) the government of Puerto Rico obtained higher petroleum import quotas for them, enabling them to import higher quantities into the United States, (2) tax exemption, which means higher profits for the particular units in Puerto Rico and, also, the possibility of transfer pricing to enhance the overall profits of the corporation, (3) less restrictive environmental regulations. With respect to this last point, it is important to keep in mind that in the United States there had been increasing opposition to the location of these industries. Thus, the massive investment in petroleum refining in Puerto Rico, the U.S. Virgin Islands and the Atlantic Provinces of Canada.

9 Allan (1975), makes the following recommendation: 'A Commonwealth Development Program which provides less jobs and less unemployment and welfare benefits ... is a positive migration policy albeit passive and unannounced'.

REFERENCES

Allan, D. M., 1975, Memorandum to the Governor of Puerto Rico, Secretary of State, Resident Commissioner, Economic Development Administrator, Secretary of Commerce, on 'Further Development and Evaluation of Development Strategy Alternatives ...', September 12.

Arbona, G. and Ramírez de Arellano, A., 1978, *Regionalization of Health Services: the Puerto Rican Experience*, Oxford University Press (forthcoming).

Baer, W., 1959, 'Puerto Rico: An Evaluation of a Successful Development Program', *Quarterly Journal of Economics*, LXVIII, November.

Boulding, K., 1961, 'The United States and Revolution', Center for the Study of Democratic Institutions, Occasional Paper, Santa Barbara.

Cardoso, F. H., 1974, 'Las Contradicciones del Desarrollo Asociado', *Revista Paraguaya de Sociología*, Año 11, No. 29, Enero-Abril.

Chase, S., 1951, *Operation Bootstrap in Puerto Rico: Report of Progress, 1951*, A Business Committee Report, National Planning Association, Washington.

Chenery, H., 1961, 'Comparative Advantage and Development Policy', *American Economic Review*, March.

Dasgupta, B. and Seers, D., 1975, *Statistical Policy in Less Developed Countries*, Communication 114, Institute of Development Studies, Brighton, England.

Daubón, R. and Robinson, W., 1975, 'Changes in Consumption Patterns During Economic Development: Puerto Rico 1940–1970', *Social and Economic Studies*, Vol. 24, No. 4, December.

Escuela Graduada de Planificación, Universidad de Puerto Rico, 1974, *Energía: Su Uso e Implicaciones en Puerto Rico*.

Furtado, C., 1969, 'Desarrollo y Estancamiento en América Latina: un Enfoque Estructuralista', in Bianchi, A. (ed.), 1969, *América Latina: Ensayos de Interpretación Económica*, Santiago, Editorial Universitaria.

1973, 'The Brazilian Model', *Social and Economic Studies*, Vol. 22, No. 1, March.

Galbraith, J. and Solo,C., 1953, 'Puerto Rican Lessons in Economic Development', *Annals of the American Academy of Political and Social Science*, Vol. 285, January.

Gutierrez, E. and Villamil, J., 1972, 'Productividad y Empleo: Un Análisis Parcial de la Experiencia en Puerto Rico', Escuela Graduada de Planificación, Universidad de Puerto Rico.

1974, 'La Toma de Decisiones Bajo Condiciones de Escasez Extrema de Recursos', *Cuadernos de la Sociedad Colombiana de Planificación*, No. 17.

1975, 'La Planificación Económica de Puerto Rico: Un Análisis Crítico', in García, E. (ed.), 1975, *La Planificación del Desarrollo en América Latina*, Fondon de Cultura Económica, México.

Herrero, J. A., 1970, 'En Torno a la Mitología del Azucar: Un Ensayo en Historia Económica de Puerto Rico, 1900–1970', CEREP, San Juan, Puerto Rico.

and Castañeda, R., 1965, 'La Distribución del Ingreso en Puerto Rico: Algunos Comentarios en Base a los Años 1953–1963', *Revista de Ciencias Sociales*, Universidad de Puerto Rico, Diciembre.

Hibben, T. and Picó, R., 1948, *Industrial Development of Puerto Rico and the Virgin Islands of the United States*, Report of the United States Section, Caribbean Commission, San Juan.

Instituto de Investigaciones Sociales y Económicas (INSE), 1978 (forthcoming), *Pobreza y Política Social*, San Juan.

International Cooperation Administration, U.S. Government, 1960, *Proceedings of the Economic Planning Seminar of the Commonwealth of Puerto Rico*, México.

Junta de Planificación de Puerto Rico, 1955, *Mid-Year 1955 Economic Report to the Governor*, San Juan.
1976, *Balance of Payments*, 1975, San Juan.
1977, *Informe Económico al Gobernador, 1976*, San Juan.
Meier, R., 1965, *Developmental Planning*, McGraw Hill, New York.
Morales, T., 1976, 'El Uso de la Ciencia y la Tecnología en Puerto Rico con Fines Coloniales', *Undécima Tesis*, Vol. II, No. 2–3, Octubre.
Moreno Plaza, G., 1976, 'El Sentido Ideológico de la Prensa en Puerto Rico', *Revista Puertorriqueña de Investigaciones Sociales*, Vol. I, No. 1, Julio–Diciembre.
Nieves Falcón, L., 1970, 'El Futuro Ideológico del Partido Popular Democrático', in his book *Diagnóstico de Puerto Rico*, Editorial Edil, San Juan, Puerto Rico.
1975, *El Emigrante Puertorriqueño*, Editorial Edil, San Juan, Puerto Rico.
Oficina del Gobernador, Estado Libre Asociado de Puerto Rico, 1974, *Documento de Integración y Síntesis, Taller de Empleo, Adiestramiento y Educación*, San Juan, Puerto Rico.
1976, *Mensaje del Gobernador a las Cámaras Legislativas*, Enero.
Pinto, A., 1971, 'El Modelo de Desarrollo Reciente en América Latina', *El Trimestre Económico*, No. 150, Abril–Junio.
Quintero Rivera, A., 1975, 'Bases Sociales de la Transformación Ideológica del PPD', *Cuadernos del CEREP*, No. 6, San Juan.
Revista Puertorriqueña de Investigaciones Sociales, Vol. 1, No. 2, Enero–Junio, 1977.
Seers, D., 1972, 'What Are We Trying to Measure?', *Journal of Development Studies*, Vol. 8, No. 3, April.
Serrano, Geyls, R., 1974, 'El Marco Constitucional del Desarrollo Económico de Puerto Rico: 1930–1974', Facultad de Derecho, Universidad de Puerto Rico, Febrero.
Sunkel, O., 1973, 'Transnational Capitalism and National Disintegration in Latin America', *Social and Economic Studies*, Vol. 22, No. 1, March.
Tavares, M. C. and Serra, J., 1972, 'Más Allá del Estancamiento: Una Discusión Sobre el Estilo de Desarrollo Reciente en Brasil', in *Teoría, Metodología y Política del Desarrollo de América Latina*, FLACSO-UNESCO, Buenos Aires.
Tobin, J., 1976, *Informe al Gobernador del Comité Para el Estudio de las Finanzas de Puerto Rico*, Editorial Universitaria, San Juan.
Vázquez Calzada, J., 1966, 'El Desbalance entre Recursos y Población en Puerto Rico', Facultad de Medicina, Universidad de Puerto Rico, San Juan.

Villamil, J., 1967, 'La Planificación en Puerto Rico', *Revista Interamericana de Planificación*, Vol. 1, No. 3.

1972, 'Puerto Rico: Una Interpretación', *Revista de Administración Pública*, Universidad de Puerto Rico, Vol. V, No. 1, Marzo.

Wells, H., 1969, *The Modernization of Puerto Rico: A Political Study of Changing Values and Institutions,* Harvard.

12

PARTNERS IN UNDERDEVELOPMENT? THE TRANSNATIONALIZATION THESIS IN A KENYAN CONTEXT

Martin Godfrey, Steven Langdon

INTRODUCTION

During the sixties the debate on dependency concentrated mainly on such economic indicators of asymmetry in international relations as commodity- and market-concentration of exports, supplier-concentration of imports, extent of foreign investment, degree of internal interdependence of economic functions, etc. More recently there has been a shift in the debate towards explicit consideration of socio-political factors in general and class analysis in particular.[1] One of the most ambitious contributions to this discussion has been that of Sunkel, who has developed the concepts of transnational capitalism and national disintegration.[2]

At the risk of over-simplification we can summarize the trans-nationalization thesis under four (overlapping) headings.[3]
(i) The capitalist system in recent years has changed from an *international system* (i.e. with nations as its most important components) to a *transnational system* (i.e. with increased importance as components for institutions, such as multinational corporations and international organizations, and individuals transcending national boundaries).

It has eliminated elements that were not part of it, 'congeries' as Sunkel and Fuenzalida call them, remnants of earlier socio-cultural systems, and has integrated the remaining elements into a whole having a remarkable consistency. At the same time it has acquired a number of new and powerful vehicles for giving substance to its meanings and diffusing them, such as new means of transportation, mass media, and new techniques of organization, of processing, storage, retrieval and analysis of information, and of marketing and advertising. This process is associated with and symbolized by the increase in the number and size of the multinational corporations and in their role in import-substituting industrialization. Transnationalization is seen as having socio-cultural as well as economic and socio-political dimensions.
(ii) As a consequence of transnationalization, national societies in

the capitalist sphere, both 'underdeveloped' and 'developed', have suffered deep changes in their social structure. In the first place a process of *disintegration,* or falling apart, has set in. This is most obvious in its effect on the economy-setting off a process of internal polarization, involving the expropriation of local entrepreneurial groups, the disruption of indigenous economic activities, and the concentration of property and income. But disintegration is also discernible in other activites, such as scientific research, architecture, sculpture and painting, and at a cultural/personal level.

(iii) At the same time national societies have generated counter-processes of *reintegration,* with a reassertion of national values and meanings, which sometimes find political expression in an attempt 'to bring the nation back to the sources of its existence as a separate entity, at all levels, social, cultural and personal'.

(iv) As a consequence of all these processes distinct communities have emerged within national societies, one of which constitutes a *transnational community* 'integrated at a world-wide level, in spite of the fact that its members live in geographically separate territories'. The other communities, incarnating different national and local socio-cultural configurations, cannot become globally integrated in this way.

There are several reasons why Sunkel's thesis deserves careful consideration. First, it suggests why the undoubted economic growth in many poorer countries should be associated with increasing dichotomization, or separation into two communities, and growing inequality there. Secondly, its concentration on the *combination* of transnational integration and national disintegration offers a more subtle concept of dependency than most earlier models, emphasizing dependency's impact on the *internal* structuring of the periphery political economy rather than simply on the periphery's asymmetrical links with a metropolis. Thus Sunkel's model suggests dependency's differential impact in a periphery political economy, and the differential response to it from groups in the periphery. Thirdly, the analysis of the way in which this differential impact cuts across the usual categories of class division seems especially important. Parts of the bourgeoisie, of the petty bourgeoisie, of the industrial working class, etc., are integrated into the transnational system while other parts are not, with the lines between integrated and non-integrated segments forcing a refinement of class analysis. Fourthly, the thesis implies a fuller, more stable incorporation of the integrated segments into the transnational system, with concomitantly greater benefits and fewer asymmetries experienced by them, than models of, say, 'comprador elites' acting as 'neo-colonialism's agents'. This suggests that the growing marginalization experienced in poor countries will be enduring and deep, which is why Sunkel stresses how 'pessimistic' he is 'about the possibilities for development in Latin America, that is, for the improvement of the living conditions of the poorer half of the Latin American population'.[4] It should be emphasized that these and other implications of the transnationalization thesis are not just descriptive statements but embody causal and in principle testable hypotheses.

The transnationalization thesis has been developed with the experience of Latin America primarily in mind, but Sunkel and Fuenzalida[5] state explicitly that they 'would like to explore the possibility of doing research on a few countries of Africa and Asia'. Among African countries an obvious test-case is Kenya. If the thesis does not retain its plausibility when measured against Kenya's experience it is hardly likely to be applicable to any other African country. For this reason we propose to look at Kenya's experience, not as an immediate leap into a full-scale test but in the hope that removal from its continent of origin will help with the pre-testing refinement and reformulation of the thesis. The scope of our approach will be defined, and to some extent limited, by the fact that we will be drawing particularly on our previous work in Kenya, on multinational corporations (Langdon), and education and labour markets (Godfrey).

FROM AN INTERNATIONAL TO A TRANSNATIONAL SYSTEM?

Since Kenya gained independence in December 1963 its economy has certainly remained exposed to external influences. Expenditure on imports, for example, as a proportion of GDP rose from 27 per cent in 1964 to 35 per cent in 1971 and remained at 30 per cent in 1973 even after the government imposed direct controls on imports. In 1971 the ratio of total current account payments to GDP had risen to an unprecedented 46 per cent. The proportion of the government's recurrent development and investment expenditure financed from external sources fell away from its post-independence level of 30 per cent to around 8 per cent in the late sixties but by 1973 it had climbed again to 13 per cent. In recent years also, in spite of the progress with Kenyanization of the civil service, the number of technical assistance personnel in Kenya has remained steady around 2,800.

Perhaps the most important index of exposure, however, is the inflow of foreign investment, some measures of which, none of them entirely satisfactory, are shown in the Table below. Such direct investment represents the heart of the transnationalization process, in so far as it incorporates the periphery into international production in new ways—generating manufacturing facilities aimed at import-substitution (or export processing) and owned by multi-national corporations.

Table 16

Net private long-term capital inflows to Kenya, 1964–1973

	1964	1965	1966	1967	1968	1969	1970	1971	1972	1973*
Total (K£mn)	− 15	2	1	8	9	13	15	17	15	16
% of total capital formation	—	3	2	9	10	14	13	12	10	9
% of capital formation by enterprises and non-profit institutions	—	4	2	12	14	19	18	16	13	12

*Provisional.

Source: Republic of Kenya, *Economic Surveys and Statistical Abstracts* (1972–74)

As Table 16 shows, international capital waited for a few years after independence before moving into Nairobi but by 1970 net private long-term capital inflows accounted for almost one-fifth of total capital formation by enterprises and non-profit institutions. If expenditure on private transport equipment is excluded from capital formation the proportion for 1970 becomes 23 per cent. In the manufacturing sector foreign capital has become particularly dominant; Needleman[6] *et al.* calculate that private long-term capital inflows accounted for 42 per cent of manufacturing invest-ment in 1968. These balance of payments data can be supplemented by figures from Langdon's 1973 survey.[7] The book value of direct foreign investment in Kenya was estimated at K£130mn in 1971–72, about 21 per cent of GNP. As well as manufacturing, where the ILO Report's[8] estimate that about 60 per cent of investment involved foreign capital was roughly confirmed, multi-national corporations were found to occupy a key position in wholesale and retail trade, banking, transportation, tourism, and primary production.

Second in importance only to the increased multinational corpo-ration presence in the flavour it gives to the Kenyan 'economic miracle' is the growth in tourism. The total number of visits of all kinds rose from 170,000 in 1964 to 428,400 in 1972, while expenditure by tourists rose in the same period from K£9mn to

K£27mn, displacing coffee as the main foreign exchange earner. That the economy became thereby no less vulnerable was emphasized in 1973, even before the oil crisis and its aftermath, when events in Uganda cut the number of visitors to 388,000 and expenditure to K£24mn.

In spite of the phenomenal expansion of the educational system, a large number of Kenyans are still studying overseas. Indeed, official estimates (somewhat unreliable) show the number to have increased between 1966 and 1971 from 3,600 to 4,600. Foreign teachers have also continued to play an important part inside Kenya. The numbers of students overseas and of foreign teachers in Kenya are merely the measurable aspects of the external orientation of the education system which remains strong. The medium of instruction after the first few standards of primary school is English and the certificates obtained in the upper reaches of the system are internationally negotiable. This works to the advantage of the holders of such certificates by trying them into the international rather than the local labour market, and to that of all salary earners, by helping to support the general level of salaries on 'comparability' grounds. With salary differentials stretched out in this way and with recruitment at every level tied to school qualifications, private demand for the continuation of the system in its present form is strong and is reflected in the rapid expansion of enrolment at every level, and in the curricular conservatism of the 'self-help' secondary schools. Continued external orientation and emphasis on qualifications are also supported by most decision-makers, who belong to the class that is able to take differential advantage of the system via its ability to buy more effective schooling.

External influence has also operated at the political and military level. The World Bank, for instance, has shaped some significant economic policies in Kenya[9] and other national aid agencies have also sought to influence policy priorities by their particular allocations. Escalations in financial assistance to Kenya have given such efforts leverage. (Kenya's total aid debt outstanding rose from $343mn to $510mn between 1968 and 1972.) Even more important has been the conscious, energetic, and active campaign by major Western embassies to influence the Kenyan government; one U.S. Ambassador in the sixties, William Attwood, offers in his memoirs a remarkably revealing picture of the intimate links his embassy developed with the Kenyatta regime and of the U.S. preoccupation with aid as a means of orienting Kenya to the Western capitalist block.[10] To these links are added military connections—particularly the presence of British Army units and advisers in the country, and the visits of U.S. warships to Mombasa.

It is easy enough, then, to show that Kenya has remained remarkably open to external influences. This has involved more, too, than straight-forward maintenance of the British colonial link in a more sophisticated neo-colonial form. The transnationalization process in Kenya has multilateralized linkages with the developed capitalist countries as a whole. This has been particularly evident in foreign assistance patterns. Some 30 per cent of technical assistance in 1969–71 (averaging $24mn annually) came from the U.K. However, the range of countries providing technical assistance has widened considerably, with West Germany (11 per cent of the total), Sweden (10 per cent), and Canada (8 per cent) now prominent, as well as the U.S. (18 per cent). In financial aid this process has gone even further, with a significant increase in the proportion provided by international organizations and by governments other than that of the U.K. Thus between 1968 and 1972, the international organizations' share in Kenya's total aid debt rose from 15 to 37 per cent, the U.K. government's fell from 53 to 28 per cent, the U.S. government's rose from 5 to 6 per cent, and the Swedish government's from 1 to 5 per cent.

The second half of the sixties, as the table shows, saw a scramble among multinational corporations to protect or win markets, by setting up manufacturing subsidiaries in Kenya. Companies participating in the scramble included many from Britain, but also non-British companies, such as Del Monte, Firestone, Union Carbide, Sterling Winthrop, and Colgate-Palmolive, all of the U.S., Philips of Holland, Sanyo of Japan, Hoechst of West Germany, Kiwi of Australia, Brollo of Italy, Birla of India, etc. Indeed, balance of payments figures show that over half of the net private long-term capital inflow in the late sixties came from outside the sterling area. This proportion fell in the early seventies to below 30 per cent and, according to 1971–72 estimates of book-value, the U.K. was still the dominant source of foreign investment with 67 per cent of the total. However, the more recent trend may be towards non-British sources of investment. The value of U.S. investment in Kenya in 1974 was estimated at K£35mn, 35 per cent higher than in 1971–72, with the opening in June 1974 of a full service branch by the First National Bank of Chicago a particularly interesting development. The largest recently announced projects have involved capital from Switzerland (a K£4.7mn textile complex), India (a K£5.3mn nylon filament plant), the U.S. (a K£2.7mn Nairobi hotel) and West Germany (a K£3.3mn alcohol/yeast distillery and a K£1.25mn cotton thread factory). Projects involving British capital have tended to be fewer and smaller.

Moreover, there is evidence of a trend towards cooperation among multinational corporations across nationalities. The oil refinery is an obvious case, with 50 per cent of its K£21.5mn capital held by the Kenyan government, 12.75 per cent by Shell, 12.75 per cent by BP, 12.75 per cent by Exxon, and 11.75 per cent by Caltex. Other examples are the Fluorspar Company of Kenya, involving Swiss, U.S. and British firms; the tannery, with joint involvement of British and Dutch firms; the resin factory, with West German and British firms involved; the paper mill, with finance from the World Bank, Canada, the U.K., and the U.S., as well as India; and the newly announced vehicle assembly plant, which will assemble Leyland trucks and buses, Land and Range Rovers as well as Volkswagen light commercial vehicles and microbuses.

One sign of cooperation among multi-nationals is the East Africa and Mauritius Association, formed in 1964 with offices in Nairobi and London to provide intelligence and liaison services for multinational corporations. Of the 150 members in 1971 one-third was non-British, roughly reflecting the composition of total investment at that time. As Leys comments,[11] the association is 'a manifestation of the fact that international companies are what they are, and have developed their own diplomatic service, transcending those of particular governments in the same way that their investments and management also do'.

This trend towards multilateralization of external links, and cooperation among developed capitalist countries and firms, is part of what distinguishes Kenya's new post-colonial pattern of incorporation into the international capitalist system from its colonial past. But the key structural change in Kenya's new 'transnational capitalist integration' remains the process of multinational-corporation-controlled industrialization. Indeed Fuenzalida—in a private communication—argues that 'transnationalization basically means the participation of some locals in the process of *production* of material and non-material goods traditionally produced in the centre of the capitalist system'.

In Kenya, this new participation has so far concentrated on manufacturing of import-substitutes. The 'transnationalization effect' of such import substitution derives from the taste transfer role of trade, or the redefinition of basic needs as desires for particular branded goods ('the translation of thirst into the need for a Coke', as Illich[12] puts it). Once such tastes have been acquired by consumers (necessarily the richer ones) in peripheral countries, import substitution means import reproduction (i.e., the production locally of goods as nearly as possible indistinguishable from those that were previously imported). This in turn implies an invitation to those firms which alone can exactly reproduce what has so far been imported—the multinational corporation. Moreover, the possibility that the multinational corporations that first produce locally can pre-empt and monopolize a protected local market, and profit accordingly, provides key material incentives for multinational firms to initiate such taste-transfer industrialization.

By the early seventies, then, Kenya, which had always dominated East Africa, via Nairobi's entrepot role, the railways, and banking and insurance systems, was well on the way to becoming a 'peripheral centre' for a much wider area. Leys[13] quotes from a 'visionary submission' by a senior civil servant to the Ndegwa commission, where this is seen as an explicit aim of policy: 'The City of Nairobi has now achieved the status of an international centre and its future planned development must be approached in that light. . . We must not spare our efforts, in keeping Nairobi facilities, etc., well above those of Johannesburg, our only competitor in this part of the world. . . By provision of suitable facilities we can force ourselves into the circuit. . . Nairobi offers all necessary advantages for industry, we can at a stroke convert it into a major industrial centre in the East and Central African region'.

NATIONAL DISINTEGRATION?

To what degree are there signs of 'national disintegration' in Kenya, moving in parallel with this 'transnational integration'? Has a process of internal polarization in the country occurred, as Sunkel analyses in Latin America, resulting in a growing marginalization of many Kenyans, in the sense of excluding them from access to the dynamic core of economic activity in Kenya?

A necessary preface is the recognition that colonial penetration itself relied on the absence of 'national integration' in Kenya (permitting tribe-by-tribe suppression of the African population), that colonial administration vigorously defended tribal differentiation in the country, and that the nationalist movement which challenged Kenyan colonialism was, for various reasons, highly regionalized in its structure. It would therefore be wrong to imply that there were 'national' institutions among the Kenyan African population which transnational integration could undermine[14]; concern must focus much more upon the *potential* for emergence of a nationally integrated Kenyan political economy, a potential which certainly *did* seem to exist in the movement-to-independence years. In the same way, it is necessary to recognize that pre-independence Kenya reflected gross social polarization in its political economy—based on race;[15] in analysing growing internal polarization, then, concern must focus primarily on the change process within the *African* population. These colonial realities complicate testing of Sunkel's model.

Nevertheless, considerable evidence has accumulated in post-independence Kenya of rapidly growing inequalities among Africans. The ILO Kenya Report[16] in particular emphasized these inequalities and related them specifically to an internal polarization in the economy between a *formal* sector and an *informal* sector—differentiating between these poles on the basis of their highly unequal access to government resources and support. This growing duality and differentiation has been reflected in increasingly highly skewed landholding patterns in rural Kenya,[17] in widening state pay differentials,[18] in Nairobi's growing economic dominance, in the marked regional differentiation evident in most indicators (favouring the Kikuyu Central Province), and in the parallel ethnic overrepresentation of Kikuyu in state institutions.[19]

'Marginalization' does seem to result for many Kenyans—with many rural households squeezed on to plots that are too small for cash crop production, while increased migration interacts, Latin American style, with growing unemployment and widespread unregulated indigenous enterprise in urban areas (as the ILO Report describes in detail). The resulting informal sector is structurally marginal to the economy in that it supplies only residual markets in which formal sector firms are not interested—as soon as small producers have developed a market to the extent that it *is* of interest, than large firms take it over (as happened recently to small-scale food kiosks in Nairobi). Burdened with very poor infrastructure,[20] generating very low wages for its employees,[21] often harassed by government, and characterized by highly competitive price-cutting, informal sector enterprise serves mainly to further surplus accumulation in the formal sector, by supplying very cheap products to firms and to wage employees in that sector.

There is, then, much evidence in Kenya of the dualistic differentiation that Sunkel's model implies. But to what extent can this polarization be explained in terms of the impact of the transnational integration traced earlier?

Certainly some aspects of Kenyan polarization are best analysed outside the transnationalization thesis. The particular pattern of regional/tribal inequality in Kenya, for instance, owes much to colonial development patterns and the associated dynamics of African nationalist dissent—both of which favoured Central Province/Kikuyu prominence in the post-independence period. The evidence also suggests that the state has been the central institution implementing Kenyan development strategy since independence, and that, too, might imply that the Sunkel model is out of focus for this context (despite the continuing expatriate presence in the bureaucracy, representing one element of transnational linkage). Yet particular elements in the transnational presence do help to explain aspect of the polarization process. In the first place, the African state itself has entered into a close symbiosis with multinational corporation subsidiaries in Kenya—marked on the one side by partnerships (institutional and personal) in such undertakings, by Africanization at executive levels, and by certain gains from corruption—and on the other side by subsidiaries' ability to avoid state constraints and to persuade government to shape out multinational corporation market privileges (tariffs, import bans, etc.). Some 76 per cent of domestic-oriented manufacturing subsidiaries interviewed in 1972–73 then had protection from imports—at least half of them as a result of direct requests to the government; requests for import protection also dominated multinational entry negotiation with government, and in 90 per cent of cases covered the request was successful. This symbiosis between the multinationals and state-dependent African insiders thus provided the former with a relatively free hand in the internal Kenyan economy—as well as generating considerable benefits for African insiders. Kristensen[22] has shown how this symbiosis has led the state to prevent locally controlled rural industry from undertaking particular projects, which have instead been allocated to the multinational sector (Kristensen discusses Kenya's alcohol factory in some detail as an example); similar government discrimination against indigenous entrepreneurs, and in favour of the multinationals, is evident in the fluorspar mining industry in Kenya.

Secondly, the freedom of multinational action that this symbiosis provides has led to a fairly specific pattern of subsidiary operations. Some 70 per cent of domestic-oriented manufacturing subsidiaries surveyed in 1972–73 reproduced precisely the brand-differentiated, quality-standardized products their parent firms sold in developed countries. And this product choice (the source of multinational oligopoly power in the world economy) was heavily promoted by mass advertising in the Kenyan market; a 1973 survey of Kenyan Swahili radio found that 80 per cent of all advertising was placed by multinationals promoting such products (from Colgate's detergents to Nestle's baby food to Glaxo's pharmaceuticals).

This product taste-transfer orientation has two effects. It establishes consumption preferences that are very difficult for small-scale indigenous entrepreneurs to meet, unless they shift, usually via dependence on government aid (hence as 'insiders'), to producing multinational-like, branded, standardized products. This seems to represent a severe blockage on the development of local industry, and can generate decline among those entrepreneurs that remain locally rather than transnationally oriented; that, at least, is the evidence from a 1973 survey of 32 African shoe manufacturers in Machakos district, the majority of whom reported that the Kenyan shoe subsidiaries' promotion efforts were destroying their business. Analysis of the Kenyan soap industry[22] shows the same pattern; multinational taste transfer was undercutting local soap manufacturers and forcing those who wished to survive to adopt the multinational pattern of product choice. Such consequences represent one sign of 'national disintegration'. But multinational taste transfer also promotes polarization in a second important sense. Sophisticated product choice dictates sophisticated, capital intensive technology choice; it also tends to require relatively sophisticated imported inputs. The latter blocks off many potential linkages to any integrated national economy (this is further blocked by parent company preferences for supplying subsidiaries with inputs). The former choice of technique restricts the employment effects of multinational investment; and it also encourages the emergence of a small, relatively well-paid work force, very differentiated in income from those in informal employment. Sophisticated techniques are also one of a number of factors which encourage multinationals to concentrate in the Nairobi area. All of these factors are also illustrated by the soap case, in which multinational product choice has led to the expansion of foreign firms, with lower employment effects, lower local linkages, and a distinct polarization impact: decentralized local soap factories (many outside Nairobi, labour-intensive and paying average 1972 wages of 286 shillings monthly) have lost ground to subsidiaries (all in Nairobi, all capital-intensive, and paying average monthly wages of K. Shillings 582 to an emerging 'labour aristocracy').

Multinationals also contribute to polarization by bringing the international labour market to Kenya's doorstep. Some 31 per cent of multinational subsidiaries (including 42 per cent of larger subsidiaries) surveyed in 1972–73 reported that they directly equated managerial salaries to Kenyans with those paid to persons in similar positions in European or North American subsidiaries; high salary levels abroad were thus directly transferred to Kenya, and in turn acted through the market mechanism on other high-level salaries in the public and the private sector.

The way in which the external orientation of the education system contributes to this stretching out of salary differentials and, given the emphasis on qualifications in formal-sector recruitment, ensures a high private rate of return on schooling has already been described. Under these circumstances schooling is seen as a means of escape from the rural environment and is used for this purpose, feeding the process of rural-urban migration and the associated growth of a marginal urban 'shadow economy'.

This increasingly skewed income distribution both generates a new ally in the multinational-state symbiosis (a 'labour aristocracy'), and also buttresses market demand for multinational-type products—as part of an ongoing self-justifying cycle. At the same time, the market power of the (protected) multinational brings it large profits, and generates consequent dividends abroad, requiring continuing multinational capital inflows to offset the outflow—and thereby strengthening multinational bargaining power in the state-subsidiary symbiosis. As Stewart concludes: 'Given industrialization based on imported technology, the dichotomy between the modern and traditional, formal and informal, protected and unprotected sectors, thus appears unavoidable'.[24] And, of course, it is transnational integration via the multinational corporation which underlies industrialization based on imported technology.

Kenyan experience, therefore, is consistent with Sunkel's model as far as polarization effects are concerned. National integration has been prevented—indeed there are signs of disintegration in some indigenous industries. Instead, increasing polarization seems evident in Kenya. It seems appropriate to see one element of this—the growth of rural-urban migration, and the accompanying emergence of a large, relatively poor informal sector—as a reflection of the same marginalization evident in the *barrios* of Latin America. And it seems possible—indeed necessary—to trace this whole process back to the pattern of transnational integration described above. This pattern, like the polarization just traced, builds on the colonial past; but it is powerfully shaped by present transnational institutions, particularly the multinational sector. The Kenyan government is a critical institution in shaping this polarization, but that government is itself closely integrated into a transnational system, and is involved in close symbiosis with the multinational sector in Kenya.

It would be presumptuous, in the absence of systematic enquiry, to attempt to deal seriously with the non-economic aspects of disintegration described by Sunkel and Fuenzalida. Casual empiricism suggests that evidence on the prevention of the emergence of (rather than disintegration of) nationally integrated research, architecture, sculpture, painting, etc., would not be difficult to gather. Even in the liveliest area of cultural activity, literature, there is a strong school, represented by Taban Io Liyong, Ali Mazrui, and Charles Mangua, which identifies itself with transnational values and styles.[25] As for psychic disturbances of the kind predicted by Sunkel, they are the stock-in-trade of Kenya's novelists and the source of some lurid stories in the press, but it is not possible to make much of such unsystematic evidence. At this point, it is sufficient to stress the more obvious socio-economic disintegration analysed in this section.

NATIONAL RE-INTEGRATION?

In many ways the most difficult part of the Sunkel/Fuenzalida thesis to apply to Kenya is their dialectical counter-process of reintegration. This is particularly so because the rhetoric of bringing 'the nation back to the sources of its existence as a separate entity, at all levels, social, cultural and personal', is much in use. Most of President Kenyatta's public speeches contain references to undesirable foreign influence. In explaining his recent decree that Swahili should be the national language, for instance, he said that 'a nation without culture is dead . . . We should not be slaves to foreign languages'. Yet such gestures always stop short of an important confrontation with transnationalism. Swahili's new status as 'national language' means merely that it will become the language of debate in the National Assembly but *not* (as would be necessary for reintegrative purposes) the medium of instruction in schools. Indeed, there is not even an examination in Swahili for primary school leavers, as a result of which they neglect the language in favour of examined subjects. Similarly, the Kenyanization programme has represented a major confrontation with Indian traders, deprived of their licences, but at most a minor inconvenience to multinational corporations forced to Africanize their management at a slightly faster pace than they would have chosen.

In general, the ties between government and subsidiaries of multinational corporations are close and friendly. This does not mean that the government never takes actions which adversely affect multinationals—in June 1974, for instance, the rates of corporation tax on multinational corporations and of withholding tax on dividends to non-residents were substantially raised, and a limit was placed on local borrowing by foreign-controlled companies—but such actions do not amount to serious constraints on multinational activities. The only potentially serious disputes arise over interpretation of the 'rules' of the symbiosis between the companies and the African insiders. Thus the American managing director of an oil company who in January 1974 threatened to cut off the President's supplies unless outstanding bills were paid was expelled, one might say, for contravening these rules.[26] The American geologist who met a similar fate in June 1974 when several prominent insiders realized the extent of the ruby deposits he had discovered in Tsavo Park might also be regarded as a victim of a dispute over rules.[26] Of course disputes over the rules of symbiosis do not amount to a process of reintegration, but should either side become too greedy there might be unpredictable consequences.

The difficulty of identifying reintegrative counter-pressures must be related to the success with which the Kikuyu ruling group has consolidated its position since independence. The Kenya African National Union (KANU) has been allowed to wither away and direct control has been exercised through the provincial administration. Odinga and the Kenya People's Union (KPU) have been crushed, even to the extent of preventing former KPU detainees from Nyanza from standing as candidates in the October 1974 elections, and the few populist members who say embarrassing things in parliament (e.g. regarding landlessness, and the situation of former Mau Mau freedom fighters), are under constant threat of harassment, imprisonment, and even death. In these circumstances one of the few sources of widely circulated critical comment is the churches, particularly the National Christian Council of Kenya. But, although the churches have shown, as in the oathing crisis of 1969, that they can act effectively to protect their members, they do not form the basis of an effective political movement.

With the strengthening of the provincial administration and the demise of KANU, political processes have devolved from the centre to the peripheries. *Harambee* (self-help) activity has become a particularly important arena for politics, which is increasingly tribalized. The *harambee* institutes of technology represent the latest stage in this process, whereby 'leaders, by promoting development activities, are able to enhance their own standing in their areas and . . . compete with each other over who will be able to initiate the largest, most successful, and most numerous development projects'.[28] In the case of the institutes of technology, this competition is at an inter-district or inter-province (i.e. inter-ethnic) level, which might be taken as a sign of tribal/regional, if not of national, reintegration. However, this would be a mistake. The leaders of these projects are certainly *not* reacting against the transnationalism of the centre by going back to their roots but are seeking to use *harambee* as a bid for resources from the centre for their communities, and as a consequent springboard for themselves into positions of access to the 'fruits' of transnationalism.

There are, as always, 'emerging contradictions'. The ever-changing Kenyan political economy is continually promoting some and extruding others, with possible consequences for the stability of existing arrangements. The scramble for educational qualifications described earlier, induced by the unequal and qualification-related structure of modern-sector rewards, means that the qualification required for any particular job has to be upgraded from time to time and that the category of school leaver that is in surplus becomes ever more senior. Ten years ago 'unemployed'[29] primary school leavers were the problem; today it is unemployed secondary school leavers; very soon it will be unemployed graduates. It is hardly surprising in these circumstances that there has been a spate of demonstrations and riots in secondary schools and the university. But these protests have usually lacked any sense of political direction. They are the protests of frustrated late-comers, using as occasions domestic issues such as bad food, crowded accommodation, and unfair examinations. It may be that, as some in high quarters fear, these protests will spill over into the streets. But, precisely because they lack political direction, it seems more likely that they will give way to resigned acceptance of the best that is available. The primary school leavers who posed such a threat a few years ago are mostly back on the farm, and their counterparts today would certainly not bother to apply for a white-collar job.

As Lamb[30] has put it, 'the groups, which are clearly perceived to present a potential threat to the existing disposition of power are those which are effectively excluded from power at the centre but are in possession of the resources and, possibly, the consciousness to make a significant impact in politics'. This means that we must look not to those who have been totally extruded by the process of cumulative differentiation—such as the rural landless and the urban unemployed—but to those who are still in the running, however far behind the leaders. Lamb suggests that there are two such groups: 'on the one hand, newly-wealthy peasants, who have benefited from the spread of cash crops and in many cases from the allocation of government settlement plots in the former White Highlands; and, secondly, those urban dwellers sometimes referred to in official documents as 'the informal sector'...' He makes out a better case for inclusion in this category of the newly-wealthy peasants than of the informal sector entrepreneurs, who seem to lack both the necessary resources and the consciousness. In particular, he draws attention to the emerging clash of interests between the capitalist large farm sector, in which insider Africans are now substantially involved, and the peasant areas. As he recognizes, it may be that this conflict is already being resolved in favour of the peasant areas by the *de facto* subdivision of many large farms. In any case it is not entirely clear why the brunt of such a conflict should be felt by the wealthy peasants who, we later argue, may even be candidates for subsidiary membership of the transnational community. Conflict seems more likely to lead to accelerated proletarianization of the weakest farmers in peasant areas. Nor need a 'threat to the existing disposition of power' take a reintegrative form; the aim might equally be a redistribution of access to the rewards of transnationalism.

The results of the October 1974 elections might be expected to yield some clues about emerging contradictions. A considered verdict requires full analysis but, at first sight, they do not seem particularly useful for this purpose. Certainly 56 per cent of the 158 sitting members lost their seats, an only slightly lower proportion than in 1969, including four cabinet ministers and thirteen assistant ministers. But the sweeping out of sitting members was not an ideological protest. Campaigning was dominated by pork-barrel issues, with the test of a member's performance being his success in attracting central government resources to his constituency. There were some interesting individual results, but most of them, far from signifying reintegrative counter-pressures, are better explained by factionalist, ethnic, or patronage factors. And, in any case, whatever the composition of the National Assembly, the administration remains in power.

This has been amply demonstrated in the recent crisis following bomb explosions in March–June 1975 in Nairobi (in one of which 26 people were killed) and the murder of J. M. Kariuki, MP for Nyandarua North, a persistent critic of government policy from a populist cross-tribal standpoint. Several days of extraordinary anger and confusion followed the discovery of his body on 11 March 1975. University students boycotted lectures and marched in demonstration through Nairobi. Shops, bars, schools, and markets were closed and bus services temporarily suspended. Members of parliament speculated with unprecedented frankness about the possible involvement of 'big men' in Mr. Kariuki's murder. At the funeral university students called for the government's resignation and the provincial commissioner was shouted down when he tried to read a message from President Kenyatta. Then, two and a half months later, the report of a select committee of 15 MPs suggested that certain members of the police force may have been involved in the murder, that the police as a whole had mounted a cover-up operation, and that no faith should be placed in police investigations. Furthermore, a government attempt to have the report 'adopted' rather than 'accepted' by the house was defeated.

Yet by July 1975 government seemed to have reasserted its authority. A minister and two assistant ministers who voted against the government's amendment had been relieved of their posts. MPs had been reminded that as members of KANU they were expected to toe the party line or resign from the party (and thus from parliament). None of the people named in the select committee's report had been arrested or suspended from duty. The administration had shown its resilience and capacity to manage the new situation. It is clearly too early to assess the consequences of the murder and its aftermath. Enough has been publicly said to ensure that things will never be quite the same again, but whether there is a serious threat to existing political arrangements and, if so, the nature of such a threat, remain much less clear.

It is worth adding a brief note on cultural activities since this area may show signs of reintegrative pressures. In opposition to the transnational literary school (of Taban and Mangua) mentioned earlier, several writers take a critical view of such values. Okot p'Bitek is perhaps the most explicit of these, emphasizing in *Song of Lawino* and *Song of Ocol* the need to return to earlier cultural roots. But Ngugi wa Thiongo is more impressive in his understanding of the processes at work. In an introduction to a book by p'Bitek, Ngugi writes: 'While I agree with p'Bitek's call for a cultural revolution, I sometimes feel that he is in danger of emphasizing culture as if it would be divorced from its political and economic basis. What makes up ape a decadent white culture? What makes up pattern ourselves on the west? What is the material base for our apemanship? And how can we seize back our creative initiative?'[31]

DISTINCT COMMUNITIES?

Finally, what of the emergence of distinct communities in Kenya— of a transnational community, integrated internationally—and of separate local communities, distinct from the transnational segment, in the sense of experiencing a different structural relationship in the economy and accordingly different life conditions?

Again, as a prelude, it is useful to recognize the colonial roots of any such distinction in Kenya. Mutiso[32] has argued persuasively that the very process of colonial penetration, focused for most Kenyan Africans around the new missionary presence and the schooling associated with it, generated profound cleavage between those accepting the new values and consequent life-style of the missions (described as the *asomi*), and those retaining the traditional tribal values and life style (the *non-asomi*, in Mutiso's terms). Such cleavage, in Mutiso's view, was basic to the nationalistic struggle, though in a rather complex way: a further division occurred among *asomi*, with some accepting their subordinate status in the new order and accordingly benefiting economically (the associative *asomi*), while others (the dissociative *asomi*) rejected the racial subordination still imposed on them despite their concession to the new values and institutions, seeking the chance to be able to rise fully to share European privilege and status; these dissociative *asomi* fell back on the traditional *non-asomi* majorities as a base from which to organize against such subordination, while the *non-asomi* used the dissociative *asomi* as allies, advisers, and spokesmen in efforts to obtain more benefits in the colonial context. Such a perspective makes it easier to understand why in post-independence Kenya nationalist politicians (dissociative *asomi*) should have found it so easy to forgive the 1950–60 collaboration of early African bureaucrats, loyalists, etc. (associative *asomi*): both groups shared Western-oriented values and emerging life-styles that distinguished them much more from the *non-asomi* than from each other.

Mutiso's analysis should give more weight to other important elements in colonial penetration, particularly African wage employment experiences (as porters, on estates, etc.). But his view of the rather fundamental cleavages generated seems persuasive. Accepting that view, to what extent might a distinct *asomi* community be said to have been transformed into a distinct transnational community in Kenya?

One important sign of such a process is the very large-scale Africanization of the multinational corporation sector which has occurred since 1966–67. Langdon's 1972–73 multinational survey illustrates this; interviews with 54 comparable subsidiaries showed that non-citizen employees fell from 11.3 per cent of total employment in 1966–67 to only 2.3 per cent in 1971–72. Such dramatic changes have given educated, urban-oriented Africans very much more of a role in the managerial levels of the direct institutions of transnational integration. And since large multinational corporations work hard to integrate such employees into the organization, by training and posting abroad for example, it is not surprising that such executives seem to be taking on an orientation to the transnational system. This impression is inescapable in interviewing such African executives; and it is underlined by such comments as the following from an expatriate subsidiary manager in Kenya:

> We are giving Kenyan citizens good chances to get on in our company. . . And the ones that we've given an opportunity to, they are also becoming definitely company oriented; I think in the beginning it's very difficult for them to feel for their company in terms of loyalty and thinking; but as they're given the chances and are getting on, you see the same thinking with these younger executives as you do with people who've been slogging on for years in the company.

Portents of the future perhaps are provided by Lonrho's appointment of its Kenyan African managing director, Udi Gecaga, to the parent company board of directors in the U.K. In turn, these executives seem clearly to be part of a wider, but nevertheless self-contained, community of Africans. The following quotations are typical of what African multinational executives reported when interviewed:

> —as an individual, I'm in very, very close contact with a lot of government officers, because these are people that I grew up with—the generation that's running the public sector and commercial sector in Kenya is my generation, and we are not too many of us (manager of U.S. subsidiary).

> —As it happens, this company is Africanized to about 98–99 per cent now; the men who run this company are Africans who went to universities and colleges with the men who run the government. . . Fifteen of the Permanent Secretaries here are my university mates, and so on (personnel director, British subsidiary).

These are the realities underlying the ILO Report's conclusion[33] that those in charge at the centre in Kenya are now more closely linked, with common interests, than ever before; 'moreover', notes the Report, 'within the circle, the influence of foreign companies appears to be growing rapidly'.

Such insiders seem to share a common relationship different from the rest of Kenyans—gaining economic benefits based on their access to the associated state and multinational sectors, being oriented to the transnational system in language and economic interest, and exhibiting life-styles that differ from those of most Kenyans. In that sense, these insiders seem to form the core of a transnational community as defined in Sunkel's model. That community is wider, then, than those employed by transnational institutions; it includes higher level civil servants, the more prominent politicians, some professionals, and more-prosperous, well-educated African businessmen. Yet does such a circle form the core of separate community oriented to the *transnational* as opposed to the *local* economy? Bienen[31], for one, certainly questions any such conclusion; in his discussion of the civil service as a class, for instance, he concludes that civil servants are in fact a vehicle for political participation, communicating views and making rural interests felt at the centre. Bienen presents no important evidence for this conclusion, but his view should perhaps still be given some weight; certainly Lamb's Murang'a analysis[35] shows that rural peasants there have been able to oppose and reshape central government policy effectively.

The real message of this Murang'a study, however, may be something else; Lamb found that a group of wealthy, relatively large-scale (Kikuyu) coffee growers were able to improve their access to production of that lucrative export crop, and to defend their self-benefiting control of local cooperative institutions in the face of government policy to the contrary. Such rich peasant exporters seem best considered as subsidiary elements in the Kenyan transnational community, whose close access to the (state, Kikuyu) core of that community has permitted them to integrate themselves further into the transnational capitalist system.

Unionized industrial workers in the multinational sector represent another such subsidiary element in the Kenyan transnational community. Sandbrook[36] has described the past role of transnational labour organizations in shaping Kenyan unions (including the ICFTU). And Amsden[37] has suggested that international firms deliberately developed a well-paid, apolitical union movement in Kenya. These transnational origins are reinforced by considerable benefits among those integrated into transnational capitalism as multinational wage workers; in twenty-four unionized industrial subsidiaries providing details, minimum monthly wages in 1972–73 averaged 335 shillings, compared to a statutory minimum wage, itself often undercut, of K. Shillings 175 in Nairobi and K. Shillings 70 in rural areas; average, as opposed to minimum, wages in these subsidiaries ranged even higher. Such better paid workers are using their income advantages to amass rural land holdings that consolidate and confirm their advantages, relative to poor informal sector workers.[38]

A brief glance at wealthier peasant exporters and unionized industrial workers, both with their links to the transnational economy, thus suggests the value of Sunkel's model in explaining the political dynamics associated with polarization in Kenya. It is widely recognized that trade unions are basically supportive of the regime in Kenya, despite this polarization.[39] Wealthier peasant support, particularly in Kikuyuland, seems to remain strong as well. It seems clear that these facts arise at least partly because, as Sunkel's model hypothesizes, the transnational community emerging in Kenya cuts across conventional class lines, emphasizing new cleavages within the usual class categories—like the peasantry and urban wage workers. This does not mean that analysis in terms of transnationalization substitutes for class analysis; it merely makes class analysis more complex.

It is, of course, even more difficult to say whether these subsidiary elements in the transnational community are distinct from the rest of Kenyans; political patron-client relations undoubtedly redistribute some benefits from wealthy peasants to poorer small-holders; and wage remissions to rural areas are often sizeable (some 13 per cent of earnings for those in Nairobi receiving K.Shs. 175 or more a month, is one estimate).[40] However, it is the *trend* in Kenya which is of greatest concern. And in that sense, a conclusion seems evident.

There *are* signs of a distinct transnational community emerging in Kenya. Its core cuts across the multinational, state, and larger-scale African-owned business sector, integrating a circle of privileged insiders in the political economy—with subsidiary elements, having good access to that core, themselves reflecting cleavages within the usual peasant, wage worker, and merchant class categories. The basic integrated/non-integrated cleavage, upon which so much of personal economic prosperity seems to depend, reflects the *asomi/non-asomi* cleavage of colonial penetration; and seems to be reflected in the Kenyan polarization discussed above. Those who have notably gained, and are gaining, since independence are part of the evolving transnational multinational corporation-state community; the great majority, who have gained relatively little, lack good access to that community.

CONCLUSION

Our limited purpose in this article has been to look at Kenya's experience with the transnationalization thesis in mind. As we have seen, that thesis suggests a model of social dynamics in periphery economies in the contemporary world capitalist system, by which their dependency is restructured (and strengthened), and through which that dependency will ultimately be challenged. To what degree does the Kenyan evidence support the model's predictions?

What we have been able to do is in many ways insufficiently systematic even for pre-testing purposes. In particular, we have neglected the cultural/psychological/intellectual implications of the thesis; even at the political/economic level it has not been possible to determine the precise boundaries of a 'transnational community' in Kenya and thus to determine the extent to which expansion in participation in the community *is* restricted (as the model predicts) in spite of GDP growth.

However, as far as we have been able to go, the Sunkel model of transnational capitalism and national disintegration travels reasonably well from Latin America to East Africa. Transnational capitalist integration in Kenya is evident in the marked process of multinational corporation import-substituting industrialization since the mid-sixties—and reinforced by the continuing external influence of expatriate personnel, aid flows, tourism, Western-bloc embassies, foreign military assistance, and internationally-oriented education. Kenya's former colonial incorporation into world capitalist exchange has been restructured. Similarly, polarization has increased to dramatic proportion among Kenyan Africans, and seems to rest on differential access to the symbiotic multinational-state sectors; this process has prevented national integration of the economy, and generated marginalization among many Kenyans (the landless, many urban migrants in the informal sector, even many smallholders with insufficient land for cash crops—such groups are cut off from the dynamic centres of growth and innovation in Kenya). This transnational integration and internal polarization/marginalization are the most clearly confirmed of Sunkel's hypotheses in Kenya. Somewhat more ambiguous signs are evident of the emergence of a distinct transnational community in Kenya. But there seems little evidence of the movements for national reintegration which the dialectic of the model anticipates.

Though the model's predictions are thus basically supported by the Kenyan evidence, some important qualifications deserve emphasis. First, it seems important to inject a time dimension in the transnationalization process. Much of the evidence reviewed has suggested trends in Kenya, rather than mature relationships, that support the Sunkel model. This suggests that transnational integration and national disintegration in Kenya have not yet reached dimensions as dramatic as in Latin America.

A second distinction to stress concerns the state's role in Kenya. Much more so than in Latin America, the state seems the critical institution shaping differential economic opportunity in Kenya—providing the resources and regulations, for instance, that permit embourgeoisement of the elite, and establishing the discrimination and harassment that contribute to the marginalization of informal sector enterprise. That state is in close symbiosis with the multinational sector. The latter and the state sector therefore together integrate the core of the transnational community in Kenya, a situation that seems distinctly different from Latin America's. This, in turn, reflects the different historical and social context of Kenya. In Latin America the local industrial capitalist bourgeoisie that is threatened by transnational integration has often had sufficient influence on the state to neutralize the chances of a multinational corporation-state symbiosis, sometimes even generating state moves to constrain and regulate the transnationalization process.[41] In Kenya the local industrial capitalist bourgeoisie was mainly Asian and (as Murray's study of the Chandarias shows)[42] it could not count on such state support; instead the African nationalist elite moved the state into symbiosis with the expanding multinationals, in a partnership aimed at its own embourgeoisement. This central role of the state in Kenya in turn also means that international organizations and foreign aid personnel and capital flows are more important elements in the transnationalization process in Kenya than in Latin America.

Third, the colonial roots of much of the transnationalization process in Kenya seem important to specify. External economic penetration accelerated under British control; social and regional polarization took shape then; and, following Mutiso, fundamental cleavage into distinct communities was initiated. The much more recent break from colonialism in Kenya, relative to Latin America, means that these colonial roots are much more evident in the contemporary political economy, and complicate any analysis set exclusively in terms of the Sunkel model.

It might be asked, therefore, if the Sunkel framework really adds much to a simpler dependency framework, which would see Kenyan development since independence as merely a neo-colonial variation on the pre-independence period.[43] Such a simple model, however does not recognize the considerable structural changes which *have* taken place in the pattern of Kenya's incorporation into international capitalism (with multinationals and international agencies—like the World Bank—now playing the role that Britain and the white settlers played under colonialism—and thereby effecting a much more stable and comprehensive incorporation of an indigenous elite than in the past). Nor does a simple dependency model find it easy to handle Kenya's undoubted progress in GDP growth after independence.[44] Sunkel's model would anticipate that growth, as transnational integration progressed, but would also hypothesize the social polarization and marginalization for most Kenyans which have accompanied it.

Some questions remain, however. The Sunkel model undercuts

conventional class analysis and does not, perhaps, sufficiently clarify the consequences of doing so. Does Sunkel's concept of distinct communities replace, supplement, or complicate class analysis? In Kenya, we have seen transnationalization as complicating and deepening class analysis, making it necessary to distinguish peasants with access to the transnational system (in the shape of rights to grow lucrative export crops with state assistance), from peasants without such access; industrial workers employed by multinational firms (a labour aristocracy) from workers in the informal sector; a petty bourgeoisie with state and multinational provided protection and privileges from small-scale businessmen without such access; etc. The dynamics of conflict among *these* classes are complex and subtle; but their analysis is likely to lead to more fruitful conclusions than approaches based on conventional class categories in Kenya.

Analysis of those dynamics, though, may not be helped by the dialectic hypothesized by Sunkel's model. Particularly in Kenya, to anticipate a political movement aimed at 'national reintegration' seems likely to obscure the actual class struggles that are emerging, in a context where the colonial inheritances colour conflict so heavily in regional and ethnic rhetoric. It would appear that the admirable subtlety of the Sunkel model's social partitioning is sacrificed in the model's much simpler notion of social dialectics.

Overall, though, the new dependency approach does seem to draw support from this Kenyan review. The Sunkel model can integrate major phenomena of contemporary Kenyan under-development: the substantial foreign role in the economy; the increasing Africanization of the institutions representing that role; the dramatic social and regional polarization which has accompanied significant GDP growth since independence; the marginalization represented by the emerging informal sector; the substantial gains of the unionized labour aristocracy and of a number of wealthy peasants; and the maturing of a powerful, well-integrated African circle controlling decision-making in the country. The transnationalization thesis needs to be reformulated somewhat in the Kenyan context, as noted above; but it does seem to offer sufficient insight into what has been happening in Kenya over the recent past to be worth carrying into further investigation.

NOTES

[We are grateful for the many comments received from colleagues, particularly the (transnational) members of the Institute of Development Studies' dependence group and participants in the Canadian African Studies Association conference in Toronto, February 1975, where the paper was first presented.]

1 For a useful survey of the dependency literature see Norman Girvan, 'The Development of Dependency Economics in the Caribbean and Latin America: Review and Comparison', 22 *Social and Economic Studies* (1973).

2 Osvaldo Sunkel, 'Transnational Capitalism and National Disintegration in Latin America, 22 *Social and Economic Studies* (1973); Sunkel, 'A Critical Commentary on the United Nations Report on Multinational Corporations in World Development' (IDS Discussion Paper No. 52, Brighton, 1974); Sunkel, 'External Economic Relations and the Process of Development' (IDS Discussion Paper No. 51, Brighton, 1974); Sunkel and Edmundo Fuenzalida, 'Transnationalization, National Disintegration and Reintegration in Contemporary Capitalism' (IDS Internal Working Paper No. 18, Brighton, 1974).

3 The version of the transnationalization thesis on which this summary is mainly based is that of Sunkel and Fuenzalida, *op. cit.*

4 Sunkel, 'External Economic Relations', 1.

5 Sunkel and Fuenzalida, *op. cit.*

6 L. Needleman, Sanjaya Lall, R. Lacey, and J. Seagrave, 'Balance of Payments Effects on Foreign Investment: Case Studies of Jamaica and Kenya' (UNCTAD document TD/B/C3/79/ADD.2/Corr. 1, 30 June 1970).

7 Steven Langdon, 'The Multinational Corporation (MNC) Sector in the Kenyan Political Economy' (mimeo, 1974). The survey covered 81 Kenyan subsidiaries, some 88 per cent of those approached, and included the great bulk of subsidiaries employing over 50 workers in the country. For more detail see Langdon, 'Multinational Corporations, Taste Transfer and Underdevelopment: A Case Study from Kenya', 2 *Review of African Political Economy* (1975), 33.

8 International Labour Office, *Employment, Incomes and Equality: A Strategy for Increasing Productive Employment in Kenya* (Geneva, 1972).

9 C. Leys, *Underdevelopment in Kenya: the Political Economy of Neo-Colonialism* (London, 1975), 161.

10 W. Attwood, *The Reds and the Blacks* (New York, 1967), 257 and 268 ff.

11 Leys, *op. cit.*, 140.

12 I. Illich, *Celebration of Awareness.*

13 Leys, *op. cit.*, 196.

14 There were of course pre-existent social organizations and it may be that disintegration of these organizations rather than *national* disintegration is what is also at issue here.

15 See, for example, Donald Rothchild, *Racial Bargaining in Independent Kenya*, (London, 1973).

16 ILO, *Employment, Incomes and Equality.*

17 See, for example, Tony Moody, 'Some Features of the Agricultural Background to the Areas Covered by Rural Industrial Development Centres' (Institute for Development Research, Project Paper D. 73.7, Copenhagen, 1973), on Nyeri district.

18 See Martin Godfrey, 'The International Market in Skills and the Transmission of Inequality', VI *Development and Change* (1975).

19 Nicholas Nyangira, 'Towards a Balanced Parliament and Government in Kenya' (IDS, Working Paper No. 110, Nairobi, 1973); D. L. Dresang and I.

Sharkansky, 'Public Corporations in Single Country and Regional Settings; Kenya and the East African Community', 27 *International Organization* (1973) *et al.*

20 See Kenya, Eastern Province Planning Team, 'Rural Industrial Development in Meru': 'Embu: Rural Industrial Development Centre'; and 'Rural Industrial Development in Machakos'; (1969–71).

21 See Frances Stewart, 'Kenya: Strategies for Development' (mimeo, 1973).

22 H. Kristensen, 'The Technology Problem in Rural Small-Scale Industries—a Case Study from Kenya' (Working Paper 7, OECD Study Group on Low-Cost Technology and Rural Industrialization, Paris, 1974).

23 Langdon, 'Multinational Corporations, Taste, Transfer and Under-development'.

24 Stewart, *op. cit.*, 22.

25 See Chris. L. Wanjala, 'Alienation in Modern East African Literature' (University of Nairobi, paper for Department of History seminar, November 1972).

26 See *The Sunday Times*, 29 September 1974, for further details.

27 See *The Sunday Times*, 29 September 1974, for further details.

28 F. Holmquist, 'Implementing Rural Development Projects', G. Hyden, R. Jackson, and J. Okumu (eds.), *Development Administration: the Kenyan Experience* (Nairobi, 1970), 222. On the institutes of technology, see Godfrey and G. C. M. Mutiso, 'The Political Economy of Self-Help: Kenya's Harambee Institutes of Technology', 8 *The Canadian Journal of African Studies* (1974).

29 'Unemployed' in this context means 'unable to obtain the sort of job that they had been led to expect'.

30 Geoff Lamb, 'Political Integration in New States: Integration and Political Change in Kenya' (IDS Internal Working Paper No. 6, April 1973), 6.

31 Introduction to Okot p'Bitek's *Cultural Revolution in Africa* quoted by Wanjala, *op. cit.*

32 Mutiso, 'Cleavage and the Organizational Base of Politics in Kenya: A Theoretical Framework', 3 *Journal of Eastern African Research and Development* (1973), 39–64.

33 ILO, *Employment, Incomes and Equality*, 101–2.

34 H. Bienen, *Kenya: The Politics of Participation and Control* (Princeton, 1974).

35 Lamb, *Peasant Politics: Conflict and Development in Muranga* (Lewes, 1974).

36 R. Sandbrook, 'Patrons, Clients and Unions: The Labour Movement and Political Conflict in Kenya', 10 *Journal of Commonwealth Political Studies* (March, 1972). 3–27.

37 Alice H. Amsden, *International Firms and Labour in Kenya, 1945–70* (London, 1971).

38 Rothchild, *op. cit.*, 181.

39 See Amsden, *op. cit.*; Bienen, *op. cit.*; Leys, *op. cit.*; Sandbrook, *op. cit. et al.*

40 See ILO, *Employment, Incomes and Equality*, 48.

41 See D. Chudnovsky, 'Foreign Manufacturing Firms' Behavior in Colombia' (unpublished DPhil thesis, Oxford, 1973), 49ff on the Colombian case.

42 R. Murray, 'The Chandarias: the development of a Kenyan multinational' (mimeo, IDS, 1975).

43 See for example A. Seidman. *Comparative Development Strategies in East Africa* (Nairobi, 1972).

44 Real GDP at constant prices was 78 per cent higher in 1973 compared with 1964, an annual average rate of increase of 6.6 per cent.

PART FOUR

ALTERNATIVE STRATEGIES

13

COLLECTIVE SELF-RELIANCE: SOME OLD AND NEW ISSUES[1]

Enrique Oteiza

INTRODUCTION

The postwar dominant order has so far failed to meet the basic needs of the world population at large. Only by strenuous sacrifice, involving wars, decolonization struggles and confrontation, have Third World peoples managed to extricate themselves in some measure from a stringent political and economic environment which blocks their possibilities for achieving independence and social progress. Dependent economic growth in the periphery has proved to be incapable of reconciling capital accumulation with social needs to a much greater degree than has occurred in the central capitalist countries.

Furthermore, any long run projection concerning the future development of the *present* world capitalist system points to an even more despairing outcome regarding the fate of the majority of the world's population. Persistent warnings are being sounded as to the distinct possibilities of disaster facing the capitalist world if action is not taken promptly to provide for the satisfaction of fundamental human needs in a more just, humane and socially responsible way.

There are many good reasons why an alternative development model should be pursued by Third World countries. First, the model for overcoming underdevelopment—dependent capitalism— advocated by 'the centre' has failed to eliminate poverty. On the contrary, it has shown inherent and almost intolerable structural, social and economic inequalities between, as well as within, countries. Second, the increasingly oppressive political régimes which seem to be required, and in many cases imposed upon so-called 'developing societies', in order to align these societies with the dependent capitalist pattern, have made the 'defence of democracy' type of justification against social change an old-fashioned souvenir. Certainly there is little to say in favour of the many dictatorships—mostly military—strongly supported by 'developed capitalist countries' and their transnational corporations, that govern a large number of Third World countries.

The lack of specificity of most alternative development proposals calls for reflection and points to the need for further work. The need for mobilizing the largely under-utilized domestic potential of Third World countries, together with the need for them to assume the responsibility for their own destiny, is urgent. Under these conditions, the attempt to clarify and develop the notion of 'collective self-reliance' (CSR) seems timely. This still somewhat vague notion is becoming more and more visible in the international arena. It is already deeply rooted in the development philosophy and practice of some Third World countries (e.g. North Korea's *juche* or Tanzania's *ujamaa*). It is also becoming a part of the language used in U.N. documents and in the discourse of many Third World politicians.

In its usage, CSR has acquired the meaning of an alternative type of development, implying participation at all levels of social life, which is an essential requisite if human effort is to be mobilized in order to overcome underdevelopment. This is necessary not only in order to obtain the amount of production needed for a population to overcome poverty, but also because genuine development also means the construction of a better society, which cannot be achieved if despotic or elitist rule is maintained.

The notion, as it has been employed so far, appears to contain some elements of pre-existing ideas concerning development alternatives. Collective self-reliance implies and incorporates at least *some* elements of earlier ideas such as autarchy, self-generated and self-sustained development, new forms of intra Third World integration and association, and independence. It does not imply breaking up the world into isolated, xenophobic states.

The notion seems to be very much connected with—and can hardly be understood outside—the dependency framework. Thus, it indirectly suggests that dependency notions, generated for the most part within the last ten years, are for the moment, the best available description of the present forms of international domination. These forms of domination are imposed upon underdeveloped countries—to their disadvantage—and provide at least a partial explanation of the nature of under-development. The dependency framework emphasizes the integrated nature of the world economic system as a whole, dependency being understood as one of the central features of a highly integrated and conflict-ridden system of domination with its own patterns of evolution.

Dependency, as has been mentioned, is a peripheral aspect of the world capitalist system whereby former colonies and underdeveloped countries are exploited economically, and thus their backwardness is maintained indefinitely (By 'economic exploitation' we mean, in this context, a relationship by virtue of which one country (or interests based in that country) exert such a degree of control over the economic process of another country, as to be able to decide where and how to allocate a significant proportion of the latter's economic surplus. Usually this implies relative stagnation and backwardness in the exploited country.). This marginalization and exploitation clearly requires a system of domination which in dependent countries takes the form of an alliance between internal privileged groups and external interests and forces, both of which benefit from the arrangement. Hence the whole question of power, and therefore the political dimension, cannot be overlooked. Consequently, some aspects of the international world order, as well as its patterns of change, and questions related with the viability of a CSR approach are touched upon in this paper.

The present international system involves not simply circulation nets, both between and within countries (through which goods, services, productive resources, knowledge, ideologies and economic surplus flow), but also transnational production structures which work for the benefit of dominant 'central capitalist' countries. It seems rather unlikely then that some degree of confrontation should not result whenever Third World countries attempt to modify their form of insertion into the world system as well as their domestic structure of production.

Therefore, it is important to consider carefully the external and internal feasibility of this type of alternative development option, together with its implications in terms of domestic social changes and international alliances. The analysis of the feasibility of this option should not rule out different types and levels of confrontation, nor of conflict at national or international levels. CSR is concerned with the attainment of fundamental structural redistribution of world production and trade, control over surplus generation and allocation, and power at both national and international levels. Its concern is the enhancement of Third World productive forces, surplus generation and the power to carry forward development strategies in its own interest and for its own benefit.

WHY SELF-RELIANCE SHOULD BE COLLECTIVE

Only very large national units have an adequate resource base, climatic diversity, and population size to be able to afford an autarchic self-reliance model. Most Third World countries are the product of colonial balkanization, constituting small or middle-sized national units. Autarky for these countries may very well mean stagnation, where the satisfaction of the population's basic needs may not be attained on account of a number of insurmountable constraints.

Since a dependent type of insertion into the world economic system has been, in fact, one of the main reasons for the perpetuation of underdevelopment, it is clear that new forms of more egalitarian co-operation should be established. Here is where collective approaches in relation to self-reliance strategies may provide the necessary answers. The new forms of co-operation require partners which are following similar strategies and who are ready not only to establish new links, but to re-define economic, technical and other forms of cooperation.

There are some aspects in particular that seem to require a collective approach, involving different forms of co-operation among Third World nations. These are, among others: the struggle, inevitably a difficult one, for improving the world order in terms of making it more responsive to the needs of the large majority of the population in Asia, Africa and Latin America; development of food production and exchange among underdeveloped countries; cooperation and complementarity in industrial development; collaboration and exchange of information in scientific and technological research efforts; sharing good quality, expensive, specialized educational facilities and resources.

The achievement of an improved world order will require joint action on the part of the underdeveloped countries. One area of such action should be aimed at making the World Bank, IMF, and regional banks democratic and more universal so their policies and their implementation become more responsive to the real needs and interests of Third World countries. A further area of common action relates to the negotiations for the re-organization of the United Nations system, so that it takes into account the needs and perceptions of underdeveloped parts of the world. Finally, the formation of different types of producer and consumer associations among Third World countries should be undertaken to improve the terms of trade and all other types of international flows, resource transfer and technical assistance. For the cooperative effort among underdeveloped countries a formal secretariat and permanent association will be needed, as it exists amongst the advanced capitalist countries (OECD).

Much potential exists for the expansion of food production in Third World countries, oriented to the satisfaction of individual needs as well as to an exchange between them. This type of trade may permit a more equitable form of exchange and provide a stimulus for meaningful expansion of agricultural production. Other forms of collaboration may be in financial terms, where, for instance, OPEC countries with territories not well suited for agricultural production may provide financial resources for the development of agriculture in underdeveloped countries with good possibilities of expansion in this field. These would, in turn, repay with food products. It may also be beneficial to exchange fertilizers or other industrial agricultural inputs for food in underdeveloped countries obtaining relative advantages from this form of complementarity.

Collective self-reliance is thus critical in agriculture as a means of overcoming present food shortages, to obtain a better distribution and avoid the negative consequences of food aid in terms of political domination.

Industrial development can also benefit from cooperation among Third World countries. At a regional level, there exists in some countries in Asia and in Latin America, significant capacity for the production of capital equipment and the development of technological and engineering skills. This existing capacity should be utilized and expanded so that Third World countries may find the solution to their industrialization problems, again aiming at a more equitable type of exchange as well as at the mobilization of existing resources and the transmission of learning experiences. Industrial integration schemes, particularly those concerning neighbouring countries, can conserve resources and contribute towards development. This is so provided integration takes place within a development framework whose objective is the satisfaction of basic human needs for the population of the countries involved, rather than simply benefit small local minorities and foreign corporations.

Technological progress, both in connection with agriculture and with industry, requires the development of significant local capabilities—not mobilized in the case of 'dependent development'. These activities require the support of an educational system and well-organized scientific research. The cost of developing these capabilities, essential in a self-reliant effort is high in terms of time and financial resources. This is an area where collaboration may prove extremely useful in the pooling of resources and the sharing of benefits.

Technological dependence is critical, not only in constituting a very effective form of exploitation, but also in terms of reproducing patterns of production, circulation and consumption insufficient for satisfactory development in underdeveloped countries. Technology, mostly supplied by transnational corporations, contributes to many of the problems of Third World countries, including the mis-allocation of resources, balance of payments difficulties and un-employment. The demand for technological inputs is outward oriented, thus promoting the stagnation of the domestic innovative potential in these countries. Insofar as technology takes the shape of proprietary assets, in the present international economic system, reliance on foreign supplied technology inputs involves alienating decision-making in favour of technology suppliers from advanced capitalist countries.

Education and information are also areas of the utmost impor-tance for self-reliant development strategies. Here colloboration can be very useful in accelerating and stimulating the exchange of knowledge and experience suited to the needs of underdeveloped societies. Collaboration in the field of the mass media will be necessary to sever a very alienating dependency on news agencies and radio and television programmes from the centre.

Before proceeding with the discussion of CSR as an alternative development strategy, it may be useful to clarify some questions related to the 'world order'. This is necessary to avoid a very com-mon confusion by which a few documents, containing ideas and pro-posals, are taken for the *real* new world order. In addition to this confusion between discourse and reality, there are many semantic (disciplinary) misunderstandings. The word 'order'—in the context of international and national politics—is necessarily connected with power. It is also associated with the way power is distributed, controlled and exercised, and with whether or not the social results of a specific 'order' are equitable for the different social groups concerned. Unfortunately, modern economics has divorced means and ends from any historical content and from social and political dimensions which are, needless to say, intimately and inseparably related to real economic decisions. Reference to this question is made to avoid falling into the trap of discussing the 'international *economic* order' as something not only different from, but also very independent of, the *international order*. Making more explicit the 'power dimension', the political implications of the questions being discussed are also more in line with the present mood of the governments of the more progressive Third World countries. These are interested in changing the mechanisms and institutions by which decisions about the world order are made rather than in discussing particular lists of concessions. It does not mean, however, that this last aspect is bound to be neglected.

From the perspective of the Third World it cannot be said that a new world order, and hence a new economic order exists. On the other hand, it seems clear that important changes have occurred since the Second World War that make it impossible for the present order to remain as it is.

In the first place, the group of socialist countries has expanded and diversified and now includes countries in Europe, Asia, Africa, and Latin America, and covers a much larger proportion of the world population and territory than it did in 1947; it accounts also for a much larger share of the world's economy and international trade. The presence of these countries has brought about a wider range of choices for Third World states and created new conditions in the world market as a whole. Secondly, a large number of countries, particularly in Africa and Asia, have obtained their formal (political) independence. Collectively they have gained some voice in world affairs, developed some economic bargaining capability and acquired sufficient power to threaten to disrupt the economies of the developed countries. Thirdly, some of these new countries have been forced to obtain their independence through protracted wars of liberation succeeding, in the extraordinary cases of Vietnam and Cambodia, against the most powerful military machine in the world, while simultaneously transforming their social systems. And fourthly, important transformations have taken place since 1945 within the OECD group of countries, particularly with regard to the expansion of productive capacity, resulting in renewed competition, increasing protectionism, unemployment and, in general, inflation and a climate of uncertainty. Partly as a consequence of the changes just mentioned, the OECD countries are undergoing a severe crisis, which does not seem to be responding to the present stock of recipes of post-Keynesian capitalist economic policy. Thus, a 'new order' seems inevitable; what is far from clear is whether it will be favourable for the people of the Third World.

It is useful to remember that, by 1945, the U.S.A. was the indisputable world power and, thus, in a position to define the new international institutional order. Europe states were in urgent need of reconstruction and the North Atlantic scheme put forward by the U.S. was accepted. Japan did not at that time have a voice in shaping the new international system. The colonial problem and the decolonization process were supposed to be more of a European concern, and the Third World, as an entity with some capacity to question the designs being implemented, did not exist as a force. Only the Soviet Union was a source of real concern for central capitalist countries, and through means to ensure peaceful coexistence such as the United Nations, including the U.N. Security Council, and a balance of power approach based on the arms race, the threat was restricted.

There is no doubt that the present world political situation is different. The number of actors with at least some power is much greater. In the dynamic process already taking place leading towards a new order, they will be active participants. No international institutions, new or reformed, will be successful if they are not established with sufficient backing by a large enough group of countries.

The Third World and particularly the non-aligned nations, is already showing its will to play a role on many different fronts. Some producer associations, particularly since OPEC's actions, have pointed to the potential advantages to be derived from new forms of association. In the U.N., these countries have obtained majority voting support for proposals dealing with the modification of present international institutions.

Wars of liberation have continued, producing not only new nations, but in many cases new social structures and socialist systems in former colonies of the capitalist metropolis. Within the OECD, social forces are being activated by the present crisis and important political changes may occur, particularly in Western Europe, and open new possibilities of transition to socialism for societies located at the centre of the capitalist system. Working classes may find new ways to press, not so much for wages, but now for social change.

THE ECONOMIC DIMENSIONS OF THE PRESENT CRISIS

A new development strategy by Third World countries should take into account the changing balance in the international system, and its deep repercussions on the patterns of the international flow and allocation of resources and the global strategy pursued by the central powers. The picture we observe today of very large reservoirs of unemployed labour and capital in central industrial countries, is one which many people believed impossible in post-war capitalism.

Neo-Keynesian policies, coupled with administered markets, a high rate of technical progress and the continuous expansion of trade and investment abroad, in the context of an unprecedented process of unification of the world economic space, was perceived by many as capable of sustaining endless and stable long-run capitalist prosperity.

Only relatively mild and entirely manageable cycles, involving inventory adjustment and innocuous pauses had been taken into account. But these were seen as an unimportant feature of an otherwise healthy and fast-growing capitalist order, endowed with fine built-in stabilizers, under the sway of the manipulative capabilities of the state and big corporations. Mutually reinforcing downward spirals at the international level were supposedly eliminated. Major depressions, therefore, were considered in many quarters to be definitely extinct.

Then, however, came the most severe depression since that of the thirties. It came as a complete surprise, a rare and almost cosmic phenomenon to be explained by resorting to 'exogenous' factors (e.g. an 'arbitrary' reversal in the terms of trade). The present depression is neither a minor 'pause' nor a definitive breakdown. It involves a critical period in a long recessive wave (i.e. an increased gap between actual and potential GNP) with a lower rate of growth, a higher rate of both inflation and unemployment and relatively deeper and longer cyclical fluctuations in contrast with the previous periods. Capitalism neither grows nor declines regularly and evenly.

Certainly the present crisis is not one of general overproduction as was the great depression. Nor does it reflect the exhaustion of the *extensive* exploitation of the world market. The conditions surrounding the present crisis are characterized by the geographical narrowing of the world capitalist market, the weakening of the national state *vis-à-vis* the transnational corporations and a big question mark concerning the capacity of capitalism to absorb the rapid growth which characterized the capitalist countries in the sixties. This occurs in the context of increasing political consciousness among vast sectors of the population, both in the Third World and in the central capitalist countries.

Clearly World War II laid the basis for post-war capitalist expansion—under new political and economic forms of organization and control—which widened economic and consequently social gaps and reinforced the concentration of power and wealth at different levels (regional, national and international). The question is how capitalism managed to maintain a fairly steady level of expansion—with its peculiar new forms of prosperity and inequality—and why it ceased to be able to do so.

One of the most plausible explanations for the long postwar prosperity cycle concerns the successive waves of technological innovations giving rise to the so-called Kondratieff prosperity cycles. One such cycle started in 1843 with the railways. Another was that of 1897, in which the electrical, chemical and motor industries played the leading role. With World War II a new long prosperity cycle was supposedly inaugurated by the so-called scientific-industrial revolution, consisting of the organic integration of science and industry. This integration, coupled with organizational innovations in key dynamic economic activities, implying a fast professionalization of management, the introduction of the computer, the concentration of decision-making, extensive internationalization and decentralization of operations, has indeed been a key factor in post-World War II economic growth.

Though this explanation has its merits (and warrants further exploration), it hardly gives the whole picture, and, used in an unqualified manner, may be misleading. For one thing, it does not, *per se*, account for cyclical fluctuations.[2] In fact, the postwar prosperity boom has been affected by more or less serious fluctuations in the general level of economic activity, particularly in employment (every 4–5 years). And now it faces the sharpest down-swing since the great depression. It is not quite clear however, whether, on the one hand, the present depression involves a definite end to the postwar prosperity boom, leading to the mobilization of the latent conflicts inherent in the system or, on the other, reveals the need for a change in the pattern of capital accumulation, which might eventually be met within the present social framework, albeit not without sacrifices in terms of stability and growth. We shall return to this question below.

Moreover, there seems to be an over-emphasis on the extent to which capital accumulation has actually been encouraged by industrial innovation. Insofar as a great many of these innovations have been both capital and labour saving, the opposite has been the case. And this is a specific aspect of the postwar long term cycle which could not have been accounted for in terms of previous Kondratieff prosperity cycles. These have been characterized by 'extensive' rather than 'intensive' industrialization (in one case 'total productivity' remains fairly constant; in the other it increases steadily).[3] This is not to suggest, as under-consumption theorists do, that there has been an exhaustion of investment outlets, but rather that the existence of serious constraints on continuous profitable accumulation is present.

However, it is beyond doubt that the innovative process, coupled with increasing concentration and centralization of capital, the state's macroeconomic devices for maintaining global demand, and sustained trade and expansion abroad, had a favourable effect on profitability until nearly the end of the last decade. High profits are one of the keys in central countries to stable 'prosperity' under capitalism. However, for the time being, it appears that profits will remain low.

All through this process, it is quite clear that, although the governments of the central economies have been using state expenditure and fiscal policies as conscious stabilizing devices to moderate fluctuations, they have paradoxically been losing their capacity to control economic behaviour both at the domestic and international levels. And this is a direct result of the pattern of long run growth pursued.

To start with, the oligopolization and 'conglomerization' of the economy, with administered prices and markets, have meant that productivity increases have not been translated into lower prices but into higher incomes for a few. Since this mechanism of appropriation of the fruits of technical progress, coupled with labour-displacing innovations, created in the long run a built-in bias against the growth of consumer demand and employment, and hence against profitable capital accumulation, the need arises for government spending to fill the gap in aggregate demand. This is intended to keep employment as high as possible and, with it, to encourage rapid capital accumulation. When it is not financed out of loans, government spending must be financed by resorting either to taxation or to money-creation. Under full or near-full employment, both are inflationary (in the first case because the most concentrated strata of industry are capable of passing at least part of the incremental burden on to consumers through higher prices). Thus defensive money/wage demands arise in order to offset higher prices and to participate as far as possible in the benefits arising from productivity increases. As a result, the whole process of capital accumulation exhibits inherent inflationary tendencies.

The inflationary process described as taking place in the industrialized capitalist countries is all the more serious when it involves an economy which is the most important single source of international liquidity. In effect, the gold exchange system stemming from the Bretton Woods agreements decreed that the American dollar was to be fully convertible to gold as an international reserve asset. Whilst war-torn nations were still recovering and hence productivity differentials were highly favourable to the U.S.A., the supply of international liquity, albeit scarce at that time, was consistent with the U.S.A. preserving external equilibrium; i.e., current account surpluses offset a steady increase in military and aid programmes abroad required for the upsurge in American long-term investment all over the world. But, starting at the end of the 1950s, with narrowing productivity differentials *vis-à-vis* Europe and Japan, current account surpluses became increasingly insufficient: a sustained gold drain began to deplete its reserves. Already in 1967 the American Secretary of the Treasury warned Europe that his country could find it necessary to 'withdraw from commitments involving the security and development of others' by taking unilateral action. Four years later, in 1971, Nixon declared the inconvertibility of the dollar. It was already clear by this time that, with America forcing its inflation on other nations, their growing dollar assets could not ultimately be convertible into gold. Thus the gold-exchange agreement could not be honoured 'down to the last bar of gold'. The role of the dollar as an international reserve asset, though aiding rapid capital development in Europe, allowed it at the same time to act as a device for exercising American control over other nations.

But this inherently unequal system was the cause of its own downfall. Under its protection, there was an unprecedented development of centralized decision-making outside and beyond the scope of the nation state. In 1970, transnational corporations controlled 196 out of 268 billion dollars available in the international economy on a short term basis. In addition, more than 30 per cent of world trade was being channelled through them. This development created increasing sources of international instability since it opened the way to mechanisms of monetary and financial manipulation well beyond the control of national governments. At the same time, the complete recovery of the productive forces and international competitiveness of the war-torn nations enabled them to start openly challenging the U.S.A.'s hegemonic powers.

At this point we return to our original question regarding the alternatives facing the capitalist order. Beyond the fact that some important attempts are being made to overcome the present depression, it has already impressed its mark upon long-run political, social and economic trends.

As to the economic dimension, some new kind of world balance may arise as considered from the standpoint of the needs of capital reproduction. Advanced capitalist countries, having reached a high degree of economic integration (almost to the point of 'saturation'), amongst themselves will look for a way out of the present crisis by a renewed drive for cheap labour and resources in Third World countries. Insofar as every significant crisis under capitalism imposes the need to reallocate resources in a more profitable way (at the expense of the weakest sectors of capital), pressures in such a direction will inevitably follow. So the already visible trend towards the integration of certain backward areas into the world capitalist industrial system will become even more accentuated. The effects of this incorporation are documented in various pieces included in this volume (e.g., Sunkel and Fuenzalida; Villamil (Puerto Rico); Fuenzalida; Godfrey and Langdon).

Social tensions will be moved from the 'centre' out to the 'periphery' by means of diverse forms of association between foreign and domestic (either private or state) capital, and increasing proletarization of Third World masses. Favourable class alliances will then be sought. Through them, efforts by Third World countries as a whole towards re-negotiating the basis of the present order *vis-à-vis* the 'centre' will be blocked and pseudo-solutions put forward as a means of by-passing the central issues that need to be dealt with. Thus, the challenge for Third World countries is not negligible. CSR can be a positive response to it.

DELINKING, RELINKING AND THE INTERNATIONAL SYSTEM

As has been mentioned in the previous paragraphs, not only did the post World War II international order create unfavourable conditions for the development of most of today's Third World countries, but the present crisis of the central industrial capitalist countries may easily result in an even more negative situation for the former group of countries.

The emphasis CSR strategies place on delinking from traditional dependency connections with the international system is therefore a reasonable reaction from the past experience of Third World countries as well as from fear of even further deterioration in their relative position and potential for development. On the other hand, the realization that an autarchic path may not be an adequate response to the problems of underdevelopment makes relinking with the aim of achieving a balanced relationship a natural response.

It is important to take into account that a process of delinking and relinking of this type is a dynamic one. Every action of this nature has a number of repercussions in the international system, not all of them economic. Changes in international flows, if sustained, should have repercussions in social structures. Therefore, the process of delinking and relinking implicit in a CSR strategy are in themselves a very dynamic and positive element in the definition of a new international order.

It is not easy, however to develop criteria which could provide a clear-cut orientation as to when to delink and when and how to relink. The need for achieving self-reliance in food has been stressed by some, in order to move away from a form of 'aid' which is uncertain in terms of supply and costly in terms of political domination. A simple rule was proposed by Nurul Islam[4] regarding the question of when to delink: 'Where a Third World country has strong individual strength—or participates in a situation of equally strong-collective-bargaining strength, it should remain connected with the international system. Otherwise delink from it'.

The linkages in the international system are many and structured in a complex way through institutions, rules and regulations which are part of the very essence of the present world order. Economic linkages such as trade, investment, loans, transfer of technologies, air and maritime transport, are very much controlled by transnational corporations and governmental and intergovernmental international agencies based in and controlled from 'developed' OECD countries. Cultural linkages such as mass media, special types of training, publishing and advanced education, are also to a very large extent controlled by transnational corporations and governmental and intergovernmental agencies similarly controlled by groups or states in the same countries. Political and military linkages also integrate large groups of Third World countries with former or new metropoli through international 'aid' or 'co-operation' treaties, and different forms of covert or overt political and military interventions. There are, thus, many more dimensions to the delinking-relinking question aside from the purely economic ones. Therefore, delinking cannot be expected to be a free, easy and zero cost process.

What is important to emphasize is that CSR development strategies, including the nature of delinking and relinking, should be adapted to the situation of each national society. Some Third World countries may have a more integrated productive structure or more resources than others. Some may have a stronger colonial or dependency heritage in terms of a more or less extroverted economy and more or less diversified system of exports. Initial conditions and characteristics of the process of transition are important aspects to be taken into account in the definition of a concrete CSR development strategy.

If socio-political changes can be brought about, the satisfaction of basic needs can produce a valuable orientation to the CSR strategy. Obviously in this perspective the production of food for local consumption becomes a high priority. This, in turn, means re-allocating labour, land and other imputs aways from export crops into the production of a domestically oriented agriculture product mix.

Exports would be affected by this reorientation. But this may be compensated to some extent by decreasing food imports, co-operation with neighbouring Third World countries in food production and exchange, and a decline in luxury imports for the privileged minorities. On the other hand, expansion of imports of capital goods required for transforming and expanding the productive structure for supplying the goods and services needed for the satisfaction of basic needs in addition to food—housing, sanitation, health, transportation, education and culture, and other basic goods such as clothing and furniture—constitutes a difficult problem to overcome. Here is an area in which adequate regional integration schemes and trade between more equal partners can be of great help.

IS THE ALTERNATIVE DEVELOPMENT STRATEGY VIABLE?

Traditionally, development models and strategies have been analysed in terms of their economic feasibility. If several alternatives are feasible in terms of some limited economic criteria, they are deemed to be equal in other respects and it is for the 'policy-maker' to decide which alternative to select.

Of course, this type of analysis is not very useful for dealing with genuine development processes, and (clearly) becomes inadequate when the alternative being considered involves breaking-away from the international system, transforming social structures in the under-developed country concerned, and establishing co-operation with other countries following a similar path—relinking.

In transformations as complex as those proposed in CSR alternative strategies, the question is not so much short-term economic considerations, but *viability* in the longer perspective. What is needed then is a long-term economic and socio-political analysis of viability, comprising both the internal and the international dimensions of the strategy. A *viability* analysis should include the question of the *initiation* of a process of development of this nature and its *sustainment* over time.

With regard to *initiation*, as long as CSR includes breaking away from the dependency linkages of exploitation beneficial to the dominant 'developed' country or countries, then it must be assumed that such an alternative strategy is to be initiated by the 'underdeveloped' countries. This implies in these countries a process of internal social transformation bringing into power new social forces to transform the orientation of the development process into a CSR alternative.

Which alliance of social groups might confront, in peripheral countries, the established order? Two main approaches are common in this respect. One poses the question in terms of alliances of élites and power groups, assuming that power can be redirected by a recombination of the top layers of society. The other tends to see the problem as involving inevitably the working class, or the majority of the population, together with progressive minorities, mobilizing contradictions that may result from the specific characteristics of the historical process. Both approaches pay attention to the specificity of the historical process of any particular country. The first approach is élitist and the second revolutionary.

One of the main difficulties with the more élitist approach, which tends to work on the assumption that the local bourgeoisie may react on a nationalistic basis, is that in dependent societies this social class derives its power and, in many ways, existence from the connection with the dominant foreign interests. Therefore, there is no 'national bourgeoisie' in dependent countries of the type that played such an important part in the European and North American industrial revolutions.

Transnational corporations (TNCs) can also become an important obstacle to a change towards a more self-reliant pattern of development. In this respect there is a significant difference between the non-industralized and the more industrialized dependent countries. As long as the TNCs are involved, not only in the business of international circulation of goods, services and technology, but also as part of the productive structure, they become a very powerful force, especially in Third World countries that follow a path of dependent industrialization. Less industrialized Third World countries should be more able, if they aim at an alternative CSR type of development, to negotiate from the beginning whatever they may need from the outside, trying at least to preserve control of their economies.

Even in a highly simplified view, it is important to consider that the relationship of the multinational corporation is not only with the state of the dependent country, but with the state of the central countries and in particular the dominant one. In turn the state of the hegemonic country has a number of ways (financial, military, etc.) to act on the state of the dependent country.

No strategy related to a CSR approach, either at the collective or at the national levels, which fails to perceive and to tackle the present power of TNCs, can succeed. The package of management, technology, capital and information in the hands of these corporations should be dismantled, the 'underdeveloped' country following an alternative strategy always retaining direct control of management. As to technology, there is a very great need to develop indigenous capabilities for the generation, adaptation and absorption of alternative solutions. Collective action and co-operation among Third World countries can increase the chances of overcoming restrictions in the technological field, and can be of immense usefulness in dealing with TNCs in general.

NOTES

1 This is a revised version of a paper presented at a Seminar on Collective Self-Reliance which took place in February 1976 in Lima (Peru) under the co-sponsorship of the National Planning Institute of the Government of Peru and of the Third World Forum. It relies on previous work done with Francisco Sercovic on this topic.
2 Schumpeter, for one, in his historical outline used a three-cycle schema: the forty month or Kitchin cycle, the ten year or Juglar cycle, and the 60 year or Kondratieff cycle. He postulates that 'each Kondratieff should contain an integral number of Juglar and each Juglar an integral number of Kitchins. . . . If waves of innovations of shorter span play around a wave of similar character but of longer span, the sequence of the phases of the latter will so determine the conditions under which the former rise and break as to make a higher unit out of them, even if the innovations which create them are entirely independent of the innovations which carry the longer wave'. *Business Cycles, A Theoretical, Historical and Statistical Analysis of the Capitalist Process*, New York, 1939, I, p. 172.
3 R. Richta, *La Civilización en la Encrucijada*, Siglo XXI, 1971.
4 During a seminar on CSR organized by the Third World Forum, in Lima, February, 1976.

14

PLANNING FOR
SELF-RELIANT GROWTH[1]

José J. Villamil

INTRODUCTION

Much of development planning theory and practice has been based
on neo-classical approaches to development (Lefeber, 1974). This
has entailed the use of highly aggregated models, an absence of
institutional and political factors in the analysis, an over-emphasis
on supply considerations, and the utilization of universal models to
explain particular national experiences. Furthermore, planning has
been considered as exogenous to the particular development model
adopted. This article is based on a contrary assumption, recognizing
that in different development contexts planning assumes different
functions and definitions. Thus, whether planning aims at achieving
significant structural transformations in society or just simply
improving the efficiency of resource allocation at the margin, will
imply very different sets of procedures. In fact, to talk of development planning without specifying the particular institutional and
political context within which it takes place, and the objectives it is
meant to achieve, may introduce a large element of confusion.

Recent work on development has questioned traditional neo-
classical thinking (as well as that of the 'modernization' school in the
social sciences), by placing emphasis on different sets of causal
relationships (see the articles by Sunkel, Sunkel and Fuenzalida,
Seers, and Valenzuela and Valenzuela in this volume). In particular,
the manner in which Third World countries have been incorporated
into the world capitalist system is seen as a determining factor in
their present condition. It has become clear that the problems of
underdevelopment are not only, and in most cases, not even
primarily problems of national insufficiencies, but relate to the
organization and functioning of the world economic system, one in
which the rules of the game have been set by the industrialized
capitalist countries and stacked in their favour. The categories of
'developed-underdeveloped' have been substituted by 'dominant-
dependent', and the process of development is seen to encompass
much more than just growth in income or GNP. Attention has been
focused on the need to achieve national self-reliance as a primary

objective of development and on the concomitant transformation
of the mode of production and the class structure. As stated by
Vasconi (1970), and suggested by Seers, Sunkel and Fuenzalida and
Godfrey in this volume, the modification of a country's dependent
condition and the change in its internal structures are parts of the
same process, and cannot occur independently of one another.

Partly as a result of this re-thinking of development approaches,
and partly due to the failure of development policies over the past
three decades, alternative development strategies have been proposed which go beyond the more limited objectives of traditional
development thinking. Included among the objectives are disengagement from the world capitalist economy, massive redistribution of income and wealth, as well as political power, much
greater control by the state of the means of production, satisfaction
of the basic needs of the population and greater collaboration
among Third World countries. Together with these proposals for
alternative development strategies, there have been a number of
proposals for changes in the international economic
order, ranging from the negotiations at UNCTAD, to the adoption
by the Sixth Special Session of the U.N. General Assembly of
1974, of a *Declaration and Action Programme on the Establishment
of a New International Economic Order* (U.N. General Assembly
Resolutions 3201 (S-VI) and 3202 (S-VI), May 1, 1974). Although
the specific content of the *Declaration and Action Programme* need
not concern us here—they deal for the most part with proposals for
improving the terms of trade of raw materials exporting countries,
improving access to markets, technology and financial resources of
the industrialized countries, and other related issues—it is important to consider two aspects related to this proposal. One is that very
little progress has been made, largely due to the opposition of the
industrialized countries (Green, 1976). The other is that, even if
some of the proposals were implemented, without significant
changes in the structure of national societies these would merely
reinforce the existing pattern of class domination.

Thus, the two must go together: changes in the international
system, and transformations in the national economic and social
structures and in development strategies. It is obvious that before
these alternative development strategies can be implemented, political conditions within a country have to change. This article deals
with the implications for planning of adopting a development
strategy which encompasses the points made above, in particular
during the transition phase which will necessarily follow the
adoption of such a strategy.

ON THE TRANSITION

In his book on the transition to socialism, Bettelheim considers two types of transition: one, which he calls a 'radical form of transition', between the capitalist mode of production and the socialist; the second a more limited and uncertain type, which characterizes those countries moving from colonial to post-colonial status, or from dependence to independence. A number of factors will affect how this latter type of transition will take place: the class nature of the state, whether or not there is a cohesive national bourgeoisie, the prevailing mode of production, and the country's 'room for manoeuvre' (Bettelheim, 1974).

In many ways, the situation under consideration is a hybrid of Bettelheim's two types of transition. We assume that political change has taken place which permits the adoption of a very different style or model of development from that which could be called the dependent capitalist model. Among the objectives pursued would be the satisfaction of the basic needs of the population, disengagement from the world capitalist economy, massive redistribution of income and wealth, greater collaboration among Third World countries, and the assumption by the state of much greater control over the means of production (Oteiza, in this volume; Amin, 1972). As mentioned, this model has been described as the 'self-reliant' model of growth.

The experience of the transition to socialism in a country such as the Soviet Union cannot be automatically transferred to the Third World (Amin, 1972). The objective conditions are so different that we are talking about very different processes. The transition which is most relevant to Third World countries today is one in which countries move from the dependent capitalist model to self-reliant growth, with the eventual transformation of the capitalist mode of production to socialism. Amin (1972) and Thomas (1974) argue that strategies for the transition are, above all, strategies for self-reliance.

Countries which adopt this model will be confronted with a number of conditions that must be considered and dealt with: (1) Serious disruptions could occur due to changes in the sources of supply of materials and consumer goods. This could be due to decisions taken by the dominant colonial or neo-colonial power, as in the case of the Cuban blockade, to internal economic conditions inherent in disengagement from the capitalist economic system, or to a conscious decision by the government. (2) Distortions in the price system will become particularly evident in the first stages of transition. The prevailing price system, which refers to the dependent growth model, will still be affecting resource allocations. This will make changes in the various economic and social policies more difficult, and will necessitate a movement away from the existing price system. (3) Discontinuities will arise in a number of areas: consumption patterns, the provision of social services, organization of the state bureaucracy and others. The handling of these discontinuities so as to prevent total disintegration in the transition phase becomes of great importance. (4) This is a period of great uncertainty, arising from the factors above, and from the fact that the country is acting in an environment which may be hostile. The reaction of the previously dominant country or countries is an unknown quantity, and the dependent country must gauge very carefully its 'room for manoeuvre'. The reactions of multinational corporations at this stage are also important, especially in those countries in which they have an important stake (Fajnzylber, 1976; Fortín, in this volume). (5) By its very nature a transition is a stage full of contradictions. Elements of the old order remain, and the new order has not established itself. The state may be completely or partially in the hands of those who seek to transform prevailing conditions, the means of production may not be. It is apparent then, that this transition phase is a very fragile one, requiring constant attention to the distribution of power, both internal and external, to creating the conditions that will make the process irreversible and that will increase its 'room for manoeuvre'. In the management of this delicate phase the role of planning is crucial.

ON PLANNING

Since the end of the Second World War, there has been an increasing interest in national planning in the capitalist world. This is a consequence of the war experience itself, the Keynesian attempts at regulating the capitalist economies, the efforts at the reconstruction of Europe and, finally, the existence of a strong bloc of socialist nations. By the late fifties and early sixties, planning had also become widely accepted and practised in the non-industrialized world. Its diffusion was stimulated by international organizations and some of the industrialized countries as a way of rationalizing their economies. Thus, in Latin America, one can be very precise as to the beginnings of development planning and the institutionalization of plan preparation. The benchmark date would be 1961 with the establishment of the Alliance for Progress. This programme required the existence of a national plan in order to qualify for United States foreign aid (Moreno, 1977; Seers, in Faber and Seers, 1972).

Perhaps the name we most associate with development planning is that of Jan Tinbergen. For Tinbergen (1964), planning is a set of procedures related to the preparation of long, medium, and short-term plans. It is also a hierarchical process which goes from the most general (long-term plans) to the most specific (annual plans). His approach to planning has been criticized as unrealistic in view of the absence of technical and human resources in most Third World countries (Leys, 1969; Faber and Seers, 1972). But perhaps the most negative aspects of Tinbergen's approach to plannings has to do with his implicit assumption that the prevailing political system is both stable and desirable, and that only tinkering at the margin is required. For him, the problem is one of maximizing the rate of growth of income and achieving maximum efficiency in the utilization of resources. In a way, planning becomes programming.

Over the past few years there has been much criticism of development planning and its results in developing countries. There has been talk of a 'crisis in planning' (Faber and Seers, 1972) and a number of reasons for this crisis mentioned: the non-implementation of plans (Meier, 1970); the inadequacy of imported planning models (Meier, 1970; Leys, 1969); theoretical inadequacies on the part of planners (Daiz-Alejandro, 1970); a disfunctional relationship between the functions of planning and its organization (Wildavsky, 1971), and others. In general, one can group these discussions on planning in three categories: those which concentrate on operational questions, those which question the disciplinary content or object of planning and finally, those which attribute to planning an ideological function, exclusively or primarily.

The failure of planning, according to those in the first category is, for the most part, attributable to problems such as lack of communication between planners and administrators or politicians, and shortcomings in the various actors involved in the planning process (Seers in Faber and Seers, 1972, and the discussion by Gooneratne). Others have pointed to the inherent conflict between planning and public administration or that planning has been ineffective because there has been no public participation in the preparation of plans (underscoring the fact that planning in many countries serves a merely formal function, or else that it is an instrument for procuring foreign aid; that it is, as Seers has called it 'pseudo-planning'). A related approach to development planning argues that it is impossible to plan the whole range of activities implied in development and thus advocates a more limited, incremental approach with a heavy emphasis on project planning. This is particularly characteristic of a number of American planners who have contributed to the language of planning such terms as '*ad hoc* opportunism', 'disjointed incrementalism', 'muddling through' and others (Bolan, 1967), but not exclusive to them (Leys, 1969; also the papers by Leys and Waterston in Faber and Seers, 1972).

A second type of critique of planning has concentrated on the need for planning to be more than economic growth planning. This view has led to efforts at developing the field of social planning as an activity to be carried out together with economic planning (Apthorpe, 1970). In the late fifties and early sixties, for example, the United Nations sponsored a number of studies and published various documents on balanced socio-economic planning. In 1969, the United Nations Research Institute on Social Development (UNRISD), launched a project to develop a 'unified approach to the analysis and planning of development' (U.N.,1972). Essentially, the objective of this project was to devise an approach to development planning which would integrate the various dimensions of the development problem. Thus, among others, it sought to introduce social elements into planning, to move away from aggregative models and look into problems of distribution. Underlying the UNRISD project was the assumption that the problem with development planning was mostly due to its having been the province of economists, for the most part, and thus lacking in interdisciplinary content, and the fact that it had placed excessive reliance on aggregate objectives such as maximizing the rate of growth of income.

The third group considers planning from a different perspective, considering it as an ideology or, at least, as one of the ideological instruments of the state. In this sense Myrdal's view (1968) that development planning became ' . . . the intellectual matrix of the modernization ideology' is accepted. Two things are entailed: on the one hand a definition of the development process in terms of categories derived from orthodox development economics or from the 'modernization' school, and on the other, a set of procedures which, if followed, would help achieve the goals derived from them. It is argued that there is complete separation of means and ends. The goals of development are assumed to be universally applicable. The specific planning procedures and instruments are assumed to have no substantive content.

Moreno (1977) has argued that it is useful to consider planning as an ideological apparatus of the state, following Althusser's definition. Viewed from this perspective, it is necessary to evaluate planning in terms of explicit and implicit objectives. Thus, regardless of whether planning has achieved the explicit objectives set out in the various plans, it has served as an instrument of class domination in preserving a particular social structure, not only because of the functions it has had in reducing social tensions inherent in capitalist development, but in a more subtle way. It has served as a means of creating a national consensus—or the appearance of a consensus—for the objectives of a dominant class.

Bettelheim (1974) has argued that capitalism and planning are incompatible, but it is clear that underlying his view is a particular definition of planning derived from the role of planning in a socialist society. It is clear that planning in capitalist countries is a very different activity with very different objectives and functions. In the capitalist underdeveloped world, planning has served as one of the means for minimizing contradictions arising from the process of capitalist growth. Thus, planning dealt with regional imbalances, urban problems, the planning of infrastructure, the various 'bottlenecks' which confronted countries at various times and other problems which could, if not dealt with, generate social tensions which could threaten the stability of the regime.

In Latin America, for example, planning has not been strictly necessary in most countries, but it has had important ancillary functions, particularly after the Alliance for Progress was established. It dealt with the rationalization of state intervention in the economy, particularly in providing infrastructure, the coordination of various sectors, sectoral programming, achieving coherence for investment programs and providing the rationale for obtaining foreign aid (Cibotti, Nuñez del Prado and Sainz, in García, 1972). If it did not achieve structural transformations in the various countries, this does not imply failure. It may very well have been successful in terms of those functions which it was called upon to perform by the dominant groups in these countries.

In any case, it is clear that countries aiming at major structural transformations have little to benefit from traditional planning theory. A new development model will require a new planning model. Neither orthodox theories of development planning, mostly from Europe and the United States, nor those which come from socialist planners are very useful for planning the transition from dependent to self-reliant growth. The work of socialist planners such as Dobb, Lange, Bettelheim, Zielinski, and Kornai is either devoted to planning in a socialist society or, as frequently happens, adopts the language and approaches of orthodox development planning. Lange, for example, has this to say:

> The essential (of economic planning) consists in assuring an amount of productive investment which is sufficient to provide for a rise of national income substantially in excess of the rise in population, so that per capita national income increases.

> By substantial productive investment I mean investment which is large enough to achieve a breakthrough, or as some economists call it—to produce the 'take-off', the passage from stagnation to intensive development. (quoted in Meier, 1974).

There are, of course, differences between socialist and non-socialist planners. One major difference is the emphasis placed by the former on investment in industries which 'produce means of production'. Another has to do with the emphasis on achieving 'material balances', which is characteristic of socialist planning. In general, however, one must look elsewhere for guidance with respect to planning the transition.

The particular structure of planning, its objectives, the variables with which it deals and the strategies adopted, are determined by the nature of the system being planned and the environment within which planning takes place. Thus, for example, the degree of control which the state has or the consensus which exists with respect to national objectives, are important determinants of how planning is organized and of how it operates. The greater the degree of control over the determinants of system behaviour the easier it is for planning to adopt a deterministic posture. The greater the degree of uncertainty or the absence of control over these factors, the more necessary it is for planning to adopt a less deterministic, contingency based approach.

It is important to define the parameters within which planning for the transition begins and which, in some cases, it seeks to modify. These include the organization and functioning of the world economy; the factors affecting the markets for the country's exports; the manner in which the national productive sector is organized and how it relates to the rest of the world; the class structure of the country and the manner in which power is allocated and maintained; the country's resource base, the market size (Vasconi, 1970; Sunkel, 1969, 1971).

As already mentioned, if a primary objective is economic independence or disengagement from the world capitalist system, this means either the closing of the system, or parts of it, or a diversification of sources of supplies or markets (Green, 1972; Gutierrez, Ortiz and Villamil, 1971). A dependent country's economy is characterized by a number of flows such as information, technology, capital, exports, imports and population, over which some measure of control must be achieved. It is essential that the foreign sector, or the channels through which the dependent relationship has been maintained, be controlled by the planning system, so that planning can regulate the external links of the country on the basis of overall objectives. Traditionally, development planning had dealt with some of these flows when, for example, implementing policies for import substitution. Recently, more and more countries have adopted measures with respect to others of these flows, such as controls on capital and even technology. However, it is important to consider also, the need for dealing with the information system at a global scale, its organization and the type of information which it generates. Just as it has become clear that world markets are organized to benefit the central capitalist economies, it has also become evident that information is produced by a few concerns in these countries, in support of the aims and objectives of the countries and the transnational capitalist system as a whole (Somavía, 1976; Sauvant, 1976). The effects on countries in the periphery range from distorting the people's perceptions of their own societies' reality, to stimulating consumption patterns and patterns of cultural behaviour which lead to increasing incorporation into the world capitalist system, and oppose an independent, self-reliant development. Thus, information flows must become one of the critical variables with which planning is concerned in the transition period (Gutierrez, Ortiz and Villamil, 1971).

If dependent capitalist growth leads to a particular type of organization of society's structures, or as Sunkel and Fuenzalida have called it, the disintegration of society's structures (see their article in this volume), then planning for self-reliant growth can also be thought of as planning for national integration or reintegration. This process has to be specified in the various contexts: social, cultural, economic and so on. Thus, in economic terms it may mean substituting internal for external linkages (Raj, 1975); in social and cultural terms it may mean dealing with variables related to language policy (de Silva, 1976), the replacement of the previous bureaucratic structures (Jones, 1975)—particularly important in recently independent nations—cultural policy and other such measures aimed at maintaining the country as an integrated whole (Scott, 1970). Obviously, what the specific measures are, and how planning is brought to bear on the problem of national integration will depend on the particular conditions of the countries. In some cases, the priorities may lie in the establishment of a national cultural policy aimed at creating a 'feeling of nationhood', as Myrdal has called it. In other cases, priorities may be related to achieving self-sufficiency in food, in some manufactured goods, and in generating industrial linkages. In yet other countries where the first two sets of problems are not critical, planning may have as its main objective, for example, minimizing external dependence on technology. What is clear is that many of the old instruments in the tool-kit of development planners and politicians in the developing countries—nationalization, localization of jobs in foreign enterprises, protective policies and integration of developing countries in common markets—are not sufficient, and may even make matters worse. Thus, Vaitsos (1977) argues that Central America became even more dependent after the establishment of the Central American Common Market. Localization of jobs may mean the strengthening of the local transnational groups who will oppose any moves toward a more self-reliant strategy (see, for example the articles by Langdon, Godfrey and Langdon, Cruise O'Brien and Sunkel and Fuenzalida in this volume). This does not mean that any of these measures is necessarily bad, but it does mean that the problem of disengagement and self-reliant development is more complex and requires measures which go beyond these.

This brings up new considerations related to planning strategies. Planning must be conceived of as a set of temporally linked actions leading to a desired and state, where each decision is aimed at making the process of national integration, or the transition to an alternative development model, less reversible. Indeed, one important criterion for planning decisions is the extent to which they contribute to making the process irreversible. Thus, actions must be taken that will provide the country with the means to resist external pressures. For example, the maintenance of foreign exchange reserves, important in any case, is crucial in the transition phase especially in the context of a hostile environment and in the case of a country which is financially dependent. Not only material but also ideological conditions must be dealt with; for example, information flows and super-structural arrangements which become crucial at least in some phases of the transition. In some African countries after independence, planning had to be concerned with basic and very crucial problems related to the formation of social, economic, cultural and political institutions. Rweyamamu (1970) argues that in a pre-industrial society such as Tanzania, national planning could 'only mean one thing, namely, nation building. . .' This had many ramifications including the more obvious ones of developing a trained group of technicians and teachers (Helleiner, 1972), framing education within a socialist ideological context (Helleiner, 1972) and emphasizing Swahili as the language of instruction in schools (Godfrey, in this volume).

A consequence of insertion into the world capitalist system is that the criteria used to evaluate behaviour in many areas are those of the dominant countries. This is true in the professions, in making investment decisions, in the organization and functioning of the educational system, in how the bureaucracy works (Jones, 1975), and in several other fields. Thus, an important objective in the planning process, is that of negating, at least in some important aspects, the cultural influence of the dominant nation or nations.

One set of problems which is important in defining a planning strategy stems from two closely related but partially contradictory requirements: the need to utilize planning as a means of social mobilization; and the definition of the optimum regime or optimum organization for the planning system. There is no question but that planning, particularly in the transition situation, both requires significant popular support and is an important means of generating it. The problem is that the use of planning as an instrument of social mobilization may conflict with the optimum organization for planning in a context such as we have been discussing. Decentralization may, for example, affect the planning system's capacity to deal with the process of structural transformation as a whole and with the complex web of interrelationships involved. Thus, one could argue that those aspects which directly relate to a country's external links must be centralized. Of course, decisions on centralization and decentralization will depend on the priorities pursued, the environment within which the process takes place and the stage at which the country finds itself. Thus, initially, planning activities could be highly centralized but as the process stabilizes, or strengthens, more and more activities can be decentralized. Again, as external constraints are reduced, the need to centralize planning could be less. Although it is beyond the scope of this paper to go into this question in detail, the issue of the optimum organization for planning deserves further study.

A consequence of having adopted neo-classical models as the basis for planning was the absence of any attention paid to the demand or consumption aspects (Lefeber, 1974; Thomas, 1974). Yet, it is important to deal with consumption during the transition for a number of reasons: by changing the pattern of consumption, possibilities are opened up for the use of alternative technologies (Raj, 1975), for the creation of internal linkages and the reduction of imports. Thomas (1974) argues that in the transition there are two 'iron laws' of transformation: converging resource use and demand, and converging needs and demand. Obviously, there are constraints to achieving this (the small size of a country being one). But it is important to alter a consumption structure which, in satisfying the needs of a small, high income bourgeoisie, creates serious distortions in the way resources are used. If one of the objectives is to satisfy the basic needs of the population, then planning must deal directly with the structure of consumption through rationing, direct allocations or other means. This is particularly true where the market mechanisms and the price system are still enforcing the rules of dependent capitalism as may very well be the case in the initial phases of the transition.

Planners are faced with a great deal of uncertainty, both because they do not control crucial variables and because they are not able to gauge the reactions of other countries. This means that the planning process must adopt a flexible posture, based on contingency planning. There is little use in drawing up very detailed, specific plans: they absorb a great deal of manpower and usually take so long to prepare that their value is limited. Rather, planning must identify strategic variables which are central to the behaviour of the system, and concentrate on them. In addition, planning in the initial stages must be seen as a 'game' in which risk is given explicit attention. It must be strategic, emphasizing policies rather than detailed programming. In an environment characterized by a great deal of uncertainty, one way of reducing this uncertainty, is to gather external intelligence in order to increase information on how the world economic system functions and how particular actors in it, such as the multinationals, conduct their operations.

Concluding remarks

It is apparent that for moving from dependent capitalist growth to a self-reliant model, the planning process must be a very different one from that which is derived from traditional neo-classical or modernization perspectives. These may, in fact, make things worse by generating conditions which lead to even greater dependence, as when, for example, a country, adopting the principle of comparative advantage, becomes an export platform because of its abundant and cheap labour supply, but thereby becomes dependent on the outside world for most of its food. Modernization schemes have, in fact, meant incorporation into the world capitalist system through various means: the adoption of advanced technologies, of consumption patterns and in other ways. This has been amply documented in the literature and in various articles in this book (Sunkel and Fuenzalida, Cruise O'Brien, Godfrey and Langdon, Luckham).

Planning, as described in this article, must be the activity concerned with making strategic choices. Certainly, this involves a very different set of activities from those associated with resource allocation and sectoral planning. It means, as Ritter (1972) has written, that planning is not only involved with a 'growth strategy', dealing with resource allocation, but also with a 'mobilization strategy', aimed at mobilizing resources and popular support, and an 'institutional strategy', whose aim is to develop the institutional basis for development. In the transition period, particularly in the early phases, planning can be looked at as the management of a process in which there is continuous disequilibrium in various areas of activity. This is, after all, what structural change is about. The task of planning is to avoid technical mistakes which would endanger the process, as for example, when wages are increased drastically and suddenly and prices frozen, with no increases in production. The result, as in Chile, was scarcity of many goods, inflation, the creation of black markets and the generation of social tensions. At this stage it is crucial to maintain internal consistency and coherence in the various policies adopted. This is, of course, always necessary, but even more so in the context of the transition phase in which the conditions described are present. Because the environment is hostile, and because there are usually serious class conflicts in the period before the consolidation of the new model, planners must be acutely aware of constraints facing them.

Planning and planners must then adopt new roles which have little to do with what has previously been called planning. As described in this paper, planning is really the management of the process of structural change, and not the process of maintaining the prevailing system or rationalizing its operation. The instruments used will necessarily have to be different. The most sophisticated mathematical tools have been developed to deal with, for the most part, problems of resource allocation and, in any case, refer for the most part to one-dimensional, sectoral planning. The statistical base for planning must also be quite different. Sunkel (1974) has proposed an economic accounting system, based on a modified Leontieff matrix, which singles out the foreign controlled sector of the economy. Certainly, in the initial phases of the transition a scheme such as this would be quite useful. Countries need to develop the capability to know precisely how the transnational capitalist system operates, and how the transnational corporations affect the countries' economies. Obtaining this information is the type of activity which would certainly benefit from multinational collaboration. Finally, countries must develop information on their own resource base and potentialities, something which is frequently lacking. In many ways, the type of planning done is a reflection of the type of statistics and accounting systems which are available. It does not appear feasible to think of a new type of planning for a new development strategy, utilizing the old tool-kit and the old statistical systems.

NOTE

1 This article is a revised version of one which appeared in the IDS Bulletin, Vol. 9, No. 1, 1977. I wish to thank my colleagues in the Dependence Cluster at IDS for many helpful suggestions.

REFERENCES

Amin, Samir, 1972, 'Le modele theorique d'accumulation et de development dans le monde contemporaine. La problematique de transition' *Tiers Monde*, No. 52, 10/12.

Apthorpe, R., 1970, *People, Planning and Development Studies: Some Reflections on Social Planning*, Frank Cass, London.

Bettelheim, 1974, *La Transición a la Economia Socialista*, Editorial Fontanella, Barcelona, (translated from the French, *La transition vers l'economie socialiste*, Maspero, Paris, 1968).

Bolan, C., 1967, 'Emerging Views of Planning', *Journal of the American Institute of Planners*, May.

de Silva, F., 1976, 'The Language of the Oracle: English as a Vehicle of Dependence', *Development Dialogue*, No. 2.

Diaz Alejandro, C., 1970, 'Planning the Foreign Sector in Latin America', *American Economic Review*, May.

Faber, M. and Seers, D., (eds.), 1972, *Crisis in Planning*, Vol. I, Chatto and Windus, London.

Fajnzylber, F., 1976, 'Las Empresas Transnacionales y el 'Collective Self-Reliance', *El Trimestre Economico*, Mexico, Oct–Dec. No. 172.

García, E., 1975, *La Planificación del Desarrollo en América Latina*, Fondo de Cultura Económica, México.

Green, R. H., 1972, 'Some Problems of National Development Planning and Foreign Financing', in S. P. Schatz (ed.), *South of the Sahara: Development in African Economies*, Macmillan, London.

1976, 'Toward a Transformation of the International Economic Order? Industrial World Responses', IDS.

Gutierrez, E., Ortiz, H., and Villamil, J., 1971, 'Open Systems Planning', *Northeast Regional Science Review*, Vol. I, April.

Helleiner, G. K., 1972, 'Socialism and Economic Development in Tanzania', *Journal of Development Studies*, Vol. 8, No. 3, January.

Jones, E., 1975, 'Tendencies and Change in Caribbean Administrative Systems', *Social and Economic Studies*, Vol. 24, No. 2, June.

Leys, Colin, 1969, 'The Analysis of Planning', in Colin Leys (ed.), *Politics and Change in Developing Countries*, Cambridge University Press, London.

Lefeber, Louis, 1974, 'Critique of Development Planning', *Indian Economic Review*, Vol. IX (new series), October.

Mallon, R., 1970, 'Planning in Crisis', *Journal of Political Economy*, July–August.

Meier, G., 1970, 'La Crisis de la Planificación en los Países en Desarrollo', *El Trimestre Económico*, octubre–deciembre.
1974, *Leading Issues in Development Economics*, Oxford University Press, New York.

Moreno, O., 1977, 'El Estado y las Técnicas de Planificacíon en America Latina', *Revista Puertorriqueña de Investigaciones Sociales*, Vol. I, No. 2.

Myrdal, G., 1968, *Asian Drama*, Random House, New York.

Raj, K. N., 1975, 'Linkages in Industrialization and Development Strategy: Some Basic Issues', *Journal of Development Planning*, No. 8.

Ritter, Arch, 1972, 'Growth Strategy and Economic Performance in Revolutionary Cuba: Past, Present and Prospective', *Social and Economic Studies*, Vol. 21, No. 3.

Rweyamamu, A., 1970, *Nation Building in Tanzania*, East African Publishing House, Nairobi.

Sauvant, K., 1976, 'His Master's Voice', *Ceres*, Vol. 9, No. 5, Sept.–Oct.

Scott, R., 1970, 'the Politics of New States: A General Review', in R. Scott (ed.), *The Politics of New States*, George Allen and Unwin, London.

Somavia, J., 1976, 'The Transnational Power Structure and International Information', *Development Dialogue*, No. 2.

Sunkel, Osvaldo, 1971, 'Capitalismo Transnacional y Desintegración Nacional en America Latina', *Estudios Internacionales*, Año IV, No. 16, Enero–Marzo.

1969, 'La Tarea Política y Teórica del Planificador en América Latina', *Estudios Internacionales*, Año 2, No. 4, Enero–Marzo. 1974, 'Dependence and Structural Heterogeneity', IDS (unpublished paper).

Thomas, Clive, 1974, *Dependence and Transformation: The Economics of the Transition to Socialism*, Monthly Review Press, New York.

Tinbergen, J., 1964, *Central Planning*, Yale University Press, New Haven.

U.N. 1972, *Report on A Unified Approach to Development Analysis and Planning, Preliminary Report of the Secretary General*, E/CN. 5/477, 25 October.

Vaitsos, C., 1977, 'The Attitudes and Role of transnational Enterprises in Economic Integration Processes Among the LDC's', Paper presented to the Millenium Conference, London School of Economics, October 14–15.

Vasconi, Tomás, 1970, 'De la Dependencia Como una Categoría Básica para el Análisis del Desarrollo Latineamericano', *Cuadernos de la Sociedad Venezolana de Planificación*, Nos. 82–83, Nov–Dic.

Wildavsky, A., 1971, 'Does Planning Work?', *The Public Interest*, Summer.

INDEX

323